WEBSTER'S NEW WORLD™

Notebook Spell Checker

The Editors
of
Webster's New World™
Dictionaries

Editor in Chief
MICHAEL AGNES

Macmillan
USA

Webster's New World Staff

Editor in Chief
Michael Agnes

Project Editor
Andrew N. Sparks

Managing Editor
James J. Heaney

Editor and Database Administrator
Donald Stewart

Editorial Staff
Jonathan L. Goldman, Senior Editor
James E. Naso
Katherine Soltis
Stephen P. Teresi
Laura Borovac Walker

Administrative, Data Processing, and Clerical Staff
Alisa Murray Davis
Cynthia M. Sadonick
Betty Dziedzic Thompson

Citation Readers
Batya Jundef
Joan Komic

Webster's New World™ Notebook Spell Checker

Copyright © 1998 by Simon & Schuster, Inc.
All rights reserved including the right of reproduction in whole or in part in any form

This book is based on and includes material from
Webster's New World™ College Dictionary, Third Edition,
copyright © 1997, 1996, 1994, 1991, 1988 by Simon & Schuster, Inc.

Macmillan General Reference
A Simon & Schuster Macmillan Company
1633 Broadway
New York, NY 10019-6785

A Webster's New World™ Book

MACMILLAN is a registered trademark of Macmillan, Inc.

WEBSTER'S NEW WORLD DICTIONARY
is a registered trademark of Simon & Schuster, Inc.

Dictionary Editorial Offices:
New World Dictionaries
850 Euclid Avenue
Cleveland, OH 44114-3354

ISBN 0-02-862377-0

Design and Typesetting
Publishing Synthesis, Ltd., New York

Manufactured in the United States of America

1 2 3 4 5 6 7   98 99 00 01 02 03

Guide to the Use of This Book

Each of the words listed alphabetically in *Webster's New World™ Notebook Spell Checker* is referred to in this guide as an *entry* or *entry word*.

1. Content

This spell checker in handy, notebook format is an authoritative, up-to-date, quick guide to the correct spelling and syllabification of 39,000 words. It is based on the widely used *Webster's New World™ College Dictionary, Third Edition.* A special feature of the *Notebook Spell Checker* is the *Table of Difficult Spellings,* which will help you locate a word even though all you know about the word is how to pronounce it.

In addition to the general guidance this book offers, there is also much information that will help to answer very specific questions. Is a certain term written as one word, or with a hyphen, or as two words? Do I want the word *anecdote* or *antidote?* When is *hanged* preferred as the past tense and past participle of *hang?* Is the word I want spelled *moot* or *mute?* When is *ringed* used correctly as a verb?

An almost infinite number of words can be formed through the addition of certain prefixes or suffixes to base words. Many of these derived words are entered, especially those whose spelling may be confusing. For example:

a·gree′a·ble   di·dac′tic
a·gree′a·bly   di·dac′ti·cal·ly

di·ag′o·nal   gar′lic
di·ag′o·nal·ly   gar′lick·y

Most obsolete, rare, and archaic forms have been omitted. Many technical terms, especially those in general use, and many colloquial words have been included.

In short, this book is designed to be as complete and timesaving an aid to spelling and syllabification as possible.

2. Word Division

All the entry words are divided into syllables. Each syllable break is indicated by a centered dot, an accent mark, or, in certain cases, a hyphen. Wherever a hyphen *is* used in an entry word, that hyphen is part of the spelling of the word.

In a piece of writing, a word can be divided from one line to the next between any two of its syllables *except* in the following cases:

a. Never separate a first or last syllable of only one letter—or, if you can avoid it, two letters—from the rest of the word.

b. If you can avoid it, do not divide a hyphenated word at any point other than the hyphen.

3. Accent Marks

Accent marks are included to help you find words more quickly. In some cases the accent mark distinguishes one word from another word that is spelled almost the same way. For example:

lo′cal / lo·cale′   kar′at / ka·ra′te

Two kinds of accent marks are used. The accent mark in heavy type shows that the syllable preceding it receives the main stress, or accent. The accent in lighter type, wherever it is used, indicates that the preceding syllable receives less stress than the main one but somewhat more stress than an unmarked syllable. For example:

ag′gra·vate′ / dem′on·stra′tion / su′per·vise′

4. Parts of Speech

Part-of-speech labels (such as *n.* = noun and *v.* = verb) are included here only in special cases. Sometimes the label gives information about current usage. In all cases, the main purpose is to help you make sure you have the word you are looking for. Here are two of these special cases:

a. Sometimes a word is accented and syllabified in one way as one part of speech and differently as another. These changes in accent and syllabification are indicated, and the word is appropriately labeled. For example:

re·cord′ *v.* / rec′ord *n.*

b. Sometimes two words are related in meaning and close in spelling and pronunciation. A part-of-speech label is all that is needed to identify each word. For example:

ad·vice′ *n.*   proph′e·cy *n.*
ad·vise′ *v.*   ·cies
 ·vised′ ·vis′ing   proph′e·sy′ *v.*
            ·sied′ ·sy′ing

5. Inflected Forms

Inflected forms include the plurals of nouns, the parts of verbs, and the comparative and superlative forms of adjectives and adverbs. Most irregularly formed inflected forms are entered as part of the entry for the base word. To save space, these forms have been shortened in most cases to show only those syllables that differ from those of the base word. For example:

please   blood′y
 pleased pleas′ing   ·i·er ·i·est
fly   ·ied ·y·ing
 flies   pic′nic
 flew flown fly′ing   ·nicked ·nick′ing
li′a·bil′i·ty   date
 ·ties   dat′ed dat′ing

For verbs, when two forms are given, the first is the past tense and past participle and the second is the present participle. When three forms are given, the first is the past tense, the second is the past participle, and the third is the present participle. Noun, adjective, and adverb forms are easy to identify.

To save space, inflected forms of some compound words and derived words have been omitted. You can easily find these forms with the entry for the base word. For example, see *man* for the plural of *policeman;* see *package* for the parts of the verb *prepackage.*

In some cases, certain inflected forms are used for particular meanings. These are identified. For example:

staff   ring
 staffs *or* staves   rang rung ring′ing
 (*stick; music*)   (*sound*)
staffs   ring
 (*people*)   ringed ring′ing
               (*circle*)

This system of entering inflected forms as part of the entry for the base word has these advantages: (1) It helps you distinguish between words that might be confused if they were entered separately, as in:

hop
 hopped hop′ping
hope
 hoped hop′ing

(2) It saves the time and trouble of searching for a word that you might think is spelled one way but that is, in fact, spelled differently, as in:

swim
 swam swum swim′ming

(3) It establishes, without further identification under a separate entry, the specific inflected form that you are looking for, as in:

hang   hang
 hung hang′ing   hanged hang′ing
 (*suspend*)   (*put to death*)

One last point: when an entry contains verb forms, this does not necessarily mean that a given form is used only as a verb. In fact, many of the entries represent the spelling for more than one part of speech. If, for example, a word used as an adjective is already entered as a verb form, and the spelling and syllabification are exactly the same for the adjective, this word is not necessarily entered again separately. You may accept the verb form as the correct spelling for the adjective (as in "a pleased customer," "a

pleasing smile": see *please* above). If a noun has the same spelling as a verb, no special notation is given (see *picnic* above). Where confusion could exist, some kind of identification is provided.

6. Use of Identifying Definitions

It should be obvious that this book is not meant to replace the dictionary. However, in attempting to learn the correct spelling for a specific word, you may find that you are confusing another word with it. There are many possibilities for such confusion in the English language. To help you find the exact word you are seeking, this book contains many cross-references. Each cross-reference supplies a very short *identifying definition* and refers you to another word that may be the one you want.

Confusion may result for any of several reasons. Two of the most common are: (1) similar (but not exactly the same) pronunciation, as in:

mou'ton'
    (*fur*; see MUTTON)

mut'ton
    (*food*; see MOUTON)

(2) exactly the same pronunciation but, usually, a different spelling, as in:

la'ma
    (*monk*; see LLAMA)

lla'ma
    (*animal*; see LAMA)

leak
    (*escape*; see LEEK)

leek
    (*vegetable*; see LEAK)

Such words are called *homonyms*.

The words involved are often very close alphabetically. In such cases only the identifying definitions are given, without cross-references. For example:

less'en
    (*make less*)

less'er
    (*smaller*)

les'son
    (*instruction*)

les'sor'
    (*one who leases*)

It is important to note here that these *identifying definitions* are meant only as an aid in locating or identifying the word you want. They are not meant to replace or cover the entire dictionary definition.

7. More Than One Accepted Spelling

Many words in the English language have more than one accepted spelling in use today. Because of space limitations, only the variant spellings of the more common words have been included in this book. To help you identify them as variants of the same word, they are, in most cases, listed together as part of the same entry. Usually, the first spelling given is the one that is used more frequently. Sometimes variants are entered separately, especially if they are far apart in the alphabet. Whichever variant spelling you decide on, be consistent and use that same spelling throughout any one piece of writing.

8. Prefixes

Many words that are formed by adding a prefix to a base word have been entered in this book. Since it is not possible to include all such words, some information on the use of a number of common prefixes is given below. Using these general rules, you can determine the usual spelling of many more of the words you need.

The prefix	is usually added to the base word
self	with a hyphen (*self-confidence*).
out	without a hyphen (*outrun*).
over	without a hyphen (*overcharge*).
anti pre pro semi un	without a hyphen *except* when the prefix is followed by a capital letter (*pretest*, *pre-Columbian*).
non	without a hyphen *except* when the prefix is followed by a capital letter or by a word that has a hyphen in it (*nonpartisan*, *non-Muslim*, *non-profit-making*).
re	without a hyphen *except* to distinguish between a word in which the prefix means "again" or "anew" and a word having a special meaning (*re-cover*, *recover*).

TABLE OF DIFFICULT SPELLINGS

At one time or another, everyone has encountered the problem of trying to look up a word without knowing how the word is spelled. In English, one letter can stand for more than one sound, and one sound can be spelled in more than one way. To make it easier for you to locate the word you want, the table below gives the most common spellings of the sound of American English.

Think of the word you want in terms of its pronounced syllables. *Be sure you are pronouncing the word correctly.*

The consonant sound of the letter or letters:	can also be spelled with the letter or letters in boldface below:
ch as in *chin*	cat**ch**, na**t**ure, ques**ti**on, **c**ello, **Cz**ech
f as in *fall*	di**ff**erent, lau**gh**, **ph**one
g as in *get*	e**gg**, **gu**ard, **gh**ost
h as in *help*	**wh**o
j as in *jump*	**g**em, ju**dg**e, gra**d**uate, a**dj**ective, exa**gg**erate
k as in *kiss*	**c**an, lu**ck**, a**cc**ount, an**ch**or, li**qu**id, li**qu**or, ex**c**ept
l as in *leg*	ca**ll**, is**l**and
m as in *meat*	ha**mm**er, cli**mb**, hy**mn**
n as in *nose*	di**nn**er, **kn**eel, **gn**ome, **pn**eumonia
ng as in *ring*	thi**n**k
r as in *red*	be**rr**y, **wr**ong, **rh**yme
s as in *see*	mi**ss**, **c**ent, **sc**ience, **ps**ychology
s as in *measure*	gara**g**e, sei**z**ure, confu**s**ion, equa**t**ion
sh as in *she*	na**ti**on, man**si**on, **s**ure, mi**ssi**on, i**ss**ue, con**sci**ence, spe**ci**al, ma**ch**ine, **sch**wa
t as in *top*	be**tt**er, **Th**omas, cook**ed**
w as in *wish*	q**u**iet, **wh**ile
y as in *yard*	on**i**on, hallelu**j**ah
z as in *zebra*	bu**s**y, bu**zz**ard, **sc**issors, **x**ylophone, **cz**ar

The vowel sound of the letter or letters:	can also be spelled with the letter or letters in boldface below:
a as in *cat*	pl**ai**d, l**au**gh
a as in *ape*	r**ai**n, p**ay**, v**ei**l, pr**ey**, w**eigh**, ob**ey**, bouqu**et**, br**ea**k
a as in *father* or *car*	**ah**, sp**o**t, h**ea**rt
a as in *fall*	**aw**ful, **au**tumn, l**o**ss, c**ou**gh, br**oa**d
e as in *ten*	h**ea**vy, th**ei**r, fri**e**nd, **a**ny, **ae**rosol, s**ai**d, s**ay**s, b**u**ry, l**eo**pard
e as in *me*	funn**y**, mach**i**ne, **ea**t, **ee**l, f**ie**ld, rec**ei**ve, k**ey**
i as in *fit*	h**y**mn, pr**e**tty, b**u**sy, b**ee**n, h**ea**r, w**ei**rd, p**ie**r, b**ui**ld
i as in *ice*	fl**y**, r**ye**, t**ie**, h**eigh**t, **ai**sle, **eye**, b**uy**
o as in *go*	**oa**t, gr**ow**, t**oe**, s**ou**l, th**ough**, plat**eau**, s**ew**
oi as in *oil*	b**oy**
ou as in *out*	n**ow**, b**ough**
u as in *up*	s**o**n, fl**oo**d, d**ou**ble, d**oe**s
u as in *rule*	t**oo**l, bl**ue**, m**o**ve, sh**oe**, s**ou**p, thr**ough**, thr**ew**, man**eu**ver, fr**ui**t
u as in *put*	w**oo**d, w**ou**ld, w**o**man
u as in *fur*	h**er**, s**ir**, c**ur**l, w**or**ry, l**ear**n, j**our**ney, w**ere**
a as in *ago***	**a**gent, penc**i**l, at**o**m, circ**u**s, cari**ou**s, fashi**o**n

*the schwa (ə)

A

aard'vark'
a·back'
ab'a·cus
  ·cus·es or ·ci'
a·baft'
ab'a·lo'ne
a·ban'don
a·ban'doned
a·ban'don·ment
a·base'
  ·based' ·bas'ing
a·base'ment
a·bash'
a·bash'ed·ly
a·bate'
  ·bat'ed ·bat'ing
a·bate'ment
ab'at·toir'
ab·bé
ab'bess
ab'bey
ab'bot
ab·bre'vi·ate'
  ·at'ed ·at'ing
ab·bre'vi·a'tion
ab'di·cate'
  ·cat'ed ·cat'ing
ab'di·ca'tion
ab'do·men
ab·dom'i·nal
ab·duct'
ab·duc'tion
ab·duc'tor
a·beam'
a·bed'
ab·er'rant
ab'er·ra'tion
ab'er·ra'tion·al
a·bet'
  ·bet'ted ·bet'ting
a·bet'tor or ·ter
a·bey'ance
ab·hor'
  ·horred' ·hor'ring
ab·hor'rence
ab·hor'rent
ab·hor'rent·ly
a·bide'
  ·bode' or ·bid'ed
  ·bid'ing
a·bid'ing
a·bil'i·ty
  ·ties
ab'ject'
ab·ject'ly
ab'ju·ra'tion
ab·jure'
  ·jured' ·jur'ing
ab·jur'er
ab·late'
  ·lat'ed ·lat'ing
ab·la'tion
ab'la·tive
a·blaze'
a'ble
  ·bler ·blest
a'ble-bod'ied
ab·lu'tion

a'bly
ab'ne·gate'
  ·gat'ed ·gat'ing
ab'ne·ga'tion
ab·nor'mal
ab'nor·mal'i·ty
  ·ties
ab·nor'mal·ly
a·board'
a·bode'
a·bol'ish
ab'o·li'tion
ab'o·li'tion·ist
a·bom'i·na·ble
a·bom'i·na·bly
a·bom'i·nate'
  ·nat'ed ·nat'ing
a·bom'i·na'tion
ab'o·rig'i·nal
ab'o·rig'i·ne
  ·nes'
a·bort'
a·bor'tion
a·bor'tion·ist
a·bor'tive
a·bound'
a·bout'
a·bout'-face'
  ·faced' ·fac'ing
a·bove'
a·bove'board'
ab'ra·ca·dab'ra
a·brade'
  ·brad'ed ·brad'ing
a·bra'sion
a·bra'sive
a·breast'
a·bridge'
  ·bridged'
  ·bridg'ing
a·bridg'ment or
  ·bridge'·
a·broad'
ab'ro·gate'
  ·gat'ed ·gat'ing
ab'ro·ga'tion
ab'ro·ga'tor
a·brupt'
a·brupt'ly
a·brupt'ness
ab'scess'
ab'scessed'
ab·scis'sa
  ·sas or ·sae
ab·scond'
ab·scond'er
ab'sence
ab'sent
ab'sen·tee'
ab'sen·tee'ism'
ab'sent·ly
ab'sent-mind'ed
ab'sent-mind'ed·ly
ab'sent-
  mind'ed·ness
ab'sinthe or ·sinth
ab'so·lute'
ab'so·lute'ly

ab'so·lu'tion
ab'so·lut'ism'
ab'so·lut'ist
ab·solve'
  ·solved' ·solv'ing
ab·sorb'
ab·sorb'en·cy
ab·sorb'ent
ab·sorb'ing
ab·sorp'tion
ab·sorp'tive
ab·stain'
ab·stain'er
ab·ste'mi·ous
ab·sten'tion
ab'sti·nence
ab'sti·nent
ab·stract'
ab·stract'ed
ab·strac'tion
ab·stract'ly
ab·struse'
ab·struse'ly
ab·struse'ness
ab·surd'
ab·surd'i·ty
ab·surd'ly
a·bun'dance
a·bun'dant
a·bun'dant·ly
a·buse'
  ·bused' ·bus'ing
a·bus'er
a·bu'sive
a·bu'sive·ly
a·but'
  ·but'ted ·but'ting
a·but'ment
a·bys'mal
a·bys'mal·ly
a·byss'
a·ca'cia
ac'a·de'mi·a
ac'a·dem'ic
ac'a·dem'i·cal·ly
a·cad'e·mi'cian
a·cad'e·my
  ·mies
a·can'thus
  ·thus·es or ·thi'
a' cap·pel'la
ac·cede'
  ·ced'ed ·ced'ing
  (agree; see
  EXCEED)
ac·cel'er·ate'
  ·at'ed ·at'ing
ac·cel'er·a'tion
ac·cel'er·a'tor
ac'cent
ac·cen'tu·ate'
  ·at'ed ·at'ing
ac·cen'tu·a'tion
ac·cept'
  (receive; see EX-
  CEPT)
ac·cept'a·bil'i·ty
ac·cept'a·ble
ac·cept'ance

ac·cept'ed
ac'cess'
  (approach; see EX-
  CESS)
ac·ces'si·bil'i·ty
ac·ces'si·ble
ac·ces'si·bly
ac·ces'sion
ac·ces'so·ry
  ·ries
ac'ci·dent
ac'ci·den'tal
ac'ci·den'tal·ly
ac'ci·dent-prone'
ac·claim'
ac'cla·ma'tion
ac·cli'mate
  ·mat·ed ·mat·ing
ac·cli'ma·tize'
  ·tized' ·tiz'ing
ac'cli·ma'tion
ac·cliv'i·ty
  ·ties
ac'co·lade'
ac·com'mo·date'
  ·dat'ed ·dat'ing
ac·com'mo·dat'ing
ac·com'mo·da'tion
ac·com'pa·ni·ment
ac·com'pa·nist
ac·com'pa·ny
  ·nied ·ny·ing
ac·com'plice
ac·com'plish
ac·com'plished
ac·com'plish·ment
ac·cord'
  ·but'ted ·but'ting
ac·cord'ance
ac·cord'ant
ac·cord'ing
ac·cord'ing·ly
ac·cor'di·on
ac·cost'
ac·count'
ac·count'a·bil'i·ty
ac·count'a·ble
ac·count'ant
ac·count'ing
ac·cou'ter
ac·cou'ter·ments or
  ·tre·ments
ac·cred'it
ac·cred'i·ta'tion
ac·cre'tion
ac·cru'al
ac·crue'
  ·crued' ·cru'ing
ac·cul'tur·ate'
  ·at'ed ·at'ing
ac·cul'tur·a'tion
ac·cu'mu·late'
  ·lat'ed ·lat'ing
ac·cu'mu·la'tion
ac·cu'mu·la'tive
ac'cu·ra·cy
ac'cu·rate
ac'cu·rate·ly
ac·curs'ed
ac'cu·sa'tion

ac·cu'sa·tive
ac·cu'sa·to'ry
ac·cuse'
  ·cused' ·cus'ing
ac·cus'er
ac·cus'tom
ac·cus'tomed
ace
  aced ac'ing
ac'er·bate'
  ·bat'ed ·bat'ing
a·cer'bic
a·cer'bi·ty
  ·ties
ac'e·ta·min'o·phen
ac'et·an'i·lide'
ac'e·tate'
a·ce'tic
  (sour; see ASCETIC)
ac'e·tone'
a·cet'y·lene'
a·ce'tyl·sal'i·cyl'ic
  acid
ache
  ached ach'ing
a·chene'
a·chiev'a·ble
a·chieve'
  ·chieved'
  ·chiev'ing
a·chieve'ment
ach'ro·mat'ic
ach'y
  ·i·er ·i·est
ac'id
a·cid'ic
a·cid'i·fy'
  ·fied' ·fy'ing
a·cid'i·ty
  ·ties
ac'id·ly
ac'i·do'sis
a·cid'u·lous
ac·knowl'edge
  ·edged ·edg'ing
ac·knowl'edg·ment
  or ·edge·
ac'me (peak)
ac'ne (pimples)
ac'o·lyte'
ac'o·nite'
a'corn'
a·cous'tic
a·cous'ti·cal
a·cous'ti·cal·ly
ac·quaint'
ac·quaint'ance
ac'qui·esce'
  ·esced' ·esc'ing
ac'qui·es'cence
ac'qui·es'cent
ac·quir'a·ble
ac·quire'
  ·quired' ·quir'ing
ac·quire'ment
ac'qui·si'tion
ac·quis'i·tive
ac·quis'i·tive·ness

ac·quit'
  ·quit'ted ·quit'ting
ac·quit'tal
a'cre
a'cre·age'
ac'rid
a·crid'i·ty
ac'rid·ly
ac'ri·mo'ni·ous
ac'ri·mo'ny
ac'ro·bat'
ac'ro·bat'ic
ac'ro·nym'
ac'ro·pho'bi·a
a·cross'
a·cros'tic
a·cryl'ic
act
act'ing
ac'ti·nide' series
ac·tin'i·um
ac'tion
ac'ti·vate'
  ·vat'ed ·vat'ing
ac'ti·va'tion
ac'ti·va'tor
ac'tive
ac'tive·ly
ac'tiv·ism'
ac'tiv·ist
ac·tiv'i·ty
  ·ties
ac'tor
ac'tress
ac'tu·al
ac'tu·al'i·ty
  ·ties
ac'tu·al·ize'
  ·ized' ·iz'ing
ac'tu·al·ly
ac'tu·ar'i·al
ac'tu·ar'y
  ·ies
ac'tu·ate'
  ·at'ed ·at'ing
ac'tu·a'tor
a·cu'i·ty
a·cu'men
ac'u·punc'ture
ac'u·punc'tur·ist
a·cute'
a·cute'ly
a·cute'ness
a·cy'clo·vir'
ad'age
a·da'gio
  ·gios
ad'a·mant
a·dapt'
  (adjust; see ADEPT,
  ADOPT)
a·dapt'a·bil'i·ty
a·dapt'a·ble
a·dapt'er or
  ·dap'tor
ad'ap·ta'tion
add
ad'dend'

ad·den'dum
·da
add'er (one who
adds)
ad'der (snake)
ad'dict
ad·dic'tion
ad·dic'tive
ad·di'tion
(an adding; see
EDITION)
ad·di'tion·al
ad·di'tion·al·ly
ad'di·tive
ad'dle
·dled ·dling
ad·dress'
ad'dress·ee'
ad·duce'
·duced' ·duc'ing
ad'e·nine'
ad'e·noids'
a·dept'
(skilled; see
ADAPT, ADOPT)
a·dept'ly
a·dept'ness
ad'e·qua·cy
ad'e·quate
ad'e·quate·ly
ad·here'
·hered' ·her'ing
ad·her'ence
ad·her'ent
ad·he'sion
ad·he'sive
ad hoc'
a·dieu'
·dieus' or ·dieux'
(goodbye; see ADO)
ad in'fi·ni'tum
a'di·os'
ad'i·pose'
ad·ja'cent
ad·ja'cent·ly
ad'jec·ti'val
ad'jec·ti'val·ly
ad'jec·tive
ad·join'
ad·join'ing
ad·journ'
ad·journ'ment
ad·judge'
·judged' ·judg'ing
ad·ju'di·cate
·cat'ed ·cat'ing
ad·ju'di·ca'tion
ad·ju'di·ca'tor
ad·ju'di·ca·to'ry
ad'junct
ad·jure'
·jured' ·jur'ing
ad·just'
ad·just'a·ble
ad·just'er or
·jus'tor
ad·just'ment
ad'ju·tant

ad'-lib'
·libbed' ·lib'bing
ad'man'
ad·min'is·ter
ad·min'is·trate'
·trat'ed ·trat'ing
ad·min'is·tra'tion
ad·min'is·tra'tor
ad'mi·ra·ble
ad'mi·ra·bly
ad'mi·ral
ad'mi·ral·ty
·ties
ad'mi·ra'tion
ad·mire'
·mired' ·mir'ing
ad·mir'er
ad·mis'si·bil'i·ty
ad·mis'si·ble
ad·mis'sion
ad·mit'
·mit'ted ·mit'ting
ad·mit'tance
ad·mit'ted·ly
ad·mix'
ad·mix'ture
ad·mon'ish
ad'mo·ni'tion
ad·mon'i·to'ry
ad nau'se·am'
a·do'
(fuss; see ADIEU)
a·do'be
ad'o·les'cence
ad'o·les'cent
A·do'nis
a·dopt'
(choose; see ADAPT,
ADEPT)
a·dop'tion
a·dop'tive
a·dor'a·ble
a·dor'a·bly
ad'o·ra'tion
a·dore'
·dored' ·dor'ing
a·dorn'
a·dorn'ment
a·dre'nal
a·dren'a·lin'
a·drift'
a·droit'
a·droit'ly
a·droit'ness
ad·sorb'
ad·sorp'tion
ad'u·late'
·lat'ed ·lat'ing
ad'u·la'tion
a·dult'
a·dul'ter·ant
a·dul'ter·ate'
·at'ed ·at'ing
a·dul'ter·a'tion
a·dul'ter·er
a·dul'ter·ess n.
a·dul'ter·ous adj.

a·dul'ter·y
a·dult'hood
ad·um'brate'
·brat'ed ·brat'ing
ad'um·bra'tion
ad' va·lo'rem
ad·vance'
·vanced' ·vanc'ing
ad·vanced'
ad·vance'ment
ad·van'tage'
·taged ·tag'ing
ad'van·ta'geous
ad'vent'
ad·ven·ti'tious
ad·ven'ture
·tured ·tur'ing
ad·ven'tur·er
ad·ven'ture·some
ad·ven'tur·ess n.
ad·ven'tur·ous adj.
ad·ven'tur·ous·ly
ad'verb'
ad·ver'bi·al
ad'ver·sar'i·al
ad'ver·sar'y
·ies
ad·verse'
(opposed; see
AVERSE)
ad·verse'ly
ad·ver'si·ty
·ties
ad·vert'
ad'ver·tise'
·tised' ·tis'ing
ad'ver·tise'ment
ad'ver·tis'er
ad'ver·tis'ing
ad·vice' n.
ad·vis'a·bil'i·ty
ad·vis'a·ble
ad·vise' v.
·vised' ·vis'ing
ad·vis'ed·ly
ad·vise'ment
ad·vi'sor or ·vis'er
ad·vi'so·ry
·ries
ad'vo·ca·cy
ad'vo·cate'
·cat'ed ·cat'ing
adz or adze
ae'gis
ae'on
a'er·ate'
·at'ed ·at'ing
a·er·a'tion
a'er·a'tor
aer'i·al
aer'i·al·ist
a'er·ie
aer'o·bat'ics
aer·o'bic
aer'o·dy·nam'ic
aer'o·dy·nam'ics
aer'o·nau'ti·cal
aer'o·nau'tics
aer'o·sol'

aer'o·space'
aes'thete'
aes·thet'ic
aes·thet'ics
a·far'
af'fa·bil'i·ty
af'fa·ble
af'fa·bly
af·fair'
af·fect'
(to influence; see
EFFECT)
af'fec·ta'tion
af·fect'ed
af·fect'ing
af·fec'tion
af·fec'tion·ate
af·fec'tion·ate·ly
af·fect'less
af'fer·ent
af·fi'ance
·anced ·anc'ing
af·fi'da·vit
af·fil'i·ate'
·at'ed ·at'ing
af·fil'i·a'tion
af·fin'i·ty
af·firm'
af'fir·ma'tion
af·firm'a·tive
af·fix'
af·fla'tus
af·flict'
af·flic'tion
af'flu·ence
af'flu·ent
(rich; see EFFLU-
ENT)
af'flu·ent·ly
af·ford'
af·ford'a·ble
af·fray'
af·front'
af'ghan'
a·fi'cio·na'do
a·field'
a·fire'
a·flame'
a·float'
a·flut'ter
a·foot'
a·fore'men'·tioned
a·fore'said'
a·fore'thought'
a·foul'
a·fraid'
Af'ri·can
aft
af'ter
af'ter·birth'
af'ter·burn'er
af'ter·ef·fect'
af'ter·life'
af'ter·math'
af'ter·noon'
af'ter·thought'
af'ter·ward (later)

af'ter·word' (epi-
logue)
a·gain'
a·gainst'
a·gape'
a'gar'
ag'ate
a·ga've
age
aged, ag'ing or
age'ing
a'ged
age'ism'
age'less
a'gen·cy
·cies
a·gen'da
a'gent
age'-old'
ag'er·a'tum
ag·glom'er·ate'
·at'ed ·at'ing
ag·glu'ti·nate'
·nat'ed ·nat'ing
ag·glu'ti·na'tion
ag·gran'dize'
·dized' ·diz'ing
ag·gran'dize·ment
ag'gra·vate'
·vat'ed ·vat'ing
ag'gra·vat'ed
ag'gra·va'tion
ag'gre·gate'
·gat'ed ·gat'ing
ag'gre·ga'tion
ag·gres'sion
ag·gres'sive
ag·gres'sive·ly
ag·gres'sive·ness
ag·gres'sor
ag·grieve'
·grieved' ·griev'ing
a·ghast'
ag'ile
ag'ile·ly
a·gil'i·ty
ag'i·tate'
·tat'ed ·tat'ing
ag'i·ta'tion
ag'i·ta'tor
a·gleam'
a·glit'ter
a·glow'
ag·nos'tic
ag·nos'ti·cism'
a·go'
a·gog'
ag'o·nize'
·nized' ·niz'ing
ag'o·ny
·nies
a·grar'i·an
a·gree'
·greed' ·gree'ing
a·gree'a·ble
a·gree'a·bly
a·gree'ment
ag'ri·busi'ness
ag'ri·cul'tur·al

ag'ri·cul'tur·al·ly
ag'ri·cul'ture
ag'ri·cul'tur·ist
a·gron'o·mist
a·gron'o·my
a·ground'
a'gue'
a·ha'
a·head'
a·hem'
a·hoy'
aid (help)
aide (assistant)
aide'-de-camp' or
aid'-
aides'- or aids'-
AIDS
ai·grette' or ·gret'
ail
(be ill; see ALE)
ai'le·ron'
ail'ment
aim
aim'less
aim'less·ly
aim'less·ness
ain't
air
(gases; see ERR,
HEIR)
air'borne'
air'brush'
air'bus'
air'-con·di'tion
air'-con·di'tioned
air conditioner
air'-cooled'
air'craft'
air'field'
air'foil'
air'head'
air'i·ly
air'i·ness
air'lift'
air'line'
air'lin'er
air'mail'
air'man'
air'plane'
air'play'
air'port'
air'ship'
air'sick'
air'sick'ness
air'space'
air'strike'
air'strip'
air'tight'
air'waves'
air'way'
air'y
·i·er ·i·est
aisle
(passage; see ISLE)
a·jar'
a·kim'bo
a·kin'
Al'a·bam'a

al'a·bas'ter
a' la carte'
a·lac'ri·ty
à' la king'
a' la mode'
a'lar
a·larm'
a·larm'ing
a·larm'ist
a·las'
A·las'ka
alb
al'ba·core'
al'ba·tross'
al·be'it
al·bi'no
·nos
al'bum
al·bu'men (egg white)
al·bu'min (class of proteins)
al'che·mist
al'che·my
al'co·hol'
al'co·hol'ic
al'co·hol'ism'
al'cove'
al'der
al'der·man
ale
(a drink; see AIL)
a'le·a·to'ry
a·lem'bic
a·lert'
a·lert'ly
a·lert'ness
A·leu'tian
ale'wife'
al·fal'fa
al·fres'co
al'gae'
al'ge·bra
al'ge·bra'ic
al'ge·bra'i·cal·ly
al'go·rithm'
a'li·as
al'i·bi'
·bis'
·bied' ·bi'ing
al'ien
al'ien·ate'
·at'ed ·at'ing
al'ien·a'tion
a·light'
light'ed or ·lit'
·light'ing
a·lign'
a·lign'ment
a·like'
al'i·men'ta·ry
(of food; see ELE-MENTARY)
al'i·mo'ny
a·line'
·lined' ·lin'ing
a·line'ment
a·live'

al'ka·li'
·lies' or ·lis'
al'ka·line'
al'ka·lin'i·ty
al'ka·lize'
·lized' ·liz'ing
al'ka·loid'
al'kyd'
all
(everything; see AWL)
all'-A·mer'i·can
all'-a·round'
al'lay'
·layed' ·lay'ing
all'-clear'
al'le·ga'tion
al·lege'
·leged' ·leg'ing
al·leged'
al·leg'ed·ly
al·le'giance
al'le·gor'i·cal
al'le·gor'i·cal·ly
al'le·go'rist
al'le·go'ry
·ries
al'le·gret'to
al·le'gro'
al·le·lu'ia
al'ler·gen
al'ler·gen'ic
al·ler'gic
al'ler·gist
al'ler·gy
·gies
al·le'vi·ate'
·at'ed ·at'ing
al·le'vi·a'tion
al'ley
·leys
(narrow lane; see ALLY)
al'ley·way'
al·li'ance
al·lied'
al'li·ga'tor
all'-im·por'tant
all'-in·clu'sive
al·lit'er·a'tion
al·lit'er·a'tive
al'lo·cate'
·cat'ed ·cat'ing
al'lo·ca'tion
al·lot'
·lot'ted ·lot'ting
al·lot'ment
all'-out'
all'o'ver
al·low'
al·low'a·ble
al·low'ance
al·lowed'
(permitted; see ALOUD)
al'loy'
all'-pur'pose'
all'-round'

all'spice'
all'-star'
all'-time'
al·lude'
·lud'ed ·lud'ing
(refer to; see ELUDE)
al·lure'
·lured' ·lur'ing
al·lur'ing
al·lu'sion
(reference; see IL-LUSION)
al·lu'sive
(referring to; see ELUSIVE, ILLUSIVE)
al·lu'sive·ly
al·lu'sive·ness
al·lu'vi·al
al·lu'vi·um
·vi·ums or ·vi·a
al'ly n. al·ly' v.
·lies
·lied' ·ly'ing
(partner; join; see ALLEY)
al'ma ma'ter
al'ma·nac'
al·might'y
al'mond
al'most'
alms
al'oe'
·oes'
a·loft'
a·lo'ha'
a·lone'
a·long'
a·long'shore'
a·long'side'
a·loof'
a·loof'ness
a·loud'
(loudly; see AL-LOWED)
al·pac'a
al'pen·stock'
al'pha
al'pha·bet'
al'pha·bet'i·cal
al'pha·bet'i·cal·ly
al'pha·bet'i·za'tion
al'pha·bet·ize'
·ized' ·iz'ing
al'pha·nu·mer'ic
al'pine'
al·read'y
al'so
al'so-ran'
al'tar (table for wor-ship)
al'ter (to change)
al'ter·a'tion
al'ter·ca'tion
al'ter e'go'
al'ter·nate
·nat'ed ·nat'ing
al'ter·nate·ly
al'ter·na'tion
al·ter'na·tive

al'ter·na'tor
al·though'
al·tim'e·ter
al'ti·tude'
al'to
·tos
al'to·geth'er
al'tru·ism'
al'tru·ist
al'tru·is'tic
al'tru·is'ti·cal·ly
al'um
a·lu'mi·num
a·lum'na fem.
·nae
a·lum'nus masc.
·ni'
al'ways
Alz'hei'mer's disease
a·mal'gam
a·mal'ga·mate'
·mat'ed ·mat'ing
a·mal'ga·ma'tion
a·man'u·en'sis
·ses'
a'ma·ret'to
am'a·ryl'lis
a·mass'
am'a·teur
am'a·teur'ish
am'a·teur·ism'
am'a·to'ry
a·maze'
·mazed' ·maz'ing
a·maze'ment
a·maz'ing
a·maz'ing·ly
am·bas'sa·dor
am·bas'sa·do'ri·al
am·bas'sa·dor·ship'
am'ber
am'ber·gris'
am'bi·dex·ter'i·ty
am'bi·dex'trous
am·bi·ence or
·ance
am'bi·ent
am·bi·gu'i·ty
·ties
am·big'u·ous
am·big'u·ous·ly
am·bi'tion
am·bi'tious
am·bi'tious·ly
am·biv'a·lence
am·biv'a·lent
am·biv'a·lent·ly
am'ble
·bled ·bling
am·bro'si·a
am'bu·lance
am'bu·late'
·lat'ed ·lat'ing
am'bu·la·to'ry
am'bus·cade'
·cad'ed ·cad'ing
am'bush'

a·me'ba
·bas or ·bae
a·me'bic
a·mel'io·rate'
·rat'ed ·rat'ing
a·mel'io·ra'tion
a'men'
a·me'na·ble
a·me'na·bly
a·mend'
(revise; see EMEND)
a·mend'a·ble
a·mend'ment
a·mends'
a·men'i·ty
·ties
am'ent
A·mer'i·can
A·mer'i·can'a
A·mer'i·can·ism'
A·mer'i·can·i·za'-tion
A·mer'i·can·ize'
·ized' ·iz'ing
am'e·thyst
a'mi·a·bil'i·ty
a'mi·a·ble
a'mi·a·bly
am'i·ca·bil'i·ty
am'i·ca·ble
am'i·ca·bly
a·mid'
am'ide'
a·mid'ships'
a·midst'
a·mi'go
·gos'
a·mi'no acid
Am'ish
a·miss'
am'i·ty
am'me'ter
am'mo
am·mo'ni·a
am·mu·ni'tion
am·ne'si·a
am'nes·ty
·ties, ·tied ·ty·ing
am'ni·o·cen·te'sis
am'ni·ot'ic
a·moe'ba
·bas or ·bae
a·mok'
a·mong'
a·mon'til·la'do
a·mor'al
a'mo·ral'i·ty
a·mor'al·ly
am'o·rous
am'o·rous·ly
a·mor'phous
am'or·ti·za'tion
am'or·tize'
·tized' ·tiz'ing
a·mount'
a·mour'
a·mour-pro'pre

am'per·age
am'pere'
am'per·sand'
am·phet'a·mine'
am·phib'i·an
am·phib'i·ous
am·phi·the'a·ter or
·tre
am'ple
·pler ·plest
am'pli·fi·ca'tion
am'pli·fi'er
am'pli·fy'
·fied' ·fy'ing
am'pli·tude'
am'ply
am'pul'
am'pu·tate'
·tat'ed ·tat'ing
am'pu·ta'tion
am'pu·tee'
a·muck'
am'u·let
a·muse'
·mused' ·mus'ing
a·muse'ment
am'yl·ase'
a·nach'ro·nism
a·nach'ro·nis'tic
an'a·con'da
an'aer·o'bic
an'aes·the'sia
an'aes·thet'ic
an'a·gram'
a'nal
an'al·ge'si·a
an'al·ge'sic
an'a·log'
a·nal'o·gize'
·gized' ·giz'ing
a·nal'o·gous
a·nal'o·gous·ly
an'a·logue'
a·nal'o·gy
·gies
a·nal'y·sand'
a·nal'y·sis
·ses'
an'a·lyst
(one who ana-lyzes; see ANNAL-IST)
an'a·lyt'ic or
·lyt'i·cal
an'a·lyt'i·cal·ly
an'a·lyze'
·lyzed' ·lyz'ing
an'a·lyz'er
an'a·pest'
an·ar'chic
an'ar·chism'
an'ar·chist'
an'ar·chis'tic
an'ar·chy
a·nath'e·ma
·mas
a·nath'e·ma·tize'
·tized' ·tiz'ing

an'a·tom'i·cal *or* ·tom'ic
a·nat'o·mist
a·nat'o·mize' ·mized' ·miz'ing
a·nat'o·my
an'ces·tor
an'ces·tral
an'ces·tress
an'ces·try
an'chor
an'chor·age
an'cho·rite'
an'cho·vy ·vies
an'cient
an'cil·lar'y
and
an·dan'te
and'i·ron
an'dro·gen
an·drog'y·nous
an'droid'
an'ec·dot'al
an'ec·dote' (*story;* see ANTI-DOTE)
a·ne'mi·a
a·ne'mic
an'e·mom'e·ter
a·nem'o·ne'
an'er·oid'
an'es·the'si·a
an'es·the'si·ol'o·gist
an'es·the'si·ol'o·gy
an'es·thet'ic
an·es'the·tist
an·es'the·ti·za'tion
an·es'the·tize' ·tized' ·tiz'ing
an'eu·rysm' *or* ·rism'
a·new'
an'gel (*spirit;* see ANGLE)
an'gel·fish'
an·gel'ic *or* ·gel'i·cal
an·gel'i·cal·ly
an'ger
an·gi'na
an'gi·o·plas'ty
an'gi·o·sperm'
an'gle gled ·gling (*corner; scheme;* see ANGEL)
an'gler
an'gle·worm'
An'gli·can
An'gli·cize' ·cized' ·ciz'ing
An'glo·phile'
An'glo-Sax'on
An·go'ra
an'gri·ly
an'gry ·gri·er ·gri·est

ang'strom
an'guish
an'guished
an'gu·lar
an'gu·lar'i·ty ·ties
an'i·line
an'i·mad·ver'sion
an'i·mad·vert'
an'i·mal
an'i·mal'cule'
an'i·mate' ·mat'ed ·mat'ing
an'i·mat'ed
an'i·ma'tion
an'i·ma'tor
an'i·mism'
an'i·mis'tic
an'i·mos'i·ty ·ties
an'i·mus
an'i·on
an·ise
an'i·sette'
ankh
an'kle
an'klet
an'nal·ist (*writer of annals;* see ANALYST)
an'nals
an·neal'
an·ne·lid'
an'nex'
an'nex·a'tion
an·ni'hi·late' ·lat'ed ·lat'ing
an·ni'hi·la'tion
an·ni'hi·la'tor
an'ni·ver'sa·ry ·ries
an'no·tate' ·tat'ed ·tat'ing
an'no·ta'tion
an'no·ta'tor
an·nounce' ·nounced' ·nounc'ing
an·nounce'ment
an·nounc'er
an·noy'
an·noy'ance
an·noy'ing
an·noy'ing·ly
an'nu·al
an'nu·al·ly
an·nu'i·ty ·ties
an·nul' ·nulled' ·nul'ling
an'nu·lar
an·nul'ment
an·nun'ci·a'tion
an'ode'
an'o·dyne'
a·noint'
a·noint'ment
a·nom'a·lous

a·nom'a·ly ·lies
an'o·mie *or* ·my
a·non'
an'o·nym'i·ty
a·non'y·mous
a·non'y·mous·ly
a·noph'e·les'
an'o·rex'i·a
an'o·rex'ic
an·oth'er
an'swer
an'swer·a·ble
ant (*insect;* see AUNT)
ant·ac'id
an·tag'o·nism'
an·tag'o·nist
an·tag'o·nis'tic
an·tag'o·nis'ti·cal·ly
an·tag'o·nize' ·nized' ·niz'ing
ant·arc'tic
an'te ·ted *or* ·teed ·te·ing
an'te- *prefix* (*before;* see ANTI-)
ant'eat'er
an'te·bel'lum
an'te·ced'ent
an'te·cham'ber
an'te·date' ·dat'ed ·dat'ing
an'te·di·lu'vi·an
an'te·lope'
an'te me·ri'di·em
an·ten'na ·nae *or* ·nas
an·te'ri·or
an'te·room'
an'them
an'ther
ant'hill'
an·thol'o·gist
an·thol'o·gize' ·gized' ·giz'ing
an·thol'o·gy ·gies
an'thra·cite'
an'thrax'
an'thro·po·cen'tric
an'thro·poid'
an'thro·po·log'i·cal
an'thro·pol'o·gist
an'thro·pol'o·gy
an'thro·po·mor'phic
an'thro·po·mor'·ph i·cal·ly
an'thro·po·mor'-phism'
an'ti' ·tis'
an'ti- *prefix* (*against;* see ANTE-)
an'ti-air'craft
an'ti-bal·lis'tic mis-sile
an'ti·bi·ot'ic

an'ti·bod'y ·ies
an'tic
an·tic'i·pate' ·pat'ed ·pat'ing
an·tic'i·pa'tion
an·tic'i·pa·to'ry
an'ti·cli·mac'tic
an'ti·cli'max'
an'ti·cline'
an'ti·co·ag'u·lant
an'ti·de·pres'sant
an'ti·dote' (*remedy;* see ANEC-DOTE)
an'ti·freeze'
an'ti·gen
an'ti·he'ro ·roes
an'ti·his'ta·mine'
an'ti·knock'
an'ti·ma·cas'sar
an'ti·mat'ter
an'ti·mis'sile
an'ti·mo'ny
an'ti·pas'to
an·tip'a·thy ·thies
an'ti·per'son·nel'
an'ti·per'spi·rant
an'ti·phon'
an·tiph'o·nal
an·tip'o·dal
an·tip'o·des'
an'ti·quar'i·an
an'ti·quar'y ·quar'ies
an'ti·quat'ed
an·tique' ·tiqued' ·tiqu'ing
an·tiq'ui·ty ·ties
an'ti·sem'ite'
an'ti·se·mit'ic
an'ti·sem'i·tism'
an'ti·sep'sis
an'ti·sep'tic
an'ti·sep'ti·cal·ly
an'ti·slav'er·y
an'ti·so'cial
an'ti·tank'
an·tith'e·sis ·ses
an'ti·thet'i·cal
an'ti·thet'i·cal·ly
an'ti·tox'in
an'ti·trust'
an'ti·vi'ral
an'ti·viv'i·sec'tion·ist
ant'ler
an'to·nym'
a'nus ·nus·es *or* ·ni'
an'vil
anx·i'e·ty ·ties
anx'ious
anx'ious·ly

an'y
an'y·bod'y
an'y·how'
an'y·more'
an'y·one'
an'y·place'
an'y·thing'
an'y·way'
an'y·where'
A'-OK'
a·or'ta ·tas *or* ·tae
a·or'tal
a·or'tic
a·pace'
a·part'
a·part'heid'
a·part'ment
ap'a·thet'ic
ap'a·thet'i·cal·ly
ap'a·thy ·thies
ap'a·tite' (*mineral;* see APPETITE)
ape aped ap'ing
ape'like'
a·per'i·tif'
ap'er·ture
a'pex' a'pex·es *or* ap'i·ces'
a·pha'si·a
a·phe'li·on ·li·ons *or* ·li·a
a'phid
aph'o·rism'
aph'o·ris'tic
aph'ro·dis'i·ac'
a'pi·a·rist
a'pi·ar'y ·ies
a·piece'
a·plen'ty
a·plomb'
a·poc'a·lypse'
a·poc'a·lyp'tic
a·poc'ry·phal
ap'o·gee'
a'po·lit'i·cal
a'po·lit'i·cal·ly
a·pol'o·get'ic
a·pol'o·get'i·cal·ly
a·pol'o·gist
a·pol'o·gize' ·gized' ·giz'ing
a·pol'o·gy ·gies
ap'o·plec'tic
ap'o·plex'y
a·pos'ta·sy ·sies
a·pos'tate
a' pos·te'ri·o'ri
a·pos'tle
ap'os·tol'ic
a·pos'tro·phe

a·poth'e·car'y ·ies
ap'o·thegm'
a·poth'e·o'sis ·ses
ap·pall'
ap'pa·loo'sa
ap'pa·ra'tus ·tus *or* ·tus·es
ap·par'el ·eled *or* ·elled ·el·ing *or* ·el·ling
ap·par'ent
ap·par'ent·ly
ap'pa·ri'tion
ap·peal'
ap·peal'ing
ap·pear'
ap·pear'ance
ap·pease' ·peased' ·peas'ing
ap·pease'ment
ap·peas'er
ap·pel'lant
ap·pel'late
ap'pel·la'tion
ap·pend'
ap·pend'age
ap'pen·dec'to·my ·mies
ap·pen'di·ci'tis
ap·pen'dix ·dix·es *or* ·di·ces'
ap'per·tain'
ap'pe·tite' (*hunger;* see AP-ATITE)
ap'pe·tiz'er
ap'pe·tiz'ing
ap·plaud'
ap·plause'
ap'ple
ap'ple·jack'
ap'ple·sauce'
ap·pli'ance
ap'pli·ca·bil'i·ty
ap'pli·ca·ble
ap'pli·cant
ap'pli·ca'tion
ap'pli·ca'tor
ap·plied'
ap·pli'er
ap·pli·qué' ·quéd' ·qué'ing
ap·ply' ·plied' ·ply'ing
ap·point'
ap·point'ee'
ap·point'ive
ap·point'ment
ap·por'tion
ap·por'tion·ment
ap'po·site
ap'po·site·ly
ap'po·site·ness
ap'po·si'tion
ap·pos'i·tive
ap·prais'al

ap·praise'
·praised'
·prais'ing
(*estimate;* see AP-PRISE)
ap·prais'er
ap·pre'ci·a·ble
ap·pre'ci·a·bly
ap·pre'ci·ate'
·at'ed ·at'ing
ap·pre'ci·a'tion
ap·pre'ci·a·tive
ap·pre'ci·a·tive·ly
ap·pre'ci·a·tor
ap'pre·hend'
ap'pre·hen'sion
ap'pre·hen'sive
ap'pre·hen'sive·ly
ap'pre·hen'sive·ness
ap·pren'tice
·ticed ·tic·ing
ap·pren'tice·ship'
ap·prise' or ·prize'
·prised' or
·prized', ·pris'ing
or ·priz'ing
(*inform;* see AP-PRAISE)
ap·proach'
ap·proach'a·ble
ap'pro·ba'tion
ap·pro'pri·ate'
·at'ed ·at'ing
ap·pro'pri·ate·ly
ap·pro'pri·ate·ness
ap·pro'pri·a'tion
ap·pro'pri·a'tor
ap·prov'al
ap·prove'
·proved' ·prov'ing
ap·prov'ing·ly
ap·prox'i·mate'
·mat'ed ·mat'ing
ap·prox'i·mate·ly
ap·prox'i·ma'tion
ap·pur'te·nance
ap'ri·cot'
A'pril
a' pri·o'ri
a'pron
ap'ro·pos'
apse
apt
ap'ti·tude'
apt'ly
apt'ness
aq'ua
aq'ua·cul'ture
aq'ua·ma·rine'
aq'ua·naut'
aq'ua·plane'
·planed' ·plan'ing
a·quar'i·um
·i·ums or ·i·a
A·quar'i·us
a·quat'ic
aq'ua·vit'
aq'ue·duct'
a'que·ous

aq'ui·fer
aq'ui·line'
ar'a·besque'
A·ra'bi·an
Ar'a·bic
ar'a·ble
a·rach'nid
ar'bi·ter
ar·bit'ra·ment
ar'bi·trar'i·ly
ar'bi·trar'i·ness
ar'bi·trar'y
ar'bi·trate'
·trat'ed ·trat'ing
ar'bi·tra'tion
ar'bi·tra'tor
ar'bor
ar·bo're·al
ar'bo·re'tum
·tums or ·ta
ar'bor·vi'tae
ar·bu'tus
arc
arced or arcked
arc'ing or arck'ing
(*curve;* see ARK)
ar·cade'
ar·cane'
arch
ar'chae·o·log'i·cal
ar'chae·o·log'i·cal·ly
ar'chae·ol'o·gist
ar'chae·ol'o·gy
ar·cha'ic
ar·cha'i·cal·ly
ar'cha·ism
arch'an'gel
arch'bish'op
arch'bish'op·ric
arch'dea'con
arch'di·oc'e·san
arch'di'o·cese'
arch'duch'ess
arch'duke'
arch'en'e·my
·mies
arch'er
arch'er·y
ar'che·typ'al or
·typ'i·cal
ar'che·type'
ar'chi·e·pis'co·pal
ar'chi·pel'a·go
·goes' or ·gos'
ar'chi·tect'
ar'chi·tec·ton'ic
ar'chi·tec·ton'ics
ar'chi·tec'tur·al
ar'chi·tec'tur·al·ly
ar'chi·tec'ture
ar'chi·trave'
ar'chive'
ar'chi·vist
arch'way
arc'tic
ar'dent
ar'dent·ly
ar'dor

ar'du·ous
ar'du·ous·ly
are
ar'e·a
(*region;* see ARIA)
a·re'na
aren't
ar'gent
Ar'gen·tine'
ar'gon'
ar'go·sy
·sies
ar'got
ar'gu·a·ble
ar'gu·a·bly
ar'gue
·gued ·gu·ing
ar'gu·ment
ar'gu·men·ta'tion
ar'gu·men'ta·tive
ar'gyle'
a'ri·a
(*melody;* see AREA)
ar'id
a·rid'i·ty
Ar'i·es'
a·right'
a·rise'
a·rose' a·ris'en
a·ris'ing
ar'is·toc'ra·cy
·cies
a·ris'to·crat
a·ris'to·crat'ic
Ar'is·to·te'li·an
a·rith'me·tic n.
ar'ith·met'ic adj.
ar'ith·met'i·cal
ar'ith·me·ti'cian
Ar'i·zo'na
ark
(*boat;* see ARC)
Ar'kan·sas'
arm
ar·ma'da
ar'ma·dil'lo
·los
Ar'ma·ged'don
ar'ma·ment
ar'ma·ture
arm'chair'
arm'ful
·fuls
arm'hole'
ar'mi·stice
arm'let
ar'mor
ar'mored
ar·mo'ri·al
ar'mor·y
·ies
arm'pit'
arm'rest'
ar'my
·mies
a·ro'ma
ar'o·mat'ic
ar'o·mat'i·cal·ly

a·rose'
a·round'
a·rous'al
a·rouse'
·roused' ·rous'ing
ar·peg'gio
·gios
ar·raign'
ar·raign'ment
ar·range'
·ranged' ·rang'ing
ar·range'ment
ar·rang'er
ar·rant'
ar·ras'
ar·ray'
ar·rears'
ar·rest'
ar·rest'ing
ar·rhyth'mi·a
ar·rhyth'mic or
·rhyth'mi·cal
ar·riv'al
ar·rive'
·rived' ·riv'ing
ar·ri've·der'ci
ar'ro·gance
ar'ro·gant
ar'ro·gant·ly
ar'ro·gate'
·gat'ed ·gat'ing
ar'ro·ga'tion
ar'row
ar'row·head'
ar'row·root'
ar·roy'o
·os
ar'se·nal
ar'se·nic'
ar'son
ar'son·ist
art
art dec'o
ar·te'ri·al adj.
ar·te'ri·ole' n.
ar·te'ri·o·scle·ro'sis
ar'ter·y
·ies
ar·te'sian
art'ful
art'ful·ly
art'ful·ness
ar·thrit'ic
ar·thri'tis
ar'thro·pod'
ar'thro·scope'
ar'thro·scop'ic
ar'ti·choke'
ar'ti·cle
ar·tic'u·late
·lat'ed ·lat'ing
ar·tic'u·late·ly
ar·tic'u·la'tion
ar'ti·fact'
ar'ti·fice
ar·tif'i·cer
ar'ti·fi'cial

ar'ti·fi'ci·al'i·ty
·ties
ar'ti·fi'cial·ly
ar·til'ler·y
ar·til'ler·y·man
art'i·ness
ar'ti·san
art'ist
ar·tis'tic
ar·tis'ti·cal·ly
art'ist·ry
art'less
art'less·ly
art'y
·i·er ·i·est
ar'um
as·bes'tos
as·cend'
as·cend'an·cy or
·en·cy
as·cend'ant or ·ent
as·cen'sion
as·cent'
(*a rising;* see AS-SENT)
as·cer'tain'
as·cet'ic
(*austere;* see ACETIC)
as·cet'i·cal·ly
as·cet'i·cism'
a·scor'bic acid
as'cot
as·cribe'
·cribed' ·crib'ing
as·crip'tion
a·sep'tic
a·sex'u·al
a·sex'u·al·ly
ash
a·shamed'
a·sham'ed·ly
ash'en
ash'es
a·shore'
ash'ram
ash'tray'
ash'y
·i·er ·i·est
A'sian
A'si·at'ic
a·side'
as'i·nine'
as'i·nin'i·ty
ask
a·skance'
ask'er
a·skew'
a·slant'
a·sleep'
a·so'cial
asp
as·par'a·gus
as·par'tame'
as'pect'
as'pen
as·per'i·ty
as·per'sion

as'phalt'
as'pho·del'
as·phyx'i·ate'
·at'ed ·at'ing
as·phyx'i·a'tion
as'pic'
as'pi·rant
as'pi·rate'
·rat'ed ·rat'ing
as'pi·ra'tion
as'pi·ra'tor
as·pire'
·pired' ·pir'ing
as'pi·rin'
ass
as·sail'
as·sail'a·ble
as·sail'ant
as·sas'sin
as·sas'si·nate'
·nat'ed ·nat'ing
as·sas'si·na'tion
as·sault'
as'say
(*analyze;* see ES-SAY)
as·say'er
as·sem'blage'
as·sem'ble
·bled ·bling
as·sem'bler
as·sem'bly
·blies
as·sem'bly·man
as·sem'bly·wom'an
as·sent'
(*consent;* see AS-CENT)
as·sert'
as·sert'er or
·sert'or
as·ser'tion
as·ser'tive
as·ser'tive·ly
as·ser'tive·ness
as·sess'
as·sess'ment
as·ses'sor
as'set
as·sev'er·ate'
·at'ed ·at'ing
as·sev'er·a'tion
as·si·du'i·ty
as·sid'u·ous
as·sid'u·ous·ly
as·sid'u·ous·ness
as·sign'
as·sign'a·ble
as'sig·na'tion
as·sign'er or
·sign'or'
as·sign'ment
as·sim'i·late'
·lat'ed ·lat'ing
as·sim'i·la'tion
as·sist'
as·sist'ance
as·sist'ant
as·siz'es

as·so'ci·ate'
 ·at'ed ·at'ing
as·so'ci·a'tion
as·so'ci·a'tive
as'so·nance
as'so·nant
as·sort'
as·sort'ed
as·sort'ment
as·suage'
 ·suaged' ·suag'ing
as·sum'a·ble
as·sume'
 ·sumed' ·sum'ing
as·sumed'
as·sump'tion
as·sur'ance
as·sure'
 ·sured' ·sur'ing
as·sured'
as·sur'ed·ly
as'ter
as'ter·isk'
a·stern'
as'ter·oid'
asth'ma
asth·mat'ic
as'tig·mat'ic
a·stig'ma·tism'
a·stir'
as·ton'ish
as·ton'ish·ing
as·ton'ish·ing·ly
as·ton'ish·ment
as·tound'
as·tound'ing
as·tound'ing·ly
a·strad'dle
as'tra·khan
as'tral
a·stray'
a·stride'
as·trin'gen·cy
as·trin'gent
as'tro·bi·ol'o·gy
as'tro·dy·nam'ics
as·trol'o·ger
as·tro·log'i·cal
as·trol'o·gy
as'tro·naut'
as'tro·nau'tics
as·tron'o·mer
as'tro·nom'ic
as'tro·nom'i·cal
as·tron'o·my
as'tro·phys'i·cist
as'tro·phys'ics
As'tro·turf'
as·tute'
as·tute'ly
as·tute'ness
a·sun'der
a·sy'lum
a·sym·met'ri·cal
a·sym'me·try
a'symp·to·mat'ic
at'a·vism'

at'a·vis'tic
a·tax'i·a
a·tax'ic
ate
at'el·ier'
a'the·ism'
a'the·ist'
a'the·is'tic
ath'er·o'scle·ro'sis
ath'lete'
ath·let'ic
ath·let'i·cal·ly
ath·let'ics
a·thwart'
a·tilt'
at'las
at'mos·phere'
at'mos·pher'ic
at'mos·pher'i·cal·ly
at'oll'
at'om
a·tom'ic
a·tom'i·cal·ly
at'om·iz'er
a·ton'al
a'to·nal'i·ty
a·tone'
 ·toned' ·ton'ing
a·tone'ment
a·top'
a'tri·um
 ·tri·a or tri·ums
a·tro'cious
a·tro'cious·ly
a·tro'cious·ness
a·troc'i·ty
 ·ties
at'ro·phy
 ·phied ·phy·ing
at'ro·pine'
at·tach'
at·tach'a·ble
at·ta·ché'
at·tach'ment
at·tack'
at·tack'er
at·tain'
at·tain'a·ble
at·tain'der
at·tain'ment
at'tar
at·tempt'
at·tend'
at·tend'ance
at·tend'ant
at·ten'tion
at·ten'tive
at·ten'tive·ly
at·ten'u·ate'
 ·at'ed ·at'ing
at·ten'u·a'tion
at·test'
at'tes·ta'tion
at'tic
at·tire'
 ·tired' ·tir'ing
at'ti·tude'

at'ti·tu'di·nal
at'ti·tu'di·nize'
 ·nized' ·niz'ing
at·tor'ney
 ·neys
at·tract'
at·trac'tion
at·trac'tive
at·trac'tive·ly
at·trac'tive·ness
at·trib'ut·a·ble
at'tri·bute' n.
at·trib'ute v.
 ·ut·ed ·ut·ing
at'tri·bu'tion
at·trib'u·tive
at·trib'u·tive·ly
at·tri'tion
at·tune'
 ·tuned' ·tun'ing
a·twit'ter
a·typ'i·cal
a·typ'i·cal·ly
au'burn
auc'tion
auc'tion·eer'
au·da'cious
au·da'cious·ly
au·da'cious·ness
au·dac'i·ty
au'di·bil'i·ty
au'di·ble
au'di·bly
au'di·ence
au'di·o'
au'di·ol'o·gist
au'di·ol'o·gy
au'di·om'e·ter
au'di·o·met'ric
au'di·o·phile'
au'di·o·vis'u·al
au'dit
au·di'tion
au'di·tor
au'di·to'ri·um
au'di·to'ry
au'ger
 (tool; see AUGUR)
aught
 (anything; see
 OUGHT)
aug·ment'
aug'men·ta'tion
aug·ment'er
au gra'tin
au'gur
 (fortuneteller; see
 AUGER)
au'gu·ry
 ·ries
au·gust'
Au'gust
au·gust'ly
au·gust'ness
au jus'
auk
aunt
 (relative; see ANT)

au'ra
 ·ras or ·rae
au'ral
 (of the ear; see
 ORAL)
au're·ole'
au' re·voir'
au'ri·cle
 (earlike part; see
 ORACLE)
au·ro'ra bo're·al'is
aus'cul·ta'tion
aus'pi·ces
aus·pi'cious
aus·pi'cious·ly
aus·tere'
aus·tere'ly
aus·ter'i·ty
 ·ties
Aus·tral'ian
Aus'tri·an
au·then'tic
au·then'ti·cal·ly
au·then'ti·cate'
 ·cat'ed ·cat'ing
au·then'ti·ca'tion
au'then·tic'i·ty
au'thor
au·thor'i·tar'i·an
au·thor'i·tar'i·an·ism'
au·thor'i·ta'tive
au·thor'i·ta'tive·ly
au·thor'i·ty
 ·ties
au·thor'i·za'tion
au'thor·ize'
 ·ized' ·iz'ing
au'thor·ship'
au'tism'
au·tis'tic
au'to
 ·tos
au'to·bi'o·graph'i·cal
au'to·bi·og'ra·phy
 ·phies
au·toc'ra·cy
 ·cies
au'to·crat'
au'to·crat'ic
au'to·crat'i·cal·ly
au'to·di'dact'
au'to·graph'
au'to·mate'
 ·mat'ed ·mat'ing
au'to·mat'ic
au'to·mat'i·cal·ly
au'to·ma'tion
au·tom'a·ton'
 ·tons' or ·ta
au'to·mo·bile'
au'to·mo'tive
au·ton'o·mic'
au·ton'o·mous
au·ton'o·mous·ly
au·ton'o·my
au'top·sy
 ·sies
au'tumn
au·tum'nal

aux·il'ia·ry
 ·ries
aux'in
a·vail'
a·vail'a·bil'i·ty
a·vail'a·ble
av'a·lanche'
a·vant'-garde'
av'a·rice
av'a·ri'cious
av'a·ri'cious·ly
a·vast'
av'a·tar'
a·venge'
 ·venged' ·veng'ing
a·veng'er
av'e·nue'
a·ver'
 ·verred' ·ver'ring
av'er·age
 ·aged ·ag·ing
a·verse'
 (unwilling; see AD-
 VERSE)
a·ver'sion
a·vert'
a'vi·an
a'vi·ar'y
 ·ar'ies
a'vi·a'tion
a'vi·a'tor
a'vi·a'trix
av'id
a·vid'i·ty
av'id·ly
a'vi·on'ics
a'vi·ta·min·o'sis
av'o·ca'do
 ·dos
av'o·ca'tion
av'o·ca'tion·al
a·void'
a·void'a·ble
a·void'a·bly
a·void'ance
av'oir·du·pois'
a·vouch'
a·vow'
a·vow'al
a·vowed'
a·vow'ed·ly
a·vun'cu·lar
a·wait'
a·wake'
 ·woke' or ·waked',
 ·waked' or
 ·wok'en, ·wak'ing
a·wak'en
a·wak'en·ing
a·ward'
a·ware'
a·ware'ness
a·wash'
a·way'
awe
 awed aw'ing
a·weigh'
awe'some
awe'some·ly

awe'strick'en
awe'-struck'
aw'ful
aw'ful·ly
aw'ful·ness
a·while'
awk'ward
awk'ward·ly
awk'ward·ness
awl
 (tool; see ALL)
awn
awn'ing
a·woke'
a·wry'
ax or axe
 ax'es
 axed ax'ing
ax'i·al
ax'i·al·ly
ax'i·om
ax'i·o·mat'ic
ax'i·o·mat'i·cal·ly
ax'is
 ax'es
ax'le
ax'le·tree'
ax'o·lotl'
ax'on'
a'ya·tol'lah
aye
a·za'lea
az'i·muth
az'ure

B

baa
bab'ble
 ·bled ·bling
bab'bler
babe
ba'bel
ba·boon'
ba·bush'ka
ba'by
 ·bies
 ·bied ·by·ing
baby boom'er
ba'by·ish
ba'by's breath
ba'by-sit'
bac'ca·lau're·ate
bac'ca·rat' or
 bac'ca·ra'
bac'cha·nal'
bac'cha·na'li·an
bach'e·lor
bach'e·lor·hood'
ba·cil'lus
 ·li'
back
back'ache'
back'bite'
back'bend'
back'board'
back'bone'

back'break'ing
back'court'
back'date'
back'door'
back'drop'
back'er
back'field'
back'fire'
back'gam'mon
back'ground'
back'hand'
back'hand'ed
back'ing
back'lash'
back'list'
back'log'
back'pack'
back'pack'er
back'ped'al
back'rest'
back'side'
back'slide'
back'space'
back'spin'
back'stage'
back'stairs'
back'stop'
back'stretch'
back'stroke'
back'-to-back'
back'track'
back'up' *or* back'-
  up'
back'ward
back'wash'
back'wa'ter
back'woods'
back'woods'man
ba'con
bac·te'ri·a
  sing. ·ri·um
bac·te'ri·al
bac·te'ri·cid'al
bac·te'ri·cide'
bac·te'ri·o·log'i·cal
bac·te'ri·ol'o·gist
bac·te'ri·ol'o·gy
bad
  worse worst
bade
  (*form of* bid)
badge
badg'er
bad'lands'
bad'min'ton
bad'-mouth'
bad'-tem'pered
baf'fle
  ·fled ·fling
baf'fler
baf'fling
bag
  bagged bag'ging
ba'gel
bag'ful'
  ·fuls'
bag'gage

bag'gie
bag'gy
  ·gi·er ·gi·est
bag'pipe'
bail
  (*money; see* BALE)
bail'iff
bail'i·wick'
bails'man
bait
bait'-and-switch'
bait'ed
  (*lured; see* BATED)
bake
  baked bak'ing
bak'er
bak'er·y
  ·ies
bal'a·lai'ka
bal'ance
  ·anced ·anc·ing
bal'co·ny
  ·nies
bald
bal'der·dash'
bald'faced'
bald'head'ed
bald'ing
bald'ness
bale
  baled bal'ing
  (*bundle; see* BAIL)
ba·leen'
bale'ful
balk
balk'y
  ·i·er ·i·est
ball
  (*round object; see*
  BAWL)
bal'lad
bal'lad·eer'
bal'lad·ry
ball'-and-sock'et
  joint
bal'last
bal'le·ri'na
bal'let
ball'game'
bal·lis'tic
bal·lis'tics
bal·loon'
bal·loon'ist
bal'lot
ball'park'
ball'play'er
ball'point'
ball'room'
bal'ly·hoo'
  ·hooed' ·hoo'ing
balm
balm'y
  ·i·er ·i·est
ba·lo'ney
bal'sa
bal'sam
bal'us·ter
bal'us·trade'

bam·bi'no
  ·nos *or* ·ni
bam·boo'
bam·boo'zle
  ·zled ·zling
ban
  banned ban'ning
ba'nal
ba·nal'i·ty
  ·ties
ba·nan'a
band
band'age
  ·aged ·ag·ing
band'-aid' *or*
  band'aid'
ban·dan'na *or*
  ban·dan'a
band'box'
ban'dit
band'mas'ter
ban'do·leer' *or*
  ·lier'
bands'man
band'stand'
band'wag'on
ban'dy
  ·died ·dy·ing
ban'dy-leg'ged
bane
bang
ban'gle
bang'-up'
ban'ish
ban'ish·ment
ban'is·ter
ban'jo
  ·jos' *or* ·joes'
ban'jo·ist
bank
bank'a·ble
bank'book'
bank'er
bank'ing
bank'roll'
bank'rupt'
bank'rupt'cy
  ·cies
ban'ner
banns (*marriage no-*
  tice)
ban'quet
ban'shee *or*
  ban'shie
ban'tam
ban'tam-weight'
ban'ter
ban'yan
ba'o·bab'
bap'tism
bap·tis'mal
Bap'tist
bap'tis·ter·y *or*
  ·tis·try
  ·ies *or* ·tries
bap'tize'
  ·tized' ·tiz'ing

bar
  barred bar'ring
barb
bar·bar'i·an
bar·bar'ic
bar'ba·rism
bar·bar'i·ty
  ·ties
bar'ba·rous
bar'be·cue'
  ·cued' ·cu'ing
barbed
bar'bel (*hairlike*
  growth)
bar'bell' (*bar with*
  weights)
bar'ber
bar'ber·ry
  ·ries
bar'ber·shop'
bar·bi'tu·rate
bard
bare
  bar'er bar'est
  bared bar'ing
  (*uncover; see*
  BEAR)
bare'back'
bare'-bones'
bare'faced'
bare'foot'
bare'foot'ed
bare'hand'ed
bare'head'ed
bare'leg'ged
bare'ly
bar'gain
barge
  barged barg'ing
bar'i·tone'
bar'i·um
bark
bar'keep'er
bark'er
bar'ley
bar'maid'
bar'man
bar mitz'vah *or* bar
  miz'vah
barn
bar'na·cle
barn'storm'
barn'yard'
ba·rom'e·ter
bar'o·met'ric
bar'on
  (*nobleman; see*
  BARREN)
bar'on·ess
bar'on·et'
ba·ro'ni·al
ba·roque'
bar'racks
bar'ra·cu'da
  ·da *or* ·das
bar·rage'
  ·raged' ·rag'ing
barred

bar'rel
  ·reled *or* ·relled
  ·rel·ing *or* ·rel·ling
bar'ren
  (*empty; see*
  BARON)
bar·rette'
  (*hair clasp; see*
  BERET)
bar'ri·cade'
  ·cad'ed ·cad'ing
bar'ri·er
bar'ring
bar'ris·ter
bar'room'
bar'row
  (*wheel barrow;*
  pile of rocks; see
  BORROW)
bar'tend'er
bar'ter
bar'y·on'
ba'sal
ba·salt'
base
  bas'es
  based bas'ing
  (*foundation; vile;*
  see BASS)
base'ball'
base'board'
base'less
base'man
base'ment
bas'es
  (*pl. of* base)
ba'ses
  (*pl. of* basis)
bash
bash'ful
bas'ic
bas'i·cal·ly
bas'il
ba·sil'i·ca
ba'sin
ba'sis
  ·ses
bask
bas'ket
bas'ket·ball'
bas'-re·lief'
bass
  (*singer; see* BASE)
bass (*fish*)
bas'set
bas'si·net'
bas·soon'
bast
bas'tard
bas'tard·i·za'tion
bas'tard·ize'
  ·ized' ·iz'ing
baste
  bast'ed bast'ing
bas'tion
bat
  bat'ted bat'ting
bate
  bat'ed bat'ing

  (*held in; see*
  BAITED)
bath
  baths
bathe
  bathed bath'ing
bath'er
bath'house'
bath'mat'
ba'thos'
bath'robe'
bath'room'
bath'tub'
bath'y·scaph'
ba·tik'
bat mitz'vah *or* bat
  miz'vah
ba·ton'
bat·tal'ion
bat'ten
bat'ter
bat'ter·y
  ·ies
bat'ting
bat'tle
  ·tled ·tling
bat'tle-ax' *or* -axe'
bat'tle-field'
bat'tle-ground'
bat'tle-ment
bat'tle-scarred'
bat'tle-ship'
bat'ty
  ·ti·er ·ti·est
bau'ble
baud
  (*measurement*)
baux'ite'
bawd (*prostitute*)
bawd'y
  ·i·er ·i·est
bawl
  (*shout; see* BALL)
bay
bay'ber'ry
  ·ries
bay'o·net'
  ·net'ed *or* ·net'ted,
  ·net'ing *or* ·net'-
  ting
bay'ou'
ba·zaar'
  (*a market; see*
  BIZARRE)
ba·zoo'ka
be
  was *or* were, been
  be'ing
  (*exist; see* BEE)
beach
  (*shore; see* BEECH)
beach'comb'er
beach'comb'ing
beach'head'
bea'con
bead
bea'dle
  (*church officer;*
  see BEETLE)

bead'y
  ·i·er ·i·est
bea'gle
beak
beak'er
beam
bean
bean'bag'
bean'stalk'
bear
  (*animal;* see BARE)
bear
  bore, borne *or*
  born, bear'ing
  (*carry;* see BARE)
bear'a·ble
beard
beard'ed
beard'less
bear'er
bear'ing
bear'ish
bear'like'
bear'skin'
beast
beast'ly
  ·li·er ·li·est
beat
  beat beat'en beat-
  'ing
beat'en
be·a·tif'ic
be·at'i·fi·ca'tion
be·at'i·fy'
  ·fied ·fy'ing
beat'ing
be·at'i·tude'
beat'-up'
beau
  beaus *or* beaux
  (*sweetheart;* see
  BOW)
beau'te·ous
beau·ti'cian
beau'ti·fi·ca'tion
beau'ti·fi'er
beau'ti·ful
beau'ti·ful·ly
beau'ti·fy'
  ·fied' ·fy'ing
beau'ty
  ·ties
bea'ver
be·calm'
be·cause'
beck'on
be·cloud'
be·come'
be·com'ing
bed
  bed'ded bed'ding
be·daz'zle
bed'bug'
bed'clothes'
bed'cov'er
bed'ding
be·deck'
be·dev'il
bed'fel'low

be·dim'
bed'lam
bed'pan'
be·drag'gle
  ·gled ·gling
bed'rid'den
bed'rock'
bed'roll'
bed'room'
bed'side'
bed'sore'
bed'spread'
bed'time'
bee
  (*insect;* see BE)
beech
  (*tree;* see BEACH)
beech'nut'
beef
  beeves *or* beefs
beef'cake'
beef'steak'
beef'y
  ·i·er ·i·est
bee'hive'
bee'keep'er
bee'keep'ing
bee'line'
been
  (*form of* be; see
  BIN)
beep
beer
  (*drink;* see BIER)
bees'wax'
beet
bee'tle
  (*insect;* see
  BEADLE)
bee'tle-browed'
be·fall'
be·fit'
be·fit'ting
be·fog'
be·fore'
be·fore'hand'
be·foul'
be·friend'
be·fud'dle
  ·dled ·dling
beg
  begged beg'ging
be·gan'
be·get'
  ·got' *or* ·gat',
  ·got'ten *or* ·got',
  ·get'ting
beg'gar
beg'gar·ly
be·gin'
  ·gan' ·gun' ·gin'ning
be·gin'ner
be·gin'ning
be·gone'
be·gon'ia
be·got'
be·got'ten
be·grime'
  ·grimed' ·grim'ing

be·grudge'
be·grudg'ing·ly
be·guile'
  ·guiled' ·guil'ing
be·gun'
be·half'
be·have'
  ·haved' ·hav'ing
be·hav'ior
be·hav'ior·al
be·head'
be·held'
be·he'moth
be·hest'
be·hind'
be·hold'
be·hold'en
be·hoove'
  ·hooved' ·hoov'ing
beige
be'ing
be·jew'el
be·la'bor
be·lat'ed
be·lay'
  ·layed' ·lay'ing
belch
be·lea'guer
bel'fry
  ·fries
Bel'gian
be·lie'
  ·lied' ·ly'ing
be·lief'
be·liev'a·ble
be·lieve'
  ·lieved' ·liev'ing
be·liev'er
be·lit'tle
  ·tled ·tling
bell (*signal device*)
bel'la·don'na
bell'-bot'tom
bell'boy'
belle (*pretty girl*)
belles-let'tres
bell'hop'
bel'li·cose'
bel'li·cos'i·ty
bel·lig'er·ence
bel·lig'er·en·cy
bel·lig'er·ent
bel'low
bel'lows'
bell'weth'er
bel'ly
  ·lies
  ·lied ·ly·ing
bel'ly·ache'
bel'ly·but'ton
bel'ly·ful'
be·long'
be·long'ings
be·lov'ed
be·low'
belt
belt'ing
belt'way'

be·moan'
be·muse'
bench
bench'-press'
bend
  bent bend'ing
bend'a·ble
be·neath'
ben'e·dic'tion
ben'e·fac'tor
ben'e·fac'tress
be·nef'i·cence
be·nef'i·cent
ben'e·fi'cial
ben'e·fi'ci·ar'y
  ·ar'ies
ben'e·fit
  ·fit·ed ·fit·ing
be·nev'o·lence
be·nev'o·lent
be·night'ed
be·nign'
be·nig'nant
be·nig'ni·ty
  ·ties
be·nign'ly
bent
bent'wood'
be·numb'
ben'zene
ben'zo·caine'
be·queath'
be·quest'
be·rate'
  ·rat'ed ·rat'ing
be·reave'
  ·reaved' *or* ·reft'
  ·reav'ing
be·reave'ment
be·ret'
  (*flat cap;* see BAR-
  RETTE)
berg
ber'i·ber'i
berm
ber'ry
  ·ries
  ·ried ·ry·ing
  (*fruit;* see BURY)
ber·serk'
berth
  (*bed;* see BIRTH)
ber'yl
be·ryl'li·um
be·seech'
  ·sought' *or*
  ·seeched'
  ·seech'ing
be·seech'ing·ly
be·set'
be·set'ting
be·side'
be·sides'
be·siege'
  ·sieged' ·sieg'ing
be·smear'
be·smirch'
be·sot'
  ·sot'ted ·sot'ting

be·sought'
  (*form of* beseech)
be·span'gle
be·spat'ter
be·speak'
  ·spoke', ·spo'ken
  or ·spoke',
  ·speak'ing
best
bes'tial
bes·ti·al'i·ty
  ·ties
be·stir'
be·stow'
be·stow'al
be·strew'
be·stride'
bet
  bet *or* bet'ted
  bet'ting
be'ta
be·take'
be·think'
be·tide'
be·to'ken
be·tray'
be·tray'al
be·tray'er
be·troth'
be·troth'al
be·trothed'
bet'ter
  (*compar. of* good)
bet'ter·ment
bet'tor *or* ·ter (*one
  who bets*)
be·tween'
be·twixt'
bev'el
  ·eled *or* ·elled,
  ·el·ing *or* ·el·ling
bev'er·age'
bev'y
  ·ies
be·wail'
be·ware'
be·wigged'
be·wil'der
be·wil'dered
be·wil'der·ment
be·witch'
be·yond'
bez'el
bi·an'nu·al
bi'as
  ·as·es
  ·ased *or* ·assed
  ·as·ing *or* ·as·sing
bi·ath'lon
bib
bi'ble
bib'li·cal
bib'li·og'ra·pher
bib'li·og'ra·phy
  ·phies
bib'li·o·phile'
bib'u·lous
bi·cam'er·al
bi·car'bon·ate

bi'cen·ten'ni·al
bi'ceps'
  ·ceps' *or* ·ceps·es'
bick'er
bi'con'cave'
bi'con'vex'
bi·cus'pid
bi'cy·cle
bi'cy'clist
bid
  bade *or* bid,
  bid'den *or* bid,
  bid'ding
  (*ask;* see BIDE)
bid'der
bid'dy
  ·dies
bide
  bode *or* bid'ed,
  bid'ed bid'ing
  (*stay;* see BID)
bi·en'ni·al
bi·en'ni·al·ly
bier
  (*coffin stand;* see
  BEER)
bi'fo'cals
bi'fur·cate'
  ·cat'ed ·cat'ing
big
  big'ger big'gest
big'a·mist
big'a·mous
big'a·my
big'-bang' theory
big'heart'ed
big'horn'
big'mouth'
big·no'ni·a
big'ot
big'ot·ed
big'ot·ry
bike
bik'er
bi·ki'ni
bi·lat'er·al
bile
bilge
bi·lin'gual
bil'ious
bilk
bill
bill'a·ble
bill'board'
bil'let
bill'fold'
bil'liard
bil'liards
bill'ing
bil'lion
bil'lion·aire'
bil'lionth
bil'low
bil'low·y
  ·i·er ·i·est
bil'ly
  ·lies
bi'me·tal'lic
bi·month'ly

bin
  (*box; see* BEEN)
bi'na·ry
  ·ries
bind
  bound bind'ing
bind'er
bind'er·y
  ·ies
bind'ing
binge
  binged binge'ing
bin'go
bin'na·cle
bin·oc'u·lar
bin·oc'u·lars
bi·no'mi·al
bi'o·chem'ist
bi'o·chem'is·try
bi'o·de·grad'a·ble
bi'o·feed'back
bi·og'ra·pher
bi'o·graph'i·cal
bi·og'ra·phy
  ·phies
bi'o·log'i·cal
bi'o·log'i·cal·ly
bi·ol'o·gist
bi·ol'o·gy
bi·on'ic
bi·on'ics
bi'o·phys'i·cal
bi'o·phys'i·cist
bi'o·phys'ics
bi·op'sy
  ·sies
bi'o·rhythm
bi'o·tin
bi·par'ti·san
bi·par'ti·san·ship'
bi'ped'
bi'plane'
bi·ra'cial
birch
bird
bird'call'
bird'er
bird'ie
bird'ing
bird'seed'
bird's'-eye'
bi·ret'ta
birth
  (*being born; see*
  BERTH)
birth'day'
birth'mark'
birth'place'
birth'rate'
birth'right'
birth'stone'
bis'cuit
  ·cuits *or* ·cuit
bi·sect'
bi·sec'tion
bi·sec'tor
bi·sex'u·al
bish'op

bish'op·ric
bis'muth
bi'son
bisque
bis'tro
bit
bitch
bite
  bit, bit'ten *or* bit,
  bit'ing
  (*eat, sting, etc.;*
  see BYTE)
bit'ing
bit'ter
bit'tern
bit'ter·ness
bit'ters
bit'ter·sweet'
bi·tu'men
bi·tu'mi·nous
bi·va'lent
bi'valve'
biv'ou·ac'
  ·acked' ·ack'ing
bi·week'ly
  ·lies
bi·zarre'
  (*odd; see* BAZAAR)
blab
  blabbed blab'bing
black
black'-and-blue'
black'ball'
black'ber'ry
  ·ries
black'bird'
black'board'
black'en
black'-eyed' Su'san
black'guard
black'head'
black'heart'ed
black'ish
black'jack'
black'list'
black'mail'
black'mail'er
black'ness
black'out'
black'smith'
black'top'
blad'der
blade
blam'a·ble *or*
  blame'·
blame
  blamed blam'ing
blame'less
blame'wor'thy
blanch
bland
blan'dish
bland'ly
bland'ness
blank
blan'ket
blank'ly
blank'ness

blare
  blared blar'ing
blar'ney
  ·neyed ·ney·ing
bla·sé'
blas·pheme'
  ·phemed'
  ·phem'ing
blas·phem'er
blas'phe·mous
blas'phe·my
  ·mies
blast
blast'off' *or* blast'-
  off'
bla'tan·cy
bla'tant
blaze
  blazed blaz'ing
blaz'er
bleach
bleach'ers
bleak
bleak'ly
bleak'ness
blear'y
  ·i·er ·i·est
blear'y-eyed'
bleat
bleed
  bled bleed'ing
bleed'er
bleep
blem'ish
blend
  blend'ed *or* blent
  blend'ing
blend'er
bless
  blessed *or* blest
  bless'ing
bless'ed
bless'ing
blew
  (*form of* blow; *see*
  BLUE)
blight
blimp
blind
blind'fold'
blind'ly
blind'ness
blind'side'
  ·sid'ed ·sid'ing
blink
blink'er
blintz
blip
bliss
bliss'ful
bliss'ful·ly
blis'ter
blithe
blitz
blitz'krieg'
bliz'zard
bloat
bloat'ed

blob
  blobbed blob'bing
bloc (*group*)
block (*solid piece*)
block·ade'
  ·ad'ed ·ad'ing
block'bust'er
block'bust'ing
block'er
block'head'
block'house'
blond
blonde
blood
blood'cur'dling
blood'ed
blood'hound'
blood'i·ly
blood'i·ness
blood'less
blood'let'ting
blood'mo·bile'
blood'shed'
blood'shot'
blood'stained'
blood'stream'
blood'suck'er
blood'thirst'y
blood'y
  ·i·er ·i·est
  ·ied ·y·ing
bloom
bloom'ers
bloom'ing
bloop'er
blos'som
blos'som·y
blot
  blot'ted blot'ting
blotch
blotch'y
  ·i·er ·i·est
blot'ter
blouse
blow
  blew blown
  blow'ing
blow'-by-blow'
blow'-dry'
  ·dried' ·dry'ing
blow'-dry'er
blow'er
blow'fly'
  ·flies'
blow'gun'
blow'hole'
blow'out'
blow'pipe'
blow'torch'
blow'up'
blow'y
  ·i·er ·i·est
blub'ber
blub'ber·y
bludg'eon
blue
  (*color; see* BLEW)
blue'bell'

blue'ber'ry
  ·ries
blue'bird'
blue'-blood'ed
blue'-chip'
blue'-col'lar
blue'gill'
blue'grass'
blue'jeans'
blue'-pen'cil
blue'print'
blu'et
bluff
blu'ing
blu'ish *or* blue'ish
blun'der
blun'der·buss'
blun'der·er
blunt
blunt'ly
blunt'ness
blur
  blurred blur'ring
blurb
blur'ri·ness
blur'ry
  ·ri·er ·ri·est
blurt
blush
blush'er
blus'ter
blus'ter·er
blus'ter·y
bo'a
boar
  (*hog; see* BORE)
board
board'er
board'ing·house'
board'walk'
boast
boast'er
boast'ful
boast'ful·ly
boat
boat'er
boat'house'
boat'ing
boat'load'
boat'man
boat'swain *or*
  bo'sun
bob
  bobbed bob'bing
bob'bin
bob'ble
  ·bled ·bling
bob'by
  ·bies
bob'cat'
bob'o·link'
bob'sled'
  ·sled'ded
  ·sled'ding
bob'white'
boc'cie *or* boc'ce
  or boc'ci

bode
  bod'ed bod'ing
bod'ice
bod'i·ly
bod'kin
bod'y
  ·ies
bod'y·guard'
bod'y·suit'
bog
  bogged bog'ging
bo'gey
  ·geys
  ·geyed ·gey·ing
  (*golf term*)
bog'gle
  ·gled ·gling
bog'gy
  ·gi·er ·gi·est
  (*like a bog*)
bo'gus
bo'gy
  ·gies
  (*spirit*)
bo'gy·man' *or*
  bo'gey·man'
boil
boil'er
boil'ing
bois'ter·ous
bok' choy'
bo'la
bold
bold'face'
bold'faced'
bold'ness
bo·le'ro
  ·ros
boll
  (*pod; see* BOWL)
bo·lo'gna
bol'ster
bolt
bo'lus
bomb
bom·bard'
bom'bar·dier'
bom·bard'ment
bom'bast'
bom·bas'tic
bom·bas'ti·cal·ly
bomb'er
bomb'shell'
bomb'sight'
bo'na fide'
bo·nan'za
bon'bon'
bond
bond'age
bond'ing
bond'man
bonds'man
bond'wom'an
bone
  boned bon'ing
bone'-dry'
bone'less
bon'er
bon'fire'

bong
bon'go
  ·gos
bon'i·ness
bo·ni'to
  ·tos ·toes
bon·jour'
bonk'ers
bon' mot'
  bons' mots'
bon'net
bon'ny *or* bon'nie
  ·ni·er ·ni·est
bon·sai'
bo'nus
  ·nus·es
bon' voy·age'
bon'y
  ·i·er ·i·est
boo
  boos
  booed boo'ing
boo'-boo' *or*
  boo'boo'
  -boos'
boo'by
  ·bies
book
book'bind'er
book'bind'er·y
  ·ies
book'bind'ing
book'case'
book'end'
book'ie
book'ing
book'ish
book'keep'er
book'keep'ing
book'let
book'mak'er
book'mark'
book'plate'
book'rack'
book'sell'er
book'shelf
  ·shelves'
book'shop'
book'stall'
book'stand'
book'store'
book'worm'
boom
boom'box'
boom'er·ang'
boon
boon'docks'
boon'dog'gle
  ·gled ·gling
boor
boor'ish
boost
boost'er
boot
boot'black'
boot'ee *or* boot'ie
  (*baby's shoe;* see
  BOOTY)
booth

boot'leg'
  ·legged' ·leg'ging
boot'leg'ger
boot'less
boot'strap'
boo'ty
  ·ties
  (*spoils;* see
  BOOTEE)
booze
  boozed booz'ing
bop
  bopped bop'ping
bo'rax'
bor'der
bor'der·line'
bore
  (*dull person;* see
  BOAR)
bore
  bored bor'ing
bore'dom
born (*brought into*
  life)
born'-a·gain'
borne
  (*form of* bear)
bo'ron'
bor'ough
  (*town;* see BURRO,
  BURROW)
bor'row
  (*take for a while;*
  see BARROW)
bor'row·er
bos'om
bos'om·y
bos'on'
boss
boss'i·ness
boss'y
  ·i·er ·i·est
bo'sun *or*
  boat'swain
bo·tan'i·cal *or*
  ·tan'ic
bot'a·nist
bot'a·ny
botch
bot'fly'
  ·flies'
both
both'er
both'er·some
bot'tle
  ·tled ·tling
bot'tle·neck'
bot'tler
bot'tom
bot'tom·less
bot'u·lism
bou·doir'
bouf·fant'
bou'gain·vil'le·a *or*
  ·lae·a
bough
  (*tree branch;* see
  BOW)
bought

bouil'lon'
  (*broth;* see BUL-
  LION)
boul'der
bou'le·vard'
bounce
  bounced bounc'ing
bounc'er
bounc'ing
bounc'y
bound
bound'a·ry
  ·ries
bound'less
boun'te·ous
boun'ti·ful
boun'ti·ful·ly
boun'ty
  ·ties
bou·quet'
bour'bon
bour·geois'
bour'geoi·sie'
bout
bou·tique'
bou'ton·niere'
bo'vine'
bow
  (*curve;* see BEAU)
bow
  (*of a ship;* see
  BOUGH)
bowd'ler·ize'
  ·ized' ·iz'ing
bow'el
bow'er
bow'ie knife
bow'knot'
bowl
  (*dish;* see BOLL)
bow'leg'
bow'leg'ged
bowl'er
bow'line
bowl'ing
bow'man
bow'sprit'
bow'string'
box
box'car'
box'er
box'ing
box'like'
boy
  (*child;* see BUOY)
boy'cott'
boy'friend'
boy'hood'
boy'ish
boy'sen·ber'ry
  ·ries
bra
brace
  braced brac'ing
brace'let
brack'et
brack'ish
bract
brad

brag
  bragged brag'ging
brag'gart
brag'ger
braid
braille
brain
brain'child'
brain'less
brain'storm'
brain'storm'ing
brain'wash'
brain'y
  ·i·er ·i·est
braise
  braised brais'ing
  (*cook;* see BRAZE)
brake
  braked brak'ing
  (*stop;* see BREAK)
brake'man
bram'ble
bran
branch
branched
branch'ing
branch'like'
brand
bran'dish
brand'-name'
brand'-new'
bran'dy
  ·dies
  ·died ·dy·ing
brash
brash'ness
brass
  brass'es
bras·siere'
brass'y
  ·i·er ·i·est
brat
brat'wurst'
bra·va'do
brave
  brav'er brav'est
  braved brav'ing
brave'ly
brave'ness
brav'er·y
bra'vo
  ·vos
bra·vu'ra
brawl
brawn
brawn'i·ness
brawn'y
  ·i·er ·i·est
bray
braze
  brazed braz'ing
  (*solder;* see
  BRAISE)
bra'zen
bra'zen·ness
bra'zier
Bra·zil'ian
breach
  (*a gap;* see
  BREECH)

bread
bread'bas'ket
bread'board'
bread'box'
breadth
  (*width;* see
  BREATH)
bread'win'ner
break
  broke bro'ken
  break'ing
  (*smash;* see
  BRAKE)
break'a·ble
break'age'
break'down'
break'er
break'fast
break'front'
break'-in'
break'neck'
break'out'
break'through'
break'up'
break'wa'ter
breast
breast'bone'
breast'-feed'
  -fed' -feed'ing
breast'plate'
breast'work'
breath
  (*air;* see BREADTH)
breath'a·ble
breathe
  breathed
  breath'ing
breath'er
breath'less
breath'less·ly
breath'tak'ing
breath'y
  ·i·er ·i·est
bred
breech
  (*rear;* see BREACH)
breech'cloth'
breech'es
breech'-load'ing
breed
  bred breed'ing
breed'er
breed'ing
breeze
  breezed breez'ing
breeze'way'
breez'i·ly
breez'i·ness
breez'y
  ·i·er ·i·est
breth'ren
bre'vi·ar'y
  ·ies
brev'i·ty
brew
brew'er
brew'er·y
  ·ies
bri'ar

brib'a·ble
bribe
  bribed brib'ing
brib'er·y
bric'-a-brac'
brick
brick'bat'
brick'lay'er
brick'lay'ing
brick'work'
brid'al
  (*of a wedding;* see
  BRIDLE)
bride
bride'groom'
brides'maid'
bridge
  bridged bridg'ing
bridge'a·ble
bridge'head'
bridge'work'
bri'dle
  bri'dled bri'dling
  (*harness;* see
  BRIDAL)
brief
brief'case'
brief'ing
brief'ly
brief'ness
bri'er
brig
bri·gade'
brig'a·dier'
brig'and
brig'an·tine'
bright
bright'en
bright'ly
bright'ness
bril'liance *or*
  bril'lian·cy
bril'liant
bril'liant·ly
brim
  brimmed
  brim'ming
brim'ful'
brim'less
brim'stone'
brin'dled
brine
bring
  brought bring'ing
brink
brink'man·ship'
brin'y
  ·i·er ·i·est
bri·quette' *or*
  ·quet'
brisk
bris'ket
brisk'ly
brisk'ness
bris'tle
  ·tled ·tling
bris'tle·cone pine
bris'tly
  ·tli·er ·tli·est

britch'es
Brit'ish
brit'tle
brit'tle·ness
broach
  (open; see BROOCH)
broad
broad'cast'
  ·cast' or ·cast'ed
  ·cast'ing
broad'cast'er
broad'cloth'
broad'en
broad'leaf'
broad'-leaved'
broad'loom'
broad'ly
broad'-mind'ed
broad'-mind'ed·ly
broad'-
  mind'ed·ness
broad'ness
broad'side'
broad'-spec'trum
broad'sword'
bro·cade'
  ·cad'ed ·cad'ing
broc'co·li
bro·chure'
bro'gan
brogue
broil
broil'er
broke
bro'ken
bro'ken-down'
bro'ken-heart'ed
bro'ken·ly
bro'ker
bro'ker·age'
bro'mide'
bro'mine'
bron'chi·al
bron·chi'tis
bron'chus
  ·chi
bron'co
  ·cos
bron'co·bust'er
bron'co·bust'ing
bron'to·saur'
bron'to·saur'us
bronze
  bronzed bronz'ing
brooch
  (a pin; see
  BROACH)
brood
brood'er
brood'mare'
brook
broom
broom'stick'
broth
broth'el
broth'er
  ·ers or breth'ren
broth'er·hood'

broth'er-in-law'
  broth'ers-in-law'
broth'er·ly
brought
brou'ha·ha'
brow
brow'beat'
  ·beat' ·beat'en
  ·beat'ing
brown
brown'-bag'
  -bagged'
  -bag'ging
brown'ie
brown'ish
brown'out'
brown'stone'
browse
  browsed brows'ing
brows'er
bruise
  bruised bruis'ing
bruis'er
brunch
bru·net' or ·nette'
brunt
brush
brush'off'
brush'wood'
brush'work'
brusque
brusque'ly
brusque'ness
Brus'sels sprouts
bru'tal
bru·tal'i·ty
  ·ties
bru'tal·i·za'tion
bru'tal·ize'
  ·ized' ·iz'ing
bru'tal·ly
brute
brut'ish
brut'ish·ly
bub'ble
  ·bled ·bling
bub'bly
bu'bo
  ·boes'
bu·bon'ic plague
buc'ca·neer'
buck
buck'board'
buck'et
buck'et·ful'
  ·fuls'
buck'eye'
buck'le
  ·led ·ling
buck'-pass'er
buck'ram
buck'saw'
buck'shot'
buck'skin'
buck'tooth'
  ·teeth'
buck'toothed'
buck'wheat'
bu·col'ic

bu·col'i·cal·ly
bud
  bud'ded bud'ding
Bud'dhism'
Bud'dhist
bud'dy
  ·dies
budge
  budged budg'ing
budg'et
budg'et·ar'y
bud'like'
buff
buf'fa·lo'
  ·loes' or ·lo'
  ·loed' ·lo'ing
buff'er
buf'fet
buf·foon'
buf·foon'er·y
bug
  bugged bug'ging
bug'a·boo'
  ·boos'
bug'bear'
bug'-eyed'
bug'gy
  ·gies
bu'gle
  ·gled ·gling
bu'gler
build
  built build'ing
build'er
build'ing
build'up' or build'-
  up'
built
built'-in'
built'-up'
bulb
bul'bous
bulge
  bulged bulg'ing
bulg'y
bu·li·ma·rex'i·a
bu·lim'i·a
bulimia ner·vo'sa
bu·lim'ic
bulk
bulk'head'
bulk'y
  ·i·er ·i·est
bull
bull'dog'
bull'doze'
  ·dozed' ·doz'ing
bull'doz'er
bul'let
bul'le·tin
bul'let·proof'
bull'fight'
bull'fight'er
bull'frog'
bull'head'ed
bull'horn'
bul'lion
  (gold; see BOUIL-
  LON)

bull'ish'
bull'ock
bull'pen'
bull's'-eye'
bull'whip'
bul'ly
  ·lies
  ·lied ·ly·ing
bul'rush'
bul'wark
bum
  bummed
  bum'ming
bum'ble
  ·bled ·bling
bum'ble·bee'
bum'bler
bum'bling
bum'mer
bump
bump'er
bump'kin
bump'tious
bump'y
  ·i·er ·i·est
bun
bunch
bun'dle
  ·dled ·dling
bun'ga·low'
bun'gle
  ·gled ·gling
bun'gler
bun'ion
bunk
bunk'er
bunk'house'
bun'ny
  ·nies
Bun'sen burner
bunt
bun'ting
buoy
  (marker; see BOY)
buoy'an·cy
buoy'ant
bur'den
bur'den·some
bur'dock'
bu'reau
  ·reaus'
bu·reauc'ra·cy
  ·cies
bu'reau·crat'
bu'reau·crat'ic
bu'reau·crat'i·cal·ly
bu·rette' or bu·ret'
burg
bur'geon
bur'ger
burgh
burgh'er
bur'glar
bur'glar·ize'
  ·ized' ·iz'ing
bur'gla·ry
  ·ries
bur'gle
  ·gled ·gling

Bur'gun·dy
  ·dies
bur'i·al
bur'lap'
bur·lesque'
  ·lesqued'
  ·lesqu'ing
bur'ley (tobacco)
bur'ly
  ·li·er ·li·est
  (muscular)
burn
  burned or burnt
  burn'ing
burn'a·ble
burn'er
bur'nish
burn'out'
burnt
burp
bur'ro
  ·ros
  (donkey; see BUR-
  ROW, BOROUGH)
bur'row
  (hole; see BURRO,
  BOROUGH)
bur'sa
  ·sae or ·sas
bur'sar
bur·si'tis
burst
  burst burst'ing
bur'y
  ·ied ·y·ing
  (cover; see BERRY)
bus
  bus'es or bus'ses
  bused or bussed
  bus'ing or bus'sing
bus'boy'
bush
bushed
bush'el
bush'ing
bush'-league'
bush'man
bush'whack'er
bush'y
  ·i·er ·i·est
bus'i·ly
busi'ness
busi'ness·like'
busi'ness·man'
busi'ness·wom'an
bus'ing or bus'sing
bust
bust'ed
bus'tle
  ·tled ·tling
bus'y
  ·i·er ·i·est
  ·ied ·y'ing
bus'y·bod'y
  ·ies
bus'y·ness
but
  (except; yet; see
  BUTT, BUTTE)
bu'tane

butch
butch'er
butch'er·y
  ·ies
but'ler
butt
  (a stub; to ram;
  see BUT, BUTTE)
butte
  (mound; see BUT,
  BUTT)
but'ter
but'ter·cup'
but'ter·fat'
but'ter·fin'gers
but'ter·fly'
  ·flies'
but'ter·milk'
but'ter·nut'
but'ter·scotch'
but'ter·y
but'tocks
but'ton
but'ton-down'
but'ton·hole'
  ·holed' ·hol'ing
but'tress
bux'om
buy
  bought buy'ing
  (purchase; see BY,
  BYE)
buy'back'
buy'er
buy'out'
buzz
buz'zard
buzz'er
by
  (near or during;
  see BUY, BYE)
by'-and-by'
bye
  (sports tourna-
  ment term; see
  BUY, BY)
bye'-bye'
by'gone'
by'law'
by'line'
by'pass'
by'play'
by'prod'uct or
  by'-prod'uct
by'stand'er
byte
  (computer unit;
  see BITE)
by'way'

C

cab
ca·bal'
cab'a·la
ca·bal·le'ro
  ·ros
ca·ban'a
cab'a·ret'

cab'bage
cab'by *or* ·bie
 ·bies
ca·ber·net'
cab'in
cab'i·net
cab'i·net·mak'er
cab'i·net·work'
ca'ble
 ·bled ·bling
ca'ble·cast'
 ·cast' ·cast'ing
ca'ble·gram'
cab'o·chon'
ca·bood'le
ca·boose'
ca·ca'o
 ·os'
cache
 cached cach'ing
 (*hiding place;* see
 CASH)
cache'pot'
ca·chet'
cack'le
 ·led ·ling
ca·coph'o·nous
ca·coph'o·ny
cac'tus
 ·tus·es *or* ·ti'
cad
CAD/CAM
ca·dav'er
ca·dav'er·ous
cad'die
 ·died ·dy·ing
 (*in golf*)
cad'dish
cad'dish·ly
cad'dish·ness
cad'dy
 ·dies
 (*container*)
ca'dence
ca·den'za
ca·det'
cadge
 cadged cadg'ing
cadg'er
cad'mi·um
ca'dre'
ca·du'ce·us
 ·ce·i'
Cae'sar
Cae·sar'e·an sec-
 tion
cae·su'ra
 ·ras *or* ·rae
ca·fe' *or* ca·fé'
caf'e·te'ri·a
caf'feine' *or* ·fein'
caf'tan
cage
 caged cag'ing
cag'er
ca'gey *or* ·gy
 ·gi·er ·gi·est
ca'gi·ly
ca'gi·ness

ca·hoots'
cairn
cais'son
cai'tiff
ca·jole'
 ·joled' ·jol'ing
ca·jol'er
ca·jol'er·y
Ca'jun *or* ·jan
cake
 caked cak'ing
cak'y *or* cak'ey
cal'a·bash'
cal'a·boose'
ca·la·ma'ri
cal'a·mine'
ca·lam'i·tous
ca·lam'i·ty
 ·ties
cal·car'e·ous
cal'ci·fi·ca'tion
cal'ci·fy'
 ·fied' ·fy'ing
cal'ci·mine'
cal'cine'
 ·cined' ·cin'ing
cal'cite'
cal'ci·um
cal'cu·la·ble
cal'cu·late'
 ·lat'ed ·lat'ing
cal'cu·la'tion
cal'cu·la'tor
cal'cu·lus
 ·li' *or* ·lus·es
cal·de'ra
cal'dron
cal'en·dar
 (*table of dates;* see
 CALENDER, COLAN-
 DER)
cal'en·der
 (*roller;* see CALEN-
 DAR, COLANDER)
calf
 calves *or* calfs
calf'skin'
cal'i·ber
cal'i·brate'
 ·brat'ed ·brat'ing
cal'i·bra'tion
cal'i·bra'tor
cal'i·co'
 ·coes' *or* ·cos'
Cal'i·for'ni·a
cal'i·pers
ca'liph
ca'liph·ate
cal'is·then'ics
calk
call
cal'la
call'er
cal·lig'ra·pher
cal'li·graph'ic
cal·lig'ra·phy
call'ing
cal·li'o·pe'
cal'lous *adj.*

cal'loused
cal'lous·ly
cal'lous·ness
cal'low
cal'low·ness
cal'lus *n.*
 ·lus·es
calm
calm'ly
calm'ness
ca·lor'ic
cal'o·rie
cal'o·rif'ic
cal'u·met'
ca·lum'ni·ate'
 ·at'ed ·at'ing
ca·lum'ni·a'tion
ca·lum'ni·a'tor
cal'um·ny
 ·nies
Cal'va·ry
 (*Biblical place;* see
 CAVALRY)
calve
 calved calv'ing
calves
Cal'vin·ism'
Cal'vin·ist
Cal'vin·is'tic
cal·vi'ti·es'
ca·lyp'so
ca'lyx'
 ·lyx'es *or* ·ly·ces'
cam
ca'ma·ra'de·rie
cam'ber
cam'bi·al
cam'bi·um
cam'bric
cam'cord'er
came
cam'el
ca·mel'li·a
cam'e·o'
 ·os'
cam'er·a
cam'er·a·man'
cam'i·sole'
cam'o·mile'
cam'ou·flage'
 ·flaged' ·flag'ing
cam'ou·flag'er
camp
cam·paign'
cam·paign'er
cam·pa·ni'le
 ·les *or* ·li
camp'er
camp'fire'
camp'ground'
cam'phor
camp'site'
cam'pus
 ·pus·es
camp'y
 ·i·er ·i·est
cam'shaft'
can
 could

cal'loused
Ca·na'di·an
ca·nal'
ca·na·pé'
 (*appetizer;* see
 CANOPY)
ca·nard'
ca·nar'y
 ·ies
ca·nas'ta
can'can'
can'cel
 ·celed *or* ·celled
 ·cel·ing *or* ·cel·ling
can'cel·la'tion
can'cer
Can'cer
can'cer·ous
can·de·la'bra
 ·bras
can·de·la'brum
 ·bra *or* ·brums
can'did
can'di·date'
can'did·ly
can'did·ness
can'died'
can'dle
 ·dled ·dling
can'dle·light'
can'dle·stick'
can'-do'
can'dor
can'dy
 ·dies
 ·died ·dy·ing
cane
 caned can'ing
cane'brake'
ca·nine'
can'is·ter
can'ker
can'ker·ous
can'na·bis'
canned
can'ner·y
 ·ies
can'ni·bal
can'ni·bal·ism'
can'ni·bal·is'tic
can'ni·bal·ize'
 ·ized' ·iz'ing
can'ni·ly
can'ni·ness
can'non
 ·nons *or* ·non
 (*large gun;* see
 CANON)
can'non·ade'
 ·ad'ed ·ad'ing
can'not
can'ny
 ·ni·er ·ni·est
ca·noe'
 ·noed' ·noe'ing
ca·noe'ist
can'on
 (*church law;* see
 CANNON)
ca'ñon (*canyon*)
ca·non'i·cal

can'on·i·za'tion
can'on·ize'
 ·ized' ·iz'ing
can'o·py
 ·pies
 ·pied ·py·ing
 (*awning;* see
 CANAPÉ)
cant
can't
can'ta·loupe' *or*
 ·loup'
can·tan'ker·ous
can·tan'ker·ous·ly
can·tan'ker·ous·
 ness
can·ta'ta
can·teen'
can'ter
 (*gallop;* see CAN-
 TOR)
can'ti·cle
can'ti·le'ver
can'to
 ·tos
can'ton
can·ton'ment
can'tor
 (*singer;* see CAN-
 TER)
can'vas (*cloth*)
can'vas·back'
can'vass (*poll*)
can'vass·er
can'yon
cap
 capped cap'ping
ca'pa·bil'i·ty
 ·ties
ca'pa·ble
ca'pa·bly
ca·pa'cious
ca·pa'cious·ly
ca·pa'cious·ness
ca·pac'i·tor
ca·pac'i·ty
 ·ties
ca·par'i·son
cape
ca'per
cap'ful'
 ·fuls'
cap'il·lar'y
 ·ies
cap'i·tal
 (*city; chief;* see
 CAPITOL)
cap'i·tal·ism'
cap'i·tal·ist
cap'i·tal·is'tic
cap'i·tal·i·za'tion
cap'i·tal·ize'
 ·ized' ·iz'ing
cap'i·tal·ly
cap'i·tol
 (*building;* see CAP-
 ITAL)
ca·pit'u·late'
 ·lat'ed ·lat'ing
ca·pit'u·la'tion

cap'let
ca'pon'
cap·puc·ci'no
ca·price'
ca·pri'cious
ca·pri'cious·ly
ca·pri'cious·ness
Cap'ri·corn'
cap'size'
 ·sized' ·siz'ing
cap'stan
cap'sule
cap'sul·ize'
 ·ized' ·iz'ing
cap'tain
cap'tain·cy
cap'tion
cap'tious
cap'tious·ly
cap'tious·ness
cap'ti·vate'
 ·vat'ed ·vat'ing
cap'ti·va'tion
cap'tive
cap·tiv'i·ty
cap'tor
cap'ture
 ·tured ·tur·ing
car
car'a·cul'
ca·rafe'
car'a·mel
car'a·mel·ize'
 ·ized' ·iz'ing
car'a·pace'
car'at
 (*gem weight;* see
 CARET, CARROT,
 KARAT)
car'a·van'
car'a·van'sa·ry
 ·ries
car'a·way'
car'bide'
car'bine'
car'bo·hy'drate
car·bol'ic acid
car'bon
car'bon·ate'
 ·at'ed, ·at'ing
car'bon·a'tion
car'bon·date'
carbon di·ox'ide'
car·bon'ic acid
car'bon·if'er·ous
carbon
 mon·ox'ide'
carbon
 tet'ra·chlo'ride'
car'bo·run'dum
car'boy'
car'bun'cle
car·bun'cu·lar
car'bu·ret'or
car'cass
car·cin'o·gen
car·ci·no·gen'ic

car′ci·no′ma
　·mas *or* ·ma·ta
card
card′board′
car′di·ac′
car′di·gan
car′di·nal
car′di·o·gram′
car′di·o·graph′
car′di·ol′o·gist
car′di·ol′o·gy
car′di·o·pul′mo·nar′y
car′di·o·vas′cu·lar
cards
card′sharp′
care
　cared car′ing
ca·reen′
ca·reer′
care′free′
care′ful
care′ful·ly
care′less
care′less·ly
care′less·ness
ca·ress′
car′et
　(*proofreader's
　mark;* see CARAT,
　CARROT, KARAT)
care′tak′er
care′worn′
car′fare′
car′go
　·goes *or* ·gos
car′hop′
car′i·bou′
car′i·ca·ture
　·tured ·tur·ing
car′i·ca·tur·ist
car′i·es′
　(*tooth decay;* see
　CARRIES)
car′il·lon′
ca·ri′tas′
car′mine
car′nage
car′nal
car·nal′i·ty
car′nal·ly
car·na′tion
car·nel′ian
car′ni·val
car′ni·vore′
car·niv′o·rous
car·niv′o·rous·ness
car′ol
　·oled *or* ·olled
　·ol·ing *or* ·ol·ling
　(*song;* see CARREL)
car′ol·er *or* ·ol·ler
car′om
ca·rot′id
ca·rous′al
　(*party;* see
　CAROUSEL)
ca·rouse′
　·roused′ ·rous′ing

car′ou·sel′
　(*merry-go-round;*
　see CAROUSAL)
carp
　carp *or* carps
car′pal (*wrist bone*)
car′pel (*flower part*)
car′pen·ter
car′pen·try
carp′er
car′pet
car′pet·bag′ger
car′pet·ing
car′port′
car′pus
　·pi
car′rel *or* ·rell
　(*study desk;* see
　CAROL)
car′riage
car′ri·er
car′ries
　(*form of* carry; see
　CARIES)
car′ri·on
car′rot
　(*vegetable;* see
　CARAT, CARET,
　KARAT)
car′rou·sel′
car′ry
　·ried ·ry·ing
car′ry-on′
car′ry-out′
car′sick′
cart
cart′age
carte′ blanche′
car·tel′
car′ti·lage
car′ti·lag′i·nous
car·tog′ra·pher
car·tog′ra·phy
car′ton
car·toon′
car·toon′ist
car′tridge
cart′wheel′
carve
　carved carv′ing
carv′er
carv′ing
car′wash′
car′y·at′id
　·ids *or* ·i·des′
ca·sa′ba
Ca′sa·no′va
cas·cade′
　·cad′ed ·cad′ing
cas·car′a
case
　cased cas′ing
case′hard′ened
ca′se·in
case′load′
case′ment
case′work′er
cash
　(*money;* see
　CACHE)

cash′ew
cash·ier′
cash′mere′
cas′ing
ca·si′no
　·nos
　(*gambling room;*
　see CASSINO)
cask
cas′ket
cas·sa′va
cas·se·role′
cas·sette′
cas′si·a
cas·si′no
　(*card game;* see
　CASINO)
cas′sock
cast
　cast cast′ing
　(*actors*)
cas′ta·nets′
cast′a·way′
caste (*social rank*)
cast′er
cas′ti·gate′
　·gat′ed ·gat′ing
cas′ti·ga′tion
cas′ti·ga′tor
cast′ing
cast′-i′ron
cas′tle
cast′off′
cas′tor oil
cas′trate′
　·trat′ed ·trat′ing
cas·tra′tion
cas′u·al
cas′u·al·ly
cas′u·al·ness
cas′u·al·ty
　·ties
cas′u·ist
cas′u·ist·ry
cat
cat′a·clysm
cat′a·clys′mic
cat′a·comb′
cat′a·falque′
cat′a·lep′sy
cat′a·lep′tic
cat′a·log′ *or* ·logue′
　·loged′ *or* ·logued′
　·log′ing *or*
　·logu′ing
cat′a·log′er *or*
　·logu′er
cat′al·pa
ca·tal′y·sis
cat′a·lyst′
cat′a·lyt′ic
cat′a·ma·ran′
cat′a·pult′
cat′a·ract′
ca·tarrh′
ca·tas′tro·phe
cat′a·stroph′ic
cat′a·to′ni·a
cat′a·ton′ic

cat′bird′
cat′call′
catch
　caught catch′ing
catch′all′
catch′er
catch′ing
catch′word′
catch′y
　·i·er ·i·est
cat′e·chism
cat′e·chize′
　·chized′ ·chiz′ing
cat′e·gor′i·cal
cat′e·gor′i·cal·ly
cat′e·go·rize′
　·rized′ ·riz′ing
cat′e·go′ry
　·ries
ca′ter
cat′er-cor′nered
ca′ter·er
cat′er·pil′lar
cat′er·waul′
cat′fish′
cat′gut′
ca·thar′sis
ca·thar′tic
ca·the′dral
cath′e·ter
cath′e·ter·ize′
　·ized′ ·iz′ing
cath′ode′
cath′ode-ray′ tube
cath′o·lic
Ca·thol′i·cism′
cath′o·lic′i·ty
cat′i·on′
cat′kin
cat′nap′
cat′nip′
cat′-o′-nine′-tails′
CAT scan
cat′s′-paw′
cat′sup
cat′tail′
cat′ti·ness
cat′tle
cat′tle·man
cat′ty
　·ti·er ·ti·est
cat′ty-cor′nered
cat′walk′
Cau·ca′sian
Cau′ca·soid′
cau′cus
　·cused *or* ·cussed
　·cus·ing *or*
　·cus·sing
cau′dal
caught
caul′dron
cau′li·flow′er
caulk
caus′al
cau·sal′i·ty
caus′al·ly
cau·sa′tion

caus′a·tive
cause
　caused caus′ing
cause′less
caus′er
cau·se·rie′
cause′way′
caus′tic
caus′ti·cal·ly
cau′ter·i·za′tion
cau′ter·ize′
　·ized′ ·iz′ing
cau′tion
cau′tion·ar′y
cau′tious
cau′tious·ly
cau′tious·ness
cav′al·cade′
cav′a·lier′
cav′a·lier′ly
cav′al·ry
　·ries
　(*troops;* see CAL-
　VARY)
cav′al·ry·man
cave
　caved cav′ing
ca′ve·at′ emp′tor′
cave′-in′
cav′ern
cav′ern·ous
cav′i·ar′ *or* ·are′
cav′il
　·iled *or* ·illed
　·il·ing *or* ·il·ling
cav′il·er *or* ·ler
cav′i·ty
　·ties
ca·vort′
caw
cay·enne′
cay′use′
　·us′es
cease
　ceased ceas′ing
cease′-fire′
cease′less
cease′less·ly
ce′cum
　·ca
ce′dar
cede
　ced′ed ced′ing
ce·dil′la
ceil′ing
cel′e·brant
cel′e·brate′
　·brat′ed ·brat′ing
cel′e·brat′ed
cel′e·bra′tion
cel′e·bra′tor
ce·leb′ri·ty
　·ties
ce·ler′i·ty
cel′er·y
ce·les′tial
cel′i·ba·cy
cel′i·bate

cell
　(*room;* see SELL)
cel′lar
celled
cel′list
cel′lo
　·los *or* ·li
cel′lo·phane′
cel′lu·lar
cel′lu·lite′
cel′lu·loid′
cel′lu·lose′
Cel′si·us
Celt
Celt′ic
ce·ment′
cem′e·ter′y
　·ies
cen′o·bite′
cen′o·taph′
Ce′no·zo′ic
cen′ser
　(*incense box;* see
　CENSOR, CENSURE,
　SENSOR)
cen′sor
　(*prohibiter;* see
　CENSER, CENSURE,
　SENSOR)
cen·so′ri·ous
cen′sor·ship′
cen′sure
　·sured ·sur·ing
　(*blame;* see
　CENSER, CENSOR,
　SENSOR)
cen′sus
cent
　(*money;* see SCENT,
　SENT)
cen′taur′
cen·ta′vo
　·vos
cen′te·nar′i·an
cen·ten′ar·y
cen·ten′ni·al
cen′ter
cen′ter·board′
cen′tered
cen′ter·fold′
cen′ter·piece′
cen′ti·grade′
cen′time′
cen′ti·me′ter
cen′ti·pede′
cen′tral
cen′tral·i·za′tion
cen′tral·ize′
　·ized′ ·iz′ing
cen′tral·ly
cen·trif′u·gal
cen′tri·fuge′
cen·trip′e·tal
cen′trist
cen·tu′ri·on
cen′tu·ry
　·ries
ce·phal′ic
ce·ram′ic
ce·ram′i·cist

ce·ram′ist
ce′re·al
  (*grain;* see SERIAL)
cer′e·bel′lum
  ·lums *or* ·la
cer′e·bral
cer′e·bra′tion
cer′e·brum
  ·brums *or* ·bra
cer′e·ment
cer′e·mo′ni·al
cer′e·mo′ni·al·ly
cer′e·mo′ni·ous
cer′e·mo′ni·ous·ly
cer′e·mo′ny
  ·nies
ce·rise′
cer′met′
cer′tain
cer′tain·ly
cer′tain·ty
  ·ties
cer′ti·fi·a·ble
cer′tif′i·cate
  ·cat′ed ·cat′ing
cer′ti·fi·ca′tion
cer′ti·fy′
  ·fied′ ·fy′ing
cer′ti·tude′
ce·ru′le·an
cer′vi·cal
cer′vix′
  cer·vi′ces′ *or*
  ·vix·es
ce′si·um
ces·sa′tion
ces′sion
  (*a giving up;* see
  SESSION)
cess′pool′
ce·ta′cean
Cha·blis′
chafe
  chafed chaf′ing
  (*rub*)
chaff (*husks of*
  grain)
chaf′ing dish
cha·grin′
  ·grined′ ·grin′ing
chain
chair
chair′lift′
chair′man
chair′man·ship′
chair′per′son
chair′wom′an
chaise
chaise′ longue′
  chaise′ longues′
chaise′ lounge′
cha·let′
chal′ice
chalk
chalk′board′
chalk′i·ness
chalk′y
  ·i·er ·i·est

chal′lenge
  ·lenged ·leng·ing
chal′leng·er
chal′lis *or* ·lie
cham′ber
cham′bered
cham′ber·lain
cham′ber·maid′
cham′bray′
cha·me′le·on
cham′ois
cham′o·mile′
champ
cham·pagne′ (*wine*)
cham·paign′ (*open*
  field)
cham′pi·on
cham′pi·on·ship′
chance
  chanced chanc′ing
chan′cel
chan′cel·ler·y
  ·ies
chan′cel·lor
chan′cer·y
  ·ies
chanc′i·ness
chan′cre
chanc′y
  ·i·er ·i·est
chan′de·lier′
chan′dler
change
  changed chang′ing
change′a·ble
change′less
change′ling
change′o′ver
change′-up′
chan′nel
  ·neled *or* ·nelled
  ·nel·ing *or*
  ·nel·ling
chan·son′
chant
chant′er
chan·teuse′
chan′tey
  ·teys
chan′ti·cleer′
Cha′nu·kah′
cha′os′
cha·ot′ic
chap
chap′ar·ral′
cha·peau′
  ·peaus′ *or* ·peaux′
chap′el
chap′er·on′ *or*
  ·one′
  ·oned′ ·on′ing
chap′er·on·age
chap′lain
chap′let
chaps
chap′ter
char
  charred char′ring
char′ac·ter

char′ac·ter·is′tic
char′ac·ter·is′ti·cal
  ·ly
char′ac·ter·i·za′-
  tion
char′ac·ter·ize′
  ·ized′ ·iz′ing
cha·rade′
char′broil′ *or*
  char′-broil′
char′coal′
chard
char′don·nay′
charge
  charged charg′ing
charge′a·ble
charg′er
char′i·ly
char′i·ness
char′i·ot
char′i·ot·eer′
cha·ris′ma
char′is·mat′ic
char′i·ta·ble
char′i·ta·bly
char′i·ty
  ·ties
char′la·tan
char′ley horse
charm
charm′er
charm′ing
charm′ing·ly
char′nel house
chart
char′ter
char·treuse′
char′wom′an
char′y
  ·i·er ·i·est
chase
  chased chas′ing
chas′er
chasm
chas′sis
  ·sis′
chaste
chaste′ly
chas′ten
chas·tise′
  ·tised′ ·tis′ing
chas·tise′ment
chas′ti·ty
chas′u·ble
chat
  chat′ted chat′ting
châ·teau′ *or*
  cha·teau′
  ·teaux′ *or* ·teaus′
chat′e·laine′
chat′tel
chat′ter
chat′ter·box′
chat′ter·er
chat′ti·ness
chat′ty
  ·ti·er ·ti·est

chauf′feur
  (*driver;* see SHO-
  FAR)
chau·tau′qua
chau′vin·ism′
chau′vin·ist
chau′vin·is′tic
chau′vin·is′ti·cal·ly
cheap
  (*inexpensive;* see
  CHEEP)
cheap′en
cheap′ly
cheap′ness
cheap′skate′
cheat
cheat′er
check
check′book′
checked
check′er
check′er·board′
check′ered
check′ers
check′list′
check′mate′
  ·mat′ed ·mat′ing
check′off′
check′out′
check′point′
check′room′
check′up′
Ched′dar
cheek
cheek′bone′
cheek′i·ness
cheek′y
  ·i·er ·i·est
cheep
  (*chirp;* see CHEAP)
cheep′er
cheer
cheer′ful
cheer′ful·ly
cheer′ful·ness
cheer′i·ly
cheer′i·ness
cheer′i·o′
cheer′lead′er
cheer′less
cheer′less·ly
cheer′less·ness
cheers
cheer′y
  ·i·er ·i·est
cheese
cheese′burg′er
cheese′cake′
cheese′cloth′
chees′y
  ·i·er ·i·est
chee′tah
chef
chem′i·cal
chem′i·cal·ly
che·mise′
chem′ist
chem′is·try

che′mo·ther′a·py
chem·ur′gy
che·nille′
cher′ish
che·root′
cher′ry
  ·ries
chert
cher′ub
  ·ubs *or* ·u·bim′ *or*
  ·u·bims
che·ru′bic
cher′vil
chess
chess′board′
chess′man
chest
ches·ter·field′
chest′nut′
chev′i·ot
che′vre
chev′ron
chew
chew′er
chew′ing gum
chew′y
  ·i·er ·i·est
Chi·an′ti
chi·a′ro·scu′ro′
chic
  (*stylish;* see CHICK,
  SHEIK)
chi·can′er·y
  ·ies
Chi·ca′no
  ·nos
chi′chi *or* chi′-chi
chick
  (*young bird;* see
  CHIC)
chick′a·dee′
chick′en
chick′en-fried′
chick′en-heart′ed
chick′en-pox′
chick′pea′
chick′weed′
chic′le
chic′o·ry
chide
  chid′ed *or* chid,
  chid′ed *or* chid *or*
  chid′den, chid′ing
chid′ing·ly
chief
chief′ly
chief′tain
chif′fon′
chig′ger
chi′gnon′
chil′blain′
child
  chil′dren
child′bear′ing
child′birth′
child′hood′
child′ish
child′ish·ly
child′ish·ness

child′less
child′like′
chil′dren
Chil′e·an
chil′i
  ·ies
  (*pepper*)
chill
chill′i·ness
chill′y
  ·i·er ·i·est
  (*cold*)
chime
  chimed chim′ing
chi·me′ra
chi·mer′i·cal
chim′ney
  ·neys
chimp
chim′pan·zee′
chin
  chinned chin′ning
chi′na
chin·chil′la
chine
Chi·nese′
chink
chi′no
  ·nos
chi·nook′
chintz
chintz′y
  ·i·er ·i·est
chip
  chipped chip′ping
chip′munk′
chip′per
chi·rop′o·dist
chi·rop′o·dy
chi′ro·prac′tic
chi′ro·prac′tor
chirp
chir′rup
chis′el
  ·eled *or* ·elled
  ·el·ing *or* ·el·ling
chis′el·er *or* ·ler
chit
chit′chat′
chi′tin
chi′ton
chit′ter·lings
chiv′al·rous
chiv′al·rous·ly
chiv′al·rous·ness
chiv′al·ry
chives
chla·myd′i·a
chlo′ride′
chlo′ri·nate′
  ·nat′ed ·nat′ing
chlo′ri·na′tion
chlo′rine′
chlo′ro·form′
chlo′ro·phyll′ *or*
  ·phyl′
chock
chock′-full′
choc′o·late

choc′o·lat·y *or* ·ey
choice
  choic′er choic′est
choir
choke
  choked chok′ing
chok′er
chol′er
chol′er·a
chol′er·ic
cho·les′ter·ol′
chomp
choose
  chose cho′sen
  choos′ing
choos′er
choos′y *or* ·ey
  ·i·er ·i·est
chop
  chopped chop′ping
chop′per
chop′pi·ness
chop′py
  ·pi′er ·pi·est
chop′sticks′
chop′ su′ey
cho′ral
  (*of a chorus;* see
  CHORALE, CORAL,
  CORRAL)
cho·rale′ *or* ·ral′
  (*hymn tune;* see
  CHORAL, CORAL,
  CORRAL)
cho′ral·ly
chord
  (*music;* see CORD)
chor′date′
chore
chor′e·o·graph′
chor′e·og′ra·pher
chor′e·o·graph′ic
chor′e·og′ra·phy
chor′is·ter
cho′roid′
chor′tle
  ·tled ·tling
chor′tler
cho′rus
chose
cho′sen
chow
chow′der
chow′ mein′
chrism
chris′ten
Chris′ten·dom
chris′ten·ing
Chris′tian
Chris′ti·an′i·ty
Chris′tian·ize′
  ·ized′ ·iz′ing
Christ′mas
chro·mat′ic
chro·mat′i·cal·ly
chro′ma·tin′
chrome
chro′mi·um
chro′mo·some′

chron′ic
chron′i·cal·ly
chron′i·cle
  ·cled ·cling
chron′i·cler
chron′o·log′i·cal
chron′o·log′i·cal·ly
chro·nol′o·gy
  ·gies
chro·nom′e·ter
chrys′a·lis
chrys·an′the·mum
chub′bi·ness
chub′by
  ·bi·er ·bi·est
chuck
chuck′-full′
chuck′hole′
chuck′le
  ·led ·ling
chuck′wal′la
chug
  chugged chug′ging
chuk′ka boot
chum
  chummed
  chum′ming
chum′mi·ness
chum′my
  ·mi·er ·mi·est
chump
chunk
chunk′i·ness
chunk′y
  ·i·er ·i·est
church
church′go′er
church′man
church′war′den
church′wom′an
church′yard′
churl
churl′ish
churl′ish·ness
churn
chute
chut′ney
chutz′pah *or* ·pa
chyme
ci·ca′da
  ·das *or* ·dae
cic′a·trix′
  cic′a·tri′ces′ *or*
  ·trix′es
ci′der
ci·gar′
cig′a·rette′ *or* ·ret′
cig′a·ril′lo
  ·los
cil′i·a
  sing. cil′i·um
ci·met′i·dine′
cinch
cin·cho′na
cinc′ture
cin′der
Cin·der·el′la
cin′e·ma
cin′e·mat′ic

cin′e·ma·tog′ra·pher
cin′e·ma·tog′ra·phy
cin′na·bar′
cin′na·mon
ci′pher
cir′ca
cir·ca′di·an
cir′cle
  ·cled ·cling
cir′clet
cir′cuit
cir·cu′i·tous
cir·cu′i·tous·ly
cir·cu′i·tous·ness
cir′cuit·ry
cir′cu·lar
cir′cu·lar′i·ty
cir′cu·lar·ize′
  ·ized′ ·iz′ing
cir′cu·lar·iz′er
cir′cu·late′
  ·lat′ed ·lat′ing
cir′cu·la′tion
cir′cu·lat′or
cir′cu·la·to′ry
cir′cum·cise′
  ·cised′ ·cis′ing
cir′cum·ci′sion
cir·cum′fer·ence
cir′cum·flex′
cir′cum·lo·cu′tion
cir′cum·nav′i·gate′
  ·gat′ed ·gat′ing
cir′cum·nav′i·ga′-
  tion
cir′cum·scribe′
  ·scribed′ ·scrib′ing
cir′cum·scrip′tion
cir′cum·spect′
cir′cum·spec′tion
cir′cum·stance′
cir′cum·stan′tial
cir′cum·stan′tial·ly
cir′cum·stan′ti·ate′
  ·at′ed ·at′ing
cir′cum·vent′
cir′cum·ven′tion
cir′cus
ci·ré′
cir·rho′sis
cir·rhot′ic
cir′rus
cis′tern
cit′a·del
ci·ta′tion
cite
  cit′ed cit′ing
  (*quote;* see SIGHT,
  SITE)
cit′i·fied′
cit′i·zen
cit′i·zen·ry
cit′i·zen·ship′
cit′ric
cit′ron
cit′ron·el·la
cit′rus

cit′y
  ·ies
civ′et
civ′ic
civ′ics
civ′il
ci·vil′ian
ci·vil′i·ty
  ·ties
civ′i·li·za′tion
civ′i·lize′
  ·lized′ ·liz′ing
civ′i·lized′
civ′il·ly
civ′vies
clack
  (*sharp sound;* see
  CLAQUE)
clad
clad′ding
claim
claim′a·ble
claim′ant
claim′er
clair·voy′ance
clair·voy′ant
clam
  clammed
  clam′ming
clam′bake′
clam′ber
clam′mer
clam′mi·ness
clam′my
  ·mi·er ·mi·est
clam′or
clam′or·ous
clamp
clan
clan·des′tine
clan·des′tine·ly
clang
clang′or
clank
clan′nish
clan′nish·ly
clan′nish·ness
clans′man
clap
  clapped clap′ping
clap′board
clap′per
clap′trap′
claque
  (*group;* see CLACK)
clar′et
clar′i·fi·ca′tion
clar′i·fy′
  ·fied′ ·fy′ing
clar′i·net′
clar′i·net′ist *or* ·tist
clar′i·on
clar′i·ty
clash
clasp
class
clas′sic
clas′si·cal

clas′si·cal·ly
clas′si·cism′
clas′si·cist
clas′si·fi·ca′tion
clas′si·fi′er
clas′si·fy′
  ·fied′ ·fy′ing
class′i·ness
class′less
class′mate′
class′room′
class′y
  ·i·er ·i·est
clat′ter
claus′al
clause
claus′tro·pho′bi·a
claus′tro·pho′bic
clav′i·chord′
clav′i·cle
cla·vier′
claw
clay
clay′ey
  ·i·er ·i·est
clean
clean′-cut′
clean′er
clean′li·ness
clean′ly
  ·li·er ·li·est
clean′ness
cleanse
  cleansed cleans′ing
cleans′er
clean′up′
clear
clear′ance
clear′-cut′
clear′ing
clear′ing·house′
clear′ly
clear′ness
cleat
cleav′age
cleave
  cleaved *or* cleft *or*
  clove, cleaved *or*
  cleft *or* clo′ven,
  cleav′ing
  (*to split*)
cleave
  cleaved cleav′ing
  (*to cling*)
cleav′er
clef
cleft
clem′a·tis
clem′en·cy
clem′ent
clench
clere′sto′ry
  ·ries
cler′gy
cler′gy·man
cler′gy·wom′an
cler′ic
cler′i·cal
cler′i·cal·ism′

cler′i·cal·ist
clerk
clev′er
clev′er·ly
clev′er·ness
clev′is
clew
  (*part of sail;* see
  CLUE)
cli·ché′
cli·chéd′
click
  (*sound;* see
  CLIQUE)
cli′ent
cli′en·tele′
cliff
cliff′hang′er *or*
  cliff′-hang′er
cli·mac′ter·ic
cli·mac′tic (*of a cli-
  max*)
cli′mate
cli·mat′ic (*of cli-
  mate*)
cli′max
climb
  climbed climb′ing
  (*ascend*)
climb′a·ble
climb′er
clime (*region*)
clinch
clinch′er
cling
  clung cling′ing
cling′er
clin′ic
clin′i·cal
clin′i·cal·ly
cli·ni′cian
clink
clink′er
cli′o·met′ric
cli′o·me·tri′cian
cli′o·met′rics′
clip
  clipped clip′ping
clip′board′
clip′per
clip′ping
clique
  (*group of people;*
  see CLICK)
cliqu′ish
clit′o·ris
  ·ris·es *or*
  cli·tor′i·des
clo·a′ca
  ·cae′ *or* ·cas
cloak
clob′ber
cloche
clock
clock′wise′
clock′work′
clod
clod′dish
clod′dy

clod'hop'per
clog
  clogged clog'ging
clog'gy
cloi'son·né'
clois'ter
clomp
clone
  cloned clon'ing
clop
  clopped clop'ping
close
  clos'er clos'est
close
  closed clos'ing
closed'-cir'cuit
close'fist'ed
close'fit'ting
close'-knit'
close'ly
close'mouthed'
close'ness
clos'et
close'-up'
clo'sure
clot
  clot'ted clot'ting
cloth *n.*
  cloths
clothe *v.*
  clothed *or* clad
  cloth'ing
clothes
clothes'pin'
cloth'ier
cloth'ing
clo'ture
cloud
cloud'burst'
cloud'i·ness
cloud'less
cloud'y
  ·i·er ·i·est
clout
clove
clo'ven
clo'ver
clo'ver·leaf'
  ·leafs'
clown
clown'ish
cloy
cloy'ing
club
  clubbed club'bing
club'foot'
club'house'
cluck
clue
  clued clu'ing
  (*helpful fact;* see
  CLEW)
clump
clump'y
  ·i·er ·i·est
clum'si·ly
clum'si·ness
clum'sy
  ·si·er ·si·est

clung
clunk
clunk'er
clus'ter
clutch
clut'ter
cni·dar'i·an
coach
coach'man
co·ad'ju·tor
co·ag'u·lant
co·ag'u·late'
  ·lat'ed ·lat'ing
co·ag'u·la'tion
coal
  (*mineral;* see
  COLE)
co'a·lesce'
  ·lesced' ·lesc'ing
co'a·les'cence
co'a·li'tion
coarse
  coars'er coars'est
  (*rough;* see
  COURSE)
coarse'ly
coars'en
coarse'ness
coast
coast'al
coast'er
coast'line'
coat
coat'ing
coat'tail'
co·au'thor
coax
co·ax'i·al
coax'ing·ly
cob
co'balt'
cob'ble
  ·bled ·bling
cob'bler
cob'ble·stone'
co'bra
cob'web'
cob'web·by
co·caine' *or* ·cain'
coc'cus
  ·ci
coc'cyx'
  coc·cy'ges'
coch'le·a
  ·ae' *or* ·as
cock
cock·ade'
cock'a·ma'mie
cock'a·too'
  ·toos'
cock'a·trice'
cock'crow'
cock'er·el
cock'eyed'
cock'fight'
cock'fight'ing
cock'i·ly
cock'i·ness
cock'le

cock'ney
  ·neys
cock'pit'
cock'roach'
cocks'comb'
cock'sure'
cock'tail'
cock'y
  ·i·er ·i·est
co'co'
  ·cos'
  (*coconut tree*)
co'coa' (*cacao pow-*
  der)
co'co·nut' *or*
  ·coa·nut'
co·coon'
cod
  cod *or* cods
co'da
cod'dle
  ·dled ·dling
code
  cod'ed cod'ing
co'de·fend'ant
co'deine'
cod'er
co'dex'
  ·di·ces'
cod'fish'
codg'er
cod'i·cil
cod'i·fi·ca'tion
cod'i·fi'er
cod'i·fy'
  ·fied' ·fy'ing
cod'-liv'er oil
co'ed' *or* co'-ed'
co'ed·u·ca'tion
co'ed·u·ca'tion·al
co'ef·fi'cient
co·e'qual
co'e·qual'i·ty
co·e'qual·ly
co·erce'
  ·erced' ·erc'ing
co·er'cion
co·er'cive
co·e'val
co'ex·ist'
co'ex·ist'ence
co'ex·ist'ent
co'ex·ten'sive
cof'fee
cof'fee·cake'
cof'fee·house'
cof'fee·pot'
cof'fer
cof'fin
cog
co'gen·cy
co'gent
cog'i·tate'
  ·tat'ed ·tat'ing
cog'i·ta'tion
cog'i·ta'tive
cog'i·ta'tor
co'gnac'

cog'nate'
cog·ni'tion
cog'ni·zance
cog'ni·zant
cog·no'men
  ·mens
cog'wheel'
co·hab'it
co·hab'i·ta'tion
co·here'
  ·hered' ·her'ing
co·her'ence
co·her'ent
co·her'ent·ly
co·he'sion
co·he'sive
co'hort'
coif
coif'fure'
coil
coin
  (*money;* see
  QUOIN)
coin'age
co'in·cide'
  ·cid'ed ·cid'ing
co·in'ci·dence
co·in'ci·dent
co·in'ci·den'tal
co·in'ci·den'tal·ly
co·i'tion
co'i·tus
coke
co'la
col'an·der
  (*strainer;* see CAL-
  ENDAR, CALENDER)
cold
cold'blood'ed
cold'ly
cold'ness
cole
  (*plant;* see COAL)
cole'slaw'
co'le·us
col'ic
col'ick·y
col'i·se'um
co·li'tis
col·lab'o·rate'
  ·rat'ed ·rat'ing
col·lab'o·ra'tion
col·lab'o·ra'tor
col·lage'
col·lapse'
  ·lapsed' ·laps'ing
col·laps'i·ble
col'lar
col'lar·bone'
col'lard
col·late'
  ·lat'ed ·lat'ing
col·lat'er·al
col·la'tion
col·la'tor
col'league'
col·lect'
col·lect'ed

col·lect'i·ble *or*
  ·a·ble
col·lec'tion
col·lec'tive
col·lec'tive·ly
col·lec'tiv·ism'
col·lec'tiv·ist
col·lec'tiv·ize'
  ·ized' ·iz'ing
col·lec'tor
col·leen'
col'lege
col·le'gian
col·le'giate
col·lide'
  ·lid'ed ·lid'ing
col'lie
col'lier
col'lier·y
  ·ies
col·li'sion
col'lo·cate'
  ·cat'ed ·cat'ing
col'lo·ca'tion
col'loid'
col·loi'dal
col·lo'qui·al
col·lo'qui·al·ism'
col·lo'qui·al·ly
col·lo'qui·um
  ·qui·a *or* ·qui·ums
col'lo·quy
  ·quies
col·lu'sion
col·lu'sive
col·lu'sive·ly
co·logne'
Co·lom'bi·an
co'lon
colo'nel
  (*officer;* see KER-
  NEL)
co·lo'ni·al
co·lo'ni·al·ism'
col'o·nist
col'o·ni·za'tion
col'o·nize'
  ·nized' ·niz'ing
col'o·niz'er
col'on·nade'
col'o·ny
  ·nies
col'o·phon'
col'or
Col'o·rad'o
col'or·ant
col'or·a'tion
col'or·a·tu'ra
col'or·blind'
col'or·blind'ness
col'ored
col'or·fast'
col'or·ful
col'or·ful·ly
col'or·ful·ness
col'or·ing
col'or·less
col'or·less·ly

col'or·less·ness
co·los'sal
co·los'sal·ly
co·los'sus
  ·si' *or* ·sus·es
co·los'to·my
  ·mies
co·los'trum
colt
colt'ish
colt'ish·ly
col'um·bine'
col'umn
co·lum'nar
col'um·nist
co'ma
  (*stupor;* see
  COMMA)
co'ma·tose'
comb
com·bat'
  ·bat'ed *or* ·bat'ted,
  ·bat'ing *or* ·bat'ting
com'bat·ant
com·bat'ive
comb'er
com'bi·na'tion
com·bine'
  ·bined' ·bin'ing
com'bo'
  ·bos'
com·bus'ti·bil'i·ty
com·bus'ti·ble
com·bus'tion
come
  came come
  com'ing
come'back'
co·me'di·an
co·me'dic
co·me'di·enne'
  fem.
come'down'
com'e·dy
  ·dies
come'li·ness
come'ly
  ·li·er ·li·est
come'-on'
co·mes'ti·ble
com'et
come'up'pance
com'fit
com'fort
com'fort·a·ble
com'fort·a·bly
com'fort·er
com'fort·ing
com'fort·less
com'fy
  ·fi·er ·fi·est
com'ic
com'i·cal
com'i·cal·ly
com'ing
com'i·ty
com'ma
  (*punctuation*
  mark; see COMA)

com·mand'
com·man·dant'
com·man·deer'
com·mand'er
com·mand'ment
com·man'do
  ·dos *or* ·does
com·mem'o·rate'
  ·rat'ed ·rat'ing
com·mem'o·ra'tion
com·mem'o·ra'tive
com·mem'o·ra'tor
com·mence'
  ·menced'
  ·menc'ing
com·mence'ment
com·mend'
com·mend'a·ble
com·mend'a·bly
com'men·da'tion
com·mend'a·to'ry
com·men'su·ra·ble
com·men'su·rate
com'ment
com'men·tar'y
  ·ies
com'men·tate'
  ·tat'ed ·tat'ing
com'men·ta'tor
com'merce
com·mer'cial
com·mer'cial·ism'
com·mer'cial·i·za'-
  tion
com·mer'cial·ize'
  ·ized' ·iz'ing
com·mer'cial·ly
com·min'gle
  ·gled ·gling
com·mis'er·ate'
  ·at'ed ·at'ing
com·mis'er·a'tion
com'mis·sar'
com'mis·sar'i·at
com'mis·sar'y
  ·ies
com·mis'sion
com·mis'sion·er
com·mit'
  ·mit'ted ·mit'ting
com·mit'ment
com·mit'tal
com·mit'tee
com·mit'tee·man
com·mit'tee·wom'
  an
com·mode'
com·mo'di·ous
com·mod'i·ty
  ·ties
com'mo·dore'
com'mon
com'mon·al·ty
  ·ties
com'mon·er
com'mon·law'
  marriage
com'mon·ly
com'mon·place'

com'mons
com'mon-sense'
com'mon·weal'
com'mon·wealth'
com·mo'tion
com'mu·nal
com·mu'nal·ize'
  ·ized' ·iz'ing
com·mu'nal·ly
com·mune' *v.*
  ·muned' ·mun'ing
com'mune *n.*
com·mu'ni·ca·bil'i·
  ty
com·mu'ni·ca·ble
com·mu'ni·cant
com·mu'ni·cate'
  ·cat'ed ·cat'ing
com·mu'ni·ca'tion
com·mu'ni·ca'tive
com·mu'ni·ca'tor
com·mun'ion
com·mu'ni·qué'
com'mu·nism'
com'mu·nist
com'mu·nis'tic
com·mu'ni·ty
  ·ties
com'mu·ta'tion
com'mu·ta'tive
com·mute'
  ·mut'ed ·mut'ing
com·mut'er
com·pact'
com·pact'ly
com·pact'ness
com·pac'tor
com·pan'ion
com·pan'ion·a·ble
com·pan'ion·ship'
com·pan'ion·way'
com'pa·ny
  ·nies
com'pa·ra·ble
com'pa·ra·bly
com·par'a·tive
com·par'a·tive·ly
com·pare'
  ·pared' ·par'ing
com·par'i·son
com·part'ment
com·part·men'tal·
  ize'
  ·ized' ·iz'ing
com'pass
com·pas'sion
com·pas'sion·ate
com·pas'sion·ate·ly
com·pat'i·bil'i·ty
com·pat'i·ble
com·pa'tri·ot
com'peer'
com·pel'
  ·pelled' ·pel'ling
com·pel'ling·ly
com·pen'di·um
  ·ums *or* ·a

com'pen·sate'
  ·sat'ed ·sat'ing
com·pen·sa'tion
com·pen'sa·to'ry
com·pete'
  ·pet'ed ·pet'ing
com'pe·tence
com'pe·ten·cy
com'pe·tent
com'pe·tent·ly
com·pe·ti'tion
com·pet'i·tive
com·pet'i·tor
com·pi·la'tion
com·pile'
  ·piled' ·pil'ing
com·pla'cen·cy
com·pla'cent
  (*smug*; see COM-
  PLAISANT)
com·plain'
com·plain'ant
com·plain'er
com·plaint'
com·plai'sance
com·plai'sant
  (*obliging*; see COM-
  PLACENT)
com·plai'sant·ly
com·plect'ed
com'ple·ment
  (*part of a whole*;
  see COMPLIMENT)
com'ple·men'ta·ry
com·plete'
  ·plet'ed ·plet'ing
com·plete'ly
com·plete'ness
com·ple'tion
com·plex'
com·plex'ion
com·plex'ioned
com·plex'i·ty
com·pli'ance
com·pli'ant
com'pli·cate'
  ·cat'ed ·cat'ing
com'pli·cat'ed
com'pli·ca'tion
com·plic'i·ty
com'pli·ment
  (*praise*; see COM-
  PLEMENT)
com'pli·men'ta·ry
com·ply'
  ·plied' ·ply'ing
com·po'nent
com·port'
com·port'ment
com·pose'
  ·posed' ·pos'ing
com·posed'
com·pos'er
com·pos'ite
com'po·si'tion
com·pos'i·tor
com'post
com·po'sure
com'pote'

com'pound
com'pre·hend'
com'pre·hen'si·ble
com'pre·hen'sion
com'pre·hen'sive
com'pre·hen'sive·ly
com'pre·hen'sive·
  ness
com·press'
com·pressed'
com·pres'sion
com·pres'sor
com·prise'
  ·prised' ·pris'ing
com'pro·mise'
  ·mised' ·mis'ing
comp·trol'ler
com·pul'sion
com·pul'sive
com·pul'sive·ly
com·pul'sive·ness
com·pul'so·ry
com·punc'tion
com·pu·ta'tion
com·pute'
  ·put'ed ·put'ing
com·put'er
com·pu'ter·i·za'-
  tion
com·put'er·ize'
  ·ized' ·iz'ing
com'rade'
com'rade·ship'
con
  (*to study*; see
  CONN)
con·cat'e·na'tion
con·cave'
con·cav'i·ty
  ·ties
con·ceal'
con·ceal'ment
con·cede'
  ·ced'ed ·ced'ing
con·ceit'
con·ceit'ed
con·ceiv'a·ble
con·ceiv'a·bly
con·ceive'
  ·ceived' ·ceiv'ing
con'cen·trate'
  ·trat'ed ·trat'ing
con'cen·tra'tion
con·cen'tric
con·cen'tri·cal·ly
con'cept'
con·cep'tion
con·cep'tu·al
con·cep'tu·al·i·za'-
  tion
con·cep'tu·al·ize'
  ·ized' ·iz'ing
con·cep'tu·al·ly
con·cern'
con·cerned'
con·cern'ing
con'cert
con·cert'ed

con·cert'ed·ly
con·cer'ti·na
con·cert·ize'
  ·ized' ·iz'ing
con'cert·mas'ter
con·cer'to
  ·tos *or* ·ti
con·ces'sion
con·ces'sion·aire'
conch
  conchs *or* conch'es
con·ci·erge'
con·cil'i·ar
con·cil'i·ate'
  ·at'ed ·at'ing
con·cil'i·a'tion
con·cil'i·a'tor
con·cil'i·a·to'ry
con·cise'
con·cise'ly
con·cise'ness
con·ci'sion
con'clave'
con·clude'
  ·clud'ed ·clud'ing
con·clu'sion
con·clu'sive
con·clu'sive·ly
con·clu'sive·ness
con·coct'
con·coc'tion
con·com'i·tant
con·com'i·tant·ly
con'cord'
Con'cord grape
con·cord'ance
con·cor'dat
con'course'
con'crete
con·crete'ly
con·crete'ness
con·cre'tion
con'cu·bine'
con·cu'pis·cence
con·cu'pis·cent
con·cur'
  ·curred' ·cur'ring
con·cur'rence
con·cur'rent
con·cur'rent·ly
con·cus'sion
con·demn'
con'dem·na'tion
con·dem'na·to'ry
con·demn'er
con'den·sa'tion
con·dense'
  ·densed' ·dens'ing
con·dens'er
con'de·scend'
con'de·scend'ing·ly
con'de·scen'sion
con·dign'
con'di·ment
con·di'tion
con·di'tion·al
con·di'tion·al·ly
con·di'tioned

con·di'tion·er
con'do'
  ·dos *or* ·does
con·dole'
  ·doled' ·dol'ing
con·do'lence
con'dom
con'do·min'i·um
con·done'
  ·doned' ·don'ing
con'dor
con·duce'
  ·duced' ·duc'ing
con·du'cive
con·duct'
con·duct'ance
con·duc'tion
con·duc'tive
con·duc·tiv'i·ty
con·duc'tor
con'du·it
cone
con'fab'
con·fec'tion
con·fec'tion·ar'y
  adj.
con·fec'tion·er
con·fec'tion·er'y *n.*
  ·ies
con·fed'er·a·cy
  ·cies
con·fed'er·ate
  ·at'ed ·at'ing
con·fed'er·a'tion
con·fer'
  ·ferred' ·fer'ring
con'fer·ee'
con'fer·ence
con·fer'ment
con·fer'ral
con·fer'rer
con·fess'
con·fess'ed·ly
con·fes'sion
con·fes'sion·al
con·fes'sor
con·fet'ti
con'fi·dant' *n.*
con'fi·dante' *fem.*
con·fide'
  ·fid'ed ·fid'ing
con'fi·dence
con'fi·dent *adj.*
con'fi·den'tial
con'fi·den'ti·al'i·ty
con'fi·den'tial·ly
con'fi·dent·ly
con·fig'u·ra'tion
con·fine'
  ·fined' ·fin'ing
con·fine'ment
con·fines'
con·firm'
con'fir·ma'tion
  (*verification*; see
  CONFORMATION)
con·firmed'
con'fis·cate'
  ·cat'ed ·cat'ing

con·fis·ca′tion
con·fis′ca·to·ry
con·fla·gra′tion
con·flict′
con·flict′ed
con·flu·ence
con·flu·ent
con·form′
con·for·ma′tion
  (*shape; see* CON-
  FIRMATION)
con·form′ism′
con·form′ist
con·form′i·ty
con·found′
con·found′ed
con·fra·ter′ni·ty
  ·ties
con′frere′
con·front′
con·fron·ta′tion
con·fron·ta′tion·al
Con·fu′cian
con·fuse′
  ·fused′ ·fus′ing
con·fus′ed·ly
con·fu′sion
con·fu·ta′tion
con·fute′
  ·fut′ed ·fut′ing
con′ga
con·geal′
con·geal′ment
con·ge′nial
con·ge′ni·al′i·ty
con·ge′nial·ly
con·gen′i·tal
con·gen′i·tal·ly
con′ger eel
con·ge′ries′
con·gest′
con·ges′tion
con·ges′tive
con·glom′er·ate
con·glom′er·a′tion
con·grat′u·late′
  ·lat′ed ·lat·ing
con·grat′u·la′tion
con·grat′u·la·to′ry
con′gre·gate′
  ·gat′ed ·gat·ing
con′gre·ga′tion
con′gre·ga′tion·al
con′gress
con·gres′sion·al
con′gress·man
con′gress·wom′an
con′gru·ence
con′gru·ent
con·gru′i·ty
  ·ties
con′gru·ous
con′gru·ous·ly
con′ic
con′i·cal
con′i·cal·ly
con′i·fer
co·nif′er·ous

con·jec′tur·al
con·jec′ture
  ·tured ·tur·ing
con·join′
con·joint′ly
con′ju·gal
con′ju·gate′
  ·gat′ed ·gat·ing
con′ju·ga′tion
con·junc′tion
con·junc·ti′va
  ·vas *or* ·vae
con·junc′tive
con·junc′ti·vi′tis
con·junc′ture
con′ju·ra′tion
con·jure
  ·jured ·jur·ing
con·jur′er *or* ·ju·ror
conk
conn
  (*direct a ship; see*
  CON)
con·nect′
Con·nect′i·cut
con·nec′tion
con·nec′tive
con·nec′tor *or*
  ·nect′er
conn′ing tower
con·niv′ance
con·nive′
  ·nived′ ·niv′ing
con·niv′er
con′nois·seur′
con′no·ta′tion
con′no·ta′tive
con′no·ta′tion·al
con·note′
  ·not′ed ·not′ing
con·nu′bi·al
con′quer
con′quer·or
con′quest′
con·quis′ta·dor′
  ·dors′ *or* ·do′res′
con′san·guin′e·ous
con′san·guin′i·ty
con′science
  (*moral judgment;*
  see CONSCIOUS)
con′science·less
con′sci·en′tious
con′sci·en′tious·ly
con′sci·en′tious·ness
con′scious
  (*aware; see* CON-
  SCIENCE)
con′scious·ly
con′scious·ness
con·script′
con·scrip′tion
con′se·crate′
  ·crat′ed ·crat′ing
con′se·cra′tion
con·sec′u·tive
con·sec′u·tive·ly
con·sen′sus
con·sent′

con′se·quence′
con′se·quent′
con′se·quen′tial
con′se·quent′ly
con′ser·va′tion
con′ser·va′tion·ist
con·serv′a·tism′
con·ser′va·tive
con·serv′a·tive·ly
con·serv′a·to′ry
  ·ries
con·serve′
  ·served′ ·serv′ing
con·sid′er
con·sid′er·a·ble
con·sid′er·a·bly
con·sid′er·ate
con·sid′er·ate·ly
con·sid′er·a′tion
con·sid′ered
con·sid′er·ing
con·sign′
con·sign′ment
con·sist′
con·sis′ten·cy
  ·cies
con·sis′tent
con·sis′tent·ly
con·sis′to·ry
  ·ries
con′so·la′tion
con·sole′
  ·soled′ ·sol′ing
con·sol′i·date′
  ·dat′ed ·dat′ing
con·sol′i·da′tion
con·sol′i·da′tor
con·sol′ing·ly
con′som·mé′
con′so·nance
con′so·nant
con·sort′
con·sor′ti·um
  ·ti·a
con·spec′tus
con·spic′u·ous
con·spic′u·ous·ly
con·spir′a·cy
  ·cies
con·spir′a·tor
con·spir′a·to′ri·al
con·spire′
  ·spired′ ·spir′ing
con·sta·ble
con·stab′u·lar′y
  ·ies
con′stan·cy
con′stant
con′stant·ly
con′stel·la′tion
con′ster·na′tion
con′sti·pate′
  ·pat′ed ·pat′ing
con′sti·pa′tion
con·stit′u·en·cy
  ·cies
con·stit′u·ent
con′sti·tute′
  ·tut′ed ·tut′ing

con′sti·tu′tion
con′sti·tu′tion·al
con′sti·tu′tion·al′i·ty
con′sti·tu′tion·al·ly
con′sti·tu′tive
con·strain′
con·straint′
con·strict′
con·stric′tion
con·stric′tor
con·struct′
con·struc′tion
con·struc′tion·ist
con·struc′tive
con·struc′tor *or*
  ·struct′er
con·strue′
  ·strued′ ·stru′ing
con′sul
  (*government offi-
  cial; see* COUNCIL,
  COUNSEL)
con′sul·ar
con′sul·ate
con·sult′
con·sult′ant
con′sul·ta′tion
con·sume′
  ·sumed′ ·sum′ing
con·sum′er
con·sum′er·ism′
con·sum′mate′ *v.*
  ·mat′ed ·mat′ing
con·sum′mate *adj.*
con′sum·ma′tion
con·sump′tion
con·sump′tive
con′tact
con·ta′gion
con·ta′gious
con·ta′gious·ness
con·tain′
con·tain′er
con·tain′er·ize′
  ·ized′ ·iz′ing
con·tain′ment
con·tam′i·nant
con·tam′i·nate′
  ·nat′ed ·nat′ing
con·tam′i·na′tion
con·temn′
con′tem·plate′
  ·plat′ed ·plat′ing
con′tem·pla′tion
con′tem·pla·tive′
con·tem′po·ra·ne′i·
  ty
con·tem′po·ra′ne·
  ous
con·tem′po·ra′ne·
  ous·ly
con·tem′po·rar′y
  ·ies
con·tempt′
con·tempt′i·ble
con·tempt′i·bly
con·temp′tu·ous
con·temp′tu·ous·ly

con·temp′tu·ous·
  ness
con·tend′
con·tend′er
con·tent′
con·tent′ed
con·tent′ed·ly
con·tent′ed·ness
con·ten′tion
con·ten′tious
con·ten′tious·ly
con·ten′tious·ness
con·tent′ment
con′tents′
con·ter′mi·nous
con·ter′mi·nous·ly
con′test′
con·test′a·ble
con·test′ant
con′text′
con·tex′tu·al
con·ti·gu′i·ty
con·tig′u·ous
con′ti·nence
con′ti·nent
con′ti·nen′tal
con·tin′gen·cy
  ·cies
con·tin′gent
con·tin′u·al
con·tin′u·al·ly
con·tin′u·ance
con·tin′u·a′tion
con·tin′ue
  ·ued ·u·ing
con′ti·nu′i·ty
  ·ties
con·tin′u·ous
con·tin′u·ous·ly
con·tin′u·um
  ·u·a *or* ·u·ums
con′tort′
con·tor′tion
con·tor′tion·ist
con′tour′
con′tra
con′tra·band′
con′tra·cep′tion
con′tra·cep′tive
con′tract′
con·trac′tile
con·trac′tion
con·trac·tor
con·trac′tu·al
con·trac′tu·al·ly
con′tra·dict′
con′tra·dic′tion
con′tra·dic′to·ry
con′tra·dis·tinc′-
  tion
con′trail′
con′tra·in′di·cate′
  ·cat′ed ·cat′ing
con·tral′to
  ·tos
con·trap′tion
con′tra·pun′tal

con·tra·ri′e·ty
con′trar′i·ly
con′trar′i·ness
con′trar′i·wise′
con′trar′y
con′trast′
con′tra·vene′
  ·vened′ ·ven′ing
con′tre·temps′
con·trib′ute
  ·ut′ed ·ut·ing
con′tri·bu′tion
con·trib′u·tor
con·trib′u·to′ry
con·trite′
con·trite′ly
con·tri′tion
con·triv′ance
con·trive′
  ·trived′ ·triv′ing
con·triv′er
con·trol′
  ·trolled′ ·trol′ling
con·trol′la·ble
con·trol′ler
con′tro·ver′sial
con′tro·ver′sy
  ·sies
con′tro·vert′
con′tro·vert′i·ble
con·tu·ma′cious
con′tu·ma·cy
con′tu·me′li·ous
con′tu·me′ly
  ·lies
con·tu′sion
co·nun′drum
con′ur·ba′tion
con′va·lesce′
  ·lesced′ ·lesc′ing
con′va·les′cence
con′va·les′cent
con·vec′tion
con·vec′tive
con·vene′
  ·vened′ ·ven′ing
con·ven′er
con·ven′ience
con·ven′ient
con·ven′ient·ly
con′vent
con·ven′ti·cle
con·ven′tion
con·ven′tion·al
con·ven′tion·al′i·ty
con·ven′tion·al·ize′
  ·ized′ ·iz′ing
con·ven′tion·al·ly
con·ven′tion·eer′
con·verge′
  ·verged′ ·verg′ing
con·ver′gence
con·ver′gent
con·ver′sant
con′ver·sa′tion
con′ver·sa′tion·al
con′ver·sa′tion·al·ist
con′ver·sa′tion·al·ly

con'verse n.
con·verse' v.
  ·versed' ·vers'ing
con'verse·ly
con·ver'sion
con·vert'
con·vert'er or
  ·ver'tor
con·vert'i·ble
con·vex'
con·vex'i·ty
con·vey'
con·vey'a·ble
con·vey'ance
con·vey'or or ·er
con·vict'
con·vic'tion
con·vince'
  ·vinced' ·vinc'ing
con·vinc'ing
con·vinc'ing·ly
con·viv'i·al
con·viv'i·al'i·ty
con·vo·ca'tion
con·voke'
  ·voked' ·vok'ing
con'vo·lut'ed
con'vo·lu'tion
con'voy'
con·vulse'
  ·vulsed' ·vuls'ing
con·vul'sion
con·vul'sive
con·vul'sive·ly
coo
cook
cook'book'
cook'er
cook'er·y
cook'ie
cook'out'
cool
cool'ant
cool'er
coo'lie
  (laborer; see
  COOLLY, COULEE)
cool'ly
  (in a cool way; see
  COOLIE, COULEE)
cool'ness
coon
coon'skin'
coop
  (cage; see COUP,
  COUPE)
co'-op'
coop'er
coop'er·age
co·op'er·ate' or
  co-op'·
  ·at'ed ·at'ing
co·op'er·a'tion or
  co-op'·
co·op'er·a·tive or
  co-op'·
co-opt'
co·or'di·nate or
  co-or'·

  ·nat'ed ·nat'ing
co·or'di·na'tion or
  co-or'·
co·or'di·na'tor or
  co-or'·
coot
coot'ie
cop
  copped cop'ping
co·part'ner
cope
  coped cop'ing
Co·per'ni·can
cop'i·er
co·pi'lot
cop'ing
co'pi·ous
co'pi·ous·ly
co'pi·ous·ness
cop'-out'
cop'per
cop'per·head'
cop'per·y
cop'pice
co'pra
copse
cop'ter
cop'u·la
  ·las
cop'u·late'
  ·lat'ed ·lat'ing
cop'u·la'tion
cop'u·la'tive
cop'y
  ·ies
  ·ied ·y'ing
cop'y·cat'
cop'y·ist
cop'y·right'
cop'y·writ'er
co·quette'
  ·quet'ted ·quet'ting
co·quet'tish
co'quet·ry
cor'al
  (shell; see CHORAL,
  CHORALE, CORRAL)
cor'bel
cord
  (string; see CHORD)
cord'age
cor'dial
cor'di·al'i·ty
cor'dial·ly
cor'dil·le'ra
cord'ite'
cord'less
cor'don
cor'do·van
cor'du·roy'
core
  cored cor'ing
co're·spond'ent
  (legal term; see
  CORRESPONDENT)
co'ri·an'der
cork
cork'screw'
corm

cor'mo·rant
corn
corn'ball'
corn'cob'
cor'ne·a
cor'ne·al
cor'ner
cor'ner·back'
cor'nered
cor'ner·stone'
cor·net'
  (a horn; see CORO-
  NET)
corn'flow'er
cor'nice
corn'meal'
corn'starch'
cor·nu·co'pi·a
corn'y
  ·i·er ·i·est
co·rol'la
cor·ol·lar'y
  ·ies
co·ro'na
  ·nas or ·nae
cor'o·nar'y
  ·ies
cor'o·na'tion
cor'o·ner
cor'o·net'
  (a crown; see COR-
  NET)
cor'po·ral
  (soldier; see COR-
  POREAL)
cor'po·rate
cor'po·ra'tion
cor·po're·al
  (bodily; see CORPO-
  RAL)
corps (group of peo-
  ple)
corpse (dead body)
cor'pu·lence
cor'pu·lent
cor'pus
  cor'po·ra
cor'pus'cle
corpus de·lic'ti'
cor·ral'
  ·ralled' ·ral'ling
  (animal pen; see
  CHORAL, CHORALE,
  CORAL)
cor·rect'
cor·rect'a·ble
cor·rec'tion
cor·rec'tion·al
cor·rec'tive
cor·rect'ly
cor·rect'ness
cor're·late'
  ·lat'ed ·lat'ing
cor're·la'tion
cor·rel'a·tive'
cor're·spond'
cor're·spond'ence
cor're·spond'ent
  (writer; see CORE-
  SPONDENT)

cor're·spond'ing·ly
cor'ri·dor
cor·rob'o·rate'
  ·rat'ed ·rat'ing
cor·rob'o·ra'tion
cor·rob'o·ra'tive
cor·rob'o·ra'tor
cor·rode'
  ·rod'ed ·rod'ing
cor·ro'sion
cor·ro'sive
cor·ro'sive·ly
cor'ru·gate'
  ·gat'ed ·gat'ing
cor'ru·ga'tion
cor·rupt'
cor·rupt'i·ble
cor·rup'tion
cor·rupt'ly
cor·sage'
cor'sair'
cor'set
cor·tege' or ·tège'
cor'tex'
  ·ti·ces'
cor'ti·cal
cor'ti·sone'
co·run'dum
cor·us·cate'
  ·cat'ed ·cat'ing
cor·us·ca'tion
cor·vette'
co'sign'
  (sign jointly; see
  COSINE)
co·sig'na·to'ry
  ·ries
co'sign'er
co'si·ly
co'sine'
  (mathematics
  term; see COSIGN)
co'si·ness
cos·met'ic
cos·met'i·cal·ly
cos·me·ti'cian
cos'me·tol'o·gist
cos'me·tol'o·gy
cos'mic
cos'mi·cal·ly
cos·mog'o·ny
cos'mo·log'i·cal
cos·mol'o·gy
cos'mo·naut'
cos'mo·pol'i·tan
cos'mos
co'spon'sor
co'spon'sor·ship'
cost
  cost cost'ing
co'star'
  ·starred' ·star'ring
cost'-ef·fec'tive
cost'-
  ef·fec'tive·ness
cost'li·ness
cost'ly
  ·li·er ·li·est

cos'tume'
  ·tumed' ·tum'ing
cot
co·tan'gent
cote
co'te·rie
co·ter'mi·nous
co·til'lion
cot'tage
cot'tag·er
cot'ter
cot'ton
cot'ton·mouth'
cot'ton·seed'
cot'ton·tail'
cot'ton·wood'
cot'ton·y
cot'y·le'don
couch
cou'gar
cough
could
cou'lee
  (ravine; see
  COOLIE, COOLLY)
cou·lomb'
coun'cil
  (legislature; see
  CONSUL, COUNSEL)
coun'cil·man
coun'ci·lor
  (council member;
  see COUNSELOR)
coun'cil·wom'an
coun'sel
  ·seled or ·selled
  ·sel·ing or ·sel·ling
  (advice; advise;
  see CONSUL, COUN-
  CIL)
coun'se·lor or
  ·sel·lor
  (adviser; see
  COUNCILOR)
count
count'down'
coun'te·nance
  ·nanced ·nanc·ing
count'er (one that
  counts)
coun'ter (opposite)
coun'ter·act'
coun'ter·ac'tion
coun'ter·at·tack'
coun'ter·bal'ance
  ·anced ·anc·ing
coun'ter·claim'
coun'ter·clock'-
  wise'
coun'ter·cul'ture
coun'ter·es'pi·o·
  nage'
coun'ter·feit'
coun'ter·feit'er
count'er·man'
coun'ter·mand'
coun'ter·meas'ure
coun'ter·pane'
coun'ter·part'
coun'ter·point'

coun'ter·poise'
  ·poised' ·pois'ing
coun'ter·pro·duc'
  tive
coun'ter·rev'o·lu'-
  tion
coun'ter·rev'o·lu'-
  tion·ar'y
  ·ies
coun'ter·sign'
coun'ter·sink'
  ·sunk' ·sink'ing
coun'ter·spy'
coun'ter·ten'or
coun'ter·weight'
count'ess
count'less
coun'tri·fied'
coun'try
  ·tries
coun'try·man
coun'try·side'
coun'ty
  ·ties
coup
  (an overthrow; see
  COOP, COUPE)
coup de grâce'
coup d'é·tat'
coupe
  (automobile; see
  COOP, COUP)
cou'ple
  ·pled ·pling
cou'pler
cou'plet
cou'pling
cou'pon'
cour'age
cou·ra'geous
cou·ra'geous·ly
cou'ri·er
course
  coursed cours'ing
  (way; to run; see
  COARSE)
cours'er
court
cour'te·ous
cour'te·ous·ly
cour'te·san
cour'te·sy
  ·sies
  (politeness; see
  CURTSY)
court'house'
cour'ti·er
court'li·ness
court'ly
  ·li·er ·li·est
court'-mar'tial
  courts'-mar'tial or
  court'-mar'tials
  ·tialed or ·tialled
  ·tial·ing or
  ·tial·ling
court'room'
court'ship'
court'yard'
cous'cous'
cous'in

cou·tu·ri·er'
cou·tu·ri·ère' *fem.*
co'va·lence
co'va·lent
cove
cov'en
cov'e·nant
cov'er
cov'er·age'
cov'er·alls'
cov'ered
cov'er·ing
cov'er·let
cov'ert
cov'ert·ly
cov'er·up'
cov'et
cov'et·ous
cov'et·ous·ness
cov'ey
 ·eys
cow
cow'ard
cow'ard·ice'
cow'ard·li·ness
cow'ard·ly
cow'boy'
cow'er
cow'girl'
cow'hand'
cow'hide'
cowl
cow'lick'
cowl'ing
co'-work'er
cow'poke'
cow'pox'
cox'comb'
cox'swain
coy
coy'ly
coy'ness
coy·o'te
coz'en
co'zi·ly
co'zi·ness
co'zy
 ·zies
 ·zi·er ·zi·est
crab
 crabbed crab'bing
crab'bed
crab'bi·ly
crab'bi·ness
crab'by
 ·bi·er ·bi·est
crack
crack'down'
cracked
crack'er
crack'er·jack'
crack'le
 ·led ·ling
crack'lings
crack'pot'
crack'up'
cra'dle
 ·dled ·dling

cra'dle·song'
craft
craft'i·ly
craft'i·ness
crafts'man
crafts'man·ship'
craft'y
 ·i·er ·i·est
crag
crag'gy
 ·gi·er ·gi·est
cram
 crammed
 cram'ming
cramp
cramped
cran'ber'ry
 ·ries
crane
 craned cran'ing
cra'ni·al
cra'ni·um
 ·ni·ums *or* ·ni·a
crank
crank'case'
crank'i·ly
crank'i·ness
crank'shaft'
crank'y
 ·i·er ·i·est
cran'ny
 ·nies
crap
crape
 (*black cloth for mourning;* see CREPE)
crap'pie
craps
crap'shoot'er
crash
crash'-land'
crass
crass'ly
crass'ness
crate
 crat'ed crat'ing
cra'ter
cra·vat'
crave
 craved crav'ing
cra'ven
cra'ven·ly
cra'ven·ness
crav'ing
craw
craw'fish'
crawl
crawl'y
 ·i·er ·i·est
cray'fish'
cray'on
craze
 crazed craz'ing
cra'zi·ly
cra'zi·ness
cra'zy
 ·zi·er ·zi·est

creak
 (*squeak;* see CREEK)
creak'i·ly
creak'i·ness
creak'y
 ·i·er ·i·est
cream
cream'er
cream'er·y
 ·ies
cream'i·ness
cream'y
 ·i·er ·i·est
crease
 creased creas'ing
cre·ate'
 ·at'ed ·at'ing
cre·a'tion
cre·a'tive
cre·a'tive·ly
cre·a'tive·ness
cre'a·tiv'i·ty
cre·a'tor
crea'ture
crèche
cre'dence
cre·den'tial
cre·den'za
cred'i·bil'i·ty
cred'i·ble (*believable*)
cred'i·bly
cred'it
cred'it·a·ble (*deserving praise*)
cred'it·a·bly
cred'i·tor
cre'do'
 ·dos'
cre·du'li·ty
cred'u·lous
cred'u·lous·ly
creed
creek
 (*stream;* see CREAK)
creel
creep
 crept creep'ing
creep'er
creep'i·ly
creep'i·ness
creep'y
 ·i·er ·i·est
cre·mains'
cre'mate'
 ·mat'ed ·mat'ing
cre·ma'tion
cre'ma·to'ri·um
 ·tor'i·ums *or* ·to'ri·a
cre'ma·to'ry
 ·ries
crème' de menthe'
crème' fraîche'
cren'el·at'ed *or* ·lat'ed

cren'el·a'tion *or* ·la'tion
Cre'ole'
cre'o·sote'
crepe *or* crêpe
 (*thin cloth;* see CRAPE)
crêpes' su·zette'
crept
cre·scen'do'
 ·dos'
cres'cent
cress
crest
crest'ed
crest'fall'en
Cre·ta'ceous
cre'tin
cre·tonne'
cre·vasse' (*deep fissure*)
crev'ice (*narrow cleft*)
crew
crew'el
 (*needlework;* see CRUEL)
crew'el·work'
crew'man
crib
 cribbed crib'bing
crib'bage'
crick
crick'et
cried
cri'er
crime
Cri·me'an
crim'i·nal
crim'i·nal'i·ty
crim'i·nal·ly
crim'i·nol'o·gist
crim'i·nol'o·gy
crimp
crim'son
cringe
 cringed cring'ing
crin'kle
 ·kled ·kling
crin'kly
 ·kli·er ·kli·est
crin'o·line'
crip'ple
 ·pled ·pling
cri'sis
 ·ses
crisp
crisp'i·ness
crisp'ly
crisp'ness
crisp'y
 ·i·er ·i·est
criss'cross'
cri·te'ri·on
 ·ri·a *or* ·ri·ons
crit'ic
crit'i·cal
crit'i·cal·ly
crit'i·cism

crit'i·ciz'a·ble
crit'i·cize'
 ·cized ·ciz'ing
cri·tique'
 ·tiqued' ·tiqu'ing
crit'ter
croak
cro·chet'
 ·cheted ·chet'ing
cro·chet'er
crock
crocked
crock'er·y
croc'o·dile'
cro'cus
 ·cus·es *or* ·ci'
crois·sant'
crone
cro'ny
 ·nies
crook
 crooked crook'ing
crook'ed
crook'ed·ly
crook'ed·ness
crook'neck'
croon
croon'er
crop
 cropped crop'ping
crop'-dust'ing
crop'per
cro·quet' (*game*)
cro·quette' (*food*)
cro'sier
cross
cross'bar'
cross'beam'
cross'bones'
cross'bow'
cross'breed'
 ·bred' ·breed'ing
cross'-coun'try
cross'-cur'rent
cross'cut' saw
cross'-ex·am'i·na'tion
cross'-ex·am'ine
 ·ined ·in'ing
cross'-eyed'
cross'hatch'
cross'ing
cross'ly
cross'o'ver
cross'piece'
cross'-pol'li·nate'
cross'-pol'li·na'tion
cross'-pur'pose
cross'-re·fer'
cross'-ref'er·ence
 ·enced ·enc'ing
cross'road'
cross'-sec'tion
cross'-town'
cross'walk'
cross'ways'
cross'wise'

cross'word' puzzle
crotch
crotch'et
crotch'et·y
crouch
croup
crou'pi·er
crou'ton'
crow
crow'bar'
crowd
crowd'ed
crown
crow's'-feet'
crow's'-nest'
cro'zier
cru'cial
cru'cial·ly
cru'ci·ble
cru'ci·fix'
cru'ci·fix'ion
cru'ci·form'
cru'ci·fy'
 ·fied' ·fy'ing
crude
 crud'er crud'est
crude'ly
crude'ness
cru·di·tés'
cru'di·ty
 ·ties
cru'el
 (*mean;* see CREWEL)
cru'el·ly
cru'el·ty
 ·ties
cru'et
cruise
 cruised cruis'ing
 (*a voyage;* see CRUSE)
cruis'er
crul'ler
crumb
crum'ble
 ·bled ·bling
crum'bly
 ·bli·er ·bli·est
crumb'y
 ·i·er ·i·est
 (*full of crumbs*)
crum'my
 ·mi·er ·mi·est
 (*inferior*)
crum'pet
crum'ple
 ·pled ·pling
crunch
crunch'y
 ·i·er ·i·est
crup'per
cru·sade'
 ·sad'ed ·sad'ing
cru·sad'er
cruse
 (*container;* see CRUISE)
crush
crush'er

crust
crus·ta′cean
crust′y
  ·i·er ·i·est
crutch
crux
  crux′es *or* cru′ces′
cry
  cries
  cried cry′ing
cry′ba·by
cry′o·gen′ics
cry′o·sur′ger·y
crypt
cryp′tic
cryp′ti·cal·ly
cryp′to·gram′
cryp·tog′ra·pher
cryp·tog′ra·phy
crys′tal
crys′tal·line
crys′tal·li·za′tion
crys′tal·lize′
  ·lized′ ·liz′ing
cub
Cu′ban
cub′by·hole′
cube
  cubed cub′ing
cu′bic
cu′bi·cal (*like a cube*)
cu′bi·cle (*compartment*)
cub′ism′
cub′ist
cu·bis′tic
cu′bit
cuck′old
cuck′old·ry
cuck′oo′
cu′cum·ber
cud
cud′dle
  ·dled ·dling
cud′dly
  ·dli·er ·dli·est
cudg′el
  ·eled *or* ·elled
  ·el·ing *or* ·el·ling
cue
  cued cu′ing *or* cue′ing
  (*a signal; see* QUEUE)
cuff
cui·sine′
cul′-de-sac′
  -sacs′
cu′li·nar′y
cull
cul′mi·nate′
  ·nat·ed ·nat·ing
cul′mi·na′tion
cu·lottes′
cul′pa·bil′i·ty
cul′pa·ble
cul′pa·bly
cul′prit

cult
cult′ism′
cult′ist
cul′ti·vate′
  ·vat′ed ·vat′ing
cul′ti·va′tion
cul′ti·va′tor
cul′tur·al
cul′tur·al·ly
cul′ture
cul′tured
cul′vert
cum′ber
cum′ber·some
cum′brous
cum′in
cum′mer·bund′
cu′mu·la′tive
cu′mu·lous *adj.*
cu′mu·lus *n.*
  ·li
cu·ne′i·form′
cun′ning
cun′ning·ly
cup
  cupped cup′ping
cup′board
cup′cake′
cup′ful′
  ·fuls′
cu′pid
cu·pid′i·ty
cu′po·la
cur
cur′a·ble
cu′ra·cy
  ·cies
cu′rate
cu′ra·tive
cu·ra′tor
cu·ra·to′ri·al
curb
curb′stone′
curd
cur′dle
  ·dled ·dling
cure
  cured cur′ing
cu·ré′
cure′-all′
cu′ret′tage′
cur′few′
cu′ri·o′
  ·os
cu′ri·os′i·ty
  ·ties
cu′ri·ous
cu′ri·ous·ly
curl
curl′er
cur′lew′
curl′i·cue′
curl′i·ness
curl′ing
curl′y
  ·i·er ·i·est
cur·mudg′eon
cur′rant (*fruit*)

cur′ren·cy
  ·cies
cur′rent (*a flow; now going on*)
cur′rent·ly
cur·ric′u·lar
cur·ric′u·lum
  ·la *or* ·lums
cur′ry
  ·ried ·ry·ing
cur′ry·comb′
curse
  cursed curs′ing
curs′ed
cur′sive
cur′sor
cur′so·ri·ly
cur′so·ri·ness
cur′so·ry
curt
cur·tail′
cur·tail′ment
cur′tain
curt′ly
curt′ness
curt′sy
  ·sies
  ·sied ·sy·ing
  (*knee bend; see* COURTESY)
cur·va′ceous
cur′va·ture
curve
  curved curv′ing
curv′y
  ·i·er ·i·est
cush′ion
cush′y
  ·i·er ·i·est
cusp
cus′pid
cus′pi·dor′
cuss
cus′tard
cus·to′di·al
cus·to′di·an
cus′to·dy
cus′tom
cus′tom·ar′i·ly
cus′tom·ar′y
cus′tom-built′
cus′tom·er
cus′tom·house′
cus′tom·ize′
  ·ized′ ·iz′ing
cus′tom-made′
cut
  cut cut′ting
cu·ta′ne·ous
cut′a·way′
cut′back′
cute
  cut′er cut′est
cute′ly
cute′ness
cute′sy *or* ·sie
  ·si·er ·si·est
cut′i·cle
cut′lass *or* ·las

cut′ler·y
cut′let
cut′off′
cut′out′
cut′-rate′
cut′ter
cut′throat′
cut′ting
cut′tle·fish′
cy′a·nide′
cy′ber·net′ics
cy′cla·men
cy′cle
  ·cled ·cling
cy′clic
cy′cli·cal
cy′clist
cy·clom′e·ter
cy′clone′
cy′clo·pe′di·a *or* ·pae′di·a
cy′clo·tron′
cyg′net
cyl′in·der
cy·lin′dri·cal
cym′bal
  (*musical instrument; see* SYMBOL)
cyn′ic
cyn′i·cal
cyn′i·cal·ly
cyn′i·cism′
cy′no·sure
cy′press
cyst
cyst′ic
cy·tol′o·gy
cy′to·plasm′
cy′to·sine′
czar
cza·ri′na
Czech
Czech′o·slo′vak *or* ·slo·vak′i·an

D

dab
  dabbed dab′bing
dab′ble
  ·bled ·bling
dachs′hund′
da′cron′
dac′tyl
dac·tyl′ic
dad
dad′dy
  ·dies
daddy long′legs′
da′do
  ·does
daf′fi·ness
daf′fo·dil′
daf′fy
  ·fi·er ·fi·est
daft
dag′ger

da·guerre′o·type′
dahl′ia
dai′ly
  ·lies
dain′ti·ly
dain′ti·ness
dain′ty
  ·ties
  ·ti·er ·ti·est
dai′qui·ri
dair′y
  ·ies
dair′y·ing
dair′y·man
da′is
  ·is·es
dai′sy
  ·sies
dale
dal′li·ance
dal′ly
  ·lied ·ly·ing
dam
  dammed
  dam′ming
  (*barrier; female animal; see* DAMN)
dam′age
  ·aged ·ag·ing
dam′age·a·ble
dam′ask
dame
damn
  damned damn′ing
  (*condemn; see* DAM)
dam′na·ble
dam′na·bly
dam·na′tion
damned
damp
damp′en
damp′en·er
damp′er
damp′ness
dam′sel
dam′sel·fly′
dam′son
dance
  danced danc′ing
danc′er
dan′de·li′on
dan′der
dan′druff
dan′dy
  ·dies
  ·di·er ·di·est
dan′ger
dan′ger·ous
dan′gle
  ·gled ·gling
Dan′ish
dank
dank′ly
dank′ness
dan·seuse′
dap′per
dap′ple
  ·pled ·pling
dap′pled

dare
  dared dar′ing
dare′dev′il
dark
dark′en
dark′en·er
dark′ly
dark′ness
dark′room′
dar′ling
darn
dart
dart′board′
dash
dash′board′
dash′ing
das′tard
das′tard·ly
da′ta
  sing. da′tum
da′ta·base′
date
  dat′ed dat′ing
date′line′
da′tive
da′tum
daub
daugh′ter
daugh′ter-in-law′
  daugh′ters-in-law′
daugh′ter·ly
daunt
daunt′less
dav′en·port′
daw′dle
  ·dled ·dling
daw′dler
dawn
day
day′bed′
day′break′
day′-care′
day′dream′
day′light′
day′long′
days
  (*pl. of* day)
day′time′
day′-to-day′
day′work′
daze
  dazed daz′ing
  (*stun*)
daz′ed·ly
daz′zle
  ·zled ·zling
daz′zler
dea′con
dea′con·ess
de·ac′ti·vate′
  ·vat′ed ·vat′ing
dead
dead′beat′
dead′bolt′
dead′en
dead′-end′
dead′head′
dead′line′

dead'li·ness
dead'lock'
dead'ly
  ·li·er ·li·est
dead'pan'
dead'wood'
deaf
deaf'en
deaf'en·ing
deaf'-mute'
deaf'ness
deal
  dealt deal'ing
deal'er
deal'er·ship'
dean
dear (*beloved*; see DEER)
dear'ly
dearth
death
death'bed'
death'blow'
death'less
death'like'
death'ly
death'trap'
death'watch'
deb
de·ba'cle
de·bar'
de·bark'
de'bar·ka'tion
de·base'
de·base'ment
de·bat'a·ble
de·bate'
  ·bat'ed ·bat'ing
de·bat'er
de·bauch'
deb'au·chee'
de·bauch'er·y
  ·ies
de·ben'ture
de·bil'i·tate'
  ·tat'ed ·tat'ing
de·bil'i·ty
  ·ties
deb'it
deb'o·nair' *or*
  ·naire'
de·brief'
de·bris'
debt
debt'or
de·bug'
de·bunk'
de·but'
deb'u·tante'
dec'ade
dec'a·dence
dec'a·dent
de·caf'fein·at·ed
de'cal'
Dec'a·logue' *or*
  ·log'
de·camp'
de·cant'

de·cant'er
de·cap'i·tate'
  ·tat'ed ·tat'ing
de·cap'i·ta'tion
de·cath'lon'
de·cay'
de·cease'
  ·ceased' ·ceas'ing
de·ceased'
de·ce'dent
de·ceit'
de·ceit'ful
de·ceit'ful·ly
de·ceive'
  ·ceived' ·ceiv'ing
de·ceiv'er
de·ceiv'ing·ly
de·cel'er·ate'
  ·at'ed ·at'ing
de·cel'er·a'tion
De·cem'ber
de'cen·cy
de·cen'ni·al
de'cent
  (*proper*; see DE-
  SCENT, DISSENT)
de'cent·ly
de·cen'tral·i·za'-
  tion
de·cen'tral·ize'
  ·ized' ·iz'ing
de·cep'tion
de·cep'tive
dec'i·bel
de·cid'a·ble
de·cide'
  ·cid'ed ·cid'ing
de·cid'ed
de·cid'ed·ly
de·cid'u·ous
dec'i·mal
dec'i·mal·ly
dec'i·mate'
  ·mat'ed ·mat'ing
dec'i·ma'tion
de·ci'pher
de·ci'sion
de·ci'sive
de·ci'sive·ly
deck
de·claim'
dec'la·ma'tion
de·clam'a·to'ry
dec'la·ra'tion
de·clar'a·tive
de·clare'
  ·clared' ·clar'ing
de·clar'er
de·clas'si·fy'
  ·fied' ·fy'ing
de·clen'sion
dec'li·na'tion
de·cline'
  ·clined' ·clin'ing
de·clin'er
de·cliv'i·ty
  ·ties
de·code'
de·col'o·ni·za'tion

de·col'o·nize'
de'com·pose'
de'com·po·si'tion
de'com·press'
de'com·pres'sion
de'con·gest'ant
de'con·tam'i·nate'
dé·cor' *or* de·cor'
dec'o·rate'
  ·rat'ed ·rat'ing
dec'o·ra'tion
dec'o·ra·tive
dec'o·ra'tor
dec'o·rous
de·co'rum
de·cou'page'
de·coy'
de·crease'
  ·creased'
  ·creas'ing
de·cree'
  ·creed' ·cree'ing
de·crep'it
de·crep'i·tude'
de·crim'i·nal·ize'
  ·ized' ·iz'ing
de·cry'
ded'i·cate'
  ·cat'ed ·cat'ing
ded'i·ca'tion
de·duce'
  ·duced' ·duc'ing
de·duc'i·ble
de·duct'
de·duct'i·ble
de·duc'tion
de·duc'tive
deed
deem
de-em'pha·sis
de-em'pha·size'
deep
deep'en
deep'freeze'
deep'-fry'
deep'ly
deep'ness
deep'-root'ed
deep'-seat'ed
deep'-six'
deer
  deer *or* deers
  (*animal*; see DEAR)
de-es'ca·late'
de·face'
de·face'ment
de fac'to
de·fal'cate'
  ·cat'ed ·cat'ing
de·fal·ca'tion
def·a·ma'tion
de·fam'a·to'ry
de·fame'
  ·famed' ·fam'ing
de·fam'er
de·fault'
de·fault'er
de·feat'

de·feat'ism'
de·feat'ist
def'e·cate'
  ·cat'ed ·cat'ing
def'e·ca'tion
de'fect'
de·fec'tion
de·fec'tive
de·fec'tor
de·fend'
de·fend'ant
de·fend'er
de·fense'
de·fense'less
de·fen'si·ble
de·fen'sive
de·fen'sive·ly
de·fer'
  ·ferred' ·fer'ring
def'er·ence
  (*respect*; see DIF-
  FERENCE)
def'er·en'tial
de·fer'ment
de·fi'ance
de·fi'ant
de·fi'ant·ly
de·fi'cien·cy
  ·cies
de·fi'cient
def'i·cit
de·file'
  ·filed' ·fil'ing
de·file'ment
de·fin'a·ble
de·fine'
  ·fined' ·fin'ing
de·fin'er
def'i·nite
def'i·nite·ly
def'i·nite·ness
def'i·ni'tion
de·fin'i·tive
de·flate'
  ·flat'ed ·flat'ing
de·fla'tion
de·fla'tion·ar'y
de·flect'
de·flec'tion
de·flec'tive
de·flec'tor
de·flow'er
de·fog'ger
de·fo'li·ant
de·fo'li·ate'
  ·at'ed ·at'ing
de·fo'li·a'tion
de·form'
de'for·ma'tion
de·formed'
de·form'i·ty
  ·ties
de·fraud'
de·fraud'er
de·fray'
de·fray'a·ble
de·fray'al
de·frost'

de·frost'er
deft
deft'ly
de·funct'
de·fuse'
de·fy'
  ·fied' ·fy'ing
de·gen'er·a·cy
de·gen'er·ate'
  ·at'ed ·at'ing
de·gen'er·a'tion
de·gen'er·a·tive
deg'ra·da'tion
de·grade'
  ·grad'ed ·grad'ing
de·gree'
de·hu'man·i·za'-
  tion
de·hu'man·ize'
  ·ized' ·iz'ing
de·hu'mid'i·fi'er
de·hu'mid'i·fy'
de·hy'drate'
de·hy·dra'tion
de·hy'dra'tor
de-ice'
de-ic'er
de'i·fi·ca'tion
de'i·fy'
  ·fied' ·fy'ing
deign
de'ism'
de'ist
de'i·ty
  ·ties
dé·jà vu'
de·ject'
de·ject'ed
de·jec'tion
Del'a·ware'
de·lay'
de·lec'ta·ble
del'e·gate'
  ·gat'ed ·gat'ing
del'e·ga'tion
de·lete'
  ·let'ed ·let'ing
del'e·te'ri·ous
de·le'tion
del'i
de·lib'er·ate
  ·at'ed ·at'ing
de·lib'er·ate·ly
de·lib'er·a'tion
del'i·ca·cy
  ·cies
del'i·cate
del'i·cate·ly
del'i·cate·ness
del'i·ca·tes'sen
de·li'cious
de·li'cious·ly
de·li'cious·ness
de·light'
de·light'ed
de·light'ful
de·light'ful·ly

de·lin'e·ate'
  ·at'ed ·at'ing
de·lin'e·a'tion
de·lin'e·a'tor
de·lin'quen·cy
  ·cies
de·lin'quent
de·lin'quent·ly
del'i·quesce'
  ·quesced'
  ·quesc'ing
del'i·ques'cent
de·lir'i·ous
de·lir'i·ous·ly
de·lir'i·um
de·liv'er
de·liv'er·a·ble
de·liv'er·ance
de·liv'er·y
  ·ies
dell
del·phin'i·um
del'ta
de·lude'
  ·lud'ed ·lud'ing
del'uge'
  ·uged' ·ug'ing
de·lu'sion
de·lu'sive
de·luxe'
delve
  delved delv'ing
de·mag'net·i·za'-
  tion
de·mag'net·ize'
dem'a·gogue' *or*
  ·gog'
dem'a·gog'y *or*
  ·gogu'er·y
de·mand'
de·mand'ing
de·mar'cate
  ·cat·ed ·cat·ing
de'mar·ca'tion
de·mean'
de·mean'or
de·ment'ed
de·men'tia
de·mer'it
dem'i·god'
de·mil'i·ta·rize'
de·mise'
  ·mised' ·mis'ing
dem'i·tasse'
dem'o
de·mo'bi·li·za'tion
de·mo'bi·lize'
de·moc'ra·cy
  ·cies
dem'o·crat'
dem'o·crat'ic
dem'o·crat'i·cal·ly
de·moc'ra·tize'
  ·tized' ·tiz'ing
de·mod'u·la'tion
de·mog'ra·pher
dem'o·graph'ic
dem'o·graph'i·cal·ly
de·mog'ra·phy

de·mol'ish
dem'o·li'tion
de'mon
de·mon'ic
de·mon'i·cal·ly
de·mon'stra·ble
de·mon'stra·bly
dem'on·strate'
  ·strat·ed ·strat'ing
dem'on·stra'tion
de·mon'stra·tive
de·mon'stra'tor
de·mor'al·i·za'tion
de·mor'al·ize'
  ·ized' ·iz'ing
de·mote'
  ·mot'ed ·mot'ing
de·mo'tion
de·mur'
  ·murred'
  ·mur'ring
  (to object)
de·mure' (coy)
de·mure'ly
de·mur'rer
den
de·na'ture
  ·tured ·tur·ing
den'drite'
de·ni'a·ble
de·ni'al
den'i·grate'
  ·grat·ed ·grat'ing
den'i·gra'tion
den'im
den'i·zen
de·nom'i·nate'
  ·nat·ed ·nat'ing
de·nom'i·na'tion
de·nom'i·na'tion·al
de·nom'i·na'tor
de'no·ta'tion
de·note'
  ·not'ed ·not'ing
de'noue·ment'
de·nounce'
  ·nounced'
  ·nounc'ing
de·nounce'ment
dense
  dens'er dens'est
dense'ly
dense'ness
den'si·ty
  ·ties
dent
den'tal
den'tal·ly
den'ti·frice
den'tin
den'tist
den'tist·ry
den'ture
de·nude'
  ·nud'ed ·nud'ing
de·nun'ci·a'tion
de·ny'
  ·nied' ·ny'ing
de·o'dor·ant

de·o'dor·ize'
  ·ized' ·iz'ing
de·o'dor·iz'er
de·part'
de·part'ed
de'part·ee'
de·part'ment
de'part·men'tal
de'part·men'tal·i·
  za'tion
de'part·men'tal·ize'
  ·ized' ·iz'ing
de·par'ture
de·pend'
de·pend'a·bil'i·ty
de·pend'a·ble
de·pend'ence
de·pend'en·cy
  ·cies
de·pend'ent
de·pend'ent·ly
de·pict'
de·pic'tion
de·pil'a·to'ry
  ·ries
de·plane'
  ·planed' ·plan'ing
de·plete'
  ·plet'ed ·plet'ing
de·ple'tion
de·plor'a·ble
de·plore'
  ·plored' ·plor'ing
de·ploy'
de·ploy'ment
de·po'lar·i·za'tion
de·po'lar·ize'
de·po·lit'i·cize'
de·pon'ent
de·pop'u·late'
de·pop'u·la'tion
de·port'
de'por·ta'tion
de·port'ment
de·pose'
  ·posed' ·pos'ing
de·pos'it
dep'o·si'tion
de·pos'i·tor
de·pos'i·to'ry
  ·ries
de'pot
dep'ra·va'tion
  (a corrupting; see
  DEPRIVATION)
de·prave'
  ·praved' ·prav'ing
de·prav'i·ty
  ·ties
dep're·cate'
  ·cat·ed ·cat'ing
dep're·ca'tion
dep're·ca·to'ry
de·pre'ci·a·ble
de·pre'ci·ate'
  ·at'ed ·at'ing
de·pre'ci·a'tion
dep're·da'tion
de·press'

de·pres'sant
de·pressed'
de·press'ing
de·pres'sion
de·pres'sive
dep'ri·va'tion
  (a taking away;
  see DEPRAVATION)
de·prive'
  ·prived' ·priv'ing
de·pro'gram'
depth
dep'u·tize'
  ·tized' ·tiz'ing
dep'u·ty
  ·ties
de·rail'
de·rail'leur
de·rail'ment
de·range'
  ·ranged' ·rang'ing
de·range'ment
der'by
  ·bies
de·reg'u·late'
de·reg'u·la'tion
der'e·lict'
der'e·lic'tion
de·ride'
  ·rid'ed ·rid'ing
de·ri'sion
de·ri'sive
de·ri'sive·ly
de·riv'a·ble
der'i·va'tion
de·riv'a·tive
de·rive'
  ·rived' ·riv'ing
der'ma·ti'tis
der'ma·tol'o·gist
der'ma·tol'o·gy
der'mis
der'o·gate'
  ·gat'ed ·gat'ing
der'o·ga'tion
de·rog'a·to'ri·ly
de·rog'a·to'ry
der'rick
der·ri·ère'
der'rin·ger
der'vish
de'sal'i·nate'
  ·nat'ed ·nat'ing
de·sal'i·na'tion
de·salt'
des'cant'
de·scend'
de·scend'ant
de·scent'
  (going down; see
  DECENT, DISSENT)
de·scrib'a·ble
de·scribe'
  ·scribed' ·scrib'ing
de·scrip'tion
de·scrip'tive
de·scry'
  ·scried' ·scry'ing

des'e·crate'
  ·crat'ed ·crat'ing
des'e·cra'tion
de·seg're·gate'
de·seg're·ga'tion
de·sen'si·tize'
de·sert'
  (abandon; see
  DESSERT)
des'ert (dry area)
de·sert'er
de·serts' (reward)
de·ser'tion
de·serve'
  ·served' ·serv'ing
de·serv'ed·ly
des'ic·cate'
  ·cat'ed ·cat'ing
des'ic·ca'tion
des'ic·ca'tor
de·sign'
des'ig·nate'
  ·nat'ed ·nat'ing
des'ig·na'tion
de·sign'er
de·sir'a·bil'i·ty
de·sir'a·ble
de·sir'a·bly
de·sire'
  ·sired' ·sir'ing
de·sir'ous
de·sist'
desk
des'o·late'
  ·lat'ed ·lat'ing
des'o·la'tion
de·spair'
des·patch'
des'per·a'do
  ·does or ·dos
des'per·ate
  (hopeless; see DIS-
  PARATE)
des'per·ate·ly
des'per·a'tion
des'pi·ca·ble
de·spise'
  ·spised' ·spis'ing
de·spite'
de·spoil'
de·spond'en·cy
de·spond'ent
des'pot
des·pot'ic
des·pot'i·cal·ly
des'pot·ism'
des·sert'
  (food; see DESERT)
des'ti·na'tion
des'tine
  ·tined ·tin·ing
des'ti·ny
  ·nies
des'ti·tute'
des'ti·tu'tion
de·stroy'
de·stroy'er
de·struct'
de·struct'i·bil'i·ty

de·struct'i·ble
de·struc'tion
de·struc'tive
de·struc'tive·ly
de·struc'tive·ness
des'ue·tude'
des'ul·to'ry
de·tach'
de·tach'a·ble
de·tached'
de·tach'ment
de·tail'
de·tain'
de·tain'ment
de·tect'
de·tect'a·ble or
  ·i·ble
de·tec'tion
de·tec'tive
de·tec'tor
dé·tente' or
  de·tente'
de·ten'tion
de·ter'
  ·terred' ·ter'ring
de·ter'gent
de·te'ri·o·rate'
  ·rat'ed ·rat'ing
de·te'ri·o·ra'tion
de·ter'ment
de·ter'mi·na·ble
de·ter'mi·na·bly
de·ter'mi·nant
de·ter'mi·nate
de·ter'mi·na'tion
de·ter'mine
  ·mined ·min·ing
de·ter'mined
de·ter'rence
de·ter'rent
de·test'
de·test'a·ble
de·test'a·bly
de'tes·ta'tion
de·throne'
  ·throned'
  ·thron'ing
det'o·nate'
  ·nat'ed ·nat'ing
det'o·na'tion
det'o·na'tor
de'tour'
de·tox'
de·tox'i·fi·ca'tion
de·tox'i·fy'
  ·fied' ·fy'ing
de·tract'
de·trac'tion
de·trac'tor
det'ri·ment
det'ri·men'tal
de·tri'tus
deuce
deu·te'ri·um
de·val'u·a'tion
de·val'ue
dev'as·tate'
  ·tat'ed ·tat'ing

dev'as·ta'tion
dev'as·ta'tor
de·vel'op
de·vel'op·er
de·vel'op·ment
de·vel'op·men'tal
de'vi·ant
de'vi·ate'
  ·at'ed ·at'ing
de'vi·a'tion
de'vi·a'tor
de·vice'
  (mechanism; see
  DEVISE)
dev'il
  ·iled or ·illed
  ·il·ing or ·il·ling
dev'il·ish
dev'il-may-care'
dev'il·ment
dev'il's-food'
dev'il·try
  ·tries
de'vi·ous
de'vi·ous·ness
de·vis'a·ble
  (that can be de-
  vised; see DIVISI-
  BLE)
de·vise'
  ·vised' ·vis'ing
  (invent; see DE-
  VICE)
de·vi'tal·ize'
de·void'
de·volve'
  ·volved' ·volv'ing
de·vote'
  ·vot'ed ·vot'ing
de·vot'ed
de·vot'ed·ly
dev'o·tee'
de·vo'tion
de·vo'tion·al
de·vour'
de·vout'
de·vout'ly
dew
  (moisture; see
  DUE)
dew'ber'ry
dew'drop'
dew'lap'
dew'y
  ·i·er ·i·est
dex·ter'i·ty
dex'ter·ous
dex'trose (sugar)
dex'trous (skillful)
di'a·be'tes
di'a·bet'ic
di'a·bol'ic
di'a·bol'i·cal
di'a·bol'i·cal·ly
di'a·crit'ic
di'a·crit'i·cal
di'a·dem'
di'ag·nos'a·ble
di'ag·nose'
  ·nosed' ·nos'ing

di·ag·no'sis
·ses'
di·ag·nos'tic
di·ag·nos'ti·cal·ly
di·ag·nos'ti·cian
di·ag'o·nal
di·ag'o·nal·ly
di'a·gram'
·gramed' or
·grammed'
·gram'ing or
·gram'ming
di'al
·aled or ·alled
·al·ing or ·al·ling
di'a·lect'
di'a·lec'tal
di'a·lec'tic
di'a·lec'ti·cal
di'a·logue' or ·log'
di·al'y·sis
·ses'
di·am'e·ter
di'a·met'ri·cal
di'a·met'ri·cal·ly
di'a·mond
di'a·mond·back'
di'a·per
di·aph'a·nous
di'a·phragm'
di'a·rist
di'ar·rhe'a or
·rhoe'a
di'a·ry
·ries
di'a·stase'
di·as'to·le'
di'a·stol'ic
di'a·tom'
di'a·tom'ic
di'a·ton'ic
di'a·tribe'
dib'ble
·bled ·bling
dice
sing. die or dice
diced dic'ing
di·chot'o·my
·mies
dick'er
dick'ey
·eys
di'cot·y·le'don
di'cot'y·le'don·ous
Dic'ta·phone'
dic'tate'
·tat'ed ·tat'ing
dic·ta'tion
dic'ta·tor
dic·ta·to'ri·al
dic·ta'tor·ship'
dic'tion
dic'tion·ar'y
·ies
dic'tum
·tums or ·ta
did
di·dac'tic
di·dac'ti·cal·ly

did'dle
·dled ·dling
die
dice
(game cube)
die
dies
died die'ing
(mold; stamp)
die
died dy'ing
(stop living; see
DYE)
die'-hard' or
die'hard'
di'e·lec'tric
di·er'e·sis
·ses'
die'sel
di'et
di'e·tar'y
di'et·er
di'e·tet'ic
di'e·ti'tian
dif'fer
dif'fer·ence
(a being different;
see DEFERENCE)
dif'fer·ent
dif'fer·en'tial
dif'fer·en'ti·ate'
·at'ed ·at'ing
dif'fer·en'ti·a'tion
dif'fi·cult'
dif'fi·cul'ty
·ties
dif'fi·dence
dif'fi·dent
dif·fract'
dif·frac'tion
dif·fuse'
·fused' ·fus'ing
dif·fus'i·ble
dif·fu'sion
dig
dug dig'ging
di'gest
di·gest'i·ble
di·ges'tion
di·ges'tive
dig'ger
dig'it
dig'i·tal
dig'i·tal'is
dig'ni·fied'
dig'ni·fy'
·fied' ·fy'ing
dig'ni·tar'y
·ies
dig'ni·ty
·ties
di·gress'
di·gres'sion
di·gres'sive
dike
di·lap'i·dat'ed
di·lap'i·da'tion
dil'a·ta'tion
di'late'
·lat'ed ·lat'ing

di·la'tion
dil'a·to'ry
di·lem'ma
dil'et·tante'
·tantes' or ·tan'ti'
dil'et·tant'ish
dil'i·gence
dil'i·gent
dill
dil'ly
·lies
dil'ly·dal'ly
·lied ·ly·ing
di·lute'
·lut'ed ·lut'ing
di·lu'tion
dim
dim'mer dim'mest
dimmed dim'ming
dime
di·men'sion
di·men'sion·al
di·min'ish
dim'i·nu'tion
di·min'u·tive
dim'ly
dim'mer
dim'ness
dim'ple
·pled ·pling
dim'ply
dim'wit'
dim'wit'ted
din
dinned din'ning
dine
dined din'ing
din'er
(person eating;
restaurant; see
DINNER)
di·nette'
ding
ding'-dong'
din'ghy
·ghies
(boat)
din'gi·ness
din'go
·goes
din'gy
·gi·er ·gi·est
(not bright)
dink'y
·i·er ·i·est
din'ner
(meal; see DINER)
din'ner·ware'
di'no·saur'
dint
di·oc'e·san
di'o·cese
di'ode'
di'o·ram'a
di·ox'ide
di·ox'in
dip
dipped dip'ping
diph·the'ri·a
diph'thong

di·plo'ma
di·plo'ma·cy
dip'lo·mat'
dip'lo·mat'ic
dip'lo·mat'i·cal·ly
di'pole'
dip'per
dip'so·ma'ni·a
dip'so·ma'ni·ac'
dip'stick'
dire
dir'er dir'est
di·rect'
di·rec'tion
di·rec'tion·al
di·rec'tive
di·rect'ly
di·rect'ness
di·rec'tor
di·rec'tor·ate
di·rec'tor·ship'
di·rec'to·ry
·ries
dirge
dir'i·gi·ble
dirt
dirt'-cheap'
dirt'i·ness
dirt'y
·i·er ·i·est
·ied ·y·ing
dis·a·bil'i·ty
·ties
dis·a'ble
·bled ·bling
dis·a·buse'
·bused' ·bus'ing
dis·ad·van'tage
dis·ad·van'taged
dis·ad'van·ta'geous
dis·af·fect'
dis·af·fect'ed
dis·af·fec'tion
dis·af·fil'i·ate'
dis·a·gree'
dis·a·gree'a·ble
dis·a·gree'a·bly
dis·a·gree'ment
dis·al·low'
dis·ap·pear'
dis·ap·pear'ance
dis·ap·point'
dis·ap·point'ment
dis·ap·prov'al
dis·ap·prove'
dis·arm'
dis·ar'ma·ment
dis·arm'ing
dis·ar·range'
dis·ar·ray'
dis·as·sem'ble
dis·as·so'ci·ate'
dis·as'ter
dis·as'trous
dis·a·vow'
dis·a·vow'al
dis·band'
dis·bar'

dis·bar'ment
dis·be·lief'
dis·be·lieve'
dis·be·liev'er
dis·burse'
·bursed' ·burs'ing
(pay out; see DIS-
PERSE)
dis·burse'ment
disc
(phonograph
record; see DISK)
dis·card'
dis·cern'
dis·cern'i·ble
dis·cern'ing
dis·cern'ment
dis·charge'
dis·ci'ple
dis·ci'ple·ship'
dis'ci·pli·nar'i·an
dis'ci·pli·nar'y
dis'ci·pline
·plined' ·plin'ing
disc jockey
dis·claim'
dis·claim'er
dis·close'
dis·clo'sure
dis'co
·cos
dis'coid
dis·col'or
dis·col'or·a'tion
dis·com'fit
dis·com'fi·ture
dis·com'fort
dis·com·pose'
dis·com·po'sure
dis·con·cert'
dis·con·nect'
dis·con·nect'ed
dis·con·nec'tion
dis·con'so·late
dis·con·tent'
dis·con·tent'ed
dis·con·tin'u·ance
dis·con·tin'ue
dis·con·tin'u·ous
dis'co·phile'
dis'cord'
dis·cord'ant
dis'co·thèque'
dis'count'
dis·coun'te·nance
·nanced ·nanc·ing
dis·cour'age
·aged ·ag·ing
dis·cour'age·ment
dis'course'
·coursed'
·cours'ing
dis·cour'te·ous
dis·cour'te·sy
dis·cov'er
dis·cov'er·er
dis·cov'er·y
·ies
dis·cred'it

dis·cred'it·a·ble
dis·creet'
(prudent; see DIS-
CRETE)
dis·creet'ly
dis·crep'an·cy
·cies
dis·crete'
(separate; see DIS-
CREET)
dis·cre'tion
dis·cre'tion·ar'y
dis·crim'i·nate'
·nat'ed ·nat'ing
dis·crim'i·nat'ing
dis·crim'i·na'tion
dis·crim'i·na·to'ry
dis·cur'sive
dis'cus (heavy disk)
dis·cuss' (talk
about)
dis·cus'sion
dis·dain'
dis·dain'ful
dis·ease'
dis·eased'
dis'em·bark'
dis'em·bod'i·ment
dis'em·bod'y
·bod'ied ·bod'y·ing
dis'em·bow'el
·eled or ·elled
·el·ing or ·el·ling
dis'en·chant'
dis'en·chant'ment
dis'en·cum'ber
dis'en·fran'chise'
dis'en·gage'
dis'en·gage'ment
dis'en·tan'gle
dis·fa'vor
dis·fig'ure
dis·fig'ure·ment
dis·fran'chise'
dis·gorge'
dis·grace'
·graced' ·grac'ing
dis·grace'ful
dis·grun'tle
·tled ·tling
dis·guise'
·guised' ·guis'ing
dis·gust'
dis·gust'ed
dis·gust'ing
dish
dis·har'mo·ny
dish'cloth'
dis·heart'en
di·shev'el
·eled or ·elled
·el·ing or ·el·ling
di·shev'el·ment
dis·hon'est
dis·hon'est·ly
dis·hon'es·ty
dis·hon'or
dis·hon'or·a·ble
dish'pan'

dish'rag'
dish'wash'er
dis·il·lu'sion
dis·il·lu'sioned
dis·il·lu'sion·ment
dis·in·cline'
dis·in·fect'
dis·in·fect'ant
dis·in·for·ma'tion
dis·in·her'it
dis·in·te·grate'
·grat·ed ·grat'ing
dis·in·te·gra'tion
dis·in·ter'
dis·in·ter·est·ed
dis·join'
dis·joint'ed
disk
(flat, circular
thing; computer
storage; see DISC)
disk·ette'
dis·like'
dis·lo·cate'
dis·lo·ca'tion
dis·lodge'
dis·loy'al
dis·loy'al·ty
dis'mal
dis'mal·ly
dis·man'tle
·tled ·tling
dis·may'
dis·mem'ber
dis·miss'
dis·miss'al
dis·mount'
dis·o·be'di·ence
dis·o·be'di·ent
dis·o·bey'
dis·or'der
dis·or'der·li·ness
dis·or'der·ly
dis·or'gan·i·za'tion
dis·or'gan·ize'
dis·o'ri·ent'
dis·o'ri·en·ta'tion
dis·own'
dis·par'age
·aged ·ag·ing
dis'pa·rate
(not alike; see DES-
PERATE)
dis·par'i·ty
·ties
dis·pas'sion·ate
dis·patch'
dis·patch'er
dis·pel'
·pelled' ·pel'ling
dis·pen'sa·ble
dis·pen'sa·ry
·ries
dis'pen·sa'tion
dis·pense'
·pensed' ·pens'ing
dis·pens'er
dis·per'sal

dis·perse'
·persed' ·pers'ing
(scatter; see DIS-
BURSE)
dis·pers'i·ble
dis·per'sion
dis·pir'it
dis·pir'it·ed
dis·place'
dis·place'ment
dis·play'
dis·please'
dis·pleas'ure
dis·pos'a·ble
dis·pos'al
dis·pose'
·posed' ·pos'ing
dis'po·si'tion
dis·pos·sess'
dis·pro·por'tion
dis·pro·por'tion·ate
dis·prove'
dis·put'a·ble
dis·pu'tant
dis·pute'
·put·ed ·put'ing
dis·qual'i·fi·ca'tion
dis·qual'i·fy'
dis·qui'et
dis·re·gard'
dis·re·pair'
dis·rep'u·ta·ble
dis·re·pute'
dis·re·spect'
dis·re·spect'ful
dis·robe'
dis·rupt'
dis·rup'tion
dis·rup'tive
dis·sat'is·fac'tion
dis·sat'is·fy'
dis·sect'
dis·sec'tion
dis·sem'blance
dis·sem'ble
·bled ·bling
dis·sem'bler
dis·sem'i·nate'
·nat·ed ·nat'ing
dis·sem'i·na'tion
dis·sen'sion
dis·sent'
(disagree; see DE-
CENT, DESCENT)
dis·sent'er
dis'ser·ta'tion
dis·serv'ice
dis'si·dence
dis'si·dent
dis·sim'i·lar
dis·sim'i·lar'i·ty
·ties
dis'si·mil'i·tude'
dis'si·pate'
·pat·ed ·pat'ing
dis'si·pa'tion
dis·so'ci·ate'
·at·ed ·at'ing
dis·so'ci·a'tion

dis'so·lute'
dis'so·lu'tion
dis·solv'a·ble
dis·solve'
·solved' ·solv'ing
dis'so·nance
dis'so·nant
dis·suade'
·suad·ed ·suad'ing
dis·sua'sion
dis·taff'
dis'tal
dis'tance
dis'tant
dis'tant·ly
dis·taste'
dis·taste'ful
dis·tem'per
dis·tend'
dis·ten'si·ble
dis·ten'tion or ·sion
dis·till' or ·til'
·tilled' ·till'ing
dis'til·late'
dis'til·la'tion
dis·till'er
dis·till'er·y
·ies
dis·tinct'
dis·tinc'tion
dis·tinc'tive
dis·tinc'tive·ly
dis·tinc'tive·ness
dis·tinct'ly
dis·tin'guish
dis·tin'guish·a·ble
dis·tin'guished
dis·tort'
dis·tor'tion
dis·tract'
dis·tract'ed
dis·tract'i·ble
dis·tract'ing
dis·trac'tion
dis·traught'
dis·tress'
dis·trib'ut·a·ble
dis·trib'ute
·ut·ed ·ut·ing
dis'tri·bu'tion
dis·trib'u·tive
dis·trib'u·tor
dis'trict
District of
Co·lum'bi·a
dis·trust'
dis·trust'ful
dis·turb'
dis·turb'ance
dis·un'ion
dis·u·nite'
dis·u'ni·ty
dis·use'
ditch
dith'er
dit'to
·tos
·toed ·to·ing

dit'ty
·ties
di'u·ret'ic
di·ur'nal
di·ur'nal·ly
di'va
·vas or ·ve
di·va'lent
di·van'
dive
dived or dove
dived div'ing
div'er
di·verge'
·verged' ·verg'ing
di·ver'gence
di·ver'gent
di'vers (various)
di·verse' (different)
di·verse'ly
di·ver'si·fi·ca'tion
di·ver'si·fy'
·fied' ·fy'ing
di·ver'sion
di·ver'sion·ar'y
di·ver'si·ty
di·vert'
di'ver·tic'u·li'tis
di'ver·tic'u·lum
·la
di·vest'
di·vest'i·ture
di·vid'a·ble
di·vide'
·vid'ed ·vid'ing
div'i·dend'
di·vid'er
div'i·na'tion
di·vine'
·vined' ·vin'ing
di·vine'ly
di·vin'i·ty
·ties
di·vis'i·bil'i·ty
di·vis'i·ble
(that can be di-
vided; see DEVIS-
ABLE)
di·vi'sion
di·vi'sive
di·vi'sive·ly
di·vi'sive·ness
di·vi'sor
di·vorce'
·vorced' ·vorc'ing
di·vor·cé' masc.
di·vor·cée' or ·cee'
fem.
div'ot
di·vulge'
·vulged' ·vulg'ing
di·vul'gence
div'vy
·vied ·vy·ing
Dix'ie·land'
diz'zi·ly
diz'zi·ness
diz'zy
·zi·er ·zi·est
·zied ·zying

do
did done do'ing
do'a·ble
Do'ber·man
pin'scher
doc
do'cent
doc'ile
doc'ile·ly
do·cil'i·ty
dock
dock'age
dock'et
dock'yard'
doc'tor
doc'tor·al
doc'tor·ate
doc'tri·naire'
doc'tri·nal
doc'trine
doc'u·ment
doc'u·men'ta·ry
·ries
doc'u·men·ta'tion
dod'der
dod'der·ing
dodge
dodged dodg'ing
dodg'er
do'do
·dos or ·does
doe
(deer; see DOUGH)
do'er
does
doe'skin'
does·n't
doff
dog
dogged dog'ging
dog'catch'er
dog'ear'
dog'eared'
dog'fish'
dog'ged
dog'ged·ly
dog'ger·el
dog'gie bag
dog'gone'
dog'goned'
dog'gy or ·gie
·gies
(dog)
dog'house'
do'gie or ·gy
·gies
(calf)
dog'ma
dog·mat'ic
dog·mat'i·cal·ly
dog'ma·tism'
dog'ma·tist
do'-good'er
dog'trot'
dog'wood'
doi'ly
·lies
do'ing

do'-it-your·self'
do'-it-your·self'er
Dol'by
dol'drums
dole
doled dol'ing
dole'ful
dole'ful·ly
doll
dol'lar
dol'lop
dol'ly
·lies
dol'men
do'lo·mite'
do'lor·ous
dol'phin
dolt
dolt'ish
do·main'
dome
do·mes'tic
do·mes'ti·cal·ly
do·mes'ti·cate'
·cat·ed ·cat'ing
do·mes'ti·ca'tion
do·mes'tic'i·ty
dom'i·cile'
·ciled' ·cil'ing
dom'i·nance
dom'i·nant
dom'i·nate'
·nat·ed ·nat'ing
dom'i·na'tion
dom'i·neer'
dom'i·neer'ing
do·min'ion
dom'i·no'
·noes' or ·nos'
don
donned don'ning
do'nate'
·nat·ed ·nat'ing
do·na'tion
done
Don' Juan'
don'key
·keys
don'ny·brook'
do'nor
do'-noth'ing
Don' Qui·xo'te
don't
do'nut'
doo'dle
·dled ·dling
doo'dler
doo'hick'ey
doom
dooms'day'
door
door'bell'
do'-or-die'
door'jamb'
door'keep'er
door'knob'
door'man'
door'mat'

door'step'
door'-to-door'
door'way'
dope
  doped dop'ing
dop'ey or dop·y
  ·i·er ·i·est
dorm
dor'man·cy
dor'mant
dor'mer
dor'mi·to'ry
  ·ries
dor'mouse'
  ·mice'
dor'sal
do'ry
  ·ries
dos'age
dose
  dosed dos'ing
do·sim'e·ter
dos'si·er'
dot
  dot'ted dot'ting
dot'age
dote
  dot'ed dot'ing
dot'ing
dot'-ma'trix
dou'ble
  ·bled ·bling
dou'ble-bar'reled
dou'ble-blind'
dou'ble-breast'ed
dou'ble-check'
dou'ble-cross'
dou'ble-cross'er
dou'ble-date'
dou'ble-deal'ing
dou'ble-deck'er
dou'ble-edged'
dou'ble-en·ten'dre
dou'ble-head'er
dou'ble-joint'ed
dou'ble-knit'
dou'ble-park
dou'ble-quick'
dou'ble-space'
dou'ble-reed'
dou'ble·speak'
dou'blet
dou·bloon'
dou'bly
doubt
doubt'er
doubt'ful
doubt'ful·ly
doubt'less
douche
  douched douch'ing
dough
  (flour; see DOE)
dough'nut'
dough'y
  ·i·er ·i·est
dour
dour'ness

douse
  doused dous'ing
dove
dove'tail'
dow'a·ger
dow'dy
  ·di·er ·di·est
dow'el
dow'er
down
down'beat'
down'cast'
down'er
down'fall'
down'grade'
down'heart'ed
down'hill'
down'play'
down'pour'
down'range'
down'right'
down'scale'
down'spout'
down'stage'
down'stairs'
down'state'
down'stream'
down'swing'
down'-to-earth'
down'town'
down'trod'den
down'turn'
down'ward
down'wind'
down'y
  ·i·er ·i·est
dow'ry
  ·ries
dox·ol'o·gy
  ·gies
doze
  dozed doz'ing
doz'en
  ·ens or ·en
doz'enth
doz'er
drab
  drab'ber drab'best
drab'ness
drach'ma
draft
draft'ee
draft'er
draft'i·ness
drafts'man
drafts'man·ship'
draft'y
  ·i·er ·i·est
drag
  dragged drag'ging
drag'gy
  ·gi·er ·gi·est
drag'net'
drag'on
drag'on·fly'
dra·goon'
drag'-race'
drain

drain'age
drain'pipe'
drake
dram
dra'ma
dram'a·mine'
dra·mat'ic
dra·mat'i·cal·ly
dram'a·tist
dram'a·ti·za'tion
dram'a·tize'
  ·tized' ·tiz'ing
drank
drape
  draped drap'ing
drap'er·y
  ·ies
dras'tic
dras'ti·cal·ly
draw
  drew drawn
  draw'ing
draw'back'
draw'bridge'
draw'er
drawers
draw'ing
drawl
drawn
draw'string'
dread
dread'ful
dread'ful·ly
dread'nought' or
  ·naught'
dream
  dreamed or
  dreamt dream'ing
dream'er
dream'i·ly
dream'land'
dream'less
dream'like'
dream'y
  ·i·er ·i·est
drear'i·ly
drear'i·ness
drear'y
  ·i·er ·i·est
dredge
  dredged dredg'ing
dregs
drench
dress
  dressed or drest
  dress'ing
dress'er
dress'i·ness
dress'ing
dress'ing-down'
dress'mak'er
dress'mak'ing
dress'y
  ·i·er ·i·est
drew
drib'ble
  ·bled ·bling
drib'bler
drib'let

dried
dri'er
  (drying agent;
  form of dry; see
  DRYER)
dri'est
drift
drift'er
drift'wood'
drill
drill'er
drill'mas'ter
dri'ly
drink
  drank drunk
  drink'ing
drink'a·ble
drink'er
drip
  dripped or dript
  drip'ping
drip'-dry'
drive
  drove driv'en
  driv'ing
drive'-in'
driv'el
  ·eled or ·elled
  ·el·ing or ·el·ling
driv'er
drive'train'
drive'way'
driz'zle
  ·zled ·zling
driz'zly
drogue
droll
droll'er·y
  ·ies
drol'ly
drom'e·dar·y
  ·ies
drone
  droned droning
drool
droop
droop'i·ly
droop'i·ness
droop'y
  ·i·er ·i·est
drop
  dropped drop'ping
drop'cloth'
drop'-forge'
drop'-kick'
drop'let
drop'-off'
drop'out'
drop'per
drop'sy
dross
drought
drove
drown
drowse
  drowsed drows'ing
drows'i·ly
drows'i·ness
drows'y
  ·i·er ·i·est

drub
  drubbed drub'bing
drub'bing
drudge
  drudged drudg'ing
drudg'er·y
  ·ies
drug
  drugged drug'ging
drug'gie
drug'gist
drug'store'
dru'id
drum
  drummed
  drum'ming
drum'beat'
drum'head'
drum'lin
drum ma·jor·ette'
drum'mer
drum'stick'
drunk
drunk'ard
drunk'en
drunk'en·ly
drunk'en·ness
drupe
drupe'let
dry
  dri'er dri'est
  dried dry'ing
dry'ad'
dry'-clean'
dry cleaner
dry cleaning
dry'er
  (machine that
  dries; see DRIER)
dry'-eyed'
dry ice
dry'ly
dry'ness
dry'wall'
du'al
  (of two; see DUEL)
du'al·is'tic
du·al'i·ty
du'al-pur'pose
dub
  dubbed dub'bing
du'bi·ous
du'cal
duc'at
duch'ess
duch'y
  ·ies
duck
duck'bill'
duck'ling
duck'pins'
duck'y
  ·i·er ·i·est
duct
duc'tile
duc·til'i·ty
duct'less
dud (a failure)
dude (a dandy)

due
  (owed; see DEW)
due bill
du'el
  ·eled or ·elled
  ·el·ing or ·el·ling
  (fight; see DUAL)
du'el·ist or
  du'el·list
du·et'
duf'fel or ·fle
duff'er
dug
dug'out'
duke
duke'dom
dul'cet
dul'ci·mer
dull
dull'ard
dull'ness
dul'ly (in a dull
  way)
du'ly (as due)
dumb
dumb'bell'
dumb'found' or
  dum'·
dumb'ly
dumb'wait'er
dum'dum'
dum'my
  ·mies
dump
dump'ling
dump'ster
dump'y
  ·i·er ·i·est
dunce
dune
dung
dun'ga·ree'
dun'geon
dung'hill'
dunk
du'o
  ·os
du'o·de'nal
du'o·de'num
  ·na or ·nums
dupe
  duped dup'ing
du'plex'
du'pli·cate
  ·cat'ed ·cat'ing
du'pli·ca'tion
du·plic'i·ty
du'ra·bil'i·ty
du'ra·ble
du'ra·bly
du'ra ma'ter
du·ra'tion
du·ress'
dur'ing
du'rum
dusk
dusk'y
  ·i·er ·i·est

dust
dust'er
dust'i·ness
dust'pan'
dust'y
·i·er ·i·est
Dutch
du'te·ous
du'ti·a·ble
du'ti·ful
du'ti·ful·ly
du'ty
·ties
du'ty-free'
dwarf
dwarfs *or* dwarves
dwarf'ish
dwell
dwelt *or* dwelled
dwell'ing
dwell'er
dwell'ing
dwin'dle
·dled ·dling
dyb'buk
dye
dyed dye'ing
(*color;* see DIE)
dyed'-in-the-wool'
dy'er
(*one who dyes;* see DIRE)
dye'stuff'
dy'ing
dy·nam'ic
dy·nam'i·cal·ly
dy'na·mite'
·mit'ed ·mit'ing
dy'na·mo'
·mos'
dy·nas'tic
dy'nas·ty
·ties
dyne
dys'en·ter'y
dys·func'tion
dys·func'tion·al
dys·lex'i·a
dys·lex'ic *or* ·lec'tic
dys·pep'si·a
dys·pep'tic
dys'tro·phy

E

each
ea'ger
ea'ger·ly
ea'ger·ness
ea'gle
ea'gle-eyed'
ea'glet
ear
ear'ache'
ear'drum'
earl
earl'dom
ear'li·ness

ear'ly
·li·er ·li·est
ear'mark'
ear'muffs'
earn
earn'er
ear'nest
ear'nest·ly
ear'nest·ness
earn'ings
ear'phone'
ear'plug'
ear'ring'
ear'shot'
ear'split'ting
earth
Earth
earth'en
earth'en·ware'
earth'ling
earth'ly
earth'quake'
earth'ward
earth'work'
earth'worm'
earth'y
·i·er ·i·est
ease
eased eas'ing
ea'sel
ease'ment
eas'i·ly
eas'i·ness
east
Eas'ter
east'er·ly
east'ern
east'ern·er
east'ward
eas'y
·i·er ·i·est
eas'y·go'ing
eat
ate eat'en eat'ing
eat'a·ble
eat'er
eat'er·y
·ies
eaves
eaves'drop'
eaves'drop'per
ebb
eb'on·y
e·bul'lience
e·bul'lient
eb'ul·li'tion
ec·cen'tric
ec·cen'tri·cal·ly
ec·cen'tric'i·ty
·ties
ec·cle'si·as'tic
ec·cle'si·as'ti·cal
ech'e·lon'
e·chi'no·derm'
ech'o
·oes, ·oed ·o·ing
e·cho'ic
é·clair'

ec·lec'tic
ec·lec'ti·cal·ly
e·clipse'
·clipsed' ·clips'ing
e·clip'tic
ec'o·cide'
ec'o·log'i·cal
ec'o·log'i·cal·ly
e·col'o·gist
e·col'o·gy
ec'o·nom'ic
ec'o·nom'i·cal
ec'o·nom'i·cal·ly
e·con'o·mist
e·con'o·mize'
·mized' ·miz'ing
e·con'o·my
·mies
ec'o·sys'tem
ec·sta·sy
·sies
ec·stat'ic
ec·stat'i·cal·ly
ec'u·men'i·cal
ec'u·men'i·cal·ly
ec'u·men'ism'
ec'u·men·ist
ec'ze·ma
ed'dy
·dies
·died ·dy'ing
e'del·weiss'
e·de'ma
·mas *or* ·ma·ta
E'den
edge
edged edg'ing
edg'er
edge'ways'
edge'wise'
edg'i·ness
edg'y
·i·er ·i·est
ed'i·bil'i·ty
ed'i·ble
e'dict'
ed'i·fi·ca'tion
ed'i·fice
ed'i·fy'
·fied' ·fy'ing
ed'it
e·di'tion
(*form of book;* see ADDITION)
ed'i·tor
ed'i·to'ri·al
ed'i·to'ri·al·ize'
·ized' ·iz'ing
ed'i·to'ri·al·ly
ed'u·ca·bil'i·ty
ed'u·ca·ble
ed'u·cate'
·cat'ed ·cat'ing
ed'u·ca'tion
ed'u·ca'tion·al
ed'u·ca'tor
e·duce'
·duced' ·duc'ing
eel

ee'rie *or* ee·ry
·ri·er ·ri·est
ee'ri·ly
ee'ri·ness
ef·face'
·faced' ·fac'ing
ef·face'ment
ef·fect'
(*result;* see AFFECT)
ef·fec'tive
ef·fec'tive·ly
ef·fec'tive·ness
ef·fec'tu·al
ef·fec'tu·al·ly
ef·fec'tu·ate'
·at'ed ·at'ing
ef·fem'i·na·cy
ef·fem'i·nate
ef'fer·ent
ef'fer·vesce'
·vesced' ·vesc'ing
ef'fer·ves'cence
ef'fer·ves'cent
ef·fete'
ef'fi·ca'cious
ef'fi·ca'cious·ly
ef'fi·ca·cy
ef·fi'cien·cy
ef·fi'cient
ef·fi'cient·ly
ef'fi·gy
·gies
ef'flu·ence
ef'flu·ent
(*contaminated outflow;* see AF-FLUENT)
ef·flu'vi·um
·vi·a *or* ·vi·ums
ef'fort
ef'fort·less
ef'fort·less·ly
ef·fron'ter·y
ef·ful'gence
ef·ful'gent
ef·fuse'
·fused' ·fus'ing
ef·fu'sion
ef·fu'sive
ef·fu'sive·ly
ef·fu'sive·ness
e·gal'i·tar'i·an
egg
egg'beat'er
egg' foo yong' *or* young'
egg'head'
egg'nog'
egg'plant'
eg'lan·tine'
e'go
·gos
e'go·cen'tric
e'go·cen'tri·cal·ly
e'go·ism'
e'go·ist
e'go·is'tic
e'go·tism

e'go·tist
e'go·tis'tic *or* ·tis'ti·cal
e·gre'gious
e·gre'gious·ly
e'gress'
e'gret'
ei'der
ei'der·down'
eight
eight'een'
eight'eenth'
eighth
eight'i·eth
eight'y
·ies
ei'ther
e·jac'u·late'
·lat'ed ·lat'ing
e·jac'u·la'tion
e·ject'
e·jec'tion
e·jec'tor
eke
eked ek'ing
e·lab'o·rate'
·rat'ed ·rat'ing
e·lab'o·rate·ly
e·lab'o·rate·ness
e·lab'o·ra'tion
é·lan'
e·lapse'
·lapsed' ·laps'ing
e·las'tic
e·las·tic'i·ty
e·las'ti·cize'
·cized' ·ciz'ing
e·late'
·lat'ed ·lat'ing
e·la'tion
el'bow'
el'bow·room'
eld'er
el'der·ber'ry
eld'er·ly
eld'est
e·lect'
e·lect'a·bil'i·ty
e·lect'a·ble
e·lec'tion
e·lec'tive
e·lec'tor
e·lec'tor·al
e·lec'tor·ate
e·lec'tric
e·lec'tri·cal
e·lec'tri·cal·ly
e·lec·tri'cian
e·lec·tric'i·ty
e·lec'tri·fi·ca'tion
e·lec'tri·fy'
·fied' ·fy'ing
e·lec'tro·car'di·o·gram'
e·lec'tro·car'di·o·graph'
e·lec'tro·cute'
·cut'ed ·cut'ing

e·lec'tro·cu'tion
e·lec'trode'
e·lec'tro·en·ceph'a·lo·gram'
e·lec'tro·en·ceph'a·lo·graph'
e·lec'trol'y·sis
e·lec'tro·lyte'
e·lec'tro·lyt'ic
e·lec'tro·mag'net
e·lec'tro·mag·net'ic
e·lec'tro·mo'tive
e·lec'tron'
e·lec'tron'i·cal·ly
e·lec'tro·plate'
·plat'ed ·plat'ing
e·lec'tro·scope'
e·lec'tro·scop'ic
e·lec'tro·shock'
e·lec'tro·type'
el'e·gance
el'e·gant
el'e·gant·ly
el'e·gy
·gies
el'e·ment
el'e·men'tal
el'e·men'ta·ry
(*basic;* see ALIMENTARY)
el'e·phant
el'e·phan·ti'a·sis
el'e·phan'tine
el'e·vate'
·vat'ed ·vat'ing
el'e·va'tion
el'e·va'tor
e·lev'en
e·lev'enth
elf
elves
elf'in
elf'ish
e·lic'it
(*to draw forth;* see ILLICIT)
el'i·gi·bil'i·ty
el'i·gi·ble
e·lim'i·nate'
·nat'ed ·nat'ing
e·lim'i·na'tion
e·li'sion
e·lite'
e·lit'ism'
e·lit'ist
e·lix'ir
E·liz'a·be'than
elk
el·lipse'
el·lip'sis
·ses'
el·lip'ti·cal
el·lip'ti·cal·ly
elm
el'o·cu'tion
el'o·cu'tion·ist
e·lo'de·a

e·lon'gate'
  ·gat'ed ·gat'ing
e'lon·ga'tion
e·lope'
  ·loped' ·lop'ing
e·lope'ment
el'o·quence
el'o·quent
el'o·quent·ly
else
else'where'
e·lu'ci·date'
  ·dat'ed ·dat'ing
e·lu'ci·da'tion
e·lude'
  ·lud'ed ·lud'ing
  (escape; see AL-
  LUDE)
e·lu'sion
  (an escape; see AL-
  LUSION, ILLUSION)
e·lu'sive
  (hard to grasp; see
  ALLUSIVE,
  ILLUSIVE)
e·lu'sive·ness
e·ma'ci·ate'
  ·at'ed ·at'ing
e·ma'ci·a'tion
em'a·nate'
  ·nat'ed ·nat'ing
em'a·na'tion
e·man'ci·pate'
  ·pat'ed ·pat'ing
e·man'ci·pa'tion
e·man'ci·pa'tor
e·mas'cu·late'
  ·lat'ed ·lat'ing
e·mas'cu·la'tion
em·balm'
em·balm'er
em·bank'
em·bank'ment
em·bar'go
  ·goes
  ·goed ·go·ing
em·bark'
em'bar·ka'tion
em·bar'rass
em·bar'rass·ing
em·bar'rass·ment
em'bas·sy
  ·sies
em·bat'tled
em·bed'
em·bel'lish
em·bel'lish·ment
em'ber
em·bez'zle
  ·zled ·zling
em·bez'zle·ment
em·bez'zler
em·bit'ter
em·bla'zon
em'blem
em'blem·at'ic
em·bod'i·ment
em·bod'y
  ·ied ·y·ing
em·bold'en

em'bo·lism
em·boss'
em·boss'er
em·brace'
  ·braced' ·brac'ing
em·brace'a·ble
em·broi'der
em·broi'der·y
  ·ies
em·broil'
em·broil'ment
em'bry·o'
em'bry·ol'o·gist
em'bry·ol'o·gy
em'bry·on'ic
em·cee'
  ·ceed' ·cee'ing
e·mend'
  (to correct; see
  AMEND)
e'men·da'tion
em'er·ald
e·merge'
  ·merged'
  ·merg'ing
  (appear; see IM-
  MERGE)
e·mer'gence
e·mer'gen·cy
  ·cies
e·mer'gent
e·mer'i·tus
em'er·y
e·met'ic
em'i·grant
em'i·grate'
  ·grat'ed ·grat'ing
  (leave; see IMMI-
  GRATE)
em'i·gra'tion
é'mi·gré' or
  e'mi·gré'
em'i·nence
em'i·nent
  (prominent; see
  IMMANENT, IMMI-
  NENT)
em'i·nent·ly
e·mir'
em'is·sar'y
  ·ies
e·mis'sion
e·mit'
  ·mit'ted ·mit'ting
e·mit'ter
e·mol'li·ent
e·mol'u·ment
e·mote'
  ·mot'ed ·mot'ing
e·mo'tion
e·mo'tion·al
e·mo'tion·al·ism'
e·mo'tion·al·ize'
  ·ized' ·iz'ing
e·mo'tion·al·ly
em'pa·thet'ic
em'pa·thize'
  ·thized' ·thiz'ing
em'pa·thy
em'per·or

em'pha·sis
  ·ses'
em'pha·size'
  ·sized' ·siz'ing
em·phat'ic
em·phat'i·cal·ly
em'phy·se'ma
em'pire'
em·pir'i·cal
em·pir'i·cal·ly
em·pir'i·cism'
em·place'ment
em·ploy'
em·ploy'a·ble
em·ploy'ee or
  ·ploy'e
em·ploy'er
em·ploy'ment
em·po'ri·um
  ·ri·ums or ·ri·a
em·pow'er
em'press
emp'ti·ly
emp'ti·ness
emp'ty
  ·ties
  ·ti·er ·ti·est
  ·tied ·ty·ing
emp'ty-hand'ed
e'mu'
em'u·late'
  ·lat'ed ·lat'ing
em'u·la'tion
em'u·la'tive
em'u·la'tor
e·mul'si·fi·ca'tion
e·mul'si·fi'er
e·mul'si·fy'
  ·fied' ·fy'ing
e·mul'sion
en·a'ble
  ·bled ·bling
en·act'
en·act'ment
en·am'el
  ·eled or ·elled
  ·el·ing or ·el·ling
en·am'el·er or
  ·el·ler
en·am'or
en·camp'
en·camp'ment
en·cap'su·late'
  ·lat'ed ·lat'ing
en·cap'su·la'tion
en·case'
  ·cased' ·cas'ing
en·ceph'a·li'tis
en·chain'
en·chant'
en·chant'er
en·chant'ing
en·chant'ment
en'chi·la'da
en·cir'cle
  ·cled ·cling
en'clave'
en·close'
  ·closed' ·clos'ing

en·clo'sure
en·code'
  ·cod'ed ·cod'ing
en·co'mi·um
  ·mi·ums or ·mi·a
en·com'pass
en'core'
en·coun'ter
en·cour'age
  ·aged ·ag·ing
en·cour'age·ment
en·croach'
en·croach'ment
en·crust'
en'crus·ta'tion
en·cum'ber
en·cum'brance
en·cyc'li·cal
en·cy'clo·pe'di·a or
  ·pae'di·a
en·cy'clo·pe'dic or
  ·pae'dic
end
en·dan'ger
en·dear'
en·dear'ing
en·dear'ment
en·deav'or
en·dem'ic
en·dem'i·cal·ly
end'ing
en'dive
end'less
end'less·ly
end'less·ness
end'most'
en'do·crine'
en·dorse'
  ·dorsed' ·dors'ing
en·dorse'ment
en·dors'er
en'do·scope'
en·dow'
en·dow'ment
en·dur'a·ble
en·dur'ance
en·dure'
  ·dured' ·dur'ing
end'ways'
en'e·ma
  ·mas
en'e·my
  ·mies
en'er·get'ic
en'er·get'i·cal·ly
en'er·gize'
  ·gized' ·giz'ing
en'er·giz'er
en'er·gy
  ·gies
en·rich'
en'er·vate'
  ·vat'ed ·vat'ing
en'er·va'tion
en·fee'ble
  ·bled ·bling
en'fi·lade'
en·fold'
en·force'
  ·forced' ·forc'ing

en·force'a·ble
en·force'ment
en·forc'er
en·fran'chise'
en·fran'chise·ment
en·gage'
  ·gaged' ·gag'ing
en·gage'ment
en·gag'ing·ly
en·gen'der
en'gine
en'gi·neer'
en'gi·neer'ing
Eng'lish
en·gorge'
  ·gorged' ·gorg'ing
en·grave'
  ·graved' ·grav'ing
en·grav'er
en·gross'
en·gulf'
en·hance'
  ·hanced' ·hanc'ing
en·hance'ment
e·nig'ma
e·nig·mat'ic
en·join'
en·joy'
en·joy'a·ble
en·joy'ment
en·large'
  ·larged' ·larg'ing
en·large'ment
en·light'en
en·light'en·ment
en·list'
en·list'ment
en·liv'en
en masse'
en·mesh'
en'mi·ty
  ·ties
en·no'ble
  ·bled ·bling
en·no'ble·ment
en·nui'
e·nor'mi·ty
  ·ties
e·nor'mous
e·nor'mous·ly
e·nough'
en·plane'
en·quire'
  ·quired' ·quir'ing
en·quir'y
  ·ies
en·rage'
en·rap'ture
  ·tured ·tur·ing
en·rich'
en·rich'ment
en·roll' or ·rol'
  ·rolled' ·roll'ing
en·roll'ment or
  ·rol'ment
en·sconce'
  ·sconced' ·sconc'-
  ing
en·sem'ble

en·shrine'
  ·shrined'
  ·shrin'ing
en·shroud'
en·sign'
en·slave'
en·slave'ment
en·snare'
en·sue'
  ·sued' ·su'ing
en·sure'
  ·sured' ·sur'ing
en·tail'
en·tan'gle
en·tan'gle·ment
en'ter
en'ter·i'tis
en'ter·prise'
en'ter·pris'ing
en'ter·tain'
en'ter·tain'er
en'ter·tain'ment
en·thrall' or ·thral'
  ·thralled'
  ·thrall'·ing
en·throne'
en·thuse'
  ·thused' ·thus'ing
en·thu'si·asm'
en·thu'si·ast'
en·thu'si·as'tic
en·thu'si·as'ti·cal·ly
en·tice'
  ·ticed' ·tic'ing
en·tice'ment
en·tire'
en·tire'ly
en·tire'ty
  ·ties
en·ti'tle
en·ti'tle·ment
en·ti·ty
  ·ties
en·tomb'
en·tomb'ment
en'to·mo·log'i·cal
en'to·mol'o·gist
en'to·mol'o·gy
  (insect study; see
  ETYMOLOGY)
en·tou·rage'
en'trails
en'trance n.
en·trance' v.
  ·tranced'
  ·tranc'ing
en'trant
en·trap'
en·treat'
en·treat'y
  ·ies
en'tree' or ·trée'
en·trench'
en·trench'ment
en'tre·pre·neur'
en'tro·py
en·trust'
en'try
  ·tries

en·twine′
e·nu′mer·ate′
　·at′ed ·at′ing
e·nu′mer·a′tion
e·nun′ci·ate′
　·at′ed ·at′ing
e·nun′ci·a′tion
en·vel′op v.
en′ve·lope′ n.
en·vel′op·ment
en·ven′om
en′vi·a·ble
en′vi·a·bly
en′vi·ous
en′vi·ous·ly
en·vi′ron·ment
en·vi′ron·men′tal
en·vi′ron·men′tal·ist
en·vi′rons
en·vi′sion
en′voy′
en′vy
　·vied ·vy·ing
en′zyme′
e′on
　(time period; see
　ION)
ep′au·let′ or ·lette′
e·pee′ or é·pée′
e·phed′rine
e·phem′er·al
ep′ic
　(poem; see EPOCH)
ep′i·cen′ter
ep′i·cure′
ep′i·cu·re′an
ep′i·dem′ic
ep′i·de·mi·ol′o·gy
ep′i·der′mal
ep′i·der′mic
ep′i·der′mis
ep′i·glot′tis
ep′i·gram′
ep′i·gram·mat′ic
ep′i·lep′sy
ep′i·lep′tic
ep′i·logue′ or ·log′
e·piph′a·ny
　·nies
e·pis′co·pa·cy
　·cies
e·pis′co·pal
E·pis′co·pa′lian
e·pis′co·pate
ep′i·sode′
ep′i·sod′ic
ep′i·sod′i·cal·ly
e·pis′tle
e·pis′to·lar′y
ep′i·taph′
ep′i·the′li·al
ep′i·the′li·um
　·li·ums or ·li·a
ep′i·thet′
e·pit′o·me′
e·pit′o·mize′
　·mized′ ·miz′ing

ep′och
　(period; see EPIC)
ep′och·al
ep·ox′y
　·ies
ep′si·lon′
Ep′som salts
eq′ua·bil′i·ty
eq′ua·ble
eq′ua·bly
e′qual
　·qualed or
　·qualled, ·qual·ing
　or ·qual·ling
e·qual′i·ty
　·ties
e′qual·i·za′tion
e′qual·ize′
　·ized′ ·iz′ing
e′qual·iz′er
e′qual·ly
e′qua·nim′i·ty
e·quat′a·ble
e·quate′
　·quat′ed ·quat′ing
e·qua′tion
e·qua′tor
e·qua·to′ri·al
e·ques′tri·an
e·ques′tri·enne′
　fem.
e′qui·dis′tant
e′qui·lat′er·al
e′qui·lib′ri·um
　·ri·ums or ·ri·a
e′quine′
e′qui·noc′tial
e′qui·nox′
e·quip′
　·quipped′
　·quip′ping
eq′ui·page′
e·quip′ment
eq′ui·poise′
eq′ui·ta·ble
eq′ui·ta·bly
eq′ui·ta′tion
eq′ui·ty
　·ties
e·quiv′a·lence
e·quiv′a·lent
e·quiv′o·cal
e·quiv′o·cal·ly
e·quiv′o·cate′
　·cat′ed ·cat′ing
e·quiv′o·ca′tion
e·quiv′o·ca′tor
e′ra
e·rad′i·cate′
　·cat′ed ·cat′ing
e·rad′i·ca′tion
e·rad′i·ca′tor
e·ras′a·ble
e·rase′
　·rased′ ·ras′ing
e·ras′er
e·ra′sure
e·rect′
e·rec′tile

e·rec′tion
e·rect′ly
e·rect′ness
e·rec′tor
erg
er′go
er·gos′ter·ol′
er′mine
e·rode′
　·rod′ed ·rod′ing
e·rog′e·nous
e′ros′
e·ro′sion
e·ro′sive
e·rot′ic
e·rot′i·ca
e·rot′i·cal·ly
err
　(be wrong; see AIR,
　HEIR)
er′rand
er′rant
er·rat′ic
er·rat′i·cal·ly
er·ra′tum
　·ta
er·ro′ne·ous
er·ro′ne·ous·ly
er′ror
er′satz′
erst′while′
e·ruct′
e′ruc·ta′tion
er′u·dite′
er′u·dite′ly
er′u·di′tion
e·rupt′
e·rup′tion
e·ryth′ro·cyte′
es′ca·late′
　·lat′ed ·lat′ing
es′ca·la′tion
es′ca·la′tor
es′ca·pade′
es·cape′
　·caped′ ·cap′ing
es·cap′ee′
es·cape′ment
es·cap′ism′
es·cap′ist
es·car·got′
es′ca·role′
es·carp′ment
es·chew′
es′cort′
es·cri·toire′
es′crow′
es·cutch′eon
Es′ki·mo′
　·mos′ or ·mo′
e·soph′a·gus
　·gi′
es′o·ter′ic
es·pal′ier
es·pe′cial
es·pe′cial·ly
Es·pe·ran′to
es′pi·o·nage′

es′pla·nade′
es·pous′al
es·pouse′
　·poused′ ·pous′ing
es·pres′so
　·sos
es·py′
　·pied′ ·py′ing
es′quire
es·say′
　(try; see ASSAY)
es·say′er
es′say·ist
es′sence
es·sen′tial
es·sen′tial·ly
es·tab′lish
es·tab′lish·ment
es·tate′
es·teem′
es′ter
es′thete′
es·thet′ics
es′ti·ma·ble
es′ti·mate′
　·mat′ed ·mat′ing
es′ti·ma′tion
es′ti·ma′tor
es·trange′
　·tranged′
　·trang′ing
es·trange′ment
es′tro·gen
es′trous adj.
es′trus n.
es·tu·ar′y
　·ies
et cet′er·a
etch
etch′er
etch′ing
e·ter′nal
e·ter′nal·ly
e·ter′nal·ness
e·ter′ni·ty
　·ties
eth′ane′
e′ther
e·the′re·al
e·the′re·al·ly
eth′ic
eth′i·cal
eth′i·cal·ly
eth′nic
eth′ni·cal·ly
eth·nic′i·ty
eth′no·log′i·cal
eth·nol′o·gist
eth·nol′o·gy
e′thos′
eth′yl
eth′yl·ene′
e′ti·o·log′ic
e′ti·ol′o·gy
　·gies
et′i·quette′
é′tude′
et′y·mo·log′i·cal

et′y·mol′o·gist
et′y·mol′o·gy
　·gies
　(word study; see
　ENTOMOLOGY)
eu·ca·lyp′tus
　·tus·es or ·ti′
Eu′cha·rist
eu′chre
eu·gen′ic
eu·gen′i·cal·ly
eu·gen′i·cist
eu·gen′ics
eu′lo·gist
eu′lo·gis′tic
eu′lo·gize′
　·gized′ ·giz′ing
eu′lo·giz′er
eu′lo·gy
　·gies
eu′nuch
eu′phe·mism
eu′phe·mis′tic
eu′phe·mis′ti·cal·ly
eu·pho′ni·ous
eu′pho·ny
　·nies
eu·pho′ri·a
eu·phor′ic
Eur·a′sian
eu·re′ka
Eu·ro·pe′an
eu·ryth′mics
eu·sta′chi·an
eu·tha·na′si·a
eu′than·ize′
　·ized′ ·iz′ing
eu·then′ics
e·vac′u·ate′
　·at′ed ·at′ing
e·vac′u·a′tion
e·vac′u·ee′
e·vade′
　·vad′ed ·vad′ing
e·vad′er
e·val′u·ate′
　·at′ed ·at′ing
e·val′u·a′tion
ev′a·nes′cence
ev′a·nes′cent
e·van·gel′i·cal
e·van′ge·lism′
e·van′ge·list
e·van′ge·lize′
　·lized′ ·liz′ing
e·vap′o·rate′
　·rat′ed ·rat′ing
e·vap′o·ra′tion
e·vap′o·ra′tor
e·va′sion
e·va′sive
e·va′sive·ly
e·va′sive·ness
eve
e′ven
e′ven·hand′ed
eve′ning
e′ven·ly
e′ven·ness

e·vent′
e′ven-tem′pered
e·vent′ful
e·vent′ful·ly
e′ven·tide′
e·ven′tu·al
e·ven′tu·al′i·ty
　·ties
e·ven′tu·al·ly
e·ven′tu·ate′
　·at′ed ·at′ing
ev′er
ev′er·glade′
ev′er·green′
ev′er·last′ing
ev′er·more′
ev′er·y
ev′er·y·bod′y
ev′er·y·day′
ev′er·y·one′
ev′er·y·thing′
ev′er·y·where′
e·vict′
e·vic′tion
ev′i·dence
　·denced ·denc·ing
ev′i·dent
ev′i·den′tial
ev′i·dent·ly
e′vil
e′vil-do′er
e′vil-do′ing
e′vil·ly
e·vince′
　·vinced′ ·vinc′ing
e·vis′cer·ate′
　·at′ed ·at′ing
e·vis′cer·a′tion
ev′o·ca′tion
e·voke′
　·voked′ ·vok′ing
ev′o·lu′tion
ev′o·lu′tion·ar′y
ev′o·lu′tion·ist
e·volve′
　·volved′ ·volv′ing
ewe
　(sheep; see YEW)
ex·ac′er·bate′
　·bat′ed ·bat′ing
ex·ac′er·ba′tion
ex·act′
ex·act′ing
ex·ac′tion
ex·ac′ti·tude′
ex·act′ly
ex·act′ness
ex·ag′ger·ate′
　·at′ed ·at′ing
ex·ag′ger·a′tion
ex·ag′ger·a′tor
ex·alt′
ex′al·ta′tion
ex·am′i·na′tion
ex·am′ine
　·ined ·in·ing
ex·am′in·er
ex·am′ple

ex·as'per·ate'
  ·at'ed ·at'ing
ex·as'per·a'tion
ex'ca·vate'
  ·vat'ed ·vat'ing
ex'ca·va'tion
ex'ca·va'tor
ex·ceed'
  (*surpass;* see AC-
  CEDE)
ex·ceed'ing·ly
ex·cel'
  ·celled' ·cel'ling
ex'cel·lence
ex'cel·len·cy
  ·cies
ex'cel·lent
ex·cel'si·or·
ex·cept'
  (*omit;* see ACCEPT)
ex·cep'tion
ex·cep'tion·a·ble
ex·cep'tion·al
ex·cep'tion·al·ly
ex·cerpt'
ex·cess'
  (*surplus;* see AC-
  CESS)
ex·ces'sive
ex·ces'sive·ly
ex·change'
  ·changed'
  ·chang'ing
ex·change'a·ble
ex·cheq'uer
ex'cise' *n.*
ex·cise' *v.*
  ·cised' ·cis'ing
ex·ci'sion
ex·cit'a·bil'i·ty
ex·cit'a·ble
ex·ci·ta'tion
ex·cite'
  ·cit'ed ·cit'ing
ex·cit'ed·ly
ex·cite'ment
ex·claim'
ex·cla·ma'tion
ex·clam'a·to·ry
ex·clude'
  ·clud'ed ·clud'ing
ex·clu'sion
ex·clu'sion·ar·y
ex·clu'sive
ex·clu'sive·ly
ex·clu'sive·ness
ex'com·mu'ni·cate'
ex'com·mu'ni·ca'-
  tion
ex·co'ri·ate'
  ·at'ed ·at'ing
ex·co'ri·a'tion
ex'cre·ment
ex·cres'cence
ex·cre'ta
ex·crete'
  ·cret'ed ·cret'ing
ex·cre'tion
ex'cre·to'ry

ex·cru'ci·at'ing
ex'cul·pate'
  ·pat'ed ·pat'ing
ex'cul·pa'tion
ex·cur'sion
ex·cur'sive
ex·cus'a·ble
ex·cuse'
  ·cused' ·cus'ing
ex'e·cra·ble
ex'e·crate'
  ·crat'ed ·crat'ing
ex'e·cra'tion
ex'e·cute'
  ·cut'ed ·cut'ing
ex'e·cu'tion
ex'e·cu'tion·er
ex·ec'u·tive
ex·ec'u·tor
ex'e·ge'sis
  ·ge'ses'
ex·em'plar
ex·em'pla·ry
ex·em'pli·fi·ca'tion
ex·em'pli·fy'
  ·fied' ·fy'ing
ex·empt'
ex·emp'tion
ex'er·cise'
  ·cised' ·cis'ing
  (*use;* see EXORCISE)
ex'er·cis'er
ex·ert'
ex·er'tion
ex'ha·la'tion
ex·hale'
  ·haled' ·hal'ing
ex·haust'
ex·haust'i·ble
ex·haus'tion
ex·haus'tive
ex·hib'it
ex'hi·bi'tion
ex'hi·bi'tion·ism'
ex'hi·bi'tion·ist
ex·hib'i·tor
ex·hil'a·rate'
  ·rat'ed ·rat'ing
ex·hil'a·ra'tion
ex·hil'a·ra'tive
ex·hort'
ex·hor·ta'tion
ex·hu·ma'tion
ex·hume'
  ·humed' ·hum'ing
ex'i·gen·cy
  ·cies
ex'i·gent
ex·ig'u·ous
ex'ile'
  ·iled' ·il'ing
ex·ist'
ex·ist'ence
ex·ist'ent
ex'is·ten'tial
ex'is·ten'tial·ism'
ex'is·ten'tial·ist
ex'it
ex'o·dus

ex of·fi'ci·o'
ex·on'er·ate'
  ·at'ed ·at'ing
ex·on'er·a'tion
ex·or'bi·tance
ex·or'bi·tant
ex'or·cise' *or* ·cize'
  ·cised' *or* ·cized'
  ·cis'ing *or* ·ciz'ing
  (*expel;* see EXER-
  CISE)
ex'or·cism'
ex'or·cist
ex'o·skel'e·ton
ex'o·ther'mic
ex·ot'ic
ex·ot'i·cal·ly
ex·pand'
ex·pand'a·ble
ex·panse'
ex·pan'si·ble
ex·pan'sion
ex·pan'sive
ex·pan'sive·ly
ex·pa'ti·ate'
  ·at'ed ·at'ing
ex·pa'ti·a'tion
ex·pa'tri·ate'
  ·at'ed ·at'ing
ex·pa'tri·a'tion
ex·pect'
ex·pect'an·cy
  ·cies
ex·pect'ant
ex·pec·ta'tion
ex·pec'to·rant
ex·pec'to·rate'
  ·rat'ed ·rat'ing
ex·pec'to·ra'tion
ex·pe'di·ence
ex·pe'di·en·cy
  ·cies
ex·pe'di·ent
ex'pe·dite'
  ·dit'ed ·dit'ing
ex'pe·dit'er
ex'pe·di'tion
ex'pe·di'tion·ar'y
ex'pe·di'tious
ex·pel'
  ·pelled' ·pel'ling
ex·pel'la·ble
ex·pel'ler
ex·pend'
ex·pend'a·ble
ex·pend'i·ture
ex·pense'
ex·pen'sive
ex·pe'ri·ence
  ·enced ·enc·ing
ex·per'i·ment
ex·per'i·men'tal
ex·per'i·men'tal·ly
ex·per'i·men·
  ta'tion
ex·per'i·ment'er
ex'pert
ex'per·tise'
ex'pert·ly

ex'pert·ness
ex'pi·ate'
  ·at'ed ·at'ing
ex'pi·a'tion
ex'pi·a·to'ry
ex·pire'
  ·pired' ·pir'ing
ex·plain'
ex·plain'a·ble
ex'pla·na'tion
ex·plan'a·to'ry
ex'ple·tive
ex'pli·ca·ble
ex'pli·cate'
  ·cat'ed ·cat'ing
ex·plic'it
ex·plic'it·ly
ex·plic'it·ness
ex·plode'
  ·plod'ed ·plod'ing
ex'ploit'
ex·ploit'a·ble
ex'ploi·ta'tion
ex·ploit'a·tive
ex·ploit'er
ex·ploi'tive
ex'plo·ra'tion
ex·plor'a·to'ry
ex·plore'
  ·plored' ·plor'ing
ex·plor'er
ex·plo'sion
ex·plo'sive
ex·plo'sive·ly
ex·plo'sive·ness
ex·po'nent
ex'po·nen'tial
ex'po·nen'tial·ly
ex·port'
ex'por·ta'tion
ex·port'er
ex·pose'
  ·posed' ·pos'ing
ex'po·sé'
ex'po·si'tion
ex·pos'i·tor
ex·pos'i·to'ry
ex post fac'to
ex·pos'tu·late'
  ·lat'ed ·lat'ing
ex·pos'tu·la'tion
ex·po'sure
ex·pound'
ex·press'
ex·press'i·ble
ex·pres'sion
ex·pres'sion·ism'
ex·pres'sion·ist
ex·pres'sion·is'tic
ex·pres'sion·less
ex·pres'sive
ex·pres'sive·ly
ex·pres'sive·ness
ex·press'ly
ex·press'way'
ex·pro'pri·ate'
  ·at'ed ·at'ing

ex·pro'pri·a'tion
ex·pul'sion
ex·punge'
  ·punged' ·pung'ing
ex'pur·gate'
  ·gat'ed ·gat'ing
ex'pur·ga'tion
ex'qui·site
ex'tant
  (*existing;* see EX-
  TENT)
ex·tem'po·ra'ne·ous
ex·tem'po·ra'ne·
  ous·ly
ex·tem'po·rize'
  ·rized' ·riz'ing
ex·tend'
ex·tend'er
ex·tend'i·ble *or*
  ex·tend'a·ble
ex·ten'si·ble
ex·ten'sion
ex·ten'sive
ex·ten'sive·ly
ex·ten'sive·ness
ex·tent'
  (*scope;* see EXTANT)
ex·ten'u·ate'
  ·at'ed ·at'ing
ex·ten'u·a'tion
ex·te'ri·or
ex·ter'mi·nate'
  ·nat'ed ·nat'ing
ex·ter'mi·na'tion
ex·ter'mi·na'tor
ex·ter'nal
ex·ter'nal·ly
ex·tinct'
ex·tinc'tion
ex·tin'guish
ex·tin'guish·er
ex'tir·pate'
  ·pat'ed ·pat'ing
ex'tir·pa'tion
ex·tol' *or* ·toll'
  ·tolled' ·tol'ling
ex·tort'
ex·tor'tion
ex·tor'tion·ate
ex·tor'tion·er
ex·tor'tion·ist
ex'tra
ex·tract'
ex·trac'tion
ex·trac'tive
ex·trac'tor
ex'tra·cur·ric'u·lar
ex'tra·dite'
  ·dit'ed ·dit'ing
ex'tra·di'tion
ex'tra·le'gal
ex'tra·mar'i·tal
ex·tra'ne·ous
ex·tra'ne·ous·ly
ex'tra·or'di·nar'y
ex·trap'o·late'
  ·lat'ed ·lat'ing
ex·trap'o·la'tion
ex'tra·sen'so·ry

ex'tra·ter·res'tri·al
ex·trav'a·gance
ex·trav'a·gant
ex·trav'a·gan'za
ex'tra·ve·hic'u·lar
ex·treme'
ex·treme'ly
ex·treme'ness
ex·trem'ism'
ex·trem'ist
ex·trem'i·ty
  ·ties
ex'tri·cate'
  ·cat'ed ·cat'ing
ex'tri·ca'tion
ex·trin'sic
ex·trin'si·cal·ly
ex'tro·ver'sion
ex'tro·vert'
ex·trude'
  ·trud'ed ·trud'ing
ex·tru'sion
ex·tru'sive
ex·u'ber·ance
ex·u'ber·ant
ex·u'ber·ant·ly
ex'u·da'tion
ex·ude'
  ·ud'ed ·ud'ing
ex·ult'
ex·ult'ant
ex·ul·ta'tion
ex·ur'ban
eye
  eyed eye'ing *or*
  ey'ing
eye'ball'
eye'brow'
eye'ful'
eye'glass'
eye'lash'
eye'let
  (*hole;* see ISLET)
eye'lid'
eye'-o'pen·er
eye'piece'
eye'sight'
eye'sore'
eye'strain'
eye'tooth'
eye'wash'
eye'wit'ness

F

fa'ble
fa'bled
fab'ric
fab'ri·cate'
  ·cat'ed ·cat'ing
fab'ri·ca'tion
fab'ri·ca'tor
fab'u·lous
fab'u·lous·ly
fa·çade' *or* ·cade'
face
  faced fac'ing

face'less
face'-lift'
face'-off'
face'-sav'ing
fac'et
  fac'et·ed *or* ·et·ted
fa·ce'tious
fa·ce'tious·ly
fa'cial
fac'ile
fa·cil'i·tate'
  ·tat'ed ·tat'ing
fa·cil'i·ta'tion
fa·cil'i·ty
  ·ties
fac'ing
fac·sim'i·le
fact
fac'tion
fac'tion·al
fac'tion·al·ism'
fac'tious
fac·ti'tious
  (*artificial;* see FIC-
  TITIOUS)
fac'tor
fac'to·ry
  ·ries
fac'tu·al
fac'tu·al·ly
fac'ul·ty
  ·ties
fad
fad'dish
fade
  fad'ed fad'ing
fagged
fag'ot·ing *or*
  fag'got·ing
Fahr'en·heit'
fail
fail'ing
fail'-safe'
fail'ure
fain
  (*gladly;* see FEIGN)
faint
  (*weak;* see FEINT)
faint'ly
faint'ness
fair
  (*just; bazaar;* see
  FARE)
fair'ground'
fair'-haired'
fair'ly
fair'ness
fair'way'
fair'-weath'er
fair'y
  ·ies
  (*tiny being;* see
  FERRY)
fair'y·land'
fait ac·com·pli'
faith
faith'ful
faith'ful·ly
faith'ful·ness

faith'less
faith'less·ly
faith'less·ness
fake
  faked fak'ing
fak'er (*fraud*)
fa·kir' (*Muslim beg-
  gar*)
fa·la'fel
fal'con
fal'con·er
fal'con·ry
fall
  fell fall'en fall'ing
fal·la'cious
fal·la'cious·ly
fal'la·cy
  ·cies
fall'en
fal·li·bil'i·ty
fal'li·ble
fal'li·bly
fall'ing-out'
fall'off'
fal·lo'pi·an tube
fall'out'
fal'low
false
  fals'er fals'est
false'hood'
false'ly
fal·set'to
fal'si·fi·ca'tion
fal'si·fi'er
fal'si·fy'
  ·fied' ·fy'ing
fal'si·ty
fal'ter
fal'ter·ing·ly
fame
famed
fa·mil'ial
fa·mil'iar
fa·mil'i·ar'i·ty
  ·ties
fa·mil'iar·i·za'tion
fa·mil'iar·ize'
  ·ized' ·iz'ing
fa·mil'iar·ly
fam'i·ly
  ·lies
fam'ine
fam'ish
fa'mous
fa'mous·ly
fan
  fanned fan'ning
fa·nat'ic
fa·nat'i·cal
fa·nat'i·cal·ly
fa·nat'i·cism'
fan'ci·er
fan'ci·ful
fan'ci·ful·ly
fan'ci·ly
fan'ci·ness
fan'cy
  ·cies

  ·ci·er ·ci·est
  ·cied ·cy·ing
fan'cy-free'
fan'cy·work'
fan'dom
fan'fare'
fang
fan·ta'si·a
fan'ta·size'
  ·sized' ·siz'ing
fan·tas'tic
fan·tas'ti·cal·ly
fan'ta·sy
  ·sies
far
  far'ther far'thest
far'ad
far'a·way'
farce
far'ci·cal
fare
  fared far'ing
  (*fee; get along;* see
  FAIR)
fare·well'
far'-fetched'
far'-flung'
fa·ri'na
farm
farm'er
farm'hand'
farm'house'
farm'ing
farm'yard'
far'o
far-off'
far'-out'
far·ra'go
  ·goes
far'-reach'ing
far'row
far'sight'ed
far'sight'ed·ness
far'ther
far'thest
far'thing
fas'ces
fas'ci·cle
fas'ci·nate'
  ·nat'ed ·nat'ing
fas'ci·na'tion
fas'ci·na'tor
fas'cism
fas'cist
fash'ion
fash'ion·a·ble
fash'ion·a·bly
fash'ion·er
fast
fas'ten
fas'ten·er
fas'ten·ing
fast'-food'
fas·tid'i·ous
fas·tid'i·ous·ly
fas·tid'i·ous·ness
fast'ness
fast'-talk'

fat
  fat'ter fat'test
fa'tal
fa'tal·ism'
fa'tal·ist
fa'tal·is'tic
fa'tal·is'ti·cal·ly
fa·tal'i·ty
  ·ties
fa'tal·ly
fat'back'
fate
fat'ed
fate'ful
fate'ful·ly
fa'ther
fa'ther·hood'
fa'ther-in-law'
  fa'thers-in-law'
fa'ther·land'
fa'ther·less
fa'ther·li·ness
fa'ther·ly
fath'om
fath'om·a·ble
fath'om·less
fa·tigue'
  ·tigued' ·tigu'ing
fat'ness
fat'ten
fat'ty
  ·ti·er ·ti·est
fa·tu'i·ty
fat'u·ous
fat'u·ous·ly
fau'cet
fault
fault'find'ing
fault'i·ly
fault'i·ness
fault'less
fault'y
  ·i·er ·i·est
faun
  (*deity;* see FAWN)
fau'na
faux pas'
fa'vor
fa'vor·a·ble
fa'vor·a·bly
fa'vored
fa'vor·ite
fa'vor·it·ism'
fawn
  (*deer; act
  servilely;* see
  FAUN)
fawn'er
faze
  fazed faz'ing
  (*disturb;* see
  PHASE)
fe'al·ty
fear
fear'ful
fear'ful·ly
fear'ful·ness
fear'less
fear'less·ly

fear'some
fea'si·bil'i·ty
fea'si·ble
fea'si·bly
feast
feat
  (*deed;* see FEET)
feath'er
feath'er·bed'ding
feath'er·weight'
feath'er·y
fea'ture
  ·tured ·tur·ing
fe'brile
Feb'ru·ar'y
fe'cal
fe'ces'
feck'less
fe'cund
fe'cun·date'
  ·dat'ed ·dat'ing
fe·cun'di·ty
fed'er·al
fed'er·al·ism'
fed'er·al·ist
fed'er·al·ize'
  ·ized' ·iz'ing
fed'er·ate'
  ·at'ed ·at'ing
fed'er·a'tion
fe·do'ra
fee
fee'ble
  ·bler ·blest
fee'ble·ness
fee'bly
feed
  fed feed'ing
feed'back'
feed'er
feed'stock'
feel
  felt feel'ing
feel'er
feel'ing
feet
  (*pl. of* foot; see
  FEAT)
feign
  (*pretend;* see FAIN)
feint
  (*pretense;* see
  FAINT)
feld'spar'
fe·lic'i·tate'
  ·tat'ed ·tat'ing
fe·lic'i·ta'tion
fe·lic'i·ta'tor
fe·lic'i·tous
fe·lic'i·ty
  ·ties
fe'line
fell
fel'low
fel'low·ship'
fel'on
fe·lo'ni·ous
fel'o·ny
  ·nies

felt
fe'male'
fem'i·nine
fem'i·nin'i·ty
fem'i·nism'
fem'i·nist
fem'o·ral
fe'mur
fen
fence
  fenced fenc'ing
fenc'er
fenc'ing
fend
fend'er
fen'es·tra'tion
fen'nel
fe'ral
fer'ment'
fer'men·ta'tion
fer'mi·on'
fern
fe·ro'cious
fe·ro'cious·ly
fe·roc'i·ty
fer'ret
fer'ric
Fer'ris wheel
fer'rous
fer'rule
  (*metal ring;* see
  FERULE)
fer'ry
  ·ries
  ·ried ·ry·ing
  (*boat;* see FAIRY)
fer'ry·boat'
fer'tile
fer·til'i·ty
fer·til·i·za'tion
fer'til·ize'
  ·ized' ·iz'ing
fer'til·iz'er
fer'ule
  (*stick;* see
  FERRULE)
fer'ven·cy
fer'vent
fer'vent·ly
fer'vid
fer'vid·ly
fer'vor
fes'cue
fes'tal
fes'ter
fes'ti·val
fes'tive
fes'tive·ly
fes'tive·ness
fes·tiv'i·ty
  ·ties
fes·toon'
fe'tal
fetch
fetch'ing
fete *or* fête
  fet'ed *or* fêt'ed
  fet'ing *or* fêt'ing
fet'id

fet'ish
fet'ish·ism'
fet'ish·ist
fet'lock'
fe'to·scope'
fet'ter
fet'tle
fet·tuc·ci'ne
fe'tus
  ·tus·es
feud
feu'dal
feu'dal·ism'
fe'ver
fe'ver·ish
fe'ver·ish·ly
few
fey
fez
  fez'zes
fi·an·cé' masc.
fi·an·cée' fem.
fi·as'co
  ·coes or ·cos
fi'at'
fib
  fibbed fib'bing
fib'ber (liar)
fi'ber (tissue)
fi'ber·board'
fi'ber·glass'
fi'ber-op'tic
fi·bril·la'tion
fi'broid'
fi·bro'sis
fi'brous
fib'u·la
  ·lae' or ·las
fick'le
fic'tion
fic'tion·al
fic'tion·al·ize'
  ·ized' ·iz'ing
fic·ti'tious
  (imaginary; see
  FACTITIOUS)
fic'tive
fi'cus
fid'dle
  ·dled ·dling
fid'dler
fid'dle·sticks'
fi·del'i·ty
  ·ties
fidg'et
fidg'et·y
fi·du'ci·ar'y
  ·ies
fie
fief'dom
field
field'er
field'-test'
field'work'
fiend
fiend'ish
fierce
  fierc'er fierc'est

fierce'ly
fierce'ness
fi'er·y
  ·i·er ·i·est
fi·es'ta
fife
fif'teen'
fif'teenth'
fifth
fif'ti·eth
fif'ty
  ·ties
fig
fight
  fought fight'ing
fight'er
fig'ment
fig'ur·a·tive'
fig'ur·a·tive'ly
fig'ure
  ·ured ·ur·ing
fig'ure·head'
fig'u·rine'
fil'a·ment
fil'bert
filch
file
  filed fil'ing
fil'er
fi·let' mi·gnon'
fil'i·al
fil'i·bus'ter
fil'i·gree'
fil'i·greed'
fil'ings
fill
fill'er
fil·let'
fill'-in'
fill'ing
fil'lip
fil'ly
  ·lies
film
film'strip'
film'y
  ·i·er ·i·est
fil'ter
  (strainer; see
  PHILTER)
fil'ter·a·ble
filth
filth'i·ly
filth'i·ness
filth'y
  ·i·er ·i·est
fil·tra'tion
fin
fi·na'gle
  ·gled ·gling
fi·na'gler
fi'nal
fi·na'le
fi'nal·ist
fi·nal'i·ty
fi'nal·i·za'tion
fi'nal·ize'
  ·ized' ·iz'ing

fi'nal·ly
fi·nance'
  ·nanced' ·nanc'ing
fi·nan'cial
fi·nan'cial·ly
fin·an·cier'
finch
find
  found find'ing
find'er
fine
  fin'er fin'est
  fined fin'ing
fine'ly
fine'ness
fin'er·y
fi·nesse'
  ·nessed' ·ness'ing
fine'-toothed'
fin'ger
fin'ger·board'
fin'ger·ling
fin'ger·nail'
fin'ger-paint'
fin'ger·print'
fin'ger·tip'
fin'i·al
fin'ick·i·ness
fin'ick·y
fin'is
fin'ish
fin'ished
fin'ish·er
fi'nite'
fink
Finn'ish
fin'ny
fiord
fir
  (tree; see FUR)
fire
  fired fir'ing
fire'arm'
fire'bomb'
fire'brand'
fire'break'
fire'brick'
fire'bug'
fire'crack'er
fire'damp'
fire'fight'
fire'fight'er
fire'fly'
fire'man
fire'place'
fire'plug'
fire'pow'er
fire'proof'
fire'side'
fire'storm'
fire'trap'
fire'truck'
fire'wa'ter
fire'wood'
fire'works'
firm
fir'ma·ment
firm'ly

firm'ness
first
first'-aid'
first'born'
first'-class'
first'hand'
first'ly
first'-rate'
first'-string'
firth
fis'cal
fis'cal·ly
fish
fish'er
fish'er·man
fish'er·y
  ·ies
fish'hook'
fish'i·ness
fish'ing
fish'tail'
fish'y
  ·i·er ·i·est
fis'sion
fis'sion·a·ble
fis'sure
fist
fist'i·cuffs'
fis'tu·la
  ·las or ·lae'
fit
  fit'ter fit'test
  fit'ted fit'ting
fit'ful
fit'ful·ly
fit'ful·ness
fit'ly
fit'ness
fit'ter
fit'ting
five
fix
fix'a·ble
fix'ate'
  ·at'ed ·at'ing
fix·a'tion
fix'a·tive
fixed
fix'ed·ly
fix'er
fix'ings'
fix'i·ty
fix'ture
fizz
fiz'zle
  ·zled ·zling
flab
flab'ber·gast'
flab'bi·ly
flab'bi·ness
flab'by
  ·bi·er ·bi·est
flac'cid
flack
flag
  flagged flag'ging
flag'el·late'
  ·lat'ed ·lat'ing

flag'el·la'tion
fla·gel'lum
  ·la or ·lums
flag'on
flag'pole'
fla'gran·cy
fla'grant
fla'grant·ly
flag'ship'
flag'staff'
flag'stone'
flail
flair
  (knack; see FLARE)
flak
flake
  flaked flak'ing
flak'i·ness
flak'y
  ·i·er ·i·est
flam·bé'
flam·boy'ance
flam·boy'ant
flam·boy'ant·ly
flame
  flamed flam'ing
fla·men'co
flame'out'
flame'throw'er
fla·min'go'
  ·gos' or ·goes'
flam'ma·bil'i·ty
flam'ma·ble
flange
flank
flan'nel
flan'nel·ette' or
  flan'nel·et'
flan'nel-mouthed'
flap
  flapped flap'ping
flap'jack'
flap'per
flare
  flared flar'ing
  (blaze; see FLAIR)
flare'-up'
flash
flash'back'
flash'bulb'
flash'cube'
flash'er
flash'-for'ward
flash'i·ly
flash'i·ness
flash'ing
flash'light'
flash'y
  ·i·er ·i·est
flask
flat
  flat'ter flat'test
  flat'ted flat'ting
flat'bed'
flat'boat'
flat'car'
flat'fish'
flat'-foot'ed

flat'i'ron
flat'ly
flat'ness
flat'-out'
flat'ten
flat'ter
flat'ter·er
flat'ter·ing·ly
flat'ter·y
flat'tish
flat'u·lence
flat'u·lent
flat'ware'
flaunt
flaunt'ing·ly
flau'tist
fla'vor
fla'vor·ful
fla'vor·ing
fla'vor·less
flaw
flaw'less
flaw'less·ly
flaw'less·ness
flax
flax'en
flax'seed'
flay
flea (insect)
fleck
fledg'ling
flee
  fled flee'ing
  (run)
fleece
  fleeced fleec'ing
fleec'er
fleec'i·ness
fleec'y
  ·i·er ·i·est
fleet
fleet'ing
fleet'ing·ly
fleet'ing·ness
fleet'ness
flesh
flesh'i·ness
flesh'y
  ·i·er ·i·est
fleur'-de-lis'
  fleurs'-de-lis'
flew
  (form of fly; see
  FLU, FLUE)
flex
flex'i·bil'i·ty
flex'i·ble
flex'i·bly
flex'time'
flick
flick'er
flied
fli'er
flight
flight'i·ness
flight'less
flight'y
  ·i·er ·i·est

flim′si·ly
flim′si·ness
flim′sy
  ·si·er ·si·est
flinch
fling
  flung fling′ing
flint
flint′y
  ·i·er ·i·est
flip
  flipped flip′ping
flip′pan·cy
flip′pant
flip′pant·ly
flip′per
flirt
flir·ta′tion
flir·ta′tious
flit
  flit′ted flit′ting
float
float′er
flock
flock′ing
floe
  (ice; see FLOW)
flog
  flogged flog′ging
flog′ger
flood
flood′gate′
flood′light′
floor
floor′board′
floor′ing
flop
  flopped flop′ping
flop′house′
flop′py
  ·pi·er ·pi·est
flo′ra
flo′ral
flo·res′cence
  (blooming; see
  FLUORESCENCE)
flo·res′cent
flo′ret
flor′id
Flor′i·da
flo·rid′i·ty
flor′in
flo′rist
floss
floss′y
  ·i·er ·i·est
flo·ta′tion
flo·til′la
flot′sam
flounce
  flounced
  flounc′ing
floun′der
flour
flour′ish
flour′y
flout
flout′er

flow
  (glide; see FLOE)
flow′chart′
flow′er
flow′ered
flow′er·i·ness
flow′er·pot′
flow′er·y
  ·i·er ·i·est
flown
flu
  (influenza; see
  FLEW, FLUE)
flub
  flubbed flub′bing
fluc′tu·ate′
  ·at′ed ·at′ing
fluc′tu·a′tion
flue
  (pipe; see FLEW,
  FLU)
flu′en·cy
flu′ent
flu′ent·ly
fluff
fluff′i·ness
fluff′y
  ·i·er ·i·est
flu′id
flu·id′i·ty
flu′id·ly
fluke
flung
flunk
flunk′y
  ·ies
flu′o·res′cence
  (light; see FLORES-
  CENCE)
flu′o·res′cent
flu′o·ri·date′
  ·dat′ed ·dat′ing
flu′o·ri·da′tion
flu′o·ride′
flu′o·rine′
flu′o·rite′
flu′o·ro·car′bon
flu′o·ro·scope′
flur′ry
  ·ries ·ried ·ry·ing
flush
flus′ter
flute
flut′ed
flut′ing
flut′ist
flut′ter
flut′ter·y
flux
fly
  flies
  flied fly′ing
  (baseball term)
fly
  flies
  flew flown fly′ing
  (insect; move
  through the air)
fly′a·ble
fly′by′ or fly′-by′

fly′-cast′
fly′catch′er
fly′leaf′
  ·leaves′
fly′pa′per
fly′speck′
fly′way′
fly′weight′
fly′wheel′
f′-num′ber
foal
foam
foam′y
  ·i·er ·i·est
fob
fo′cal
fo′cus
  ·cus·es or ·ci′
  ·cused or ·cussed
  ·cus·ing or
  ·cus·sing
fod′der
foe
fog
  fogged fog′ging
fog′gi·ness
fog′gy
  ·gi·er ·gi·est
fog′horn′
fo′gy
  ·gies
foi′ble
foil
foist
fold
fold′a·way′
fold′er
fo′li·age′
fo′lic acid
fo′li·o′
  ·os′
folk
  folk or folks
folk′lore′
folk′sy
  ·si·er ·si·est
fol′li·cle
fol′low
fol′low·er
fol′low·ing
fol′low-through′
fol′low-up′
fol′ly
  ·lies
fo·ment′
fo′men·ta′tion
fond
fon′dant
fon′dle
  ·dled ·dling
fond′ly
fond′ness
fon·due′
font
fon′ta·nel′ or
  fon′ta·nelle′
food
food′stuff′
fool

fool′er·y
fool′har·di·ness
fool′har·dy
fool′ish
fool′ish·ly
fool′ish·ness
fool′proof′
fools′cap′
foot
  feet
foot′age
foot′ball′
foot′bridge′
foot′-can′dle
foot′ed
foot′fall′
foot′hill′
foot′hold′
foot′ing
foot′less
foot′lights′
foot′lock′er
foot′loose′
foot′man
foot′note′
foot′path′
foot′-pound′
foot′print′
foot′sore′
foot′step′
foot′stool′
foot′wear′
foot′work′
fop
fop′pish
fop′pish·ly
for
  (in place of; see
  FORE, FOUR)
for′age
  ·aged ·ag·ing
for′ag·er
for′ay′
for·bear′
  (abstain; see FORE-
  BEAR)
for·bear′ance
for·bid′
  ·bade′ or ·bad′
  ·bid′den ·bid′ding
for·bid′ding
for·bid′ding·ly
force
  forced forc′ing
forced
forc′ed·ly
force′-feed′
force′ful
force′ful·ly
force′ful·ness
for′ceps′
for′ci·ble
for′ci·bly
ford
fore
  (front; see FOR,
  FOUR)
fore′arm′

fore′bear′
  (ancestor; see FOR-
  BEAR)
fore·bode′
  ·bod′ed ·bod′ing
fore·bod′ing
fore·cast′
  ·cast′ or ·cast′ed
  ·cast′ing
fore′cast′er
fore′cas·tle
fore·close′
fore·clo′sure
fore·doom′
fore′fa′ther
fore′fin′ger
fore′foot′
fore′front′
fore·go′
  ·went′ ·gone′
  ·go′ing
  (precede; see
  FORGO)
fore·go′ing
fore·gone′
fore′ground′
fore′hand′
fore′head′
for′eign
for′eign-born′
for′eign·er
fore′knowl′edge
fore′leg′
fore′lock′
fore′man
fore′mast′
fore′most′
fore′noon′
fo·ren′sic
fo·ren′si·cal·ly
fore·or·dain′
fore′paw′
fore′play′
fore′run′ner
fore′sail′
fore·see′
fore·see′a·ble
fore·se′er
fore·shad′ow
fore·short′en
fore′sight′
fore′skin′
for′est
fore·stall′
for′est·a′tion
for′est·er
for′est·ry
fore′taste′
fore·tell′
fore′thought′
for·ev′er
for·ev′er·more′
fore·warn′
fore′wom′an
fore′word′
  (preface; see FOR-
  WARD)
for′feit
for′fei·ture

for·gave′
forge
  forged forg′ing
forg′er
forg′er·y
  ·ies
for·get′
  ·got′, ·got′ten or
  ·got′, ·get′ting
for·get′ful
for·get′ful·ly
for·get′ful·ness
for·get′-me-not′
for·get′ta·ble
for·giv′a·ble
for·give′
  ·gave′ ·giv′en
  ·giv′ing
for·give′ness
for·giv′er
for·giv′ing
for·giv′ing·ly
for·go′
  ·went′ ·gone′
  ·go′ing
  (do without; see
  FOREGO)
for·got′
for·got′ten
fork
fork′lift′
for·lorn′
for·lorn′ly
form
for′mal
form·al′de·hyde′
for′mal·ism′
for·mal′i·ty
  ·ties
for′mal·i·za′tion
for′mal·ize′
  ·ized′ ·iz′ing
for′mal·ly
  (of form; see FOR-
  MERLY)
for′mat′
for·ma′tion
form′a·tive
for′mer
for′mer·ly
  (in the past; see
  FORMALLY)
for′mic
For·mi′ca
for′mi·da·ble
form′less
for′mu·la
  ·las or ·lae′
for′mu·late′
  ·lat′ed ·lat′ing
for′mu·la′tion
for′mu·la′tor
for′ni·cate′
  ·cat′ed ·cat′ing
for′ni·ca′tion
for′ni·ca′tor
for·sake′
  ·sook′ ·sak′en
  ·sak′ing

for·swear'
.swore' .sworn'
.swear'ing
for·syth'i·a
fort (*fortified place*)
forte (*special skill*)
forth
(*forward;* see
FOURTH)
forth'com'ing
forth'right'
forth'with'
for'ti·eth
for'ti·fi·ca'tion
for'ti·fi'er
for'ti·fy'
.fied' .fy'ing
for·tis'si·mo'
for'ti·tude'
fort'night'
fort'night'ly
for'tress
for·tu'i·tous
for·tu'i·tous·ly
for'tu·nate
for'tu·nate·ly
for'tune
for'tune·tell'er
for'tune·tell'ing
for'ty
.ties
fo'rum
for'ward
(*to the front;* see
FOREWORD)
fos'sil
fos'sil·ize'
.ized' .iz'ing
fos'ter
fought
foul
(*filthy;* see FOWL)
foul'mouthed'
foul'-up'
found
foun·da'tion
found'er *n.*
foun'der *v.*
found'ling'
found'ry
.ries
foun'tain
foun'tain·head'
four
(*number;* see FOR,
FORE)
four'-foot'ed
four'-in-hand'
four'score'
four'some
four'square'
four'teen'
four'teenth'
fourth
(*number;* see
FORTH)
fourth'-class'
four'-wheel'

fowl
(*bird;* see FOUL)
fox
fox'glove'
fox'hole'
fox'hound'
fox'y
.i·er .i·est
foy'er
fra'cas
frac'tion
frac'tion·al
frac'tious
frac'ture
.tured .tur·ing
frag'ile
fra·gil'i·ty
frag'ment
frag'men·tar'y
frag'men·ta'tion
fra'grance
fra'grant
frail
frail'ly
frail'ty
.ties
frame
framed fram'ing
fram'er
frame'-up'
frame'work'
franc (*coin*)
fran'chise'
.chised' .chis'ing
fran'gi·ble
frank (*candid*)
Frank'en·stein'
frank'furt·er
frank'in·cense'
frank'ly
frank'ness
fran'tic
fran'ti·cal·ly
frap·pé' *or* **frappe**
fra·ter'nal
fra·ter'ni·ty
.ties
frat'er·ni·za'tion
frat'er·nize'
.nized' .niz'ing
frat'ri·cide'
fraud
fraud'u·lence
fraud'u·lent
fraud'u·lent·ly
fraught
fray
fraz'zle
.zled .zling
freak
freak'ish
freak'out'
freck'le
.led .ling
free
fre'er fre'est
freed free'ing
free'bie *or* **·bee**

free'boot'er
freed'man
free'dom
free'-for-all'
free'-form'
free'hand'
free'hold'
free'lance' *or*
free'-lance'
.lanced' .lanc'ing
free'lanc'er *or*
free'-lanc'er
free'load'
free'load'er
free'ly
free'man
Free'ma'son
free'-stand'ing
free'stone'
free'think'er
free'way'
free'-wheel'ing
freez'a·ble
freeze
froze fro'zen
freez'ing
(*become ice;* see
FRIEZE)
freeze'-dry'
-dried' -dry'ing
freez'er
freight
freight'er
French
fre·net'ic
fre·net'i·cal·ly
fren'zied
fren'zy
.zies
fre'quen·cy
.cies
fre'quent
fre'quent·ly
fres'co
.coes *or* .cos
fresh
fresh'en
fresh'et
fresh'ly
fresh'man
fresh'ness
fresh'wa'ter
fret
fret'ted fret'ting
fret'ful
fret'ful·ly
fret'ful·ness
fret'work'
Freud'i·an
fri'a·ble
fri'ar
fric'as·see'
.seed' .see'ing
fric'tion
Fri'day
fried
fried'cake'
friend

friend'less
friend'li·ness
friend'ly
.li·er .li·est
friend'ship'
frieze
(*decoration;* see
FREEZE)
frig'ate
fright
fright'en
fright'en·ing·ly
fright'ful
fright'ful·ly
frig'id
fri·gid'i·ty
frig'id·ly
frill
frill'y
.i·er .i·est
fringe
fringed fring'ing
frip'per·y
.ies
fris'bee
frisk
frisk'i·ly
frisk'i·ness
frisk'y
.i·er .i·est
frit'ter
fri·vol'i·ty
.ties
friv'o·lous
friv'o·lous·ly
frizz *or* **friz**
frizzed friz'zing
friz'zi·ness
friz'zle
.zled .zling
friz'zly *or* **friz'zy**
fro
frock
frog
frog'man'
frol'ic
·icked ·ick·ing
frol'ick·er
frol'ic·some
from
frond
front
front'age
fron'tal
fron·tier'
fron·tiers'man
fron'tis·piece'
front'-run'ner
frost
frost'bite'
frost'bit'ten
frost'ing
frost'y
.i·er .i·est
froth
froth'y
.i·er .i·est
frown
frow'zi·ly

frow'zi·ness
frow'zy
.zi·er .zi·est
froze
fro'zen
fruc'ti·fy'
.fied' .fy'ing
fruc'tose'
fru'gal
fru·gal'i·ty
fru'gal·ly
fruit
fruit'cake'
fruit'ful
fru·i'tion
fruit'less
fruit'less·ly
fruit'wood'
fruit'y
.i·er .i·est
frump
frump'ish *or*
frump'y
frus'trate'
.trat'ed .trat'ing
frus·tra'tion
fry
fries
fried fry'ing
fry'er
fuch'sia
fud'dy-dud'dy
.dies
fudge
fudged fudg'ing
fu'el
.eled *or* .elled
.el·ing *or* .el·ling
fu'gi·tive
fugue
ful'crum
ful·fill' *or* **·fil'**
.filled' .fill'ing
ful·fill'ment *or*
.fil'ment
full
full'back'
full'-blood'ed
full'-blown'
full'-bod'ied
full'er
full'-fledged'
full'ness
full'-scale'
full'-time'
full'y
ful'mi·nate'
.nat'ed .nat'ing
ful'mi·na'tion
ful'some
fum'ble
.bled .bling
fum'bler
fume
fumed fum'ing
fu'mi·gate'
.gat'ed .gat'ing
fu'mi·ga'tion
fu'mi·ga'tor

fum'y
.i·er .i·est
fun
func'tion
func'tion·al
func'tion·ar'y
.ies
func'tion·less
fund
fun'da·men'tal
fun'da·men'tal·ism'
fun'da·men'tal·ist
fun'da·men'tal·ly
fund'-rais'er
fu'ner·al
fu·ne're·al
fu·ne're·al·ly
fun'gi·cide'
fun'gous *adj.*
fun'gus *n.*
.gi' *or* ·gus·es
fu·nic'u·lar
funk
funk'y
.i·er .i·est
fun'nel
-neled *or* -nelled
.nel·ing *or*
.nel·ling
fun'nies
fun'ni·ness
fun'ny
.ni·er .ni·est
fur
(*hair;* see FIR)
fur'be·low'
fur'bish
fu'ri·ous
fu'ri·ous·ly
furl
fur'long'
fur'lough
fur'nace
fur'nish
fur'nish·ings
fur'ni·ture
fu'ror'
fur'ri·er
fur'ri·ness
fur'ring
fur'row
fur'ry
.ri·er .ri·est
fur'ther
fur'ther·ance
fur'ther·more'
fur'thest
fur'tive
fur'tive·ly
fur'tive·ness
fu'ry
furze
fuse
fused fus'ing
fu'se·lage'
fu'si·ble
fu'si·lier' *or*
fu'sil·eer'

fu'sil·lade'
fu'sion
fuss
fuss'budg'et
fuss'i·ness
fuss'y
 ·i·er ·i·est
fus'tian
fus'ti·ness
fus'ty
 ·ti·er ·ti·est
fu'tile
fu·til'i·ty
fu'ton'
fu'ture
fu'tur·is'tic
fu·tu'ri·ty
 ·ties
fuzz
fuzz'i·ness
fuzz'y
 ·i·er ·i·est

G

gab
 gabbed gab'bing
gab'ar·dine'
gab'ble
 ·bled ·bling
gab'by
 ·bi·er ·bi·est
ga'ble
gad
 gad'ded gad'ding
gad'a·bout'
gad'fly'
gadg'et
gaff (a spar)
gaffe (blunder)
gag
 gagged gag'ging
gage
 (pledge; see
 GAUGE)
gag'gle
gai'e·ty
gai'ly
gain
gain'er
gain'ful
gain'ful·ly
gain'say'
gain'say'er
gait
 (way of walking;
 see GATE)
gai'ter
gal
ga'la
ga·lac'tic
gal'ax·y
 ·ies
gale
ga·le'na
gall
gal'lant

gal'lant·ry
 ·ries
gall'blad'der
gal'le·on
gal·le·ri'a
gal'ler·y
 ·ies
gal'ley
 ·leys
gal'li·um
gal'li·vant'
gal'lon
gal'lop
gal'lows
 ·lows or ·lows·es
gall'stone'
ga·lore'
ga·losh' or ·loshe'
gal·van'ic
gal'va·nism'
gal'va·nize'
 ·nized' ·niz'ing
gal·va·nom'e·ter
gam'bit
gam'ble
 ·bled ·bling
 (risk; see GAMBOL)
gam'bler
gam'bol
 ·boled or ·bolled
 ·bol·ing or
 ·bol·ling
 (frolic; see
 GAMBLE)
gam'brel
game
 gamed gam'ing
game'cock'
game'keep'er
game'ly
game'ness
games'man·ship'
gam'ete
gam'in
gam'i·ness
gam'ma
gam'ut
gam'y
 ·i·er ·i·est
gan'der
gang
gan'gling
gan'gli·on
 ·gli·a or ·gli·ons
gan'gly
gang'plank'
gang'grene'
gan'gre·nous
gang'ster
gang'ster·ism'
gang'way'
gant'let
 (punishment; see
 GAUNTLET)
gan'try
 ·tries
gap
 gapped gap'ping
gape
 gaped gap'ing

gar
 gar or gars
ga·rage'
garb
gar'bage
gar'ble
 ·bled ·bling
gar·çon'
gar'den
gar'den·er
gar·de'ni·a
gar·gan'tu·an
gar'gle
 ·gled ·gling
gar'goyle'
gar'ish
gar'land
gar'lic
gar'lick·y
gar'ment
gar'ner
gar'net
gar'nish
gar'nish·ee'
 ·eed' ·ee'ing
gar'nish·ment
gar'ret
gar'ri·son
gar·rote'
 ·rot'ed or ·rot'ted
 ·rot'ing or ·rot'ting
gar·ru'li·ty
gar'ru·lous
gar'ter
gas
 gas'es or gas'ses
 gassed gas'sing
gas'e·ous
gash
gas'ket
gas'light'
gas'o·hol'
gas'o·line'
gasp
gas'sy
 ·si·er ·si·est
gas'tric
gas·tri'tis
gas'tro·nom'ic or
 ·nom'i·cal
gas·tron'o·my
gas'tro·pod'
gate
 (door; see GAIT)
gate'-crash'er
gate'way'
gath'er
gath'er·ing
ga'tor or 'ga'·
gauche
 (lacking grace; see
 GOUACHE)
gau'che·rie
gau'cho
 ·chos
gaud'i·ly
gaud'i·ness
gaud'y
 ·i·er ·i·est

gauge
 gauged gaug'ing
 (measure; see
 GAGE)
gaunt
gaunt'let
 (armored glove;
 see GANTLET)
gauze
gauz'y
 ·i·er ·i·est
gave
gav'el
gawk
gawk'i·ness
gawk'y
 ·i·er ·i·est
gay
gay'e·ty
gay'ly
gay'ness
gaze
 gazed gaz'ing
ga·ze'bo
 ·bos or ·boes
ga·zelle'
ga·zette'
gaz'et·teer'
gaz·pa'cho
gear
gear'box
gear'shift'
gear'wheel'
geck'o
 ·os or ·oes
gas
geese
gee'zer
ge·fil'te fish
Gei'ger counter
gei'sha
 ·sha or ·shas
gel
 gelled gel'ling
gel'a·tin
ge·lat'i·nous
geld
 geld'ed or gelt
 geld'ing
gel'id
gem
Gem'i·ni'
gem·ol'o·gy or
 gem·mol'·
gem·ol'o·gist or
 gem·mol'·
gem'stone'
gen·darme'
gen'der
gene
ge'ne·a·log'i·cal
ge'ne·al'o·gist
ge'ne·al'o·gy
 ·gies
gen'er·a
gen'er·al
gen'er·al'i·ty
 ·ties
gen'er·al·ize'
 ·ized' ·iz'ing

gen'er·al·ly
gen'er·al·ship'
gen'er·ate'
 ·at'ed ·at'ing
gen'er·a'tion
gen'er·a'tion·al
gen'er·a'tive
gen'er·a'tor
ge·ner'ic
ge·ner'i·cal·ly
gen'er·os'i·ty
gen'er·ous
gen'er·ous·ly
gen'e·sis
ge·net'ic
ge·net'i·cal·ly
ge·net'i·cist
gen'i·al
ge·ni·al'i·ty
gen'i·al·ly
ge'nie
gen'i·tal
gen'i·tals or
 gen'i·ta'li·a
gen'i·tive
gen'i·us
gen'o·cide'
gen're
gent
gen·teel'
gen'tian
gen'tile'
gen·til'i·ty
gen'tle
 ·tler ·tlest
gen'tle·folk'
gen'tle·man
gen'tle·man·ly
gen'tle·ness
gen'tle·wom'an
gen'tly
gen'tri·fi·ca'tion
gen'tri·fy'
 ·fied' ·fy'ing
gen'try
gen'u·flect'
gen'u·flec'tion
gen'u·ine
gen'u·ine·ly
ge'nus
 gen'er·a or
 ge'nus·es
ge'o·cen'tric
ge'o·cen'tri·cal·ly
ge'ode'
ge'o·des'ic
ge'o·det'ic
ge·og'ra·pher
ge'o·graph'ic
ge'o·graph'i·cal
ge'o·graph'i·cal·ly
ge·og'ra·phy
ge'o·log'ic
ge'o·log'i·cal
ge'o·log'i·cal·ly
ge·ol'o·gist
ge·ol'o·gy

ge'o·mag·net'ic
ge'o·mag'ne·tism'
ge'o·met'ric
ge'o·met'ri·cal
ge'o·met'ri·cal·ly
ge·om'e·try
ge'o·phys'i·cal
ge'o·phys'ics
Geor'gia
ge'o·sta'tion·ar'y
ge'o·syn'chro·nous
ge'o·ther'mic
ge·ra'ni·um
ger'bil
ger'i·at'ric
germ
Ger'man
ger·mane'
ger·ma'ni·um
ger'mi·ci'dal
ger'mi·cide'
ger'mi·nal
ger'mi·nate'
 ·nat'ed ·nat'ing
ger'mi·na'tion
ger'on·tol'o·gist
ger'on·tol'o·gy
ger'ry·man'der
ger'und
ges'tate
 ·tat·ed ·tat·ing
ges·ta'tion
ges·tic'u·late'
 ·lat'ed ·lat'ing
ges·tic'u·la'tion
ges'ture
 ·tured ·tur·ing
get
 got, got'ten or got,
 get'ting
get'a·way'
get'-to·geth'er
get'-up'
gew'gaw'
gey'ser
ghast'ly
 ·li·er ·li·est
gher'kin
ghet'to
 ·tos or ·toes
ghet'to·ize'
 ·ized' ·iz'ing
ghost
ghost'ly
ghost'write'
ghost'writ'er
ghoul
ghoul'ish
gi'ant
gi'ant·ess fem.
gib'ber
gib'ber·ish
gib'bet
gib'bon
gibe
 gibed gib'ing
 (taunt; see JIBE)
gib'let

gid'di·ness
gid'dy
  ·di·er ·di·est
gift
gift'ed
gig
gi·gan'tic
gig'gle
  ·gled ·gling
gig'gly
gig'o·lo'
  ·los
Gi'la monster
gild
  gild'ed or gilt
  gild'ing
  (coat with gold;
  see GUILD)
gild'ing
gill
gilt
  (gold; see GUILT)
gilt'-edged'
gim'bals
gim'crack'
gim'let
gim'mick
gimp'y
gin
gin'ger
gin'ger·bread'
gin'ger·ly
gin'ger·snap'
gin'ger·y
ging'ham
gin·gi·vi'tis
gink'go
  ·goes
gi·raffe'
gird
  gird'ed or girt
  gird'ing
gird'er
gir'dle
  ·dled ·dling
girl
girl'hood'
girl'ish
girth
gist
give
  gave giv'en giv'ing
give'a·way'
give'back'
giv'er
giz'mo
  ·mos
giz'zard
gla·cé'
  ·céed' ·cé'ing
gla'cial
gla'cier
glad
  glad'der glad'dest
glad'den
glade
glad'-hand'er
glad'i·a'tor
glad'i·a·to'ri·al

glad'i·o'lus
  ·lus·es or ·li'
glad'ly
glad'ness
glad'some
glam'or·i·za'tion
glam'or·ize'
  ·ized' ·iz'ing
glam'or·ous or
  ·our·ous
glam'our or ·or
glance
  glanced glanc'ing
gland
glan'du·lar
glans
glare
  glared glar'ing
glar'ing·ly
glas'nost
glass
glass'ful'
glass'i·ness
glass'ware'
glass'y
  ·i·er ·i·est
glau·co'ma
glaze
  glazed glaz'ing
gla'zier
gleam
glean
glean'ings
glee
glee'ful
glen
glib
  glib'ber glib'best
glib'ly
glib'ness
glide
  glid'ed glid'ing
glid'er
glim'mer
glimpse
  glimpsed
  glimps'ing
glint
glis·san'do
  ·di or ·dos
glis'ten
glitch
glit'ter
glit'ter·y
glitz
glitz'y
  ·i·er ·i·est
gloam'ing
gloat
glob
glob'al
glob'al·ism'
glob'al·ly
globe
globe'-trot'ter
glob'u·lar
glob'ule'
glob'u·lin

gloom
gloom'y
  ·i·er ·i·est
glop
glop'py
  ·pi·er ·pi·est
glo·ri·fi·ca'tion
glo'ri·fy'
  ·fied' ·fy'ing
glo'ri·ous
glo'ri·ous·ly
glo'ry
  ·ries
  ·ried ·ry·ing
gloss
glos'sa·ry
  ·ries
glos'so·la'li·a
gloss'y
  ·i·er ·i·est
glot'tal
glot'tis
glove
  gloved glov'ing
glow
glow'er
glow'ing·ly
glow'worm'
glu'cose'
glue
  glued glu'ing
glu'ey
  glu'i·er glu'i·est
glum
  glum'mer
  glum'mest
glum'ly
glut
  glut'ted glut'ting
glu'ten
glu'ten·ous (having
  gluten)
glu'ti·nous (gluey)
glut'ton
glut'ton·ous
  (greedy)
glut'ton·y
glyc'er·in
glyc'er·ol'
gly'co·gen
gly'col'
gnarl
gnash
gnat
gnaw
gneiss
gnome
gno'mic
gnom'ish
gnu
go
  goes
  went gone go'ing
goad
go'-a·head'
goal
goal'ie
goal'keep'er
goal'ten'der

goat
goat'ee'
goat'herd'
goat'skin'
gob
gob'ble
  ·bled ·bling
gob'ble·dy·gook'
gob'bler
go'-be·tween'
gob'let
gob'lin
god
god'child'
god'daugh'ter
god'dess
god'fa'ther
god'head'
god'hood'
god'less
god'like'
god'li·ness
god'ly
  ·li·er ·li·est
god'moth'er
god'par'ent
god'send'
god'son'
go'fer or go'-fer
go'-get'ter
gog'gle
  ·gled ·gling
go'-go'
go'ing-ov'er
go'ings-on'
goi'ter or ·tre
gold
gold'brick'
gold'en
gold'en·rod'
gold'-filled'
gold'finch'
gold'fish'
gold'smith'
golf
golf'er
gol'ly
go'nad'
gon'do·la
gon'do·lier'
gone
gon'er
gong
gon'or·rhe'a or
  ·rhoe'a
goo
goo'ber
good
  bet'ter best
good'bye' or
  good'-bye'
good'-heart'ed
go'-a·head'
good'-hu'mored
good'-look'ing
good'ly
  ·li·er ·li·est
good'-na'tured

good'-na'tured·ly
good'ness
good'-sized'
good'-tem'pered
good'will'
good'y
  ·ies
goo'ey
  goo'i·er goo'i·est
goof
goof'y
  ·i·er ·i·est
gook
goon
goop
goose
  geese
goose'ber'ry
go'pher
gore
gorge
  gorged gorg'ing
gor'geous
gor'geous·ly
go·ril'la
  (ape; see GUER-
  RILLA)
gor'mand·ize'
  ·ized' ·iz'ing
gorp
gorse
gor'y
  ·i·er ·i·est
gosh
gos'ling
gos'pel
gos'sa·mer
gos'sip
gos'sip·y
got
Goth'ic
got'ten
gouache
  (painting; see
  GAUCHE)
Gou'da cheese
gouge
  gouged goug'ing
gou'lash'
gou'ra·mi
  ·mies or ·mi
gourd
gour·mand'
gour'met
gout
gov'ern
gov'ern·a·ble
gov'ern·ance
gov'ern·ess
gov'ern·ment
gov'ern·men'tal
gov'er·nor
gov'er·nor·ship'
gown
grab
  grabbed grab'bing
grace
  graced grac'ing
grace'ful

grace'ful·ly
grace'ful·ness
grace'less
grace'less·ly
grace'less·ness
gra'cious
gra'cious·ly
gra'cious·ness
grack'le
grad
gra·da'tion
grade
  grad'ed grad'ing
gra'di·ent
grad'u·al
grad'u·al·ism'
grad'u·al·ly
grad'u·ate'
  ·at'ed ·at'ing
grad'u·a'tion
graf·fi'to
  ·ti
graft
gra'ham
grain
grain'i·ness
grain'y
  ·i·er ·i·est
gram
gram'mar
gram·mar'i·an
gram·mat'i·cal
gram·mat'i·cal·ly
gran'a·ry
  ·ries
grand
grand'child'
grand'daugh'ter
gran·dee'
gran'deur
grand'fa'ther
gran·dil'o·quence
gran·dil'o·quent
gran'di·ose'
grand'ma
grand'mas'ter
grand'moth'er
grand'pa
grand'par'ent
grand'son'
grand'stand'
grange
gran'ite
gran'ny or ·nie
  ·nies
gran·o'la
grant
grant'-in-aid'
  grants'-in-aid'
gran'u·lar
gran'u·lar'·i·ty
gran'u·late'
  ·lat'ed ·lat'ing
gran'u·la'tion
gran'ule
grape
grape'fruit'
grape'vine'

graph
graph'ic
graph'i·cal·ly
graph'ite
graph·ol'o·gist
graph·ol'o·gy
grap'nel
grap'ple
　·pled ·pling
grasp
grass
grass'hop'per
grass'y
　·i·er ·i·est
grate
　grat'ed grat'ing
grate'ful
grate'ful·ly
grat'er
grat'i·fi·ca'tion
grat'i·fy'
　·fied' ·fy'ing
gra'tis
grat'i·tude'
gra·tu'i·tous
gra·tu'i·ty
　·ties
gra·va'men
　·va'mens or
　·vam'i·na
grave
　grav'er grav'est
grav'el
grav'el·ly (full of
　gravel)
grave'ly (seriously)
grav'en
grave'ness
grave'stone'
grave'yard'
grav'id
grav'i·tate'
　·tat'ed ·tat'ing
grav'i·ta'tion
grav'i·ta'tion·al
grav'i·ty
　·ties
gra'vy
　·vies
gray
gray'beard'
gray'ish
gray'ness
graze
　grazed graz'ing
grease
　greased greas'ing
grease'paint'
greas'i·ness
greas'y
　·i·er ·i·est
great
great'-grand'·child'
great'-
　grand'·par'ent
great'heart'ed
great'ly
great'ness
grebe

greed
greed'i·ly
greed'i·ness
greed'y
　·i·er ·i·est
Greek
green
green'back'
green'belt'
green'bri'er
green'er·y
green'gro'cer
green'horn'
green'house'
green'ish
green'ness
green'room'
greens'keep'er
green'sward'
green'wood'
greet
greet'ing
gre·gar'i·ous
grem'lin
gre·nade'
gren'a·dier'
gren'a·dine'
grew
grey'hound'
grid
grid'dle
grid'dle·cake'
grid'i·ron
grid'lock'
grief
griev'ance
grieve
　grieved griev'ing
griev'ous
grif'fin
grill (barbecue)
grille (grating)
grim
　grim'mer
　grim'mest
gri·mace'
　·maced' ·mac'ing
grime
grim'ly
grim'y
　·i·er ·i·est
grin
　grinned grin'ning
grind
　ground grind'ing
grind'er
grind'stone'
grin'go
　·gos
grip
　gripped or gript
　grip'ping
gripe
　griped grip'ing
grippe
grip'per
gris'li·ness

gris'ly
　·li·er ·li·est
　(horrible)
grist
gris'tle
gris'tly (of gristle)
grist'mill'
grit
　grit'ted grit'ting
grit'ty
　·ti·er ·ti·est
griz'zled
griz'zly
　·zlies
　·zli·er ·zli·est
groan
gro'cer
gro'cer·y
　·ies
grog
grog'gi·ness
grog'gy
　·gi·er ·gi·est
groin
grom'met
groom
groove
　grooved groov'ing
groov'y
　·i·er ·i·est
grope
　groped grop'ing
grop'er
gros'beak'
gros'grain'
gross
gross'ly
gro·tesque'
gro·tesque'ly
grot'to
　·toes or ·tos
grouch
grouch'y
　·i·er ·i·est
ground
ground'er
ground'hog'
ground'less
grounds'keep'er
ground'work'
group
grou'per
group'ie
grouse
　grouse
　groused grous'ing
grout
grove
grov'el
　·eled or ·elled
　·el·ing or ·el·ling
grow
　grew grown
　grow'ing
grow'er
growl
grown'-up'
growth
grub
　grubbed grub'bing

grub'by
　·bi·er ·bi·est
grub'stake'
grudge
　grudged grudg'ing
grudg'ing·ly
gru'el
gru'el·ing or ·ling
grue'some
gruff
gruff'ly
grum'ble
　·bled ·bling
grump'y
　·i·er ·i·est
grun'gy
　·gi·er ·gi·est
grun'ion
grunt
Gru·yère' cheese
gua'no
guar'an·tee'
　·teed' ·tee'ing
guar'an·tor'
guar'an·ty
　·ties
　·tied ·ty·ing
guard
guard'ed
guard'house'
guard'i·an
guard'i·an·ship'
guard'rail'
gua'va
gu·ber·na·to'ri·al
Guern'sey
guer·ril'la or gue·
　(soldier; see GO-
　RILLA)
guess
guess'work'
guest
guff
guf·faw'
guid'ance
guide
　guid'ed guid'ing
guide'book'
guide'line'
guild
　(union; see GILD)
guil'der
guile
guile'less
guil'lo·tine'
　·tined' ·tin'ing
guilt
　(blame; see GILT)
guilt'i·ly
guilt'less
guilt'y
　·i·er ·i·est
guin'ea
guise
gui·tar'
gui·tar'ist
gulch
gulf
gull

gul'let
gul'li·bil'i·ty
gul'li·ble
gul'ly
　·lies
gulp
gum
　gummed
　gum'ming
gum'bo
gum'drop'
gum'my
　·mi·er ·mi·est
gump'tion
gun
　gunned gun'ning
gun'boat'
gun'fight'
gun'fire'
gung'-ho'
gunk
gun'man
gun'met'al
gun'ner
gun'ner·y
gun'ny
　·nies
gun'ny·sack'
gun'play'
gun'pow'der
gun'ship'
gun'shot'
gun'-shy'
gun'smith'
gun'wale
gup'py
　·pies
gur'gle
　·gled ·gling
gur'ney
　·neys
gu'ru'
gush
gush'er
gush'y
　·i·er ·i·est
gus'set
gus'sy or gus'sie
　·sied ·sy·ing
gust
gus'ta·to'ry
gus'to
gust'y
　·i·er ·i·est
gut
　gut'ted gut'ting
gut'less
guts'y
　·i·er ·i·est
gut'ter
gut'tur·al
guy
guz'zle
　·zled ·zling
gym
gym·na'si·um
　·si·ums or ·si·a
gym'nast'
gym·nas'tic

gym'no·sperm'
gy'ne·col'o·gist
gy'ne·col'o·gy
gyp
　gypped gyp'ping
gyp'sum
Gyp'sy
　·sies
gy'rate'
　·rat'ed ·rat'ing
gy·ra'tion
gy'ro
　·ros
gy'ro·scope'

H

ha'be·as cor'pus
hab'er·dash'er
hab'er·dash'er·y
hab'it
hab'it·a·ble
hab'i·tat'
hab'i·ta'tion
hab'it-form'ing
ha·bit'u·al
ha·bit'u·al·ly
ha·bit'u·ate'
　·at'ed ·at'ing
ha·bit'u·é'
ha'ci·en'da
hack
hack'er
hack'le
hack'ney
　·neys
hack'neyed'
hack'saw'
had
had'dock
Ha'des'
haft
hag
hag'gard
hag'gish
hag'gle
　·gled ·gling
hag'gler
hah
hai'ku'
hail
　(ice; to call out to;
　see HALE)
hail'stone'
hail'storm'
hair
　(fur; see HARE)
hair'ball'
hair'breadth'
hair'cut'
hair'do'
　·dos'
hair'dress'er
hair'i·ness
hair'less
hair'like'
hair'line'

hair'piece'
hair'pin'
hair'-rais'ing
hairs'breadth'
hair'split'ting
hair'spring'
hair'y
  ·i·er ·i·est
  (*hair-covered;* see
  HARRY)
hake
hal'berd
hal'cy·on
hale
  hal'er hal'est
  (*healthy;* see HAIL)
half
  halves
half'-and-half'
half'back'
half'heart'ed
half'heart'ed·ly
half'-life'
half'-mast'
half'pen·ny
  ·pence *or* ·pen·nies
half'track'
half'way'
half'-wit'
half'-wit'ted
hal'i·but
hal'ite'
hal'i·to'sis
hall
  (*room;* see HAUL)
hal'le·lu'jah *or* ·iah
hall'mark'
hal·loo'
  ·looed' ·loo'ing
hal'low
  (*venerate;* see
  HALO)
hal'lowed
Hal'low·een'
hal·lu'ci·nate'
  ·nat'ed ·nat'ing
hal·lu'ci·na'tion
hal·lu'ci·na·to'ry
hal·lu'ci·no·gen
hall'way'
ha'lo
  ·los *or* ·loes
  (*ring of light;* see
  HALLOW)
hal'o·gen
halt
hal'ter
halve
  halved halv'ing
  (*cut in half;* see
  HAVE)
halves
hal'yard
ham
ham'burg
ham'burg·er
ham'let
ham'mer
ham'mer·er
ham'mer·head'

ham'mer·toe'
ham'mock
ham'my
  ·mi·er ·mi·est
ham'per
ham'ster
ham'string'
ham'strung'
hand
hand'bag'
hand'ball'
hand'bar'row
hand'bill'
hand'book'
hand'breadth'
hand'car'
hand'cart'
hand'clasp'
hand'craft'
hand'cuff'
hand'ful'
  ·fuls'
hand'gun'
hand'i·cap'
  ·capped' ·cap'ping
hand'i·cap'per
hand'i·craft'
hand'i·ly
hand'i·ness
hand'i·work'
hand'ker·chief'
han'dle
  ·dled ·dling
han'dle·bar'
han'dler
hand'made' (*made
  by hand*)
hand'maid' (*ser-
  vant*)
hand'maid'en
hand'-me-down'
hand'out'
hand'pick'
hand'rail'
hand'set'
hand'shake'
hands'-off'
hand'some
  (*good-looking;* see
  HANSOM)
hand'spring'
hand'-to-hand'
hand'-to-mouth'
hand'work'
hand'writ'ing
hand'writ'ten
hand'y
  ·i·er ·i·est
hand'y·man'
hang
  hung hang'ing
  (*suspend*)
hang
  hanged hang'ing
  (*put to death*)
hang'ar (*aircraft
  shed*)

hang'er (*garment
  holder*)
hang'ing
hang'man
hang'nail'
hang'o'ver
hang'-up'
hank
han'ker
han'ker·ing
han'ky-pan'ky
han'som
  (*carriage;* see
  HANDSOME)
Ha'nu·ka'
hap
hap'haz'ard
hap'less
hap'loid'
hap'pen
hap'pen·ing
hap'pen·stance'
hap'pi·ly
hap'pi·ness
hap'py
  ·pi·er ·pi·est
hap'py-go-luck'y
har'a·kir'i
ha·rangue'
  ·rangued' ·ran-
  gu'ing
ha·rangu'er
har·ass'
har·ass'ment
har'bin·ger
har'bor
hard
hard'back'
hard'ball'
hard'-bit'ten
hard'-boiled'
hard'-bound'
hard'-core'
hard'cov'er
hard'en
hard'en·er
hard'head'ed
hard'heart'ed
har'di·hood'
har'di·ly
  (*in a hardy way;*
  see HARDLY,
  HEARTILY)
har'di·ness
hard'-line'
hard'-lin'er
hard'ly
  (*barely;* see
  HARDILY, HEARTILY)
hard'ness
hard'-nosed'
hard'ship'
hard'stand'
hard'tack'
hard'top'
hard'ware'
hard'wood'
har'dy
  ·di·er ·di·est

hare
  (*rabbit;* see HAIR)
hare'brained'
hare'lip'
ha'rem
hark
hark'en
har'le·quin
har'lot
har'lot·ry
harm
harm'ful
harm'ful·ly
harm'less
harm'less·ly
har·mon'ic
har·mon'i·ca
har·mon'i·cal·ly
har·mo'ni·ous
har·mo'ni·ous·ly
har'mo·ni·za'tion
har'mo·nize'
  ·nized' ·niz'ing
har'mo·niz'er
har'mo·ny
  ·nies
har'ness
harp
harp'ist
har·poon'
harp'si·chord'
Har'py
  ·pies
har'ri·dan
har'ri·er
har'row
har'row·ing
har'ry
  ·ried ·ry·ing
  (*harass;* see HAIRY)
harsh
harsh'ly
harsh'ness
hart
  (*deer;* see HEART)
har'te·beest'
har'um-scar'um
har'vest
har'vest·er
has
has'-been'
hash
hash'ish'
hasp
has'sle
  ·sled ·sling
has'sock
hast
haste
has'ten
hast'i·ly
hast'i·ness
hast'y
  ·i·er ·i·est
hat
hatch
hatch'back'
hat'check'

hatch'er·y
  ·ies
hatch'et
hatch'way'
hate
  hat'ed hat'ing
hate'ful
hate'ful·ly
hate'ful·ness
hat'er
hath
ha'tred
hat'ter
haugh'ti·ly
haugh'ti·ness
haugh'ty
  ·ti·er ·ti·est
haul
  (*pull;* see HALL)
haunch
haunt
haunt'ed
haunt'ing
hau·teur'
have
  had hav'ing
  (*possess;* see
  HALVE)
ha'ven
have'-not'
hav'er·sack'
hav'oc
haw
Ha·wai'i
Ha·wai'ian
hawk
hawk'er
hawk'-eyed'
haw'ser
haw'thorn'
hay
  (*dried grass;* see
  HEY)
hay'loft'
hay'stack'
hay'wire'
haz'ard
haz'ard·ous
haze
  hazed haz'ing
ha'zel
ha'zel·nut'
ha'zi·ly
ha'zi·ness
ha'zy
  ·zi·er ·zi·est
H'-bomb'
he
  they
head
head'ache'
head'board'
head'dress'
head'first'
head'gear'
head'ing
head'land'
head'less
head'light'

head'line'
  ·lined' ·lin'ing
head'long'
head'mas'ter
head'mis'tress
head'-on'
head'phone'
head'quar'ters
head'rest'
head'room'
head'set'
head'stone'
head'strong'
head'wa'ters
head'way'
head'y
  ·i·er ·i·est
heal
  (*cure;* see HEEL,
  HE'LL)
heal'er
health
health'ful
health'i·ness
health'y
  ·i·er ·i·est
heap
hear
  heard hear'ing
  (*listen;* see HERE)
heard
  (*form of* hear; see
  HERD)
hear'er
hear'ing
heark'en
hear'say'
hearse
heart
  (*organ;* see HART)
heart'ache'
heart'beat'
heart'break'
heart'bro'ken
heart'burn'
heart'en
heart'felt'
hearth
heart'i·ly
  (*in a hearty way;*
  see HARDILY,
  HARDLY)
heart'i·ness
heart'land'
heart'less
heart'less·ly
heart'-rend'ing
heart'sick'
heart'strings'
heart'-to-heart'
heart'warm'ing
heart'y
  ·i·er ·i·est
heat
heat'ed
heat'ed·ly
heat'er
heath
hea'then

heath'er
heat'stroke'
heave
   heaved *or* hove
   heav'ing
heave'-ho'
heav'en
heav'en·ly
heav'i·ly
heav'i·ness
heav'y
   ·ies
   ·i·er ·i·est
heav'y-du'ty
heav'y-hand'ed
heav'y-heart'ed
heav'y-set'
heav'y-weight'
He·bra'ic
He'brew'
heck
heck'le
   ·led ·ling
heck'ler
hec'tare'
hec'tic
hec'ti·cal·ly
hedge
   hedged hedg'ing
hedge'hog'
he'don·ism'
he'don·ist
he'do·nis'tic
heed
heed'ful
heed'less
heed'less·ly
heed'less·ness
hee'haw'
heel
   (*part of foot;* see
   HEAL, HE'LL)
heft
heft'i·ness
heft'y
   ·i·er ·i·est
he·gem'o·ny
he·gi'ra
heif'er
height
height'en
Heim'lich
   maneuver
hei'nous
hei'nous·ly
hei'nous·ness
heir
   (*inheritor;* see AIR,
   ERR)
heir'ess
heir'loom'
heist
held
hel'i·cal
hel'i·cop'ter
he'li·o·cen'tric
he'li·o·trope'
hel'i·port'

he'li·um
he'lix'
   ·lix·es' *or* hel'i·ces'
hell
he'll
   (*he will;* see HEAL,
   HEEL)
hell'bent'
hell'cat'
hel'le·bore'
Hel·len'ic
Hel'len·ism'
Hel'len·is'tic
hel'lion
hell'ish
hell'ish·ly
hell'ish·ness
hel·lo'
   ·los'
   ·loed' lo'ing
helm
hel'met
helms'man
hel'ot
help
help'er
help'ful
help'ful·ly
help'ful·ness
help'ing
help'less
help'less·ly
help'less·ness
help'mate'
hel'ter-skel'ter
helve
hem
   hemmed
   hem'ming
he'-man'
hem'a·tite'
he'ma·tol'o·gist
he'ma·tol'o·gy
he'ma·to'ma
   ·mas *or* ·ma·ta
heme
hem'i·sphere'
hem'i·spher'i·cal *or*
   ·spher'ic
hem'line'
hem'lock'
he'mo·glo'bin
he'mo·phil'i·a
he'mo·phil'i·ac'
hem'or·rhage'
   ·rhaged' ·rhag'ing
hem'or·rhag'ic
hem'or·rhoid'
hem'or·rhoi'dal
he'mo·stat'
hemp
hemp'en
hem'stitch'
hen
hence
hence·forth'
hench'man
hen'na

hen'peck'
hen'pecked'
hep
hep'a·rin
he·pat'ic
hep'a·ti'tis
her
her'ald
he·ral'dic
her'ald·ry
   ·ries
herb
her·ba'ceous
herb'age
herb'al
herb'al·ist
her'bi·ci'dal
her'bi·cide'
her'bi·vore'
her·biv'o·rous
her'cu·le'an
Her'cu·les'
herd
   (*group;* see HEARD)
herds'man
here
   (*on this place;* see
   HEAR)
here'a·bout'
here·af'ter
here·by'
he·red'i·tar'y
he·red'i·ty
   ·ties
here·in'
here·of'
her'e·sy
   ·sies
her'e·tic
he·ret'i·cal
here'to·fore'
here·up·on'
here·with'
her'it·a·ble
her'it·age'
her·maph'ro·dite'
her·maph'ro·dit'ic
her·met'ic
her·met'i·cal·ly
her'mit
her'mit·age'
her'ni·a
   ·as *or* ·ae'
her'ni·al
her'ni·ate'
   ·at'ed ·at'ing
her'ni·a'tion
he'ro
   ·roes
he·ro'ic
he·ro'i·cal·ly
her'o·in (*narcotic*)
her'o·ine (*female
   hero*)
her'o·ism'
her'on
her'pes'
herpes sim'plex'

herpes zos'ter
her'pe·tol'o·gist
her'pe·tol'o·gy
her'ring
her'ring·bone'
hers
her·self'
hertz
   hertz
Hertz'i·an waves
hes'i·tan·cy
hes'i·tant
hes'i·tant·ly
hes'i·tate'
   ·tat'ed ·tat'ing
hes'i·tat'ing·ly
hes'i·ta'tion
het'er·o·dox'
het'er·o·dox'y
het'er·o·ge'ne·ous
het'er·o·sex'u·al
heu·ris'tic
hew
   hewed, hewed *or*
   hewn, hew'ing
   (*to chop;* see HUE)
hex
hex'a·gon'
hex·ag'o·nal
hex·am'e·ter
hey
   (*look!; wow!;* see
   HAY)
hey'day'
hi·a'tus
   ·tus·es *or* ·tus
hi·ba'chi
   ·chis
hi'ber·nate'
   ·nat'ed ·nat'ing
hi'ber·na'tion
hi·bis'cus
hic'cup'
   ·cuped' *or* ·cupped'
   ·cup'ing *or*
   ·cup'ping
hic'cough'
hick
hick'ey
   ·eys *or* ·ies
hick'o·ry
   ·ries
hid'den
hide
   hid, hid'den *or*
   hid, hid'ing
hide'a·way'
hide'bound'
hid'e·ous
hid'e·ous·ly
hid'e·ous·ness
hide'-out'
hie
   hied, hie'ing *or*
   hy'ing
hi'er·ar'chi·cal
hi'er·ar'chy
   ·chies
hi'er·o·glyph'ic
hi'-fi'

high
high'ball'
high'born'
high'boy'
high'brow'
high'chair'
high'-class'
high'er-up'
high'fa·lu'tin *or*
   ·ting
high'-flown'
high'hand'ed
high'hand'ed·ly
high'hand'ed·ness
high'land
high'land·er
high'-lev'el
high'light'
high'ly
high'-mind'ed
high'-mind'ed·ly
high'ness
high'-pres'sure
high'-rise'
high'road'
high'-spir'it·ed
high'-strung'
high'-tech'
high'-ten'sion
high'way'
high'way·man
hi'jack'
hi'jack'er
hike
   hiked hik'ing
hik'er
hi·lar'i·ous
hi·lar'i·ty
hill
hill'bil'ly
   ·lies
hill'i·ness
hill'side'
hill'top'
hill'y
   ·i·er ·i·est
hilt
him
him·self'
hind
hin'der
hind'most'
hind'quar'ter
hin'drance
hind'sight'
Hin'du'
Hin'du·ism'
hinge
   hinged hing'ing
hint
hin'ter·land'
hip
hip'pie
hip'po'
   ·pos
Hip'po·crat'ic oath
hip'po·drome'

hip'po·pot'a·mus
   ·mus·es *or* ·mi'
hire
   hired hir'ing
hire'ling
hir'sute'
his
His·pan'ic
hiss
hist
his'ta·mine'
his·tol'o·gist
his·tol'o·gy
his·to'ri·an
his·tor'ic
his·tor'i·cal
his·tor'i·cal·ly
his·to·ric'i·ty
his·to'ri·og'ra·phy
his'to·ry
   ·ries
his'tri·on'ic
his'tri·on'ics
hit
   hit hit'ting
hit'-and-run'
hitch
hitch'hike'
   ·hiked' ·hik'ing
hitch'hik'er
hith'er
hith'er·to'
hit'-or-miss'
hit'-skip'
hit'ter
hive
   hived hiv'ing
hives
hoa'gie *or* ·gy
   ·gies
hoard
   (*accumulate;* see
   HORDE)
hoard'er
hoard'ing
hoar'frost'
hoar'i·ness
hoarse
   (*with a rough
   voice;* see HORSE)
hoarse'ness
hoar'y
   ·i·er ·i·est
hoax
hob
hob'ble
   ·bled ·bling
hob'by
   ·bies
hob'by·horse'
hob'by·ist
hob'gob'lin
hob'nail'
hob'nob'
   ·nobbed' ·nob'bing
ho'bo'
   ·bos' *or* ·boes'
hock
hock'ey

hock'shop'
ho'cus-po'cus
hod
hodge'podge'
Hodg'kin's disease
hoe
  hoed hoe'ing
hoe'down'
hog
  hogged hog'ging
ho'gan'
hog'gish
hog'gish·ly
hogs'head'
hog'tie'
hog'wash'
hoi' pol·loi'
hoist
hok'ey
ho'kum
hold
  held hold'ing
hold'er
hold'ing
hold'o'ver
hold'up'
hole
  holed hol'ing
  (*cavity;* see
  WHOLE)
hole'y
  (*with holes;* see
  HOLY, WHOLLY)
hol'i·day'
ho'li·er-than-thou'
ho'li·ness
ho·lis'tic
ho·lis'ti·cal·ly
hol'lan·daise'
  sauce
hol'ler
hol'low'
hol'low·ness
hol'ly
  ·lies
hol'ly·hock'
hol'o·caust'
Hol'o·cene'
hol'o·graph'
hol'o·graph'ic
ho·log'ra·phy
Hol'stein
hol'ster
ho'ly
  ·li·er ·li·est
  (*sacred;* see
  HOLEY, WHOLLY)
hom'age
hom'burg'
home
  homed hom'ing
home'com'ing
home'land'
home'less
home'li·ness
home'ly
  ·li·er ·li·est
home'made'
home'mak'er

hom'er
Ho·mer'ic
home'sick'
home'sick'ness
home'spun'
home'stead'
home'stead'er
home'stretch'
home'ward
home'work'
home'y
  ·i·er ·i·est
home'y·ness
hom'i·ci'dal
hom'i·cide'
hom'i·let'ics
hom'i·ly
  ·lies
hom'i·nid
hom'i·noid'
hom'i·ny
ho'mo·ge·ne'i·ty
ho'mo·ge'ne·ous
ho·mog'e·nize'
  ·nized' ·niz'ing
hom'o·graph'
ho·mol'o·gous
hom'o·nym'
ho'mo·pho'bi·a
ho'mo·pho'bic
hom'o·phone'
Ho'mo sa'pi·ens'
ho'mo·sex'u·al
ho'mo·sex'ual'i·ty
hone
  honed hon'ing
hon'est
hon'est·ly
hon'es·ty
hon'ey
  ·eys, ·eyed *or* ·ied,
  ·ey·ing
hon'ey·bee'
hon'ey·comb'
hon'ey·dew'
hon'ey·lo'cust
hon'ey·moon'
hon'ey·suck'le
honk
hon'ky-tonk'
hon'or
hon'or·a·ble
hon'or·a·bly
hon'or·ar'i·ly
hon'o·ra'ri·um
  ·ri·ums *or* ·ri·a
hon'or·ar'y
hon'or·if'ic
hood
hood'ed
hood'lum
hood'wink'
hoo'ey
hoof
  hoofs *or* hooves
hoofed
hook
hook'ah *or* ·a

hooked
hook'er
hook'up'
hook'worm'
hoo'li·gan
hoop
hoop'la'
hoo·ray'
hoose'gow'
hoot
hoot'en·an'ny
  ·nies
hoot'er
hooves
hop
  hopped hop'ping
hope
  hoped hop'ing
hope'ful
hope'ful·ly
hope'less
hope'less·ly
hop'head'
hop'per
hop'sack'ing
hop'scotch'
horde
  hord'ed hord'ing
  (*crowd;* see HOARD)
hore'hound'
ho·ri'zon
hor'i·zon'tal
hor'i·zon'tal·ly
hor·mo'nal
hor'mone'
horn
horn'blende'
horned
hor'net
horn'i·ness
horn'less
horn'pipe'
horn'y
  ·i·er ·i·est
hor'o·scope'
hor·ren'dous
hor'ri·ble
hor'ri·bly
hor'rid
hor'rid·ly
hor·rif'ic
hor'ri·fy'
  ·fied' ·fy'ing
hor'ror
hors' d'oeu·vre'
  ·vres'
horse
  horsed hors'ing
  (*animal;* see
  HOARSE)
horse'back'
horse'feath'ers
horse'fly'
horse'hair'
horse'hide'
horse'laugh'
horse'man
horse'man·ship'

horse'play'
horse'pow'er
horse'rad'ish
horse'shoe'
horse'tail'
horse'whip'
horse'wom'an
hors'i·ness
hors'y
  ·i·er ·i·est
hor'ta·to'ry
hor'ti·cul'tur·al
hor'ti·cul'ture
ho·san'na
hose
  hosed hos'ing
ho'sier·y
hos'pice
hos'pi·ta·ble
hos'pi·ta·bly
hos'pi·tal
hos'pi·tal'i·ty
  ·ties
hos'pi·tal·i·za'tion
hos'pi·tal·ize'
  ·ized' ·iz'ing
host
hos'tage
hos'tel (*inn*)
hos'tel·er
hos'tel·ry
  ·ries
host'ess
hos'tile (*unfriendly*)
hos'tile·ly
hos·til'i·ty
  ·ties
hos'tler
hot
  hot'ter hot'test
hot'bed'
hot'blood'ed
ho·tel'
hot'head'
hot'head'ed
hot'house'
hot'ly
hot' rod'der
hot'shot'
hot'-tem'pered
hound
hour
hour'glass'
hou'ri
  ·ris
hour'ly
house
  housed hous'ing
house'boat'
house'break'ing
house'bro'ken
house'fly'
house'hold'
house'hold'er
house'hus'band
house'keep'er
house'maid'
house'plant'

house'wares'
house'warm'ing
house'wife'
house'work'
hous'ing
hove
hov'el
hov'er
how
how·ev'er
how'itz·er
howl
howl'er
how'so·ev'er
hoy'den
hub
hub'bub'
hub'cap'
hu'bris
huck'le·ber'ry
  ·ries
huck'ster
hud'dle
  ·dled ·dling
hue
  (*color;* see HEW)
huff
huff'y
  ·i·er ·i·est
hug
  hugged hug'ging
huge
  hug'er hug'est
huge'ly
huge'ness
huh
hu'la
hulk
hulk'ing
hull
hul'la·ba·loo'
hum
  hummed
  hum'ming
hu'man
hu·mane'
hu·mane'ly
hu·mane'ness
hu'man·ism'
hu'man·ist
hu'man·is'tic
hu'man·is'ti·cal·ly
hu·man'i·tar'i·an
hu·man'i·tar'i·an·
  ism'
hu·man'i·ty
  ·ties
hu'man·i·za'tion
hu'man·ize'
  ·ized' ·iz'ing
hu'man·iz'er
hu'man·kind'
hu'man·ly
hu'man·ness
hu'man·oid'
hum'ble
  ·bler ·blest
  ·bled ·bling
hum'ble·ness

hum'bly
hum'bug'
hum'drum'
hu·mec'tant
hu'mer·al
hu'mer·us
  ·mer·i'
  (*a bone;* see HU-
  MOROUS)
hu'mid
hu·mid'i·fi'er
hu·mid'i·fy'
  ·fied' ·fy'ing
hu·mid'i·ty
hu'mi·dor'
hu·mil'i·ate'
  ·at'ed ·at'ing
hu·mil'i·a'tion
hu·mil'i·ty
hum'ming·bird'
hum'mock
hum'mus
  (*chickpea paste;*
  see HUMUS)
hu·mon'gous
hu'mor
hu'mor·ist
hu'mor·less
hu'mor·ous
  (*funny;* see
  HUMERUS)
hu'mor·ous·ly
hump
hump'back'
hump'backed'
hu'mus
  (*soil;* see HUMMUS)
hunch
hunch'back'
hun'dred
hun'dred·fold'
hun'dredth
hun'dred·weight'
hung
Hun·gar'i·an
hun'ger
hun'gri·ly
hun'gry
  ·gri·er ·gri·est
hunk
hun'ker
hunt
hunt'er
hunt'ress
hunts'man
hur'dle
  ·dled ·dling
  (*barrier;* see HURTLE)
hur'dler
hur'dy-gur'dy
  ·dies
hurl
hurl'er
hurl'y-burl'y
  ·burl'ies
hur·rah'
hur·ray'
hur'ri·cane'
hur'ried·ly

hur′ry
·ried ·ry·ing
hurt
hurt hurt′ing
hurt′ful
hur′tle
·tled ·tling
(to rush; see HUR-DLE)
hus′band
hus′band·man
hus′band·ry
hush
hush′-hush′
husk
hus′ky
·kies
(dog)
husk′y
·i·er ·i·est
(hoarse; burly)
hus·sar′
hus′sy
·sies
hus′tings
hus′tle
·tled ·tling
hus′tler
hut
hutch
hy′a·cinth′
hy′brid
hy′brid·ism′
hy′brid·ize′
·ized′ ·iz′ing
hy′dra
·dras or ·drae′
hy′drant
hy′drate′
·drat′ed ·drat′ing
hy·dra′tion
hy·drau′lic
hy·drau′li·cal·ly
hy·drau′lics
hy′dro·car′bon
hy′dro·chlo′ric acid
hy′dro·e·lec′tric
hy′dro·e·lec′tric′i·ty
hy′dro·foil′
hy′dro·gen
hy·drog′e·nate′
·nat′ed ·nat′ing
hy·drol′o·gy
hy·drol′y·sis
hy·drom′e·ter
hy·drom′e·try
hy′dro·pho′bi·a
hy′dro·phone′
hy′dro·plane′
hy′dro·pon′ics
hy′dro·sphere′
hy′dro·ther′a·py
hy′drous
hy·drox′ide′
hy·e′na
hy′giene′
hy′gi·en′ic
hy′gi·en′i·cal·ly

hy·gi·en′ist
hy·grom′e·ter
hy′men
hy′me·ne′al
hymn
hym′nal
hymn′book′
hype
hyped hyp′ing
hy′per
hy′per- prefix
(over or more than; see HYPO-)
hy·per′bo·la
·las or ·lae′
(curve)
hy·per′bo·le (exaggeration)
hy′per·bol′ic
hy′per·crit′i·cal
(too critical; see HYPOCRITICAL)
hy′per·sen′si·tive
hy′per·sen′si·tiv′i·ty
hy′per·ten′sion
(high blood pressure; see HYPOTENSION)
hy′per·thy′roid′
hy′per·ven′ti·late′
·lat′ed ·lat′ing
hy′per·ven′ti·la′tion
hy′phen
hy′phen·ate′
·at′ed ·at′ing
hy′phen·a′tion
hyp·no′sis
hyp·not′ic
hyp·not′i·cal·ly
hyp′no·tism′
hyp′no·tist
hyp′no·tize′
·tized′ ·tiz′ing
hy′po
·pos
hy·po- prefix
(under or less than; see HYPER-)
hy′po·chon′dri·a
hy′po·chon′dri·ac′
hy·poc′ri·sy
·sies
hyp′o·crite′
hyp′o·crit′i·cal
(deceitful; see HYPERCRITICAL)
hy′po·der′mic
hy′po·gly·ce′mi·a
hy′po·ten′sion
(low blood pressure; see HYPERTENSION)
hy·pot′e·nuse′
hy′po·thal′a·mus
·mi′
hy′po·ther′mi·a
hy·poth′e·sis
·ses′
hy·poth′e·size′
·sized′ ·siz′ing

hy′po·thet′i·cal
hy′po·thet′i·cal·ly
hy′po·thy′roid′
hys′sop
hys′ter·ec′to·my
·mies
hys·te′ri·a
hys·ter′i·cal or ·ter′ic
hys·ter′i·cal·ly

I

i·am′bic
i′bex′
i′bex′es i′bi·ces′
i′bis
i′bu·pro′fen
ice
iced ic′ing
ice′berg′
ice′bound′
ice′box′
ice′break′er
ice′cap′
ice′-cream′
ice′house′
ice′man′
ice′-skate′
ich′thy·ol′o·gist
ich′thy·ol′o·gy
i′ci·cle
i′ci·ly
i′ci·ness
ic′ing
ick′y
·i·er ·i·est
i′con
i·con′o·clast′
i·con′o·clas′tic
i′cy
i′ci·er i′ci·est
I′da·ho′
i·de′a
i·de′al
i·de′al·ism′
i·de′al·ist
i·de′al·is′tic
i·de′al·is′ti·cal·ly
i·de′al·i·za′tion
i·de′al·ize′
·ized′ ·iz′ing
i·de′al·ly
i·den′ti·cal
i·den′ti·cal·ly
i·den′ti·fi′a·ble
i·den′ti·fi·ca′tion
i·den′ti·fi′er
i·den′ti·fy′
·fied′ ·fy′ing
i·den′ti·ty
·ties
id′e·o·gram′
id′e·o·graph′
id′e·o·graph′ic
i·de′o·log′i·cal
i·de′o·log′i·cal·ly

i·de·ol′o·gist
i·de·ol′o·gy
·gies
ides
id′i·o·cy
·cies
id′i·om
id′i·o·mat′ic
id′i·o·mat′i·cal·ly
id′i·o·path′ic
id′i·o·syn′cra·sy
·sies
id′i·o·syn·crat′ic
id′i·o·syn·crat′i·cal·ly
id′i·ot
id′i·ot′ic
id′i·ot′i·cal·ly
i′dle
i′dler i′dlest i′dled i′dling
(not active; see IDOL, IDYLL)
i′dle·ness
i′dler
i′dly
i′dol
(image worshiped; see IDLE, IDYLL)
i·dol′a·ter
i·dol′a·trous
i·dol′a·try
·tries
i′dol·ize′
·ized′ ·iz′ing
i′dyll or i·dyl
(pastoral poem; see IDLE, IDOL)
i·dyl′lic
if′fy
ig′loo′
·loos
ig′ne·ous
ig·nit′a·ble or ·i·ble
ig·nite′
·nit′ed ·nit′ing
ig·ni′tion
ig·no′ble
ig·no′bly
ig′no·min′i·ous
ig′no·min′y
·ies
ig′no·ra′mus
·mus·es
ig′no·rance
ig′no·rant
ig·nore′
·nored′ ·nor′ing
i·gua′na
il′e·um (intestine)
il′i·um (bone)
ilk
ill
worse worst
ill′-ad·vised′
ill′-bred′
ill′-con·sid′ered
il·le′gal
il·le·gal′i·ty
·ties

il·le′gal·ly
il·leg′i·ble
il·leg′i·bly
il·le·git′i·ma·cy
·cies
il·le·git′i·mate
ill′-fat′ed
ill′-fa′vored
ill′-found′ed
ill′-hu′mored
il·lic′it
(unlawful; see ELICIT)
Il′li·nois′
il·lit′er·a·cy
il·lit′er·ate
ill′-man′nered
ill′-na′tured
ill′ness
il·log′i·cal
il·log′i·cal·ly
ill′-spent′
ill′-suit′ed
ill′-tem′pered
ill′-timed′
ill′-treat′
il·lu′mi·na·ble
il·lu′mi·nate′
·nat′ed ·nat′ing
il·lu′mi·na′tion
il·lu′mine
·mined ·min·ing
ill′-use′
il·lu′sion
(false idea; see ALLUSION, ELUSION)
il·lu′sive
(deceptive; see ALLUSIVE, ELUSIVE)
il·lu′so·ry
il′lus·trate′
·trat′ed ·trat′ing
il′lus·tra′tion
il·lus′tra·tive
il′lus·tra′tor
il·lus′tri·ous
im′age
·aged ·ag·ing
im′age·ry
i·mag′i·na·ble
i·mag′i·na·bly
i·mag′i·nar′y
i·mag′i·na′tion
i·mag′i·na·tive
i·mag′ine
·ined ·in·ing
im·bal′ance
im·be·cile
im·bed′
im·bibe′
·bibed′ ·bib′ing
im·bib′er
im·bro′glio
·glios
im·bue′
·bued′ ·bu′ing
im′i·tate′
·tat′ed ·tat′ing
im′i·ta′tion

im′i·ta′tive
im′i·ta′tor
im·mac′u·late
im′ma·nent
(inherent; see EMINENT, IMMINENT)
im′ma·te′ri·al
im′ma·ture′
im′ma·tu′ri·ty
im·meas′ur·a·ble
im·meas′ur·a·bly
im·me′di·a·cy
im·me′di·ate
im·me′di·ate·ly
im′me·mo′ri·al
im·mense′
im·mense′ly
im·men′si·ty
im·merge′
·merged′ ·merg′ing
(plunge; see EMERGE)
im·merse′
·mersed′ ·mers′ing
im·mers′i·ble
im·mer′sion
im′mi·grant
im′mi·grate′
·grat′ed ·grat′ing
(arrive; see EMIGRATE)
im′mi·gra′tion
im′mi·nent
(impending; see EMINENT, IMMANENT)
im·mo′bile
im′mo·bil′i·ty
im·mo′bi·lize′
im·mod′er·ate
im·mod′est
im·mod′es·ty
im′mo·late′
·lat′ed ·lat′ing
im′mo·la′tion
im·mor′al
im′mo·ral′i·ty
·ties
im·mor′al·ly
im·mor′tal
im′mor·tal′i·ty
im·mor′tal·i·za′tion
im·mor′tal·ize′
·ized′ ·iz′ing
im·mov′a·ble
im·mune′
im·mu′ni·ty
·ties
im′mu·ni·za′tion
im′mu·nize′
·nized′ ·niz′ing
im′mu·nol′o·gist
im′mu·nol′o·gy
im·mure′
·mured′ ·mur′ing
im·mu′ta·ble
im·mu′ta·bly
imp

im·pact′
im·pact′ed
im·pair′
im·pair′ment
im·pa′la
  -la *or* -las
im·pale′
  ·paled′ ·pal′ing
im·pal′pa·ble
im·pan′el
  ·eled *or* ·elled
  ·el·ing *or* ·el·ling
im·part′
im·par′tial
im·par′ti·al′i·ty
im·par′tial·ly
im·pass′a·ble
  (*not passable;* see
  IMPASSIBLE)
im′passe′
im·pas′si·ble
  (*unfeeling;* see IM-
  PASSABLE)
im·pas′sioned
im·pas′sive
im·pa′tience
im·pa′tient
im·peach′
im·peach′a·ble
im·peach′ment
im·pec′ca·ble
im·pec′ca·bly
im·pe·cu′ni·ous
im·ped′ance
im·pede′
  ·ped′ed ·ped′ing
im·ped′i·ment
im·pel′
  ·pelled′ ·pel′ling
im·pel′ler
im·pend′
im·pend′ing
im·pen′e·tra·ble
im·pen′i·tent
im·per′a·tive
im′per·cep′ti·ble
im′per·cep′ti·bly
im·per′fect
im·per·fec′tion
im·per′fect·ly
im·pe′ri·al
im·pe′ri·al·ism′
im·pe′ri·al·ist
im·pe′ri·al·is′tic
im·pe′ri·al·ly
im·per′il
im·pe′ri·ous
im·per′ish·a·ble
im·per′ma·nent
im·per′me·a·ble
im·per′son·al
im·per′son·al·ly
im·per′son·ate′
  ·at·ed ·at·ing
im·per′son·a′tion
im·per′son·a′tor
im·per′ti·nence
im·per′ti·nent

im′per·turb′a·ble
im·per′vi·ous
im·pe·ti′go
im·pet′u·os′i·ty
im·pet′u·ous
im′pe·tus
im·pinge′
  ·pinged′ ·ping′ing
im·pinge′ment
im′pi·ous
imp′ish
im·pla′ca·ble
im·pla′ca·bly
im·plant′
im′ple·ment
im′ple·men·ta′tion
im′pli·cate′
  ·cat′ed ·cat′ing
im′pli·ca′tion
im·plic′a·tive
im·plic′it
im·plode′
  ·plod′ed ·plod′ing
im·plore′
  ·plored′ ·plor′ing
im·plor′ing·ly
im·plo′sion
im·plo′sive
im·ply′
  ·plied′ ·ply′ing
im′po·lite′
im·pon′der·a·ble
im·port′
im·port′a·ble
im·por′tance
im·por′tant
im′por·ta′tion
im·port′er
im·por′tu·nate
im′por·tune′
  ·tuned′ ·tun′ing
im′por·tu′ni·ty
  ·ties
im·pose′
  ·posed′ ·pos′ing
im·pos′ing
im′po·si′tion
im·pos′si·bil′i·ty
  ·ties
im·pos′si·ble
im·pos′si·bly
im·pos′tor *or*
  ·post′er (*deceiver*)
im·pos′ture (*decep-
tion*)
im′po·tence
im′po·ten·cy
im′po·tent
im·pound′
im·pov′er·ish
im·prac′ti·ca·ble
im·prac′ti·cal
im′pre·cate′
  ·cat′ed ·cat′ing
im′pre·ca′tion
im′pre·cise′

im′pre·ci′sion
im·preg′na·bil′i·ty
im·preg′na·ble
im·preg′na·bly
im·preg′nate′
  ·nat′ed ·nat′ing
im′preg·na′tion
im′pre·sa′ri·o′
  ·os′
im·press′
im·press′i·ble
im·pres′sion
im·pres′sion·a·ble
im·pres′sion·ism′
im·pres′sion·ist
im·pres′sion·is′tic
im·pres′sive
im·pres′sive·ly
im′pri·ma′tur
im′print′
im·pris′on
im·pris′on·ment
im′prob·a·bil′i·ty
im·prob′a·ble
im·promp′tu′
im·prop′er
im′pro·pri′e·ty
  ·ties
im·prov′a·ble
im·prove′
  ·proved′ ·prov′ing
im·prove′ment
im·prov′i·dent
im·prov′i·sa′tion
im·prov′i·sa′·tion·al
im′pro·vise′
  ·vised′ ·vis′ing
im·pru′dence
im·pru′dent
im′pu·dence
im′pu·dent
im·pugn′
im′pulse′
im·pul′sive
im·pul′sive·ly
im·pu′ni·ty
im·pure′
im·pu′ri·ty
  ·ties
im′pu·ta′tion
im·pute′
  ·put′ed ·put′ing
in
in′a·bil′i·ty
in ab·sen′ti·a
in′ac·ces′si·ble
in·ac′cu·ra·cy
  ·cies
in·ac′cu·rate
in·ac′tion
in·ac′ti·vate′
in·ac′ti·va′tion
in·ac′tive
in′ac·tiv′i·ty
in·ad′e·qua·cy
  ·cies
in·ad′e·quate
in′ad·mis′si·ble

in′ad·vert′ence
in′ad·vert′ent
in′ad·vert′ent·ly
in′ad·vis′a·bil′i·ty
in′ad·vis′a·ble
in·al′ien·a·ble
in·al′ien·a·bly
in·al′ter·a·ble
in·ane′
in·an′i·mate
in·ap′pli·ca·ble
in′ap·pre′ci·a·ble
in′ap·proach′a·ble
in′ap·pro′pri·ate
in·ar·tic′u·late
in′as·much′ as′
in′at·ten′tion
in′at·ten′tive
in·au′di·ble
in·au′gu·ral
in·au′gu·rate′
  ·rat′ed ·rat′ing
in·au′gu·ra′tion
in′aus·pi′cious
in′au·then′tic
in′board′
in′born′
in′bound′
in′bred′
in′breed′
in·cal′cu·la·ble
in·cal′cu·la·bly
in′can·des′cence
in′can·des′cent
in′can·ta′tion
in′ca·pa·bil′i·ty
in·ca′pa·ble
in′ca·pac′i·tate′
  ·tat′ed ·tat′ing
in′ca·pac′i·ty
in·car′cer·ate′
  ·at′ed ·at′ing
in·car′cer·a′tion
in·car′nate′
  ·nat′ed ·nat′ing
in′car·na′tion
in·cen′di·ar′y
  ·ies
in′cense′ *n.*
in·cense′ *v.*
  ·censed′ ·cens′ing
in·cen′tive
in·cep′tion
in·cer′ti·tude′
in·ces′sant
in′cest
in·ces′tu·ous
inch
in·cho′ate
in′ci·dence
in′ci·dent
in′ci·den′tal
in′ci·den′tal·ly
in·cin′er·ate′
  ·at′ed ·at′ing
in·cin′er·a′tion
in·cin′er·a′tor
in·cip′i·ent

in·cise′
  ·cised′ ·cis′ing
in·ci′sion
in·ci′sive
in·ci′sor
in·cite′
  ·cit′ed ·cit′ing
  (*rouse;* see
  INSIGHT)
in·cite′ment
in·cit′er
in·clem′en·cy
in·clem′ent
in′cli·na′tion
in·cline′
  ·clined′ ·clin′ing
in·close′
in·clo′sure
in·clude′
  ·clud′ed ·clud′ing
in·clu′sion
in·clu′sive
in·cog′ni·to′
in′co·her′ence
in′co·her′ent
in′come′
in′com′ing
in′com·mu′ni·ca·ble
in′com·mu′ni·ca′do
in·com′pa·ra·ble
in′com·pat′i·bil′i·ty
  ·ties
in′com·pat′i·ble
in·com′pe·tence
in·com′pe·tent
in′com·plete′
in′com·pre·hen′si·
ble
in·com·put′a·ble
in′con·ceiv′a·ble
in′con·clu′sive
in·con′gru·ent
in′con·gru′i·ty
  ·ties
in·con′gru·ous
in′con·se·quen′tial
in′con·sid′er·a·ble
in′con·sid′er·ate
in′con·sid′er·a′tion
in′con·sis′ten·cy
  ·cies
in′con·sis′tent
in′con·sol′a·ble
in′con·spic′u·ous
in·con′stan·cy
in·con′stant
in′con·test′a·ble
in′con·test′a·bly
in·con′ti·nence
in·con′ti·nent
in′con·trol′la·ble
in′con·tro·vert′i·ble
in′con·ven′ience
  ·ienced ·ienc·ing
in′con·ven′ient
in·cor′po·rate′
  ·rat′ed ·rat′ing
in·cor′po·ra′tion

in′cor·rect′
in·cor′ri·gi·bil′i·ty
in·cor′ri·gi·ble
in·cor′ri·gi·bly
in′cor·rupt′i·ble
in·crease′
  ·creased′
  ·creas′ing
in·creas′ing·ly
in·cred′i·ble
in·cred′i·bly
in′cre·du′li·ty
in·cred′u·lous
in′cre·ment
in′cre·men′tal
in·crim′i·nate′
  ·nat′ed ·nat′ing
in·crim′i·na′tion
in·crust′
in′crus·ta′tion
in′cu·bate′
  ·bat′ed ·bat′ing
in′cu·ba′tion
in′cu·ba′tor
in·cul′cate′
  ·cat′ed ·cat′ing
in′cul·ca′tion
in·culp′a·ble
in·cum′ben·cy
  ·cies
in·cum′bent
in·cur′
  ·curred′ ·cur′ring
in·cur′a·ble
in·cur′sion
in·debt′ed
in·debt′ed·ness
in·de′cen·cy
  ·cies
in·de′cent
in′de·ci′pher·a·ble
in′de·ci′sion
in′de·ci′sive
in′de·ci′sive·ly
in′de·ci′sive·ness
in·deed′
in·de·fat′i·ga·ble
in′de·fen′si·ble
in·def′i·nite
in·def′i·nite·ly
in·del′i·ble
in·del′i·bly
in·del′i·ca·cy
  ·cies
in·del′i·cate
in·dem′ni·fi·ca′tion
in·dem′ni·fy′
  ·fied′ ·fy′ing
in·dem′ni·ty
  ·ties
in·dent′
in′den·ta′tion
in·den′ture
  ·tured ·tur·ing
in′de·pend′ence
in′de·pend′ent
in′de·pend′ent·ly
in′-depth′

in'de·scrib'a·ble
in'de·scrib'a·bly
in'de·struct'i·ble
in'de·ter'mi·nate
in'dex'
  ·dex'es or ·di·ces'
In'di·an
In'di·an'a
in'di·cate'
  ·cat'ed ·cat'ing
in'di·ca'tion
in·dic'a·tive
In'di·ca'tor
in·dict'
  (accuse formally; see INDITE)
in·dict'a·ble
in·dict'ment
in·dif'fer·ence
in·dif'fer·ent
in'di·gence
in·dig'e·nous
in'di·gent
in·di·gest'i·ble
in·di·ges'tion
in·dig'nant
in'dig·na'tion
in·dig'ni·ty
  ·ties
in'di·go'
in'di·rect'
in'di·rect'ly
in'dis·creet'
in'dis·cre'tion
in'dis·crim'i·nate
in'dis·crim'i·nate·ly
in'dis·pen'sa·ble
in'dis·pose'
in'dis·posed'
in·dis'pu·ta·ble
in'dis·tinct'
in'dis·tin'guish·a·ble
in·dite'
  ·dit'ed ·dit'ing
  (write; see INDICT)
in'di·vid'u·al
in'di·vid'u·al·ism'
in'di·vid'u·al·ist
in'di·vid'u·al·is'tic
in'di·vid'u·al'i·ty
in'di·vid'u·al·ize'
  ·ized' ·iz'ing
in'di·vid'u·al·ly
in'di·vis'i·bil'i·ty
in'di·vis'i·ble
in·doc'tri·nate'
  ·nat'ed ·nat'ing
in·doc'tri·na'tion
in'do·lence
in'do·lent
in·dom'i·ta·ble
in·dom'i·ta·bly
in'door'
in'doors'
in·dorse'
  ·dorsed' ·dors'ing
in·du'bi·ta·ble
in·du'bi·ta·bly

in·duce'
  ·duced' ·duc'ing
in·duce'ment
in·duc'er
in·duct'
in·duct'ance
in'duct·ee'
in·duc'tion
in·duc'tive
in·dulge'
  ·dulged' ·dulg'ing
in·dul'gence
in·dul'gent
in'du·rate'
  ·rat'ed ·rat'ing
in'du·ra'tion
in·dus'tri·al
in·dus'tri·al·ism'
in·dus'tri·al·ist
in·dus'tri·al·i·za'-
  tion
in·dus'tri·al·ize'
  ·ized' ·iz'ing
in·dus'tri·al·ly
in·dus'tri·ous
in'dus·try
  ·tries
in·e'bri·ate'
  ·at'ed ·at'ing
in·e'bri·a'tion
in·ed'i·ble
in·ed'u·ca·ble
in·ef'fa·ble
in·ef'fa·bly
in'ef·fec'tive
in'ef·fec'tu·al
in·ef'fi·ca·cy
in'ef·fi'cien·cy
in'ef·fi'cient
in'e·las'tic
in'e·las·tic'i·ty
in·el'e·gance
in·el'e·gant
in·el'i·gi·bil'i·ty
in·el'i·gi·ble
in'e·luc'ta·ble
in'e·luc'ta·bly
in·ept'
in·ep'ti·tude'
in·ept'ness
in'e·qual'i·ty
  ·ties
in·eq'ui·ta·ble
in·eq'ui·ty
  ·ties
  (unfairness; see INIQUITY)
in·ert'
in·er'ti·a
in·er'tial
in'es·cap'a·ble
in'es·cap'a·bly
in·es'ti·ma·ble
in·ev'i·ta·bil'i·ty
in·ev'i·ta·ble
in·ev'i·ta·bly
in·ex'act'
in'ex·cus'a·ble

in'ex·haust'i·ble
in·ex'o·ra·ble
in·ex'o·ra·bly
in'ex·pe'di·ent
in'ex·pen'sive
in'ex·pe'ri·ence
in'ex·pe'ri·enced
in·ex'pert
in·ex'pi·a·ble
in·ex'pli·ca·ble
in·ex'pli·ca·bly
in'ex·press'i·ble
in'ex·tin'guish·a·ble
in ex·tre'mis
in·ex'tri·ca·ble
in·ex'tri·ca·bly
in·fal'li·bil'i·ty
in·fal'li·ble
in·fal'li·bly
in'fa·mous
in'fa·my
  ·mies
in'fan·cy
  ·cies
in'fant
in·fan'ti·cide'
in'fan·tile'
in'fan·try
  ·tries
in'fan·try·man
in'farct'
in·farc'tion
in·fat'u·ate'
  ·at'ed ·at'ing
in·fat'u·a'tion
in·fect'
in·fec'tion
in·fec'tious
in·fec'tive
in'fe·lic'i·tous
in'fe·lic'i·ty
  ·ties
in·fer'
  ·ferred' ·fer'ring
in'fer·a·ble
in'fer·ence
in'fer·en'tial
in·fe'ri·or
in·fe'ri·or'i·ty
in·fer'nal
in·fer'no'
  ·nos'
in·fer'tile
in·fest'
in'fes·ta'tion
in'fi·del'
in'fi·del'i·ty
in'field'
in'fight'er
in'fight'ing
in'fil'trate'
  ·trat'ed ·trat'ing
in'fil·tra'tion
in'fil·tra'tor
in'fi·nite
in'fi·nite·ly
in·fin'i·tes'i·mal
in·fin'i·tes'i·mal·ly

in·fin'i·tive
in·fin'i·tude'
in·fin'i·ty
  ·ties
in·firm'
in·fir'ma·ry
  ·ries
in·fir'mi·ty
  ·ties
in·flame'
  ·flamed' ·flam'ing
in·flam'ma·bil'i·ty
in·flam'ma·ble
in'flam·ma'tion
in·flam'ma·to'ry
in·flat'a·ble
in·flate'
  ·flat'ed ·flat'ing
in·fla'tion
in·fla'tion·ar'y
in·flect'
in·flec'tion
in·flec'tion·al
in·flex'i·bil'i·ty
in·flex'i·ble
in·flict'
in·flic'tion
in'·flight'
in'flow'
in'flo·res'cence
in'flow'
in'flu·ence
  ·enced ·enc·ing
in'flu·en'tial
in'flu·en'za
in'flux'
in'fo
in·form'
in·for'mal
in'for·mal'i·ty
  ·ties
in·for'mal·ly
in·form'ant
in'for·ma'tion
in·form'a·tive
in·form'er
in·frac'tion
in·fran'gi·ble
in·fran'gi·bly
in'fra·red'
in'fra·son'ic
in'fra·struc'ture
in·fre'quen·cy or
  ·quence
in·fre'quent
in·fringe'
  ·fringed' ·fring'ing
in·fringe'ment
in·fu'ri·ate'
  ·at'ed ·at'ing
in·fuse'
  ·fused' ·fus'ing
in·fu'sion
in·gen'ious
  (clever; see INGEN-UOUS)
in'gé·nue'
in'ge·nu'i·ty

in·gen'u·ous
  (frank; see INGE-NIOUS)
in·gest'
in·ges'tion
in·glo'ri·ous
in'got
in·grained'
in'grate'
in·gra'ti·ate'
  ·at'ed ·at'ing
in·grat'i·tude'
In·gre'dl·ent
in'gress'
in'-group'
in'grown'
in'gui·nal
in·hab'it
in·hab'it·a·ble
in·hab'it·ant
in·hal'ant
in'ha·la'tion
in'ha·la'tor
in·hale'
  ·haled' ·hal'ing
in·hal'er
in·here'
  ·hered' ·her'ing
in·her'ent
in·her'it
in·her'it·a·ble
in·her'it·ance
in·her'i·tor
in·hib'it
in'hi·bi'tion
in·hib'i·tor or ·it·er
in·hos'pi·ta·ble
in'-house'
in·hu'man
in'hu·mane'
in'hu·man'i·ty
in·im'i·cal
in·im'i·ta·ble
in·iq'ui·tous
in·iq'ui·ty
  ·ties
  (wickedness; see INEQUITY)
in·i'tial
  ·tialed or ·tialled
  ·tial·ing or
  ·tial·ling
in·i'tial·ly
in·i'ti·ate'
  ·at'ed ·at'ing
in·i'ti·a'tion
in·i'ti·a·tive
in·i'ti·a'tor
in·ject'
in·jec'tion
in·jec'tor
in·ju·di'cious
in·junc'tion
in·jure'
  ·jured ·jur·ing
in·ju'ri·ous
in'ju·ry
  ·ries
in·jus'tice

ink
ink'blot'
ink'i·ness
ink'ling
ink'well'
ink'y
  ·i·er ·i·est
in'laid'
in'land
in'-law'
in'lay'
  ·laid' ·lay'ing
  ·lays'
in'let'
in'mate'
in' me·mo'ri·am'
in'most'
inn
in'nards'
in·nate'
in'ner
in'ner·most'
in'ner·vate'
  ·vat'ed ·vat'ing
in'ner·va'tion
in'ning
inn'keep'er
in'no·cence
in'no·cent
in·noc'u·ous
in'no·vate'
  ·vat'ed ·vat'ing
in'no·va'tion
in'no·va'tive
in'no·va'tor
in·nu·en'do'
  ·does' or ·dos'
in·nu'mer·a·ble
in·oc'u·late'
  ·lat'ed ·lat'ing
in·oc'u·la'tion
in·of'fen·sive
in·op'er·a·ble
in·op'er·a·tive
in'op·por·tune'
in·or'di·nate
in'or·gan'ic
in·pa'tient
in'put'
in'quest'
in'qui'e·tude'
in·quire'
  ·quired' ·quir'ing
in'quir·y
  ·ies
in'qui·si'tion
in·quis'i·tive
in·quis'i·tive·ness
in·quis'i·tor
in'road'
in·sane'
in·san'i·ty
  ·ties
in·sa'ti·a·ble
in·sa'ti·a·bly
in·scribe'
  ·scribed' ·scrib'ing
in·scrip'tion

in·scru·ta·bil′i·ty
in·scru′ta·ble
in·scru′ta·bly
in′seam′
in′sect′
in·sec′ti·cide′
in·sec′ti·vore′
in′sec·tiv′o·rous
in′se·cure′
in′se·cu′ri·ty
 ·ties
in·sem′i·nate′
 ·nat′ed ·nat′ing
in·sem′i·na′tion
in·sen′sate′
in·sen′si·bil′i·ty
in·sen′si·ble
in·sen′si·tive
in·sen′si·tiv′i·ty
in·sen′ti·ence
in·sen′ti·ent
in·sep′a·ra·ble
in·sert′
in·ser′tion
in′set′
in′side′
in·sid′er
in·sid′i·ous
in′sight′
 (understanding;
 see INCITE)
in·sig′ni·a
in′sig·nif′i·cance
in′sig·nif′i·cant
in′sin·cere′
in′sin·cer′i·ty
in·sin′u·ate′
 ·at′ed ·at′ing
in·sin′u·a′tion
in·sin′u·a′tive
in·sip′id
in·sist′
in·sist′ence
in·sist′ent
in′so·far′
in′sole′
in′so·lence
in′so·lent
in·sol′u·bil′i·ty
in·sol′u·ble
in·sol′ven·cy
in·sol′vent
in·som′ni·a
in·som′ni·ac′
in′so·much′
in·sou′ci·ance
in·sou′ci·ant
in·spect′
in·spec′tion
in·spec′tor
in′spi·ra′tion
in′spi·ra′tion·al
in·spire′
 ·spired′ ·spir′ing
in′sta·bil′i·ty
in·stall′ or ·stal′
 ·stalled′ ·stall′ing
in′stal·la′tion

in·stall′er
in·stall′ment or
 in·stal′ment
in′stance
in′stant
in′stan·ta′ne·ous
in′stant·ly
in·state′
 ·stat′ed ·stat′ing
in·stead′
in′step′
in′sti·gate′
 ·gat′ed ·gat′ing
in′sti·ga′tion
in′sti·ga·tor
in·still′ or ·stil′
 ·stilled′ ·still′ing
in′stinct′
in·stinc′tive
in·stinc′tu·al
in′sti·tute′
 ·tut′ed ·tut′ing
in′sti·tu′tion
in′sti·tu′tion·al
in′sti·tu′tion·al·i·za′
 tion
in′sti·tu′tion·al·ize′
 ·ized′ ·iz′ing
in·struct′
in·struc′tion
in·struc′tive
in·struc′tor
in′stru·ment
in′stru·men′tal
in′stru·men′tal·ist
in′stru·men′tal′i·ty
 ·ties
in′stru·men·ta′tion
in′sub·or′di·nate
in′sub·or′di·na′tion
in′sub·stan′tial
in·suf′fer·a·ble
in′suf·fi′cien·cy
 ·cies
in′suf·fi′cient
in′su·lar
in′su·late′
 ·lat′ed ·lat′ing
in′su·la′tion
in′su·la′tor
in′su·lin
in·sult′
in·su′per·a·ble
in′sup·port′a·ble
in′sup·press′i·ble
in·sur′a·bil′i·ty
in·sur′a·ble
in·sur′ance
in·sure′
 ·sured′ ·sur′ing
in·sured′
in·sur′er
in·sur′gence
in·sur′gent
in′sur·mount′a·ble
in′sur·rec′tion
in′sur·rec′tion·ist
in·tact′

in·ta′glio′
 ·glios′
in′take′
in·tan′gi·ble
in′te·ger
in′te·gral
in′te·grate′
 ·grat′ed ·grat′ing
in′te·gra′tion
in·teg′ri·ty
in·teg′u·ment
in′tel·lect′
in′tel·lec′tu·al
in′tel·lec′tu·al·ize′
 ·ized′ ·iz′ing
in′tel·lec′tu·al·ly
in·tel′li·gence
in·tel′li·gent
in·tel′li·gent′si·a
in·tel′li·gi·bil′i·ty
in·tel′li·gi·ble
in·tel′li·gi·bly
in·tem′per·ance
in·tem′per·ate
in·tend′
in·tense′
in·tense′ly
in·ten′si·fi·ca′tion
in·ten′si·fy′
 ·fied′ ·fy′ing
in·ten′si·ty
 ·ties
in·ten′sive
in·tent′
in·ten′tion
in·ten′tion·al
in·ten′tion·al·ly
in·tent′ly
in·ter′
 ·terred′ ·ter′ring
in′ter- prefix
 (between; to-
 gether; see INTRA-)
in′ter·act′
in′ter·ac′tion
in′ter·ac′tive
in′ter·breed′
in′ter·cede′
 ·ced′ed ·ced′ing
in′ter·cept′
in′ter·cep′tion
in′ter·cep′tor
in′ter·ces′sion
in′ter·ces′sor
in′ter·change′
in′ter·change′a·ble
in′ter·col·le′gi·ate
in′ter·com′
in′ter·com·mu′ni·
 cate′
in′ter·com·mu′ni·
 ca′tion
in′ter·con·nect′
in′ter·con·nec′tion
in′ter·con·ti·nen′-
 tal
in′ter·cos′tal
in′ter·course′

in′ter·de·nom′i·na′
 tion·al
in′ter·de′part·men′
 tal
in′ter·de·pend′ence
in′ter·de·pend′ent
in′ter·dict′
in′ter·dic′tion
in′ter·dis′ci·pli·nar′y
in′ter·est
in′ter·est·ed
in′ter·est·ing
in′ter·face′
in′ter·faith′
in′ter·fere′
 ·fered′ ·fer′ing
in′ter·fer′ence
in′ter·fer′on′
in′ter·gen′er·a′tion
 ·al
in′ter·im
in·te′ri·or
in·te′ri·or·ize′
 ·ized′ ·iz′ing
in′ter·ject′
in′ter·jec′tion
in′ter·lace′
in′ter·lard′
in′ter·leu′kin
in′ter·lock′
in′ter·loc′u·to·ry
in′ter·lop·er
in′ter·lude′
in′ter·mar′riage
in′ter·mar′ry
in′ter·me′di·ar′y
 ·ar′ies
in′ter·me′di·ate
in·ter′ment
in′ter·mez′zo′
 ·zos′ or ·zi′
in·ter′mi·na·ble
in·ter′mi·na·bly
in′ter·min′gle
in′ter·mis′sion
in′ter·mit′tent
in′tern
in·ter′nal
in·ter′nal·ize′
 ·ized′ ·iz′ing
in·ter′nal·ly
in′ter·na′tion·al
in′ter·na′tion·al·ize′
in′ter·na′tion·al·ly
in′ter·ne′cine
in′tern·ee′
in′tern′ist
in·tern′ment
in′tern′ship′
in′ter·of′fice
in′ter·per′son·al
in′ter·plan′e·tar′y
in′ter·play′
in·ter′po·late′
 ·lat′ed ·lat′ing
in·ter′po·la′tion
in′ter·pose′
in·ter′pret
in·ter′pre·ta′tion

in·ter′pret·er
in·ter′pre·tive
in′ter·ra′cial
in′ter·re·late′
in′ter·re·la′tion
in′ter·re·la′tion·ship
in·ter′ro·gate′
 ·gat′ed ·gat′ing
in·ter′ro·ga′tion
in·ter·rog′a·tive
in·ter′ro·ga·tor
in·ter′ro·ga·to′ry
in′ter·rupt′
in′ter·rup′tion
in′ter·scho·las′tic
in′ter·sect′
in′ter·sec′tion
in′ter·ses′sion
in′ter·sperse′
 ·spersed′ ·spers′-
 ing
in′ter·state′
in′ter·stel′lar
in·ter′stice
 ·sti·ces′
in′ter·twine′
in′ter·ur′ban
in′ter·val
in′ter·vene′
 ·vened′ ·ven′ing
in′ter·ven′tion
in′ter·view′
in′ter·view·ee′
in′ter·view′er
in′ter·weave′
in·tes′ta·cy
in·tes′tate′
in·tes′tin·al
in·tes′tine
in′ti·ma·cy
 ·cies
in′ti·mate′
 ·mat′ed ·mat′ing
in′ti·mate·ly
in·tim′i·date′
 ·dat′ed ·dat′ing
in·tim′i·da′tion
in′to
in·tol′er·a·ble
in·tol′er·a·bly
in·tol′er·ance
in·tol′er·ant
in′to·na′tion
in·tone′
in to′to
in·tox′i·cant
in·tox′i·cate′
 ·cat′ed ·cat′ing
in·tox′i·ca′tion
in′tra- prefix
 (within; inside;
 see INTER-)
in′tra·cel′lu·lar
in·trac′ta·ble
in′tra·der′mal
in′tra·mu′ral
in′tra·mus′cu·lar
in·tran′si·gence

in·tran′si·gent
in·tran′si·tive
in′tra·state′
in′tra·u′ter·ine
in′tra·ve′nous
in·trep′id
in′tri·ca·cy
 ·cies
in′tri·cate
in·trigue′
 ·trigued′ ·trigu′ing
in·trigu′er
in·trigu′ing·ly
in·trin′sic
in·trin′si·cal·ly
in′tro·duce′
 ·duced′ ·duc′ing
in′tro·duc′tion
in′tro·duc′to·ry
in·tro′it
in′tro·spec′tion
in′tro·spec′tive
in′tro·ver′sion
in′tro·vert′
in′tro·vert′ed
in·trude′
 ·trud′ed ·trud′ing
in·trud′er
in·tru′sion
in·tru′sive
in·trust′
in′tu·bate′
 ·bat′ed ·bat′ing
in·tu·i′tion
in·tu′i·tive
in′un·date′
 ·dat′ed ·dat′ing
in′un·da′tion
in·ure′
 ·ured′ ·ur′ing
in·vade′
 ·vad′ed ·vad′ing
in·vad′er
in′va·lid (sick per-
 son)
in·val′id (not valid)
in·val′i·date′
 ·dat′ed ·dat′ing
in·val′i·da′tion
in·val′u·a·ble
in·val′u·a·bly
in·var′i·a·ble
in·var′i·a·bly
in·va′sion
in·vec′tive
in·veigh′
in·vei′gle
 ·gled ·gling
in·vei′gler
in·vent′
in·ven′tion
in·ven′tive
in·ven′tor
in′ven·to′ry
 ·ries
 ·ried ·ry·ing
in·verse′
in·verse′ly

in·ver′sion
in·vert′
in·ver′te·brate
in·vest′
in·ves′ti·gate′
  ·gat′ed ·gat′ing
in·ves′ti·ga′tion
in·ves′ti·ga′tor
in·ves′ti·ture
in·vest′ment
in·ves′tor
in·vet′er·ate
in·vid′i·ous
in·vig′or·ate′
  ·at′ed ·at′ing
in·vin′ci·bil′i·ty
in·vin′ci·ble
in·vin′ci·bly
in·vi′o·la·bil′i·ty
in·vi′o·la·ble
in·vi′o·late
in·vis′i·bil′i·ty
in·vis′i·ble
in·vis′i·bly
in′vi·ta′tion
in′vi·ta′tion·al
in·vite′
  ·vit′ed ·vit′ing
in′vit·ee′
in·vit′ing
in vi′tro
in′vo·ca′tion
in′voice
  ·voiced′ ·voic′ing
in·voke′
  ·voked′ ·vok′ing
in·vol′un·tar′i·ly
in·vol′un·tar′y
in′vo·lu′tion
in·volve′
  ·volved′ ·volv′ing
in·volved′
in·volve′ment
in·vul′ner·a·ble
in′ward
i′o·dine′
i′on
  (atom; see EON)
i′on·i·za′tion
i′on·ize′
  ·ized′ ·iz′ing
i′on·iz′er
i·on′o·sphere′
i·o′ta
I′o·wa
ip′e·cac′
ip′so fac′to
I·ra′ni·an
I·ra′qi
i·ras′ci·ble
i·rate′
ire
i·ren′ic
ir′i·des′cence
ir′i·des′cent
i·rid′i·um
i′ris
I′rish

irk
irk′some
i′ron
i′ron·clad′
i·ron′ic
i·ron′i·cal·ly
i′ron·ware′
i′ron·work′
i′ro·ny
  ·nies
ir·ra′di·ate′
  ·at′ed ·at′ing
ir·ra′di·a′tion
ir·ra′tion·al
ir·ra′tion·al′i·ty
  ·ties
ir·ra′tion·al·ly
ir′re·claim′a·ble
ir′rec·on·cil′a·ble
ir′re·cov′er·a·ble
ir′re·deem′a·ble
ir·ref′u·ta·ble
ir·reg′u·lar
ir·reg′u·lar′i·ty
  ·ties
ir·rel′e·vance
ir·rel′e·vant
ir′re·li′gious
ir′re·me′di·a·ble
ir′re·me′di·a·bly
ir·rep′a·ra·ble
ir′re·place′a·ble
ir′re·press′i·ble
ir′re·proach′a·ble
ir′re·sist′i·ble
ir·res′o·lute′
ir′re·spec′tive
ir′re·spon′si·ble
ir′re·triev′a·ble
ir·rev′er·ence
ir·rev′er·ent
ir′re·vers′i·ble
ir·rev′o·ca·ble
ir·rev′o·ca·bly
ir′ri·ga·ble
ir′ri·gate′
  ·gat′ed ·gat′ing
ir′ri·ga′tion
ir′ri·ta·bil′i·ty
ir′ri·ta·ble
ir′ri·ta·bly
ir′ri·tant
ir′ri·tate′
  ·tat′ed ·tat′ing
ir′ri·ta′tion
ir·rupt′
ir·rup′tion
ir·rup′tive
i′sin·glass′
Is′lam′
Is·lam′ic
is′land
is′land·er
isle
  (island; see AISLE)
is′let
  (small island; see
  EYELET)

ism
i′so·bar′
i′so·late′
  ·lat′ed ·lat′ing
i′so·la′tion
i′so·la′tion·ism′
i′so·la′tion·ist
i′so·la′tor
i′so·mer
i′so·met′ric
i′so·met′ri·cal·ly
i·sos′ce·les′
i′so·therm′
i′so·tope′
Is·rae′li
is′su·ance
is′sue
  ·sued ·su·ing
isth′mus
  ·mus·es or ·mi′
it
  they
I·tal′ian
i·tal′ic
i·tal′i·cize′
  ·cized′ ·ciz′ing
itch
itch′i·ness
itch′y
  ·i·er ·i·est
i′tem
i′tem·i·za′tion
i′tem·ize′
  ·ized′ ·iz′ing
it′er·ate′
  ·at′ed ·at′ing
it′er·a′tion
i·tin′er·ant
i·tin′er·ar′y
  ·ies
its (of it)
it′s (it is)
it·self′
it′ty-bit′ty
i′vied
i′vo·ry
  ·ries
i′vy
  i′vies

J

jab
  jabbed jab′bing
jab′ber
jab′ber·er
ja·bot′
jack
jack′al
jack′ass′
jack′daw′
jack′et
jack′ham′mer
jack′-in-the-box′
  -box′es
jack′-in-the-pul′pit
  ·pits

jack′knife′
  ·knives′
  ·knifed′ ·knif′ing
jack′-o′-lan′tern
  ·terns
jack′pot′
jade
  jad′ed jad′ing
jade′ite
jag′ged
jag′ged·ly
jag′ged·ness
jag′uar′
jai′ a·lai′
jail
jail′break′
jail′er or ·or
ja·la·pe′ño
ja·lop′y
  ·ies
jal′ou·sie′
  (window; see JEAL-
  OUSY)
jam
  jammed jam′ming
  (jelly; to crowd)
jamb (door frame)
jam′bo·ree′
jam′packed′
jan′gle
  ·gled ·gling
jan′i·tor
jan′i·to′ri·al
Jan′u·ar′y
ja·pan′
  ·panned′
  ·pan′ning
Jap′a·nese′
jape
  japed jap′ing
jar
  jarred jar′ring
jar′di·niere′
jar′gon
jas′mine
jas′per
jaun′dice
  ·diced ·dic·ing
jaunt
jaun′ti·ly
jaun′ti·ness
jaun′ty
  ·ti·er ·ti·est
jav′e·lin
jaw
jaw′bone′
jaw′break′er
jay
jay′walk′
jay′walk′er
jazz
jazz′y
  ·i·er ·i·est
jeal′ous
jeal′ous·ly
jeal′ous·y
  (envy; see
  JALOUSIE)
jeans
jeep

jeer
je·june′
je·ju′num
  ·na
jell
jel′ly
  ·lies
  ·lied ·ly·ing
jel′ly·fish′
jel′ly·roll′
jeop′ard·ize′
  ·ized′ ·iz′ing
jeop′ard·y
jerk
jerk′i·ly
jer′kin
jerk′wa′ter
jerk′y
  ·i·er ·i·est
  (moving by jerks)
jer′ky (dried beef)
jer′ry-built′
jer′sey
  ·seys
jest
jest′er
jet
  jet′ted jet′ting
jet′port′
jet′-pro·pelled′
jet′sam
jet′-set′ter
jet′ti·son
jet′ty
  ·ties
jew′el
  ·eled or ·elled
  ·el·ing or ·el·ling
jew′el·er or ·ler
jew′el·ry
Jew′ish
Jew′ry
jib
jibe
  jibed jib′ing
  (agree; see GIBE)
jif′fy
jig
  jigged jig′ging
jig′ger
jig′gle
  ·gled ·gling
jig′saw′
jilt
jim′my
  ·mies
  ·mied ·my·ing
jim′son weed
jin′gle
  ·gled ·gling
jin′go·ism′
jin′go·ist
jin′go·is′tic
jin·ni′
  jinn
jinx
jit′ter·bug′
jit′ters
jit′ter·y
jive

job
  jobbed job′bing
job′ber
job′hold′er
job′less
jock
jock′ey
  ·eys
  ·eyed ·ey·ing
jock′strap′
jo·cose′
jo·cose′ly
jo·cos′i·ty
joc′u·lar
joc′u·lar′i·ty
joc′u·lar·ly
joc′und
joc′und·ly
jodh′purs
jog
  jogged jog′ging
jog′ger
jog′gle
  ·gled ·gling
join
join′er
joint
joint′ly
joist
joke
  joked jok′ing
jok′er
jok′ey
jok′ing·ly
jok′y
jol′li·ly
jol′li·ness
jol′li·ty
jol′ly
  ·li·er ·li·est
jolt
jon′quil
josh
josh′er
jos′tle
  ·tled ·tling
jot
  jot′ted jot′ting
jot′ter
joule
jounce
  jounced jounc′ing
jour′nal
jour′nal·ese′
jour′nal·ism′
jour′nal·ist
jour′nal·is′tic
jour′ney
  ·neys
  ·neyed ·ney·ing
jour′ney·er
jour′ney·man
joust
jo′vi·al
jo′vi·al′i·ty
jo′vi·al·ly
jowl
joy

joy'ful
joy'ful·ly
joy'ous
joy'ous·ly
joy'ous·ness
joy'stick'
ju'bi·lant
ju'bi·la'tion
ju'bi·lee'
Ju·da'ic
Ju'da·ism'
judge
 judged judg'ing
judge'ship'
judg'ment or
 judge'·
judg·men'tal
ju'di·ca·to'ry
 ·ries
ju'di·ca·ture
ju·di'cial
ju·di'ci·ar'y
 ·ies
ju·di'cious
ju·di'cious·ly
ju'do
jug
jug'ger·naut'
jug'gle
 ·gled ·gling
jug'gler
jug'u·lar
juice
 juiced juic'ing
juic'er
juic'i·ness
juic'y
 ·i·er ·i·est
ju·jit'su'
ju'ju·be'
juke'box'
ju'lep
ju'li·enne'
Ju·ly'
jum'ble
 ·bled ·bling
jum'bo
 ·bos
jump
jump'er
jump'i·ly
jump'i·ness
jump'-start'
jump'suit'
jump'y
 ·i·er ·i·est
jun'co'
 ·cos'
junc'tion
junc'ture
June
jun'gle
jun'ior
ju'ni·per
junk
junk'er
jun'ket

junk'ie or ·y
 ·ies
 (an addict)
junk'y
 ·i·er ·i·est
 (worthless)
junk'yard'
jun'ta
Ju'pi·ter
Ju·ras'sic
ju·rid'i·cal
ju'ris·dic'tion
ju'ris·dic'tion·al
ju'ris·pru'dence
ju'rist
ju·ris'tic
ju'ror
ju'ry
 ·ries
just
jus'tice
jus·ti'ci·a·ble
jus'ti·fi'a·ble
jus'ti·fi·ca'tion
jus'ti·fy'
 ·fied' ·fy'ing
just'ly
just'ness
jut
 jut'ted jut'ting
jute
ju've·nile'
jux'ta·pose'
 ·posed' ·pos'ing
jux'ta·po·si'tion

K

kad'dish
kaf'fee·klatsch'
kai'ser
kale
ka·lei'do·scope'
ka·lei'do·scop'ic
ka'mi·ka'ze
kan'ga·roo'
Kan'sas
ka'o·lin
ka'pok'
ka·put'
kar'a·kul'
kar'at
 (gold measure; see
 CARAT, CARET, CAR-
 ROT)
ka·ra'te
kar'ma
kart
ka'ty·did'
kay'ak'
kay'o'
 ·oed' ·o'ing
ka·zoo'
ke·bab' or ·bob'
keel
keen
keen'ly
keen'ness

keep
 kept keep'ing
keep'er
keep'sake'
keg
kelp
Kel'vin
ken
ken'nel
 ·neled or ·nelled
 ·nel·ing or
 ·nel·ling
Ken·tuck'y
kept
ker'a·tin
ker'chief
ker'nel
 (grain; see
 COLONEL)
ker'o·sene'
kes'trel
ketch
ketch'up
ket'tle
ket'tle·drum'
key
 keys
 keyed key'ing
 (reef; see QUAY)
key'board'
key'hole'
key'note'
key'stone'
key'stroke'
kha'ki
 ·kis
khan
kib·butz'
 kib'but·zim'
kib'itz
kib'itz·er
ki'bosh'
kick
kick'back'
kick'er
kick'off'
kick'stand'
kick'y
 ·i·er ·i·est
kid
 kid'ded kid'ding
kid'die or ·dy
 ·dies
kid'nap'
 ·napped' or
 ·naped', ·nap'ping
 or ·nap'ing
kid'nap'per or
 ·nap'er
kid'ney
 ·neys
kiel·ba'sa
 ·si or ·sas
kill
kill'er
kill'ing
kill'joy'
kiln
ki'lo
 ·los

kil'o·byte'
kil'o·cy'cle
kil'o·gram'
kil'o·hertz'
 ·hertz'
kil·o'me·ter
kil'o·watt'
kilt
kil'ter
ki·mo'no
 ·nos
kin
kind
kin'der·gar'ten
kin'der·gart'ner or
 ·gar'ten·er
kind'heart'ed
kin'dle
 ·dled ·dling
kind'li·ness
kin'dling
kind'ly
 ·li·er ·li·est
kind'ness
kin'dred
ki·net'ic
kin'folk'
king
king'dom
king'fish'er
king'ly
king'pin'
king'-size'
kink
kin'ka·jou'
kink'y
 ·i·er ·i·est
kin'ship'
kins'man
kins'wom'an
ki'osk'
kip'per
kis'met
kiss
kiss'a·ble
kit
kitch'en
kitch'en·ette' or
 ·et'
kitch'en·ware'
kite
kitsch
kitsch'y
kit'ten
kit'ten·ish
kit'ty
 ·ties
ki'wi
 ·wis
Klee'nex'
klep'to·ma'ni·a
klep'to·ma'ni·ac'
klez'mer
klieg light
klutz
knack
knack'wurst'
knap'sack'

knave
 (rogue; see NAVE)
knav'er·y
knav'ish
knead
 (press; see NEED)
knead'er
knee
 kneed knee'ing
knee'cap'
knee'-deep'
knee'-jerk'
kneel
 knelt or kneeled
 kneel'ing
knell
knew
knick'ers
knick'knack'
knife
 knives
 knifed knif'ing
knight
 (rank; see NIGHT)
knight'-er'rant
 knights'-er'rant
knight'hood'
knight'ly
knit
 knit'ted or knit
 knit'ting
knit'ter
knit'wear'
knob
knob'by
 ·bi·er ·bi·est
knock
knock'er
knock'-kneed'
knock'out'
knock'wurst'
knoll
knot
 knot'ted knot'ting
knot'hole'
knot'ty
 ·ti·er ·ti·est
know
 knew known
 know'ing
know'-how'
know'ing·ly
know'-it-all'
knowl'edge
knowl'edge·a·ble
knowl'edge·a·bly
known
knuck'le
knuck'le·head'
knurl
ko·a'la
kohl·ra'bi
 ·bies
kook
kook'a·bur'ra
kook'y or ·ie
 ·i·er ·i·est
ko'peck' or ·pek'
Ko·ran'
Ko·re'an

ko'sher
kow'tow'
ku'chen
ku'dos
kud'zu
kum'quat'
kung' fu'

L

lab
la'bel
 ·beled or ·belled
 ·bel·ing or
 ·bel·ling
la'bi·al
la'bi·um
 ·bi·a
la'bor
lab'o·ra·to'ry
 ·ries
la'bor·er
la·bo'ri·ous
la·bo'ri·ous·ly
la·bur'num
lab'y·rinth'
lace
 laced lac'ing
lac'er·ate'
 ·at'ed ·at'ing
lac'er·a'tion
lace'work'
lach'ry·mal
lach'ry·mose'
lac'i·ness
lack
lack'a·dai'si·cal
lack'ey
 ·eys
lack'lus'ter
la·con'ic
la·con'i·cal·ly
lac'quer
lac'ri·mal
la·crosse'
lac'tate'
 ·tat'ed ·tat'ing
lac·ta'tion
lac'te·al
lac'tic
lac'tose'
la·cu'na
 ·nas or ·nae
lac'y
 ·i·er ·i·est
lad
lad'der
lad'en
lad'ing
la'dle
 ·dled ·dling
la'dy
 ·dies
la'dy·bird'
la'dy·bug'
la'dy·fin'ger
la'dy·like'
la'dy·ship'

la'dy-slip'per
lag
  lagged lag'ging
la'ger (*beer*)
lag'gard
lag'ger (*one who*
  lags)
la·gniappe' *or*
  ·gnappe'
la·goon'
laid
laid'-back'
lain
lair
lais'sez faire'
la'i·ty
  ·ties
lake
lal'ly·gag'
  ·gagged' ·gag'ging
lam
  (*escape;* see LAMB)
la'ma
  (*monk;* see LLAMA)
la'ma·ser'y
  ·ies
La·maze'
lamb
  (*a young sheep;*
  see LAM)
lam·baste'
  ·bast'ed ·bast'ing
lam'bent
lamb'kin
lame
  lamed lam'ing
  (*crippled*)
la·mé' (*cloth*)
la·mel'la
  ·lae *or* ·las
lame'ly
lame'ness
la·ment'
lam'en·ta·ble
lam'en·ta'tion
lam'i·na
  ·nae' *or* ·nas
lam'i·nate'
  ·nat'ed ·nat'ing
lam'i·na'tion
lamp
lamp'black'
lam·poon'
lamp'post'
lam'prey
  ·preys
lamp'shade'
la·na'i
lance
  lanced lanc'ing
lanc'er
lan'cet
land
land'fall'
land'fill'
land'hold'er
land'hold'ing
land'la'dy
land'locked'

land'lord'
land'lub'ber
land'mark'
land'mass'
land'scape'
  ·scaped' ·scap'ing
land'scap'er
land'slide'
land'ward
lane
lan'guage
lan'guid
lan'guid·ly
lan'guish
lan'guor
lan'guor·ous
lank
lank'i·ness
lank'ness
lank'y
  ·i·er ·i·est
lan'o·lin'
lan'tern
lan'yard
lap
  lapped lap'ping
la·pel'
lap'i·dar'y
  ·ies
lap'is laz'u·li'
lapse
  lapsed laps'ing
lar'ce·nist
lar'ce·nous
lar'ce·ny
  ·nies
larch
lard
lard'er
large
  larg'er larg'est
large'heart'ed
large'ly
large'ness
large'-scale'
lar·gess' *or* ·gesse'
larg'ish
lar'go
lar'i·at
lark
lark'spur'
lar'va
  ·vae' *or* ·vas
lar'val
lar'yn·gi'tis
lar'ynx
  ·ynx·es *or*
  la·ryn'ges'
la·sa'gna *or* ·gne
las·civ'i·ous
la'ser
lash
lass
las'si·tude'
las'so'
  ·sos' *or* ·soes'
  ·soed' ·so'ing
last
last'ing

last'ing·ly
last'ly
latch
late
  lat'er *or* lat'ter
  lat'est *or* last
late'ly
la'ten·cy
late'ness
la'tent
lat'er·al
lat'er·al·ly
la'tex'
lath (*wood strip*)
lathe
  lathed lath'ing
  (*shaping machine*)
lath'er
lath'er·y
Lat'in
lat'ish
lat'i·tude'
la·trine'
lat'ter
lat'tice
lat'tice·work'
laud
laud'a·ble
lau'da·num
laud'a·to'ry
laugh
laugh'a·ble
laugh'a·bly
laugh'ing·stock'
laugh'ter
launch
laun'der
laun'der·er
laun'dress
Laun'dro·mat'
laun'dry
  ·dries
laun'dry·man'
laun'dry·wom'an
lau're·ate
lau'rel
la'va
lav'a·to'ry
  ·ries
lav'en·der
lav'ish
lav'ish·ly
law
law'-a·bid'ing
law'break'er
law'ful
law'ful·ly
law'giv'er
law'less
law'less·ness
law'mak'er
law'man
lawn
law'suit'
law'yer
law'yer·ly
lax

lax'a·tive
lax'i·ty
lay
  laid lay'ing
  (*put;* see LIE)
lay'a·way'
lay'er
lay·ette'
lay'man
lay'off'
lay'out'
lay'o'ver
laze
  lazed laz'ing
la'zi·ly
la'zi·ness
la'zy
  ·zi·er ·zi·est
la'zy·bones'
leach
  (*to filter;* see
  LEECH)
lead
  led lead'ing
  (*to direct others*)
lead
  lead'ed lead'ing
  (*heavy metal*)
lead'en
lead'er
lead'er·ship'
leaf
  leaves
leaf'less
leaf'let
leaf'y
  ·i·er ·i·est
league
  leagued leagu'ing
leagu'er
leak
  (*escape;* see LEEK)
leak'age
leak'y
  ·i·er ·i·est
lean
  leaned *or* leant
  lean'ing
  (*incline;* see LIEN)
lean'ness
lean'-to'
  -tos'
leap
  leapt *or* lept *or*
  leaped
  leap'ing
leap'er
leap'frog'
  ·frogged'
  ·frog'ging
learn
  learned *or* learnt
  learn'ing
learn'ed *adj.*
learn'er
lease
  leased leas'ing
lease'hold'
lease'hold'er
leas'er
leash

least
least'wise'
leath'er
leath'er·y
leave
  left leav'ing
  (*go away*)
leave
  leaved leav'ing
  (*to bear leaves*)
leav'en
leav'er
  (*one who leaves;*
  see LEVER)
leaves
lech'er
lech'er·ous
lech'er·y
lec'i·thin
lec'tern
lec'ture
  ·tured ·tur·ing
lec'tur·er
led
ledge
ledg'er
lee
leech
  (*worm;* see LEACH)
leek
  (*vegetable;* see
  LEAK)
leer
leer'y
lees
lee'ward
lee'way'
left
left'-hand'ed
left'ist
left'o'ver
left'-wing'er
left'y
  ·ies
leg
  legged leg'ging
leg'a·cy
  ·cies
le'gal
le'gal·ese'
le'gal·is'tic
le·gal'i·ty
  ·ties
le'gal·i·za'tion
le'gal·ize'
  ·ized' ·iz'ing
le'gal·ly
leg'ate
leg'a·tee'
le·ga'tion
le·ga'to
leg'end
leg'end·ar'y
leg'er·de·main'
leg'gy
  ·gi·er ·gi·est
leg'horn'
leg'i·bil'i·ty
leg'i·ble

leg'i·bly
le'gion
le'gion·naire'
leg'is·late'
  ·lat'ed ·lat'ing
leg'is·la'tion
leg'is·la'tive
leg'is·la'tive·ly
leg'is·la'tor
leg'is·la'ture
le·git'i·ma·cy
le·git'i·mate
le·git'i·mate·ly
le·git'i·ma·tize'
  ·tized' ·tiz'ing
le·git'i·mi·za'tion
le·git'i·mize'
  ·mized' ·miz'ing
leg'room'
leg'ume'
le·gu'mi·nous
leg'work'
lei
lei'sure
lei'sure·ly
leit'mo·tif' *or* ·tiv'
lem'ming
lem'on
lem'on·ade'
lem'on·y
le'mur
lend
  lent lend'ing
lend'er
length
length'en
length'i·ly
length'wise'
length'y
  ·i·er ·i·est
le'ni·en·cy
le'ni·ent
le'ni·ent·ly
len'i·tive
lens
lent
Lent'en
len'til
  (*pea;* see LINTEL)
Le'o
le'o·nine'
leop'ard
le'o·tard'
lep'er
lep're·chaun'
lep'ro·sy
lep'rous
lept
les'bi·an
les'bi·an·ism'
le'sion
less
les·see'
less'en (*make less*)
less'er (*smaller*)
les'son (*instruction*)

les'sor' (one who
   leases)
lest
let
   let let'ting
let'down'
le'thal
le·thar'gic
le·thar'gi·cal·ly
leth·ar·gy
let'ter
let'ter·er
let'ter·head'
let'ter·ing
let'ter-per'fect
let'tuce
let'up'
leu·ke'mi·a
leu'ko·cyte'
lev'ee
   (embankment; see
   LEVY)
lev'el
   ·eled or ·elled
   ·el·ing or ·el·ling
lev'el·er or ·ler
lev'el·head'ed
lev'er
   (lifting device; see
   LEAVER)
lev'er·age
le·vi'a·than
lev'i·tate'
   ·tat'ed ·tat'ing
lev'i·ta'tion
lev'i·ty
lev'y
   ·ies
   ·ied ·y·ing
   (tax; see LEVEE)
lewd
lewd'ly
lewd'ness
lex'i·cog'ra·pher
lex'i·cog'ra·phy
lex'i·con'
li'a·bil'i·ty
   ·ties
li'a·ble
li'ai·son'
li'ar
   (one who tells lies;
   see LYRE)
li·ba'tion
li'bel
   ·beled or ·belled
   ·bel·ing or
   ·bel·ling
li'bel·er or ·ler
li'bel·ous or ·lous
lib'er·al
lib'er·al·ism'
lib'er·al'i·ty
lib'er·al·i·za'tion
lib'er·al·ize'
   ·ized' ·iz'ing
lib'er·al·ly
lib'er·al·ness
lib'er·ate'
   ·at'ed ·at'ing

lib'er·a'tion
lib'er·a'tor
lib'er·tar'i·an
lib'er·tine'
lib'er·ty
   ·ties
li·bid'i·nous
li·bi'do
Li'bra
li·brar'i·an
li'brar'y
   ·ies
li·bret'tist
li·bret'to
   ·tos or ·ti
lice
   sing. louse
li'cense
   ·censed ·cens·ing
li'cen·see'
li'cens·er or
   ·cen·sor
li·cen'tious
li·cen'tious·ness
li'chen
lic'it
lic'it·ly
lick
lic'o·rice
lid
lid'ded
lie
   lay lain ly'ing
   (recline; see LAY)
lie
   lied ly'ing
   (tell a falsehood;
   see LYE)
liege
li·en'
   (a claim; see LEAN)
lieu
lieu·ten'an·cy
lieu·ten'ant
life
   lives
life'blood'
life'boat'
life'guard'
life'less
life'like'
life'line'
life'long'
lif'er
life'sav'er
life'-size'
life'style'
life'time'
life'work'
lift
lift'er
lift'off'
lig'a·ment
lig'a·ture
light
   light'ed or lit
   light'ing
light'en
   ·ened ·en·ing

light'en·ing
   (making light or
   less heavy; see
   LIGHTNING)
light'er
light'-foot'ed
light'head'ed
light'heart'ed
light'heart'ed·ly
light'heart'ed·ness
light'house'
light'ing
light'ly
light'ness
light'ning
   (flash of light in
   the sky; see LIGHT-
   ENING)
light'weight'
light'-year'
lig'nite'
lik'a·bil'i·ty
lik'a·ble or like'·
lik'a·ble·ness
like
   liked lik'ing
like'li·hood'
like'ly
   ·li·er ·li·est
like'-mind'ed
lik'en
like'ness
lik'er
like'wise'
li'lac'
Lil'li·pu'tian
lilt
lil'y
   ·ies
lil'y-liv'ered
li'ma bean
limb
   (branch; see LIMN)
lim'ber
limb'less
lim'bo'
   ·bos'
lime
   limed lim'ing
lime'ade'
lime'light'
lim'er·ick
lime'stone'
lim'it
lim·i·ta'tion
lim'it·ed
lim'it·er
lim'it·less
limn
   limned limn'ing
   (draw; see LIMB)
lim·nol'o·gy
lim'o
   ·os
lim'ou·sine'
limp
limp'et
lim'pid
limp'ly

limp'ness
lim'y
   ·i·er ·i·est
lin'age
   (printed lines; see
   LINEAGE)
linch'pin'
lin'den
line
   lined lin'ing
lin'e·age
   (ancestry; see
   LINAGE)
lin'e·al
lin'e·a·ment
   (feature; see LINI-
   MENT)
lin'e·ar
line'back'er
line'man
lin'en
lin'er
lines'man
line'up'
lin'ger
lin'ger·er
lin'ge·rie'
lin'ger·ing
lin'go'
   ·goes'
lin'gual
lin·gui'ne or ·ni
lin'guist
lin·guis'tic
lin'i·ment
   (medication; see
   LINEAMENT)
link
link'age
link'up'
lin'net
li·no'le·um
lin'seed'
lint
lin'tel
   (piece above door;
   see LENTIL)
lint'y
li'on
li'on·ess
li'on-heart'ed
li'on·ize'
   ·ized' ·iz'ing
lip
   lipped lip'ping
lip'id
lip'py
lip'-read'
lip'stick'
lip'-sync' or -
   synch'
liq'ue·fac'tion
liq'ue·fy'
   ·fied' ·fy'ing
li·queur'
   (a sweet liquor;
   see LIQUOR)
liq'uid
liq'ui·date'
   ·dat'ed ·dat'ing

liq'ui·da'tion
liq'ui·da'tor
liq·uid'i·ty
liq'uid·ize'
   ·ized' ·iz'ing
liq'uor
   (alcoholic drink;
   see LIQUEUR)
lisle
lisp
lis'some or ·som
list
lis'ten
lis'ten·er
list'less
list'less·ness
lit
lit'a·ny
   ·nies
li'tchi'
li'ter
   (metric unit; see
   LITTER)
lit'er·a·cy
lit'er·al
   (exact; see LIT-
   TORAL)
lit'er·al·ly
lit'er·ar'y
lit'er·ate
lit'e·ra'ti
lit'er·a·ture'
lithe
lith'i·um
lith'o·graph'
li·thog'ra·pher
lith'o·graph'ic
li·thog'ra·phy
lith'o·sphere'
lit'i·gant
lit'i·gate'
   ·gat'ed ·gat'ing
lit'i·ga'tion
lit'i·ga'tor
li·ti'gious
li·ti'gious·ness
lit'mus
lit'ter
   (rubbish; see
   LITER)
lit'ter·bug'
lit'tle
   lit'tler or less or
   less'er
   lit'tlest or least
lit'tle·ness
lit'to·ral
   (along the shore;
   see LITERAL)
li·tur'gi·cal
lit'ur·gy
   ·gies
liv'a·ble or live'·
live
   lived liv'ing
live'bear'er
live'li·hood'
live'li·ness
live'long'

live'ly
   ·li·er ·li·est
liv'en
liv'er
liv'er·wurst'
liv'er·y
   ·ies
lives
live'stock'
liv'id
liz'ard
lla'ma
   (animal; see LAMA)
lla'no
   ·nos
load
   (burden; see LODE)
load'er
loaf
   loaves
loaf'er
loam
loam'y
loan
   (something lent;
   see LONE)
loan'er
loath (reluctant)
loathe
   loathed loath'ing
   (dislike)
loath'ing
loath'some
loaves
lob
   lobbed lob'bing
lob'by
   ·bies
   ·bied ·by·ing
lob'by·ist
lobe
lo·bot'o·my
   ·mies
lob'ster
lo'cal
lo·cale'
lo·cal'i·ty
   ·ties
lo'cal·ize'
   ·ized' ·iz'ing
lo'cal·ly
lo'cate'
   ·cat'ed ·cat'ing
lo·ca'tion
lock
lock'er
lock'et
lock'jaw'
lock'out'
lock'smith'
lock'up'
lo'co
lo'co·mo'tion
lo'co·mo'tive
lo'co·weed'
lo'cus
   ·ci'
lo'cust
lo·cu'tion

lode
(*ore;* see LOAD)
lode'stone'
lodge
lodged lodg'ing
(*house;* see LOGE)
lodg'er
lodg'ing
loft
loft'i·ness
loft'y
·i·er ·i·est
log
logged log'ging
lo'gan·ber'ry
log'a·rithm
log'a·rith'mic
loge
(*theater box;* see LODGE)
log'ger·heads'
log'ic
log'i·cal
log'i·cal·ly
lo·gi'cian
lo·gis'tic
lo·gis'tics
lo·gis'ti·cal
lo·gis'ti·cal·ly
log'jam'
log'o'
log'o·type'
lo'gy
·gi·er ·gi·est
loin
loin'cloth'
loi'ter
loi'ter·er
loll
lol'li·pop' *or* ·ly·
lol'ly·gag'
·gagged' ·gag'ging
lone
(*solitary;* see LOAN)
lone'li·ness
lone'ly
·li·er ·li·est
lon'er
lone'some
long
long'-dis'tance
lon·gev'i·ty
long'hand'
long'ing
lon'gi·tude'
lon'gi·tu'di·nal
long'-lived'
long'-range'
long'shore'man
long'-stand'ing
long'-suf'fer·ing
long'-term'
long'-wind'ed
look
look'er
look'out'
look'-see'
loom

loon
loon'y
·i·er ·i·est
loop
loop'hole'
loop'y
·i·er ·i·est
loose
loos'er loos'est
loosed loos'ing
(*set free;* see LOSE)
loose'-leaf'
loose'ly
loos'en
loose'ness
loot
(*stolen goods;* see LUTE)
lop
lopped lop'ping
(*cut*)
lope
loped lop'ing
(*canter*)
lop'sid'ed
lo·qua'cious
lo·quac'i·ty
lord
lord'ly
lord'ship'
lore
lor·gnette'
lo'ris
lor'ry
·ries
lose
lost los'ing
(*mislay;* see LOOSE)
los'er
loss
lot
lo'tion
lot'ter·y
·ies
lot'to
lo'tus
loud
loud'ly
loud'mouthed'
loud'ness
loud'speak'er
Lou·i'si·an'a
lounge
lounged loung'ing
louse
lice
lous'y
·i·er ·i·est
lout
lout'ish
lou'ver
lov'a·ble
love
loved lov'ing
love'bird'
love'less
love'li·ness
love'lorn'

love'ly
·li·er ·li·est
lov'er
lov'ing·ly
low
low'born'
low'boy'
low'brow'
low'down'
low'er
low'er·case'
low'er·class'man
low'er·ing
low'-grade'
low'-key'
low'land'
low'li·ness
low'ly
·li·er ·li·est
low'ness
lox
loy'al
loy'al·ist
loy'al·ly
loy'al·ty
·ties
loz'enge
lu'au'
lube
lu'bri·cant
lu'bri·cate'
·cat'ed ·cat'ing
lu'bri·ca'tion
lu'bri·ca'tor
lu'cid
lu·cid'i·ty
lu'cid·ly
luck
luck'i·ly
luck'i·ness
luck'less
luck'y
·i·er ·i·est
lu'cra·tive
lu'cre
lu'cu·bra'tion
lu'di·crous
lu'di·crous·ly
lu'di·crous·ness
lug
lugged lug'ging
lug'gage
lu·gu'bri·ous
lu·gu'bri·ous·ly
lu·gu'bri·ous·ness
luke'warm'
luke'warm'ly
lull
lull'a·by'
·bies'
lum·ba'go
lum'bar (*of the loins*)
lum'ber (*timber*)
lum'ber·er
lum'ber·jack'
lum'ber·man

lu'mi·nar'y
·ies
lu'mi·nes'cence
lu'mi·nes'cent
lu'mi·nos'i·ty
lu'mi·nous
lum'mox
lump
lump'i·ness
lump'y
·i·er ·i·est
lu'na·cy
·cies
lu'nar
lu'na·tic
lunch
lunch'eon
lunch'eon·ette'
lung
lunged lung'ing
lunge
lung'fish'
lunk'head'
lu'pine'
lu'pus
lurch
lure
lured lur'ing
lu'rid
lu'rid·ness
lurk
lus'cious
lus'cious·ly
lus'cious·ness
lush
lust
lus'ter
lust'ful
lust'ful·ly
lust'i·ly
lust'i·ness
lus'trous
lust'y
·i·er ·i·est
lute
(*musical instrument;* see LOOT)
lu'te·nist
Lu'ther·an
lut'ist
lux·u'ri·ance
lux·u'ri·ant
lux·u'ri·ate'
·at'ed ·at'ing
lux·u'ri·ous
lux·u'ri·ous·ly
lux'u·ry
·ries
ly·ce'um
Ly'cra
lye
(*strong alkali;* see LIE)
ly'ing
ly'ing-in'
lymph
lym·phat'ic
lymph'oid'
lym·pho'ma

lynch
lynx
lyre
(*small harp;* see LIAR)
lyr'ic
lyr'i·cal
lyr'i·cist

M

ma·ca'bre
mac·ad'am
mac'a·ro'ni
mac'a·roon'
ma·caw'
mace
mac'er·ate'
·at'ed ·at'ing
mac'er·a'tion
ma·che'te
Mach'i·a·vel'li·an
mach'i·na'tion
ma·chine'
·chined' ·chin'ing
ma·chin'er·y
ma·chin'ist
ma·chis'mo
ma'cho
mack'er·el
·el *or* ·els
mack'i·naw'
mac'ra·mé'
mac'ro- *prefix*
(*large;* see MICRO-)
mac'ro·bi·ot'ic
mac'ro·bi·ot'ics
mac'ro·cosm'
ma'cron
mad
mad'der mad'dest
mad'am
mad'ams *or* mes·dames'
ma·dame'
mes'dames'
mad'cap'
mad'den
mad'den·ing
mad'den·ing·ly
mad'der
made
(*form of* make; see MAID)
ma'de·moi·selle'
mes·de·moi·selles'
made'-to-or'der
made'-up'
mad'house'
mad'man'
mad'ness
ma'dras
mad'ri·gal
mad'wom'an
mael'strom
ma·es'tro
·tros *or* ·tri
Ma·fi·a

Ma·fi·o'so'
·si
mag'a·zine'
ma·gen'ta
mag'got
mag'got·y
mag'ic
mag'i·cal
mag'i·cal·ly
ma·gi'cian
mag'is·te'ri·al
mag'is·trate'
mag'ma
mag'na·nim'i·ty
mag·nan'i·mous
mag'nate
(*influential person;* see MAGNET)
mag·ne'sia
(*laxative*)
mag·ne'si·um (*element*)
mag'net
(*iron attracter;* see MAGNATE)
mag·net'ic
mag·net'i·cal·ly
mag'net·ism'
mag'net·ite'
mag'net·ize'
·ized' ·iz'ing
mag·ne'to
·tos
mag·ne·tom'e·ter
mag'ni·fi·ca'tion
mag·nif'i·cence
mag·nif'i·cent
mag·nif'i·cent·ly
mag'ni·fi'er
mag'ni·fy'
·fied' ·fy'ing
mag'ni·tude'
mag·no'li·a
mag'num
mag'pie'
ma·ha·ra'jah *or* ·ja
ma·ha·ra'ni *or* ·nee
ma·ha·ri'shi
ma·hat'ma
mah'-jongg' *or* **mah'jong'**
ma·hog'a·ny
maid
(*servant;* see MADE)
maid'en
maid'en·hair'
maid'en·head'
maid'en·hood'
maid'en·ly
maid'ser'vant
mail
(*letters;* see MALE)
mail'box'
mail'er
mail'man'
mail'-or'der
maim

main
(*most important;* see MANE)
Maine
main'frame'
main'land'
main'line'
main'ly
main'mast'
main'sail'
main'spring'
main'stay'
main'stream'
main·tain'
main·tain'a·ble
main'te·nance
mai'tre d''
maî·tre d'hô·tel'
maize
(*corn;* see MAZE)
ma·jes'tic
ma·jes'ti·cal·ly
maj'es·ty
·ties
ma·jol'i·ca
ma'jor
ma'jor-do'mo
·mos
ma·jor'i·ty
·ties
make
made mak'ing
make'-be·lieve'
mak'er
make'shift'
make'up' *or* make'-
up'
mal'ad·just'ed
mal'a·droit'
mal'a·dy
·dies
ma·laise'
mal'a·mute'
mal'a·prop'ism'
ma·lar'i·a
ma·lar'i·al
ma·lar'key *or* ·ky
mal'a·thi'on
mal'con·tent'
male
(*masculine;* see
MAIL)
mal'e·dic'tion
mal'e·fac'tion
mal'e·fac'tor
ma·lef'i·cent
ma·lev'o·lence
ma·lev'o·lent
mal·fea'sance
mal'for·ma'tion
mal·formed'
mal·func'tion
mal'ice
ma·li'cious
ma·li'cious·ly
ma·lign'
ma·lig'nan·cy
·cies

ma·lig'nant
ma·lig'ni·ty
ma·lin'ger
ma·lin'ger·er
mall
(*promenade;* see
MAUL)
mal'lard
mal'le·a·bil'i·ty
mal'le·a·ble
mal'let
mal'low
mal·nour'ished
mal·nu·tri'tion
mal·oc·clu'sion
mal·o'dor·ous
mal·prac'tice
malt
malt'ed
malt'ose'
mal·treat'
mal·treat'ment
ma'ma *or* mam'ma
mam'mal
mam·ma'li·an
mam'ma·ry
mam'mo·gram'
mam·mog'ra·phy
mam'mon
mam'moth
man
men, manned
man'ning
man'a·cle
·cled ·cling
man'age
·aged ·ag·ing
man'age·a·ble
man'age·ment
man'ag·er
man'a·ge'ri·al
ma·ña'na
man'a·tee'
man'da·rin
man'date'
·dat'ed ·dat'ing
man'da·to'ry
man'di·ble
man'do·lin'
man'drake'
man'drel *or* ·dril
(*metal spindle*)
man'drill (*baboon*)
mane
(*long hair;* see
MAIN)
man'-eat'er
man'-eat'ing
ma·neu'ver
ma·neu'ver·a·ble
man'ful
man'ful·ly
man'ga·nese'
mange
man'ger
man'gi·ness
man'gle
·gled ·gling

man'go
·goes *or* ·gos
man'grove
man'gy
·gi·er ·gi·est
man'han'dle
·dled ·dling
man'hole'
man'hood'
man'-hour'
man'hunt'
ma'ni·a
ma'ni·ac'
ma·ni'a·cal
man'ic
man'ic-de·pres'-
sive
man'i·cot'ti
man'i·cure'
·cured' ·cur'ing
man'i·cur'ist
man'i·fest'
man'i·fes·ta'tion
man'i·fest'ly
man'i·fes'to
·toes *or* ·tos
man'i·fold'
man'i·kin
ma·nip'u·late'
·lat'ed ·lat'ing
ma·nip'u·la'tion
ma·nip'u·la'tive
ma·nip'u·la'tor
man'kind'
man'li·ness
man'ly
·li·er ·li·est
man'-made'
man'na
man'ne·quin
man'ner
(*way;* see MANOR)
man'nered
man'ner·ism'
man'ner·ly
man'nish
man'-of-war'
men'-of-war'
ma·nom'e·ter
man'or
(*residence;* see
MANNER)
ma·no'ri·al
man'pow'er
man'sard
manse
man'ser'vant
men'ser'vants
man'sion
man'-sized'
man'slaugh'ter
man'ta
man'tel
(*fireplace facing;*
see MANTLE)
man'tel·piece'
man·til'la
man'tis
·tis·es *or* ·tes'

man·tis'sa
man'tle
·tled ·tling
(*cloak;* see
MANTEL)
man'tra
man'u·al
man'u·al·ly
man'u·fac'ture
·tured ·tur·ing
man'u·fac'tur·er
man'u·mis'sion
man'u·mit'
·mit'ted ·mit'ting
ma·nure'
man'u·script'
man'y
more most
man'y-sid'ed
map
mapped map'ping
ma'ple
mar
marred mar'ring
mar'a·bou'
ma·ra'ca
mar'a·schi'no
mar'a·thon'
ma·raud'ing
ma·raud'er
mar'ble
·bled ·bling
mar'ble·ize'
·ized' ·iz'ing
march
March
mar'chion·ess
Mar'di Gras'
mare
mare's'-nest'
mar'ga·rine'
mar'gin
mar'gin·al
mar'gin·al·ly
mar'gi·na'li·a
mar'gin·al·ized'
ma·ri·a'chi
·chis
mar'i·gold'
mar'i·jua'na *or*
·hua'na
ma·rim'ba
ma·ri'na
mar'i·nade'
mar'i·nate'
·nat'ed ·nat'ing
ma·rine'
mar'i·ner'
mar'i·o·nette'
mar'i·tal
(*of marriage;* see
MARTIAL)
mar'i·tal·ly
mar'i·time'
mar'jo·ram
mark
mark'down'
marked
mark'ed·ly

mark'er
mar'ket
mar'ket·a·bil'i·ty
mar'ket·a·ble
mar'ket·eer'
mar'ket·er
mar'ket·ing
mar'ket·place'
mark'ing
marks'man
marks'man·ship'
mark'up'
mar'lin (*fish*)
mar'line (*cord*)
mar'line·spike'
mar'ma·lade'
mar'mo·set'
mar'mot
ma·roon'
mar·quee' (*theater
awning*)
mar'quess (*British
nobleman*)
mar'quis (*European
nobleman*)
mar'riage
mar'riage·a·ble
mar'ried
mar'row
mar'ry
·ried ·ry·ing
(*wed;* see MERRY)
Mars
marsh
mar'shal
·shaled *or*
·shalled, ·shal·ing
or ·shal·ling
marsh'mal'low
marsh'y
·i·er ·i·est
mar·su'pi·al
mart
mar'ten
(*small mammal;*
see MARTIN)
mar'tial
(*military;* see MAR-
TIAL)
Mar'tian
mar'tin
(*bird;* see MARTEN)
mar'ti·net'
mar·ti'ni
·nis
mar'tyr
mar'tyr·dom
mar'vel
·veled *or* ·velled
·vel·ing *or*
·vel·ling
mar'vel·ous
Marx'ism'
Marx'ist *or*
Marx'i·an
Mar'y·land'
mar'zi·pan'
mas·car'a
·aed ·a·ing

mas'cot'
mas'cu·line
mas'cu·lin'i·ty
ma'ser
mash
mash'er
mask
(*cover;* see
MASQUE)
masked
mas'o·chism'
mas'o·chist
mas'o·chis'tic
mas'o·chis'ti··cal·ly
ma'son
Ma·son'ic
ma'son·ry
masque
(*masked ball;* see
MASK)
mas'quer·ade'
·ad'ed ·ad'ing
mass
Mas'sa·chu'setts
mas'sa·cre
·cred ·cring
mas·sage'
·saged' ·sag'ing
(*a rubbing;* see
MESSAGE)
mas·seur' *masc.*
mas·seuse' *fem.*
mas'sive
mast
mas·tec'to·my
·mies
mas'ter
mas'ter·ful
mas'ter·ful·ly
mas'ter·ly
mas'ter·mind'
mas'ter·piece'
mas'ter·work'
mas'ter·y
mast'head'
mas'tic
mas'ti·cate'
·cat'ed ·cat'ing
mas'ti·ca'tion
mas'tiff
mas'to·don'
mas'toid'
mas'tur·bate'
·bat'ed ·bat'ing
mas'tur·ba'tion
mat
mat'ted mat'ting
(*floor covering;* see
MATTE)
mat'a·dor'
match
match'book'
match'box'
match'less
match'mak'er
match'stick'
mate
mat'ed mat'ing

ma·te'ri·al
(*of matter;* see MA-
TERIEL)
ma·te'ri·al·ism'
ma·te'ri·al·ist
ma·te'ri·al·is'tic
ma·te'ri·al·i·za'tion
ma·te'ri·al·ize'
·ized' ·iz'ing
ma·te'ri·al·ly
ma·te·ri·el' *or* ·té'·
(*equipment;* see
MATERIAL)
ma·ter'nal
ma·ter'nal·ly
ma·ter'ni·ty
math'e·mat'i·cal
math'e·mat'·i·cal·ly
math'e·ma·ti'cian
math'e·mat'ics
mat'i·nee' *or* ·i·née'
mat'ins
ma'tri·arch'
ma'tri·ar'chal
ma'tri·arch'y
·ies
ma·tric'u·late'
·lat'ed ·lat'ing
ma·tric'u·la'tion
mat'ri·mo'ni·al
mat'ri·mo'ny
ma'trix'
·tri·ces' *or* ·trix'es
ma'tron
ma'tron·ly
matte
(*not shiny;* see
MAT)
mat'ted
mat'ter
mat'ter-of-fact'
mat'ting
mat'tock
mat'tress
mat'u·ra'tion
ma·ture'
·tured' ·tur'ing
ma·tu'ri·ty
mat'zo
·zot *or* ·zoth *or*
·zos
maud'lin
maul
(*mallet; injure;*
see MALL)
maun'der
mau·so·le'um
·le'ums *or* ·le'a
mauve
mav'er·ick
maw
mawk'ish
max·il'la
·lae
max'im
max'i·mal
max'i·mize'
·mized' ·miz'ing
max'i·mum
·mums *or* ·ma

may
might
May
may'be
may'flow'er
may'fly'
may'hem
may'o'
may'on·naise'
may'or
may'or·al
may'or·al·ty
may'pole'
maze
(*labyrinth;* see
MAIZE)
maz'el tov'
ma·zur'ka *or*
·zour'·
mead
mead'ow
mea'ger
mea'ger·ness
meal
meal'time'
meal'y
·i·er ·i·est
meal'y-mouthed'
mean *v.*
meant mean'ing
mean *adj., n.*
(*middle; low;* see
MIEN)
me·an'der
mean'ie *or* ·y
·ies
mean'ing
mean'ing·ful
mean'ing·less
mean'ness
means
meant
mean'time'
mean'while'
mea'sles
mea'sly
·sli·er ·sli·est
meas'ur·a·ble
meas'ur·a·bly
meas'ure
·ured ·ur·ing
meas'ured
meas'ure·less
meas'ure·ment
meat
(*flesh;* see MEET,
METE)
meat'y
·i·er ·i·est
me·chan'ic
me·chan'i·cal
me·chan'i·cal·ly
me·chan'ics
mech'a·nism'
mech'a·nis'tic
mech'a·ni·za'tion
mech'a·nize'
·nized' ·niz'ing

med'al
(*award;* see MED-
DLE)
med'al·ist
me·dal'lion
med'dle
·dled ·dling
(*interfere;* see
MEDAL)
med'dler
med'dle·some
me'di·a
me'di·al
me'di·an
me'di·ate'
·at'ed ·at'ing
me'di·a'tion
me'di·a'tor
med'ic
Med'ic·aid'
med'i·cal
med'i·cal·ly
Med'i·care'
med'i·cate'
·cat'ed ·cat'ing
med'i·ca'tion
me·dic'i·nal
med'i·cine
me'di·e'val
me'di·o'cre
me'di·oc'ri·ty
·ties
med'i·tate'
·tat'ed ·tat'ing
med'i·ta'tion
med'i·ta'tive
med'i·ta'tor
Med'i·ter·ra'ne·an
me'di·um
·di·ums *or* ·di·a
med'ley
·leys
me·dul'la
·las *or* ·lae
meek
meek'ly
meek'ness
meer'schaum
meet
met meet'ing
(*come upon;* see
MEAT, METE)
meet'ing
meg'a·byte'
meg'a·hertz'
meg'a·lo·ma'ni·a
meg'a·lop'o·lis
·lis·es
meg'a·phone'
meg'a·ton'
mel'a·mine'
mel'an·cho'li·a
mel'an·chol'ic
mel'an·chol'y
mé·lange'
mel'a·nin
mel'a·no'ma
·mas *or* ·ma·ta

meld
(*cards; blend;* see
MELT)
me·lee' *or* mê'lée'
mel'io·rate'
·rat'ed ·rat'ing
mel·lif'lu·ous
mel'low
me·lod'ic
me·lod'i·cal·ly
me·lo'di·ous
mel'o·dra'ma
mel'o·dra·mat'ic
mel'o·dra·mat'ics
mel'o·dy
·dies
mel'on
melt
(*dissolve;* see
MELD)
melt'down'
mem'ber
mem'ber·ship'
mem'brane'
mem'bra·nous
me·men'to
·tos *or* ·toes
mem'o
·os
mem'oirs
mem'o·ra·bil'i·a
mem'o·ra·ble
mem'o·ra·bly
mem'o·ran'dum
·dums *or* ·da
me·mo'ri·al
me·mo'ri·al·ize'
·ized' ·iz'ing
mem'o·ri·za'tion
mem'o·rize'
·rized' ·riz'ing
mem'o·ry
·ries
men
men'ace
·aced ·ac·ing
men'ac·ing·ly
me·nag'er·ie
mend
men·da'cious
men·dac'i·ty
men'di·cant
men'folk'
men·ha'den
·den *or* ·dens
me'ni·al
me'ni·al·ly
me·nin'ges
men'in·gi'tis
me·nis'cus
·cus·es *or* ·ci'
Men'non·ite'
men'o·pause'
me·no'rah
men'ses'
men'stru·al
men'stru·ate'
·at'ed ·at'ing
men'stru·a'tion

men'sur·a·ble
men'su·ra'tion
men'tal
men·tal'i·ty
·ties
men'tal·ly
men'thol'
men'tho·lat'ed
men'tion
men'tor
men'u
·us
me·ow' *or* ·ou'
mer'can·tile'
mer'can·til·ism'
mer'ce·nar'y
·ies
mer'chan·dise'
·dised' ·dis'ing
mer'chan·dis'er
mer'chant
mer·ci'
mer'ci·ful
mer'ci·ful·ly
mer'ci·less
mer·cu'ri·al
mer'cu·ry
Mer'cu·ry
mer'cy
mere
mer'est
mere'ly
mer·gan'ser
merge
merged merg'ing
merg'er
me·rid'i·an
me·ringue'
me·ri'no
·nos
mer'it
mer'i·to'ri·ous
mer'maid'
mer'ri·ly
mer'ri·ment
mer'ri·ness
mer'ry
·ri·er ·ri·est
(*happy;* see
MARRY)
mer'ry-go-round'
mer'ry·mak'er
mer'ry·mak'ing
me'sa
mes·cal'
mes'ca·line
mes·dames'
mes·de·moi·selles'
mesh
mes'mer·ize'
·ized' ·iz'ing
mes'on'
Mes·o·zo'ic
mes·quite' *or* ·quit'
mess
mes'sage
(*communication;*
see MASSAGE)
mes'sen·ger

mes·si'ah
mes'sieurs
mess'i·ly
mess'i·ness
mess'y
·i·er ·i·est
mes·ti'zo
·zos *or* ·zoes
met
met'a·bol'ic
me·tab'o·lism'
me·tab'o·lize'
·lized' ·liz'ing
met'a·car'pal
met'al
(*mineral;* see MET-
TLE)
me·tal'lic
me·tal'li·cal·ly
met'al·lur'gi·cal
met'al·lur'gist
met'al·lur'gy
met'a·mor'phic
met'a·mor'phose'
·phosed' ·phos'ing
met'a·mor'pho·sis
·ses'
met'a·phor'
met'a·phor'ic *or*
met'a·phor'i·cal
met'a·phor'i·cal·ly
met'a·phys'i·cal
met'a·phys'ics
me·tas'ta·sis
·ses'
me·tas'ta·size'
·sized' ·siz'ing
met'a·tar'sal
me·tath'e·sis
·ses'
mete
met'ed met'ing
(*allot;* see MEAT,
MEET)
me·tem'psy·cho'sis
me'te·or
me'te·or'ic
me'te·or·ite'
me'te·or·oid'
me'te·or·o·log'i·cal
me'te·or·ol'o·gist
me'te·or·ol'o·gy
me'ter
meth'a·done'
meth'ane'
meth'a·nol'
meth'od
me·thod'i·cal
me·thod'i·cal·ly
Meth'od·ist
meth'od·ol'o·gy
·gies
Me·thu'se·lah
meth'yl
me·tic'u·lous
me·tic'u·lous·ly
mé·tier'
met'ric
met'ri·cal

met'ri·cate'
  ·cat'ed ·cat'ing
met'ri·ca'tion
met'ro
  ·ros
met'ro·nome'
me·trop'o·lis
  ·lis·es
met'ro·pol'i·tan
met'tle
  (*spirit;* see METAL)
met'tle·some
mew
Mex'i·can
mez'za·nine'
mez'zo-so·pra'no
  ·nos *or* ·ni
mi·as'ma
mi'ca
mice
Mich'i·gan
mi'cro- *prefix*
  (*small;* see MACRO-)
mi'crobe'
mi'cro·bi·ol'o·gist
mi'cro·bi·ol'o·gy
mi'cro·chip'
mi'cro·com·put'er
mi'cro·cosm'
mi'cro·dot'
mi'cro·ec'o·nom'ics
mi'cro·fiche'
  ·fich'es *or* ·fiche'
mi'cro·film'
mi·crom'e·ter
mi'cron'
mi'cro·or'gan·ism'
mi'cro·phone'
mi'cro·proc'es'sor
mi'cro·scope'
mi'cro·scop'ic
mi'cro·scop'i·cal·ly
mi'cro·sur'ger·y
mi'cro·wave'
mid
mid'air'
mid'day'
mid'dle
mid'dle-aged'
mid'dle-brow'
mid'dle-class'
mid'dle-man'
mid'dle-of-the-
  road'
mid'dle-weight'
mid'dling
mid'dy
  ·dies
midge
midg'et
mid'land
mid'night'
mid'point'
mid'riff
mid'ship'man
mid'-size' *or*
  mid'size'

midst
  (*middle;* see MIST)
mid'stream'
mid'sum'mer
mid'term'
mid'way'
mid'week'
Mid'west'ern
Mid'west'ern·er
mid'wife'
  ·wives'
mid'wife'ry
mid'win'ter
mid'year'
mien
  (*manner;* see
  MEAN)
miff
might
  (*power;* see MITE)
might'i·ly
might'i·ness
might'y
  ·i·er ·i·est
mi'gnon·ette'
mi'graine'
mi'grant
mi'grate'
  ·grat'ed ·grat'ing
mi·gra'tion
mi'gra·to'ry
mi·ka'do
  ·dos
mil
milch
mild
mil'dew'
mild'ly
mild'ness
mile
mile'age
mile'post'
mil'er
mile'stone'
mi·lieu'
mil'i·tan·cy
mil'i·tant
mil'i·tar'i·ly
mil'i·ta·rist
mil'i·ta·ris'tic
mil'i·ta·ri·za'tion
mil'i·ta·rize'
  ·rized' ·riz'ing
mil'i·tar'y
mil'i·tate'
  ·tat'ed ·tat'ing
mi·li'tia
milk
milk'i·ness
milk'maid'
milk'man'
milk'shake'
milk'sop'
milk'weed'
milk'y
  ·i·er ·i·est
mill
mill'age

mil·len'ni·um
  ·ni·ums *or* ·ni·a
mill'er
mil'let
mil'li·bar'
mil'li·gram'
mil'li·li'ter
mil'li·me'ter
mil'li·ner
mil'li·ner'y
mil'lion
mil'lion·aire'
mil'lionth
mil'li·pede'
mill'pond'
mill'race'
mill'stone'
mill'stream'
mill'wright'
milt
mime
  mimed mim'ing
mim'e·o·graph'
mi·met'ic
mim'ic
  ·icked ·ick·ing
mim'ic·ry
mi·mo'sa
min'a·ret'
min'a·to'ry
mince
  minced minc'ing
mince'meat'
minc'ing
mind
mind'ful
mind'less
mine
  mined min'ing
min'er
  (*mine worker;* see
  MINOR)
min'er·al
min'er·al'o·gist
min'er·al'o·gy
mi'ne·stro'ne
min'gle
  ·gled ·gling
min'i·a·ture
min'i·a·tur'i·za'-
  tion
min'i·a·tur·ize'
  ·ized' ·iz'ing
min'i·bike
min'i·bus'
min'i·cam'
min'i·com·put'er
min'im
min'i·mal
min'i·mal·ism'
min'i·mal·ist
min'i·mal·ly
min'i·mize'
  ·mized' ·miz'ing
min'i·mum
  ·mums *or* ·ma
min'ion
min'i·se'ries

min'i·skirt'
min'is·ter
min'is·te'ri·al
min'is·trant
min'is·tra'tion
min'is·try
  ·tries
mink
Min'ne·so'ta
min'now
mi'nor
  (*lesser;* see MINER)
mi·nor'i·ty
  ·ties
min'strel
mint
mint'age
min'u·end'
min'u·et'
mi'nus
mi·nus'cule'
min'ute *n.*
mi·nute' *adj.*
mi·nute'ly
min'ute-man'
mi·nu'ti·ae'
  sing. ·ti·a
minx
mir'a·cle
mi·rac'u·lous
mi·rage'
mire
  mired mir'ing
mir'ror
mirth
mirth'ful
mis'ad·ven'ture
mis·an'thrope'
mis·an'throp'ic
mis·an'thro·py
mis·ap·ply'
mis'ap·pre·hend'
mis'ap·pre·hen'-
  sion
mis'ap·pro'pri·ate'
mis'ap·pro'pri·a'-
  tion
mis'be·got'ten
mis'be·have'
mis'be·hav'ior
mis·cal'cu·late'
mis·cal·cu·la'tion
mis·call'
mis·car'riage
mis·car'ry
mis·cast'
mis'ce·ge·na'tion
mis'cel·la'ne·ous
mis'cel·la'ny
mis·chance'
mis·chief
mis'chie·vous
mis'chie·vous·ly
mis'ci·ble
mis'con·ceive'
mis'con·cep'tion
mis'con·duct'

mis'con·struc'tion
mis'con·strue'
mis·count'
mis·cre·ant
mis·cue'
mis·date'
mis·deal'
mis·deed'
mis'de·mean'or
mis'di·rect'
mis'di·rec'tion
mis·do'ing
mi'ser
mis'er·a·ble
mis'er·a·bly
mi'ser·li·ness
mi'ser·ly
mis'er·y
  ·ies
mis'file'
mis'fire'
mis'fit'
mis·for'tune
mis·giv'ing
mis·gov'ern
mis·gov'ern·ment
mis·guid'ance
mis·guide'
mis·han'dle
mis·hap'
mis·hear'
mish'mash'
mis'in·form'
mis'in·for·ma'tion
mis·in·ter'pret
mis·in·ter'pre·ta'-
  tion
mis·judge'
mis·la'bel
mis·lay'
  ·laid' ·lay'ing
mis·lead'
  ·led' ·lead'ing
mis·man'age
mis·man'age·ment
mis·match'
mis·mate'
mis·name'
mis·no'mer
mi·sog'y·nist
mi·sog'y·ny
mis·place'
mis·play'
mis·print'
mis·pri'sion
mis'pro·nounce'
mis'pro·nun'ci·a'-
  tion
mis'quo·ta'tion
mis·quote'
mis·read'
mis'rep·re·sent'
mis'rep·re·sen·ta'-
  tion
mis·rule'
miss
  miss'es

mis'sal
  (*book;* see MISSILE)
mis·shape'
mis·shap'en
mis'sile
  (*weapon;* see
  MISSAL)
mis'sile·ry *or* mis'-
  sil·ry
miss'ing
mis'sion
mis'sion·ar'y
  ·ies
Mis'sis·sip'pi
mis'sive
Mis·sou'ri
mis·speak'
mis·spell'
mis·spend'
mis·state'
mis·state'ment
mis·step'
mist
  (*water vapor;* see
  MIDST)
mis·take'
mis·tak'en
mist'i·ly
mis'time'
mist'i·ness
mis'tle·toe'
mis·treat'
mis·treat'ment
mis'tress
mis·tri'al
mis·trust'
mist'y
  ·i·er ·i·est
mis'un·der·stand'
mis'un·der·stand'ing
mis·use'
mite
  (*arachnid; tiny
  thing;* see MIGHT)
mi'ter
mit'i·gate'
  ·gat'ed ·gat'ing
mit'i·ga'tion
mi·to'sis
mi·tot'ic
mitt
mit'ten
mix
  mixed *or* mixt
  mix'ing
mixed
mix'er
mix'ture
mix'-up'
miz'zen-mast'
mne·mon'ic
moan
moat
  (*ditch;* see MOTE)
mob
  mobbed mob'bing
mo'bile
mo·bil'i·ty
mo'bi·li·za'tion

mo'bi·lize'
·lized' ·liz'ing
mob'ster
moc'ca·sin
mo'cha
mock
mock'er·y
·ies
mock'ing·bird'
mock'-up'
mod
mod'al
(of a mode; see
MODEL)
mode
mod'el
·eled or ·elled
·el·ing or ·el·ling
(a copy; see
MODAL)
mo'dem'
mod'er·ate'
·at'ed ·at'ing
mod'er·ate·ly
mod'er·a'tion
mod'er·a'tor
mod'ern
mod'ern·ism'
mod'ern·ist
mod'ern·is'tic
mod'ern·i·za'tion
mod'ern·ize'
·ized' ·iz'ing
mod'est
mod'est·ly
mod'es·ty
mod'i·cum
mod'i·fi·ca'tion
mod'i·fi'er
mod'i·fy'
·fied' ·fy'ing
mod'ish
mod'u·lar
mod'u·late'
·lat'ed ·lat'ing
mod'u·la'tion
mod'u·la'tor
mod'ule'
mo'gul'
mo'hair'
Mo·ham'med·an·
ism'
moi'e·ty
moire
moist
mois'ten
moist'ness
mois'ture
mois'tur·ize'
·ized' ·iz'ing
mois'tur·iz'er
mo'lar
mo·las'ses
mold
mold'er
mold'i·ness
mold'ing
mold'y
·i·er ·i·est

mole
mo·lec'u·lar
mol'e·cule'
mole'hill'
mole'skin'
mo·lest'
mo'les·ta'tion
mo·lest'er
mol'li·fy'
·fied' ·fy'ing
mol'lusk
mol'ly
·lies
mol'ly·cod'dle
·dled ·dling
molt
mol'ten
mo·lyb'de·num
mo'ment
mo'men·tar'i·ly
mo'men·tar'y
mo·men'tous
mo·men'tum
mon'arch
mo·nar'chi·cal
mon'ar·chist
mon'ar·chy
·chies
mon'as·ter'y
·ies
mo·nas'tic
mo·nas'ti·cism
mon·au'ral
Mon'day
mon'e·tar'i·ly
mon'e·tar'y
mon'ey
·eys or ·ies
mon'ey·bag'
mon'eyed
mon'ey·lend'er
mon'ey·mak'er
mon'ger
Mon'gol·oid'
mon'goose'
·goos'es
mon'grel
mon'ied
mon'i·ker
mo·ni'tion
mon'i·tor
monk
mon'key
·keys
mon'key·shines'
mon'o
mon'o·cle
mon'o·clon'al
mon'o·cot'y·le'don
mo·nog'a·mous
mo·nog'a·my
mon'o·gram'
mon'o·graph'
mon'o·lin'gual
mon'o·lith'
mon'o·lith'ic
mon'o·logue' or
·log'

mon'o·ma'ni·a
mon'o·ma'ni·ac'
mon'o·ma·ni'a·cal
mon'o·nu'cle·o'sis
mon'o·phon'ic
mo·nop'o·list
mo·nop'o·lis'tic
mo·nop'o·li·za'tion
mo·nop'o·lize'
·lized' ·liz'ing
mo·nop'o·ly
·lies
mon'o·rail'
mon'o·syl·lab'ic
mon'o·syl'la·ble
mon'o·the·ism'
mon'o·the·ist'
mon'o·the·is'tic
mon'o·tone'
mo·not'o·nous
mo·not'o·ny
mon·ox'ide'
mon·sieur'
mes'sieurs
Mon·si'gnor
mon·soon'
mon'ster
mon·stros'i·ty
·ties
mon'strous
mon·tage'
Mon·tan'a
month
month'ly
·lies
mon'u·ment
mon'u·men'tal
moo
moos
mooed moo'ing
mooch
mooch'er
mood
mood'i·ly
mood'i·ness
mood'y
·i·er ·i·est
moon
moon'beam'
moon'light'
moon'light'ing
moon'lit'
moon'scape'
moon'shine'
moon'shin'er
moon'stone'
moon'struck'
moor
moor'ing
moose
moose
(deer; see MOUSE,
MOUSSE)
moot
(debatable; see
MUTE)
mop
mopped mop'ping

mope
moped mop'ing
mop'ey or mop'y
mop'pet
mop'-up'
mo·raine'
mor'al (ethical)
mo·rale' (spirit)
mor'al·ist
mor'al·is'tic
mor'al·is'ti·cal·ly
mo·ral'i·ty
·ties
mor'al·ize'
·ized' ·iz'ing
mor'al·ly
mo·rass'
mor'a·to'ri·um
·ri·ums or ·ri·a
mo'ray eel
mor'bid
mor·bid'i·ty
mor'bid·ly
mor'dant
more
more·o'ver
mo'res'
morgue
mor'i·bund'
Mor'mon
morn
morn'ing
(part of day; see
MOURNING)
mo'ron'
mo·ron'ic
mo·rose'
mo·rose'ly
mor'pheme'
mor'phine'
mor·phol'o·gy
mor'row
mor'sel
mor'tal
mor·tal'i·ty
mor'tal·ly
mor'tar
mor'tar·board'
mort'gage
·gaged ·gag·ing
mort'ga·gee'
mort'ga·gor or
·gag·er
mor·ti'cian
mor'ti·fi·ca'tion
mor'ti·fy'
·fied' ·fy'ing
mor'tise
·tised ·tis·ing
mor'tu·ar'y
·ies
mo·sa'ic
mo'sey
Mos'lem
mosque
mos·qui'to
·toes or ·tos
moss

moss'back'
moss'y
·i·er ·i·est
most
most'ly
mote
(speck; see MOAT)
mo·tel'
moth
moths
moth'ball'
moth'er
moth'er·hood'
moth'er-in-law'
moth'ers-in-law'
moth'er·land'
moth'er·less
moth'er·li·ness
moth'er·ly
moth'er-of-pearl'
moth'proof'
mo·tif'
mo'tile
mo·til'i·ty
mo'tion
mo'tion·less
mo'ti·vate'
·vat'ed ·vat'ing
mo'ti·va'tion
mo'ti·va'tor
mo'tive
mot'ley
mo'to·cross'
mo'tor
mo'tor·bike'
mo'tor·boat'
mo'tor·cade'
mo'tor·car'
mo'tor·cy'cle
mo'tor·ist
mo'tor·ize'
·ized' ·iz'ing
mot'tle
·tled ·tling
mot'tled
mot'to
·toes or ·tos
mound
mount
moun'tain
moun'tain·eer'
moun'tain·ous
moun'te·bank'
mount'ing
mourn
mourn'er
mourn'ful
mourn'ing
(grieving; see
MORNING)
mouse
mice
(rodent; see
MOOSE, MOUSSE)
mouse'trap'
mous'i·ness
mousse
(food; see MOOSE,
MOUSE)

mous'tache'
mous'y
·i·er ·i·est
mouth
mouths
mouth'ful'
·fuls'
mouth'i·ness
mouth'part'
mouth'piece'
mouth'wash'
mouth'wa'ter·ing
mouth'y
·i·er ·i·est
mou'ton'
(fur; see MUTTON)
mov'a·ble or
move'·
move
moved mov'ing
move'ment
mov'er
mov'ie
mov'ie·go'er
mow
mowed, mowed or
mown, mow'ing
mow'er
moz'za·rel'la
much
more most
mu'ci·lage'
muck
muck'rake'
·raked' ·rak'ing
muck'rak'er
muck'y
·i·er ·i·est
mu'cous adj.
mu'cus n.
mud
mud'di·ness
mud'dle
·dled ·dling
mud'dle-head'ed
mud'dy
·di·er ·di·est
·died ·dy·ing
mud'sling'er
mud'sling'ing
mu·ez'zin
muff
muf'fin
muf'fle
·fled ·fling
muf'fler
muf'ti
mug
mugged mug'ging
mug'ger
mug'gi·ness
mug'gy
·gi·er ·gi·est
muk'luk'
mu·lat'to
·toes or ·tos
mul'ber'ry
·ries
mulch
mulct

mule
mu·le·teer′
mul′ish
mull
mul′let
mul·li·ga·taw′ny
mul′lion
mul·ti·col′ored
mul·ti·far′i·ous
mul·ti·lin′gual
mul·ti·mil′lion·aire′
mul·ti·na′tion·al
mul′ti·ple
mul′ti·ple-choice′
mul′ti·plex′
mul′ti·plex′er *or*
 ·or
mul′ti·pli·cand′
mul·ti·pli·ca′tion
mul·ti·plic′i·ty
mul′ti·pli′er
mul′ti·ply′
 ·plied′ ·ply′ing
mul′ti·proc′es′sor
mul′ti·stage′
mul′ti·tude′
mul·ti·tu′di·nous
mum
mum′ble
 ·bled ·bling
mum′bler
mum′bo jum′bo
mum′mer
mum′mer·y
mum′mi·fy′
 ·fied′ ·fy′ing
mum′my
 ·mies
mumps
munch
mun′dane′
mun′dane′ly
mu·nic′i·pal
mu·nic′i·pal′i·ty
 ·ties
mu·nif′i·cence
mu·nif′i·cent
mu·ni′tions
mu′ral
mu′ral·ist
mur′der
mur′der·er
mur′der·ess
mur′der·ous
mur′der·ous·ly
murk
murk′i·ness
murk′y
 ·i·er ·i·est
mur′mur
mur′mur·er
mus′cat
mus′ca·tel′
mus′cle
 ·cled ·cling
 (*body part;* see
 MUSSEL)
mus′cle-bound′

mus′cu·lar
mus′cu·lar′i·ty
mus′cu·la·ture
muse
 mused mus′ing
mu·se′um
mush
mush′room′
mush′y
 ·i·er ·i·est
mu′sic
mu′si·cal *adj.*
mu′si·cale′ *n.*
mu′si·cal·ly
mu·si′cian
mu·si·col′o·gist
mu·si·col′o·gy
musk
mus′kel·lunge′
mus′ket
mus′ket·eer′
mus′kie
musk′mel′on
musk′rat′
musk′y
 ·i·er ·i·est
Mus′lim
mus′lin
muss
mus′sel
 (*shellfish;* see
 MUSCLE)
muss′y
 ·i·er ·i·est
must
mus′tache′
mus′tang′
mus′tard
mus′ter
mus′ti·ly
mus′ti·ness
mus′ty
 ·ti·er ·ti·est
mu·ta·bil′i·ty
mu′ta·ble
mu′ta·bly
mu′tant
mu′tate′
 ·tat′ed ·tat′ing
mu·ta′tion
mute
 mut′ed mut′ing
 (*silent;* see MOOT)
mute′ly
mu′ti·late′
 ·lat′ed ·lat′ing
mu·ti·la′tion
mu′ti·la′tor
mu′ti·neer′
mu′ti·nous
mu′ti·ny
 ·nies
 ·nied ·ny·ing
mutt
mut′ter
mut′ton
 (*food;* see MOUTON)
mu′tu·al
mu·tu·al′i·ty

mu′tu·al·ly
muu′muu′
Mu′zak′
muz′zle
 ·zled ·zling
my′e·li′tis
my′lar′
my′na *or* ·nah
my·o′pi·a
my·op′ic
myr′i·ad
myr′mi·don′
myrrh
myr′tle
my·self′
mys·te′ri·ous
mys·te′ri·ous·ly
mys′ter·y
 ·ies
mys′tic
mys′ti·cal
mys′ti·cal·ly
mys′ti·cism
mys′ti·fi·ca′tion
mys′ti·fy′
 ·fied′ ·fy′ing
mys·tique′
myth
myth′i·cal
myth′o·log′i·cal
my·thol′o·gy
 ·gies

N

nab
 nabbed nab′bing
na′bob′
na′cre
na′cre·ous
na′dir
nag
 nagged nag′ging
nai′ad′
nail
na·ive′ *or* ·ïve′
na·ive′ly *or* ·ïve′·
na·ive·té′ *or* ·ïve·
na′ked
na′ked·ly
na′ked·ness
nam′by-pam′by
 ·bies
name
 named nam′ing
name′less
name′ly
name′sake′
nap
 napped nap′ping
na′palm′
nape
naph′tha
naph′tha·lene′
nap′kin
nap′less
napped

nap′per
nap′py
 ·pi·er ·pi·est
narc
nar′cis·sism′
nar′cis·sist
nar′cis·sis′tic
nar·cis′sus
 ·cis′sus *or*
 ·cis′sus·es *or*
 ·cis′si
nar·co′sis
nar·cot′ic
nar′co·tize′
 ·tized′ ·tiz′ing
nar′rate′
 ·rat′ed ·rat′ing
nar·ra′tion
nar′ra·tive
nar′row
nar′row·cast′
 ·cast′ ·cast′ing
nar′row-mind′ed
nar′row-
 mind′ed·ness
nar′whal
nar′y
na′sal
na′sal·ize′
 ·ized′ ·iz′ing
nas′cent
nas′ti·ly
nas′ti·ness
nas·tur′tium
nas′ty
 ·ti·er ·ti·est
na′tal
na′tes′
na′tion
na′tion·al
na′tion·al·ism′
na′tion·al·ist
na′tion·al·is′tic
na′tion·al′i·ty
 ·ties
na′tion·al·i·za′tion
na′tion·al·ize′
 ·ized′ ·iz′ing
na′tion·al·ly
na′tion·wide′
na′tive
na′tive-born′
na·tiv′i·ty
 ·ties
nat′ti·ly
nat′ty
 ·ti·er ·ti·est
nat′u·ral
nat′u·ral·ism′
nat′u·ral·ist
nat′u·ral·is′tic
nat′u·ral·i·za′tion
nat′u·ral·ize′
 ·ized′ ·iz′ing
nat′u·ral·ly
nat′u·ral·ness
na′ture
naught
naugh′ti·ly

naugh′ti·ness
naugh′ty
 ·ti·er ·ti·est
nau′se·a
nau′se·ate′
 ·at′ed ·at′ing
nau′seous
nau′ti·cal
nau′ti·cal·ly
nau′ti·lus
 ·lus·es *or* ·li′
na′val (*of a navy*)
nave
 (*part of a church;*
 see KNAVE)
na′vel (*umbilicus*)
nav′i·ga·bil′i·ty
nav′i·ga·ble
nav′i·gate′
 ·gat′ed ·gat′ing
nav′i·ga′tion
nav′i·ga′tor
na′vy
 ·vies
nay
 (*no;* see NEE,
 NEIGH)
nay′say·er
Na′zi
Ne·an′der·thal′
neap
near
near′by′
near′ly
near′ness
near′sight′ed
near′sight′ed·ness
neat
neat′ly
neat′ness
Ne·bras′ka
neb′u·la
 ·lae *or* ·las
neb′u·lar
neb′u·lous
nec·es·sar′i·ly
nec′es·sar′y
 ·ies
ne·ces′si·tate′
 ·tat′ed ·tat′ing
ne·ces′si·ty
 ·ties
neck
neck′er·chief
neck′lace
neck′tie′
neck′wear′
ne·crol′o·gy
 ·gies
nec′ro·man′cer
nec′ro·man′cy
ne·cro′sis
nec′tar
nec′tar·ine′
nee *or* née
 (*born;* see NAY,
 NEIGH)
need
 (*require;* see
 KNEAD)

need′ful
need′i·ness
nee′dle
 ·dled ·dling
nee′dle·point′
nee′dler
need′less
need′less·ly
nee′dle·work′
need′y
 ·i·er ·i·est
ne′er′-do-well′
ne·far′i·ous
ne·far′i·ous·ly
ne·far′i·ous·ness
ne·gate′
 ·gat′ed ·gat′ing
ne·ga′tion
neg′a·tive
neg′a·tive·ly
neg′a·tiv·ism′
ne·glect′
ne·glect′ful
neg′li·gee′
neg′li·gence
neg′li·gent
neg′li·gi·ble
ne·go′ti·a·ble
ne·go′ti·ate′
 ·at′ed ·at′ing
ne·go′ti·a′tion
ne·go′ti·a′tor
Ne′gro
 ·groes
Ne′groid′
neigh
 (*whinny;* see NAY,
 NEE)
neigh′bor
neigh′bor·hood′
neigh′bor·ing
neigh′bor·li·ness
neigh′bor·ly
nei′ther
 (*not either;* see
 NETHER)
nem′a·tode′
nem′e·sis
 ·ses′
ne′o·clas′sic
ne′o·clas′si·cal
ne′o·clas′si·cism′
ne′o·co·lo′ni·al·ism′
ne′o·lith′ic
ne·ol′o·gism′
ne′on′
ne′o·na′tal
ne′o·nate′
ne′o·phyte′
ne′o·plasm′
ne′o·prene′
neph′ew
neph′rite′
ne·phri′tis
ne·phro′sis
nep′o·tism′
Nep′tune′
nep·tu′ni·um

nerd
nerve
  nerved nerv'ing
nerve'less
nerve'less·ly
nerve'-rack'ing or
  -wrack'·
nerv'ous
nerv'ous·ly
nerv'ous·ness
nerv'y
  ·i·er ·i·est
nest
nes'tle
  ·tled ·tling
nest'ling (young
  bird)
net
  net'ted net'ting
neth'er
  (lower; see NEI-
  THER)
neth'er·most'
net'ting
net'tle
  ·tled ·tling
net'tle·some
net'work'
net'work'ing
neu'ral
neu·ral'gi·a
neu·ral'gic
neu·rit'ic
neu·ri'tis
neu·ro·log'i·cal
neu·rol'o·gist
neu·rol'o·gy
neu·ro·mus'cu·lar
neu'ron'
neu·ro'sis
  ·ses
neu'ro·sur'geon
neu'ro·sur'ger·y
neu·rot'ic
neu·rot'i·cal·ly
neu'ro·trans·mit'ter
neu'ter
neu'tral
neu·tral'i·ty
neu'tral·i·za'tion
neu'tral·ize'
  ·ized ·iz'ing
neu'tral·iz'er
neu'tral·ly
neu·tri'no
  ·nos
neu'tron'
Ne·vad'a
nev'er
nev'er·more'
nev'er·the·less'
ne'vus
  ·vi'
new
new'born'
new'com'er
new'el
new'fan'gled

new'-fash'ioned
New Hamp'shire
New Jer'sey
new'ly
new'ly·wed'
New Mex'i·co'
new'ness
news
news'boy'
news'cast'
news'cast'er
news'deal'er
news'let'ter
news'man'
news'pa'per
news'pa'per·man'
news'pa'per·wom'an
news'print'
news'stand'
news'wor'thy
newt
new'ton
New York
next
next'-door'
nex'us
  ·us·es or nex'us
ni'a·cin
nib
nib'ble
  ·bled ·bling
nib'bler
nibs
nice
  nic'er nic'est
nice'ly
ni'ce·ty
  ·ties
niche
nick
nick'el
nick'el·o'de·on
nick'name'
nic'o·tine'
niece
nif'ty
  ·ti·er ·ti·est
nig'gard
nig'gard·li·ness
nig'gard·ly
nig'gle
  ·gled ·gling
nig'gler
nig'gling
nigh
night
  (darkness; see
  KNIGHT)
night'cap'
night'clothes'
night'club'
night crawl'er
night'dress'
night'fall'
night'gown'
night'hawk'
night'ie
night'in·gale'

night'ly
night'mare'
night'mar'ish
night'shade'
night'shirt'
night'spot'
night'stick'
night'time'
night'wear'
ni'hil·ism'
ni'hil·ist
ni'hil·is'tic
nil
nim'ble
  ·bler ·blest
nim'bly
nim'bus
  ·bi or ·bus·es
nin'com·poop'
nine
nine'pins'
nine'teen'
nine'teenth'
nine'ti·eth
nine'ty
  ·ties
nin'ny
  ·nies
ninth
nip
  nipped nip'ping
nip'per
nip'ple
nip'py
  ·pi·er ·pi·est
nir·va'na
nit
ni'ter
nit'-pick'er
nit'-pick'ing
ni'trate'
  ·trat'ed ·trat'ing
ni'tric acid
ni'tro·cel'lu·lose'
ni'tro·gen
ni·trog'e·nous
ni'tro·glyc'er·in or
  ·ine
ni'trous
nit'ty-grit'ty
nit'wit'
nix
no
  noes or nos
No·bel' prize
no·bil'i·ty
no'ble
  ·bler ·blest
no'ble·man
no'ble·ness
no'bly
no'bod'y
  ·ies
noc·tur'nal
noc·tur'nal·ly
noc'turne'
nod
  nod'ded nod'ding

nod'al
node
nod'ule'
no'-fault'
nog'gin
no'-good'
noise
  noised nois'ing
noise'less
noise'less·ly
nois'i·ly
nois'i·ness
noi'some
nois'y
  ·i·er ·i·est
no'mad'
no·mad'ic
nom' de plume'
  noms' de plume'
no'men·cla'ture
nom'i·nal
nom'i·nal·ly
nom'i·nate'
  ·nat'ed ·nat'ing
nom'i·na'tion
nom'i·na·tive
nom'i·nee'
non'age
non'a·ge·nar'i·an
non'a·ligned'
non'a·lign'ment
nonce
non'cha·lance'
non'cha·lant'
non'cha·lant'ly
non'com'
non'com'bat·ant
non'com·mis'-
  sioned officer
non'com·mit'tal
non'con·form'ist
non'con·form'i·ty
non'dair'y
non'de·script'
none
non·en'ti·ty
  ·ties
non'es·sen'tial
none'such'
none'the·less'
non'ex·ist'ent
non'fer'rous
non'in·ter·ven'tion
non'judg·men'tal
no'-non'sense
non'pa·reil'
non'par'ti·san
non'per'son
non'plus'
  ·plused' or
  ·plussed'
  ·plus'ing or
  ·plus'sing
non'prof'it
non'res'i·dent
non're·stric'tive
non'sched'uled
non'sec·tar'i·an

non'sense'
non·sen'si·cal
non·sen'si·cal·ly
non' se'qui·tur
non'skid'
non'stop'
non'sup·port'
non·un'ion
non'vi'o·lence
non'vi'o·lent
noo'dle
nook
noon
noon'day'
noon'time'
noose
nor
norm
nor'mal
nor'mal·cy or
  nor·mal'i·ty
nor'mal·i·za'tion
nor'mal·ize'
  ·ized ·iz'ing
nor'mal·ly
norm'a·tive
north
North Car'o·li'na
North Da·ko'ta
north'east'
north'east'er·ly
north'east'ern
north'east'ward
north'east'wards
north'er·ly
north'ern
north'ern·er
north'ward'
north'west'
north'west'er·ly
north'west'ern
north'west'ward
north'west'wards
Nor·we'gian
nose
  nosed nos'ing
nose'bleed'
nose'-dive'
  -dived' -div'ing
no'-show'
nos·tal'gi·a
nos·tal'gic
nos'tril
nos'trum
nos'y or ·ey
  ·i·er ·i·est
not
no'ta·ble
no'ta·bly
no'ta·rize'
  ·rized' ·riz'ing
no'ta·ry
  ·ries
no·ta'tion
notch
note
  not'ed not'ing
note'book'

not'ed
note'wor'thy
noth'ing
noth'ing·ness
no'tice
  ·ticed ·tic·ing
no'tice·a·ble
no'tice·a·bly
no'ti·fi·ca'tion
no'ti·fy'
  ·fied' ·fy'ing
no'tion
no'tion·al
no·to·ri'e·ty
no·to'ri·ous
no·to'ri·ous·ly
not'with·stand'ing
nou'gat
nought
noun
nour'ish
nour'ish·ing
nour'ish·ment
nou'veau riche'
  nou'veaux riches'
nou·velle' cuisine
no'va
  ·vae or ·vas
nov'el
nov'el·ette'
nov'el·ist
nov'el·ize'
  ·ized' ·iz'ing
no·vel'la
nov'el·ty
  ·ties
No·vem'ber
no·ve'na
nov'ice
no·vi'ti·ate
No'vo·cain'
now
now'a·days'
no'where'
no'-win'
nox'ious
noz'zle
nu'ance'
nub
nub'bin
nub'by
  ·bi·er ·bi·est
nu'bile
nu'cle·ar
nu'cle·ate'
  ·at'ed ·at'ing
nu·cle·a'tion
nu·cle'ic acid
nu·cle'o·lus
  ·li'
nu'cle·us
  ·cle·i' or ·cle·us·es
nude
nudge
  nudged nudg'ing
nud'ism'
nud'ist
nu·di·ty

nu'ga·to'ry
nug'get
nui'sance
nuke
  nuked nuk'ing
null
nul'li·fi·ca'tion
nul'li·fy'
  ·fied' ·fy'ing
numb
num'ber
num'ber·less
numb'ly
numb'ness
nu'mer·al
nu'mer·ate'
  ·at'ed ·at'ing
nu'mer·a'tor
nu·mer'i·cal
nu·mer'i·cal·ly
nu'mer·ol'o·gy
nu'mer·ous
nu'mi·nous
nu'mis·mat'ics
nu·mis'ma·tist
num'skull'
nun
nun'ci·o'
  ·os'
nun'ner·y
  ·ies
nup'tial
nurse
  nursed nurs'ing
nurse'maid'
nurs'er·y
  ·ies
nurs'er·y·man
nur'ture
  ·tured ·tur·ing
nur'tur·er
nut
nu·ta'tion
nut'crack'er
nut'hatch'
nut'meat'
nut'meg'
nu'tri·ent
nu'tri·ment
nu·tri'tion
nu·tri'tion·al
nu·tri'tion·al·ly
nu·tri'tion·ist
nu·tri'tious
nu·tri'tious·ly
nu·tri'tious·ness
nu'tri·tive
nut'shell'
nut'ti·ness
nut'ty
  ·ti·er ·ti·est
nuz'zle
  ·zled ·zling
nuz'zler
ny'lon'
nymph
nym'pho·ma'ni·a
nym'pho·ma'ni·ac'

O

oaf
oaf'ish
oak
oak'en
oa'kum
oar
  (*paddle;* see OR, ORE)
oar'lock'
oars'man
o·a'sis
  ·ses'
oat
oath
oat'meal'
ob'bli·ga'to
  ·tos or ·ti
ob'du·ra·cy
ob'du·rate
ob'du·rate·ly
o·be'di·ence
o·be'di·ent
o·be'di·ent·ly
o·bei'sance
o·bei'sant
ob'e·lisk
o·bese'
o·be'si·ty
o·bey'
ob'fus·cate'
  ·cat'ed ·cat'ing
ob'fus·ca'tion
o·bit'u·ar'y
  ·ies
ob'ject
ob·jec'tion
ob·jec'tion·a·ble
ob·jec'tion·a·bly
ob·jec'tive
ob·jec'tive·ly
ob'jec·tiv'i·ty
ob·jec'tor
ob'jet d'art'
  ob'jets d'art'
ob'jur·gate'
  ·gat'ed ·gat'ing
ob'jur·ga'tion
ob'late'
ob·la'tion
ob'li·gate'
  ·gat'ed ·gat'ing
ob'li·ga'tion
ob·lig'a·to'ry
o·blige'
  o·bliged' o·blig'ing
o·blig'ing
o·blig'ing·ly
ob·lique'
ob·lique'ly
ob·liq'ui·ty
ob·lit'er·ate'
  ·at'ed ·at'ing
ob·lit'er·a'tion
ob·liv'i·on
ob·liv'i·ous
ob'long'

ob'lo·quy
  ·quies
ob·nox'ious
ob·nox'ious·ly
ob·nox'ious·ness
o'boe
o'bo·ist
ob·scene'
ob·scen'i·ty
  ·ties
ob'scur'ant·ism'
ob·scure'
  ·scured' ·scur'ing
ob·scure'ly
ob·scu'ri·ty
ob·se·quies'
ob·se'qui·ous
ob·serv'a·ble
ob·serv'ance
ob·serv'ant
ob'ser·va'tion
ob·serv'a·to'ry
  ·ries
ob·serve'
  ·served' ·serv'ing
ob·serv'er
ob·sess'
ob·ses'sion
ob·ses'sive
ob·ses'sive·ly
ob·sid'i·an
ob'so·lesce'
  ·lesced' ·lesc'ing
ob'so·les'cence
ob'so·les'cent
ob'so·lete'
ob'sta·cle
ob·stet'ric or
  ob·stet'ri·cal
ob'ste·tri'cian
ob·stet'rics
ob'sti·na·cy
ob'sti·nate
ob'sti·nate·ly
ob·strep'er·ous
ob·strep'er·ous·ly
ob·strep'er·ous·ness
ob·struct'
ob·struc'tion
ob·struc'tion·ist
ob·struc'tive
ob·struc'tive·ly
ob·struc'tive·ness
ob·tain'
ob·tain'a·ble
ob·tain'ment
ob·trude'
  ·trud'ed ·trud'ing
ob·tru'sion
ob·tru'sive
ob·tru'sive·ly
ob·tru'sive·ness
ob·tuse'
ob·tuse'ly
ob·tuse'ness
ob·verse'
ob'vi·ate'
  ·at'ed ·at'ing

ob'vi·ous
ob'vi·ous·ly
ob'vi·ous·ness
oc'a·ri'na
oc·ca'sion
oc·ca'sion·al
oc·ca'sion·al·ly
Oc'ci·den'tal
oc·cip'i·tal
oc·clude'
  ·clud'ed ·clud'ing
oc·clu'sion
oc·cult'
oc'cu·pan·cy
  ·cies
oc'cu·pant
oc'cu·pa'tion
oc'cu·pa'tion·al
oc'cu·py'
  ·pied' ·py'ing
oc·cur'
  ·curred' ·cur'ring
oc·cur'rence
o'cean
o'cean·go'ing
o'ce·an'ic
o'ce·an·og'ra·phy
o'ce·an·ol'o·gy
o'ce·lot
o'cher or o'chre
o'clock'
oc'ta·gon
oc·tag'o·nal
oc'tane
oc'ta·vo
  ·vos
oc·tet' or oc·tette'
Oc·to'ber
oc'to·ge·nar'i·an
oc'to·pus
  ·pus·es or ·pi
oc'u·lar
OD
  OD'd or ODed
  OD'ing or ODing
o'da·lisque' or
  o'da·lisk'
odd
odd'ball'
odd'i·ty
  ·ties
odd'ly
odd'ness
odds
odds'mak'er
odds'-on'
ode
o'di·ous
o'di·ous·ly
o'di·ous·ness
o'di·um
o·dom'e·ter
o'dor
o'dor·if'er·ous
o'dor·less
o'dor·ous
Od'ys·sey

Oed'i·pal
Oed'i·pus complex
oe·nol'o·gist
oe·nol'o·gy
oe'no·phile'
oeu'vre
  ·vres
off
of'fal
off'beat'
off'-col'or
of·fend'
of·fend'er
of·fense'
of·fen'sive
of·fen'sive·ly
of·fen'sive·ness
of'fer
of'fer·ing
of'fer·to'ry
  ·ries
off'hand'
of'fice
of'fice-hold'er
of'fi·cer
of·fi'cial
of·fi'cial·ly
of·fi'ci·ate'
  ·at'ed ·at'ing
of·fi'cious
of·fi'cious·ly
of·fi'cious·ness
off'ing
off'-key'
off'-lim'its
off'-line'
off'load'
off'print'
off'-put'ting
off'-road'
off'-sea'son
off·set'
  ·set' ·set'ting
off'shoot'
off'shore'
off'side'
off'spring'
  ·spring' or
  ·springs'
off'stage'
off'-track'
off'-white'
of'ten
of'ten·times'
o'gle
  ·gled ·gling
o'gler
o'gre
O·hi'o
ohm
ohm'me'ter
o·ho'
oil
oil'cloth'
oil'i·ness
oil'skin'
oil'y
  ·i·er ·i·est

oink
oint'ment
OK or O.K.
  OK's or O.K.'s
  OK'd or O.K.'d
  OK'ing or O.K.'ing
o'kay'
O'kla·ho'ma
o'kra
old
  old'er or eld'er
  old'est or eld'est
old'en
old'-fash'ioned
old'ie or old'y
  ·ies
old'-line'
old'ster
old'-time'
old'-tim'er
o'le·ag'i·nous
o'le·an'der
o'le·o·mar'ga·rine
  or ·rin
ol·fac'to·ry
ol'i·garch'
ol'i·gar'chic
ol'i·gar'chy
  ·chies
ol'ive
O·lym'pi·an
O·lymp'ic games
om'buds·man
o·me'ga
om'e·let or ·lette
o'men
om'i·nous
om'i·nous·ly
o·mis'sion
o·mit'
  ·mit'ted ·mit'ting
om'ni·bus
om·nip'o·tence
om·nip'o·tent
om'ni·pres'ence
om'ni·pres'ent
om·nis'cience
om·nis'cient
om·niv'o·rous
om·niv'o·rous·ly
om·niv'o·rous·ness
once
once'-o'ver
on'co·gene'
on·col'o·gy
on'com'ing
one
one'ness
one'-on-one'
on'er·ous
one'self'
one'-sid'ed
one'time'
one'-track'
one'-up'
one-up'man·ship'
one'-way'
on'go'ing

on′ion
on′ion·skin′
on′-line′
on′look′er
on′ly
on′o·mat′o·poe′ia
on′rush′
on·set′
on′slaught′
on′to
on·tog′e·ny
o′nus
on′ward
on′yx
oo′dles
ooze
  oozed ooz′ing
o·pac′i·ty
o′pal
o′pal·es′cent
o·paque′
o·paque′ly
Op′-Ed′
o′pen
o′pen-air′
o′pen-and-shut′
o′pen-end′ed
o′pen·er
o′pen-eyed′
o′pen-faced′
o′pen-hand′ed
o′pen-heart′ed
o′pen-hearth′
o′pen-heart′
  surgery
o′pen·ing′
o′pen·ly
o′pen-mind′ed
o′pen-mouthed′
o′pen·ness
o′pen·work′
op′er·a
op′er·a·ble
op′er·ate′
  ·at′ed ·at′ing
op′er·at′ic
op′er·a′tion
op′er·a′tion·al
op′er·a·tive′
op′er·a′tor
op′er·et′ta
oph·thal′mic
oph′thal·mol′o·gist
oph′thal·mol′o·gy
o′pi·ate
o·pin′ion
o·pin′ion·at′ed
o′pi·um
o·pos′sum
op·po′nent
op′por·tune′
op′por·tun′ism′
op′por·tun′ist
op′por·tun·is′tic
op′por·tu′ni·ty
  ·ties
op·pos′a·ble

op·pose′
  ·posed′ ·pos′ing
op′po·site
op′po·si′tion
op·press′
op·pres′sion
op·pres′sive
op·pres′sive·ly
op·pres′sor
op·pro′bri·ous
op·pro′bri·um
opt
op′tic
op′ti·cal
op′ti·cal·ly
op·ti′cian
op′tics
op′ti·mal
op′ti·mism
op′ti·mist
op′ti·mis′tic
op′ti·mis′ti·cal·ly
op′ti·mum
op′tion
op′tion·al
op′tion·al·ly
op·tom′e·trist′
op·tom′e·try
op′u·lence
op′u·lent
o′pus
  o′pe·ra or o′pus·es
or
  (conj.; see OAR,
  ORE)
or′a·cle
  (wise person; see
  AURICLE)
o·rac′u·lar
o′ral
  (of the mouth; see
  AURAL)
o′ral·ly
or′ange
or′ange·ade′
o·rang′u·tan′
o·rate′
  ·rat′ed ·rat′ing
o·ra′tion
or′a·tor
or′a·tor′i·cal
or′a·to′ri·o′
  ·os′
or′a·to′ry
orb
or′bit
or′bit·al
or′chard
or′ches·tra
or·ches′tral
or′ches·trate′
  ·trat′ed ·trat′ing
or′ches·tra′tion
or′chid
or·dain′
or·deal′
or′der
or′der·li·ness

or′der·ly
  ·lies
or′di·nal
or′di·nance
  (law; see ORD-
  NANCE)
or′di·nar′i·ly
or′di·nar′y
or′di·nate
or′di·na′tion
ord′nance
  (artillery; see OR-
  DINANCE)
or′dure
ore
  (mineral; see OAR,
  OR)
o·reg′a·no
Or′e·gon
or′gan
or′gan·dy or ·die
  ·dies
or′gan·elle′
or·gan′ic
or·gan′i·cal·ly
or′gan·ism′
or′gan·ist
or′gan·i·za′tion
or′gan·i·za′tion·al
or′gan·ize′
  ·ized′ ·iz′ing
or′gan·iz′er
or′gan′za
or′gasm
or·gas′mic
or′gi·as′tic
or′gy
  ·gies
o′ri·el
  (window; see ORI-
  OLE)
O′ri·ent n.
o′ri·ent′ v.
O′ri·en′tal
o′ri·en·ta′tion
or′i·fice
o′ri·ga′mi
or′i·gin
o·rig′i·nal
o·rig′i·nal′i·ty
o·rig′i·nal·ly
o·rig′i·nate′
  ·nat′ed ·nat′ing
o·rig′i·na′tion
o·rig′i·na′tor
o′ri·ole′
  (bird; see ORIEL)
or′lon′
or′mo·lu′
or′na·ment
or′na·men′tal
or′na·men·ta′tion
or′nate′
or′nate′ly
or′nate′ness
or′ner·i·ness
or′ner·y
or′ni·thol′o·gist
or′ni·thol′o·gy

o′ro·tund′
or′phan
or′phan·age
or′tho·don′tics
or′tho·don′tist
or′tho·dox′
or′tho·dox′y
  ·ies
or′tho·graph′ic
or·thog′ra·phy
or′tho·pe′dic or
  ·pae′.
or′tho·pe′dics or
  ·pae′.
or′tho·pe′dist or
  ·pae′.
os′cil·late′
  ·lat′ed ·lat′ing
  (fluctuate; see OS-
  CULATE)
os′cil·la′tion
os′cil·la′tor
os·cil′lo·scope′
os′cu·late′
  ·lat′ed ·lat′ing
  (kiss; see OSCIL-
  LATE)
os′cu·la′tion
o′sier
os·mo′sis
os·mot′ic
os′prey
  ·preys
os′si·fi·ca′tion
os′si·fy′
  ·fied′ ·fy′ing
os·ten′si·ble
os·ten′si·bly
os′ten·ta′tion
os′ten·ta′tious
os′te·o·ar·thri′tis
os′te·o·path′
os′te·op′a·thy
os′te·o·po·ro′sis
os′to·my
  ·mies
os′tra·cism′
os′tra·cize′
  ·cized′ ·ciz′ing
os′trich
oth′er
oth′er·wise′
oth′er·world′ly
o′ti·ose′
ot′ter
ot′to·man
  ·mans
ouch
ought
  (be obliged; see
  AUGHT)
ounce
our
ours
our·selves′
oust
oust′er
out
out′age

out′-and-out′
out′back′
out′bid′
  ·bid′ ·bid′ding
out′board′
out′bound′
out′break′
out′build′ing
out′burst′
out′cast′
out′class′
out′come′
out′crop′
out′cry′
  ·cries′
out′dat′ed
out′dis′tance
  ·tanced ·tanc·ing
out′do′
  ·did′ ·done′ ·do′ing
out′door′
out′doors′
out′er
out′er·most′
out′er·wear′
out′field′
out′field′er
out′fit′
  ·fit′ted ·fit′ting
out′fit′ter
out′flank′
out′flow′
out′fox′
out′go′ing
out′grow′
out′growth′
out′guess′
out′house′
out′ing
out′land′ish
out′last′
out′law′
out′lay′
out′let′
out′line′
out′live′
out′look′
out′ly′ing
out′man′
out′ma·neu′ver or
  ·noeu′vre
  ·vered or ·vred
  ·ver·ing or ·vring
out′mod′ed
out′num′ber
out′-of-date′
out′-of-doors′
out′-of-the-way′
out′pa′tient
out′place′ment
out′play′
out′post′
out′pour′ing
out′put′
out′rage′
  ·raged′ ·rag′ing
out·ra′geous
out·ra′geous·ly

out′rank′
ou·tré′
out′reach′
out′rid′er
out′rig′ger
out′right′
out′run′
out′sell′
out′set′
out′shine′
out′side′
out′sid′er
out′size′
out′skirts′
out′smart′
out′sourc·ing
out′spo′ken
out′spread′
out′stand′ing
out′stay′
out′stretch′
out′strip′
out′take′
out′talk′
out′think′
out′vote′
out′ward
out′ward·ly
out′wear′
out′weigh′
out′wit′
  ·wit′ted ·wit′ting
o′va
o′val
o·var′i·an
o′va·ry
  ·ries
o′vate′
o·va′tion
ov′en
o′ver
o′ver·a·chieve′
o′ver·a·chieve′-
  ment
o′ver·a·chiev′er
o′ver·act′
o′ver·age′
o′ver·all′
o′ver·alls′
o′ver·awe′
o′ver·bal′ance
o′ver·bear′ing
o′ver·bite′
o′ver·blown′
o′ver·board′
o′ver·book′
o′ver·cast′
o′ver·charge′
o′ver·cloud′
o′ver·coat′
o′ver·come′
o′ver·com′pen·sate′
o′ver·con′fi·dent
o′ver·crowd′ed
o′ver·de·ter′mine
o′ver·do′
  ·did′ ·done′ ·do′ing

o'ver·dose'
o'ver·draft'
o'ver·draw'
o'ver·dress'
o'ver·dub'
o'ver·due'
o'ver·es'ti·mate'
o'ver·flight'
o'ver·flow'
o'ver·grown'
o'ver·growth'
o'ver·hand'
o'ver·hang'
  ·hung' ·hang'ing
o'ver·haul'
o'ver·head'
o'ver·hear'
o'ver·in·dul'gence
o'ver·joy'
o'ver·kill'
o'ver·land'
o'ver·lap'
  ·lapped' ·lap'ping
o'ver·lay'
  ·laid' ·lay'ing
o'ver·lie'
  ·lay' ·lain' ·ly'ing
o'ver·load'
o'ver·look'
o'ver·lord'
o'ver·ly
o'ver·mas'ter
o'ver·much'
o'ver·night'
o'ver·pass'
o'ver·play'
o'ver·pow'er
o'ver·price'
o'ver·pro·tect'
o'ver·qual'i·fied
o'ver·rate'
o'ver·reach'
o'ver·re·act'
o'ver·ride'
  ·rode' ·rid'den
  ·rid'ing
o'ver·rule'
o'ver·run'
  ·ran' ·run' ·run'-
  ning
o'ver·seas'
o'ver·see'
o'ver·se'er
o'ver·sexed'
o'ver·shad'ow
o'ver·shoe'
o'ver·shoot'
o'ver·sight'
o'ver·sim'pli·fi·ca'-
  tion
o'ver·sim'pli·fy'
o'ver·size'
o'ver·sleep'
o'ver·state'
o'ver·state'ment
o'ver·stay'
o'ver·step'
o'ver·stock'

o'ver·strung'
o'ver·stuff'
o'ver·sup·ply'
o·vert'
o'ver·take'
o'ver·tax'
o'ver-the-count'er
o'ver·throw'
  ·threw' ·thrown'
  ·thow'ing
o'ver·time'
o·vert'ly
o'ver·tone'
o'ver·ture
o'ver·turn'
o'ver·use'
o'ver·view'
o'ver·ween'ing
o'ver·weight'
o'ver·whelm'
o'ver·whelm'ing
o'ver·work'
o'ver·wrought'
o'vi·duct'
o·vip'a·rous
o'void'
ov'u·lar
ov'u·late'
  ·lat'ed ·lat'ing
ov'u·la'tion
ov'ule'
o'vum
  o'va
owe
  owed ow'ing
ow'ing
owl
owl'ish
own
own'er
own'er·ship'
ox
  ox'en
ox'blood'
ox'bow'
ox'ford
ox'i·dant
ox'i·da'tion
ox'ide'
ox'i·dize'
  ·dized' ·diz'ing
ox'i·diz'er
ox'y·a·cet'y·lene'
ox'y·gen
ox'y·gen·ate'
  ·at'ed ·at'ing
ox'y·gen·a'tion
ox'y·mo'ron'
  ·mo'ra
oys'ter
o'zone'

P

pab'lum
pace
  paced pac'ing

pace'mak'er
pac'er
pace'set'ter
pach'y·derm'
pach'y·san'dra
pa·cif'ic
pac'i·fi·ca'tion
pac'i·fi'er
pac'i·fism'
pac'i·fist
pac'i·fy'
  ·fied' ·fy'ing
pack
pack'age
  ·aged ·ag·ing
pack'ag·er
pack'er
pack'et
pack'ing
pack'sad'dle
pact
pad
  pad'ded pad'ding
pad'ding
pad'dle
  ·dled ·dling
pad'dock
pad'dy
  ·dies
  (rice; see PATTY)
pad'lock'
pa'dre'
pae'an
  (song; see PEON)
pa'gan
pa'gan·ism'
page
  paged pag'ing
pag'eant
pag'eant·ry
  ·ries
pag'i·na'tion
pa·go'da
paid
pail
  (bucket; see PALE)
pail'ful'
  ·fuls'
pain
  (hurt; see PANE)
pain'ful
pain'ful·ly
pain'kill'er
pain'less
pains'tak'ing
pains'tak'ing·ly
paint
paint'er
paint'ing
pair
  pairs or pair
  (couple; see PARE,
  PEAR)
pais'ley
pa·ja'mas
pal
pal'ace
pal'at·a·ble
pal'a·tal

pal'ate
  (roof of mouth; see
  PALETTE, PALLET)
pa·la'tial
pal'a·tine'
pa·lav'er
pale
  pal'er pal'est
  paled pal'ing
  (white; see PAIL)
pale'face'
pale'ly
pale'ness
pa'le·o·lith'ic
pa'le·on·tol'o·gist
pa'le·on·tol'o·gy
Pa'le·o'zo·ic
Pal'es·tin'i·an
pal'ette
  (paint board; see
  PALATE, PALLET)
pal'frey
  ·freys
pal'i·mo'ny
pal'ing
pal'i·sade'
pall
  palled pall'ing
  (gloom; to bore;
  see PAWL)
pall'bear'er
pal'let
  (tool; bed; see
  PALATE, PALETTE)
pal'li·ate'
  ·at'ed ·at'ing
pal'li·a'tive
pal'lid
pal'lid·ly
pal'lor
palm
pal·met'to
  ·tos or ·toes
palm'ist
palm'is·try
palm'y
  ·i·er ·i·est
pal'o·mi'no
  ·nos
pal'pa·ble
pal'pa·bly
pal'pi·tate'
  ·tat'ed ·tat'ing
pal'pi·ta'tion
pal'sy
  ·sies
  ·sied ·sy·ing
pal'tri·ness
pal'try
  ·tri·er ·tri·est
pam'pas
pam'per
pam'phlet
pam'phlet·eer'
pan
  panned pan'ning
pan'a·ce'a
pa·nache'
Pan'-A·mer'i·can
pan'cake'

pan'chro·mat'ic
pan'cre·as
pan'cre·at'ic
pan'da
pan·dem'ic
pan'de·mo'ni·um
pan'der
pane
  (window; see PAIN)
pan'e·gyr'ic
pan'el
  ·eled or ·elled
  ·el·ing or ·el·ling
pan'el·ing or ·ling
pan'el·ist
pang
pan'han'dle
pan'han'dler
pan'ic
  ·icked ·ick·ing
pan'ick·y
pan'ic-strick'en
pan'nier or ·ier
pan'o·ply
  ·plies
pan'o·ram'a
pan'o·ram'ic
pan'sy
  ·sies
pant
pan'ta·loons'
pan'the·ism'
pan'the·ist
pan'the·on'
pan'ther
pant'ies
pan'to·mime'
  ·mimed' ·mim'ing
pan'to·mim'ic
pan'to·mim'ist
pan'to·then'ic acid
pan'try
  ·tries
pants
pant'suit'
pant'y·hose'
pap
pa'pa
pa'pa·cy
  ·cies
pa'pal
pa·paw'
pa·pa'ya
pa'per
pa'per·back'
pa'per·boy'
pa'per·girl'
pa'per·hang'er
pa'per·weight'
pa'per·work'
pa'per·y
pa'pier-mâ·ché'
pa·pil'la
  ·lae
pap'il·lar'y
pa·poose'
pa·pri'ka
Pap' test'

pa·py'rus
  ·ri' or ·rus·es
par
par'a·ble
pa·rab'o·la
par'a·bol'ic
par'a·chute'
  ·chut'ed ·chut'ing
par'a·chut'ist
pa·rade'
  ·rad'ed ·rad'ing
par'a·digm'
par'a·dise'
par'a·dox'
par'a·dox'i·cal
par'a·dox'i·cal·ly
par·af'fin
par'a·gon'
par'a·graph'
par'a·keet'
par'a·le'gal
par'al·lax'
par'al·lel'
  ·leled' or ·lelled'
  ·lel'ing or ·lel'ling
par'al·lel'ism'
par'al·lel'o·gram'
pa·ral'y·sis
  ·ses'
par'a·lyt'ic
par'a·lyze'
  ·lyzed' ·lyz'ing
par'a·me'ci·um
  ·ci·a
par'a·med'ic
par'a·med'i·cal
pa·ram'e·ter
  (a limit or factor;
  see PERIMETER)
par'a·mil'i·tar'y
par'a·mount'
par'a·mour'
par'a·noi'a
par'a·noid'
par'a·pet'
par'a·pher·na'li·a
par'a·phrase'
par'a·ple'gi·a
par'a·ple'gic
par'a·pro·fes'sion·al
par'a·psy·chol'o·gy
par'a·site'
par'a·sit'ic
par'a·sol'
par'a·troop'er
par'a·troops'
par'boil'
par'cel
  ·celed or ·celled
  ·cel·ing or ·cel·ling
parch
parch'ment
par'don
par'don·a·ble
par'don·er
pare
  pared par'ing
  (to trim; see PAIR,
  PEAR)

par'e·gor'ic
par'ent
par'ent·age
pa·ren'tal
pa·ren'the·sis
  ·ses'
par'en·thet'i·cal *or*
  ·thet'ic
par'ent·hood'
par'ent·ing
pa·re'sis
par·fait'
pa·ri'ah
par'i·mu'tu·el
par'ing
par'ish
  (*church district;*
  see PERISH)
pa·rish'ion·er
Pa·ri'sian
par'i·ty
park
par'ka
Par'kin·son's dis-
  ease
park'way'
par'lance
par'lay (*bet*)
par'ley
  ·leys
  (*confer*)
par'lia·ment
par'lia·men·tar'i·an
par'lia·men'ta·ry
par'lor
pa·ro'chi·al
par'o·dy
  ·dies, ·died ·dy·ing
pa·role'
  ·roled' ·rol'ing
pa·rol'ee'
par'ox·ysm'
par·quet'
  ·queted' ·quet'ing
par'quet·ry
par'ri·cide'
par'rot
par'ry
  ·ries, ·ried ·ry·ing
parse
  parsed pars'ing
par'sec'
par'si·mo'ni·ous
par'si·mo'ny
pars'ley
pars'nip'
par'son
par'son·age
part
par·take'
  ·took' ·tak'en
  ·tak'ing
par·tak'er
part'ed
par'the·no'gen'e·sis
par'tial
par'ti·al'i·ty
par'tial·ly
par·tic'i·pant

par·tic'i·pate'
  ·pat'ed ·pat'ing
par·tic'i·pa'tion
par·tic'i·pa'tor
par·tic'i·pa·to'ry
par'ti·cip'i·al *adj.*
par'ti·ci·ple *n.*
par'ti·cle
par·tic'u·lar
par·tic'u·lar'i·ty
  ·ties
par·tic'u·lar·ize'
  ·ized' ·iz'ing
par·tic'u·lar·ly
par·tic'u·late'
part'ing
par'ti·san
par·ti'tion
par·ti'tioned
part'ly
part'ner
part'ner·ship'
par·took'
par'tridge
part'-time'
par'tu·ri'tion
part'way'
par'ty
  ·ties, ·tied ·ty·ing
par've·nu'
pas'chal
pa·sha'
pass
pass'a·ble
pass'a·bly
pas'sage
pas'sage·way'
pass'book'
pas·sé'
passed
  (*form of* pass; see
  PAST)
pas'sen·ger
pass'er
pass'er·by'
  ·ers·by'
pass'ing
pas'sion
pas'sion·ate
pas'sion·ate·ly
pas'sive
pas'sive·ly
pas·siv'i·ty
pass'key'
Pass'o'ver
pass'port'
pass'word'
past
  (*gone by; over;* see
  PASSED)
pas'ta
paste
  past'ed past'ing
paste'board'
pas·tel'
pas'tern
pas'teur·i·za'tion

pas'teur·ize'
  ·ized' ·iz'ing
pas·tiche'
pas'time'
past'i·ness
pas'tor
pas'to·ral
pas'tor·ate
pas·tra'mi
pas'try
  ·tries
pas'tur·age
pas'ture
  ·tured ·tur·ing
past'y
  ·i·er ·i·est
pat
  pat'ted pat'ting
patch
patch'i·ness
patch'work'
patch'y
  ·i·er ·i·est
pate (*head*)
pâ·té' (*meat paste*)
pat'ent
pa·ter'nal
pa·ter'nal·ism'
pa·ter'nal·is'tic
pa·ter'ni·ty
path
pa·thet'ic
pa·thet'i·cal·ly
path'o·gen
path'o·gen'ic
path'o·log'i·cal *or*
  ·log'ic
pa·thol'o·gist
pa·thol'o·gy
  ·gies
pa'thos'
path'way'
pa'tience
pa'tient
pa'tient·ly
pat'i·na
pa'ti·o'
  ·os'
pa'tois'
pa'tri·arch'
pa'tri·ar'chal
pa'tri·arch'y
  ·ies
pa·tri'cian
pat'ri·mo'ny
  ·nies
pa'tri·ot
pa'tri·ot'ic
pa'tri·ot'i·cal·ly
pa'tri·ot·ism'
pa·trol'
  ·trolled' ·trol'ling
pa·trol'man
pa'tron
pa'tron·age
pa'tron·ess
pa'tron·ize'
  ·ized' ·iz'ing

pat'ro·nym'ic
pat'sy
  ·sies
pat'ter
pat'tern
pat'ty
  ·ties
  (*cake;* see PADDY)
pau'ci·ty
paunch
paunch'y
pau'per
pau'per·ism'
pau'per·ize'
  ·ized' ·iz'ing
pause
  paused paus'ing
pave
  paved pav'ing
pave'ment
pa·vil'ion
pav'ing
paw
pawl
  (*ratchet;* see PALL)
pawn
pawn'bro'ker
pawn'shop'
pay
  paid pay'ing
  (*give*)
pay
  payed pay'ing
  (*let out rope*)
pay'a·ble
pay'check'
pay'day'
pay'ee'
pay'er
pay'load'
pay'mas'ter
pay'ment
pay'off'
pay·o'la
pay'out'
pay'roll'
pea
  peas
peace
  (*harmony;* see
  PIECE)
peace'a·ble
peace'ful
peace'ful·ly
peace'mak'er
peace'mak'ing
peace'time'
peach
pea'cock'
pea'fowl'
pea'hen'
peak
  (*highest point;* see
  PEEK, PIQUE)
peak'ed (*thin and
  drawn*)
peaked (*pointed*)
peal
  (*sound;* see PEEL)

pea'nut'
pear
  (*fruit;* see PAIR,
  PARE)
pearl
  (*gem;* see PURL)
pearl'y
  ·i·er i·est
peas'ant
peas'ant·ry
peat
peb'ble
peb'bly
  ·bli·er ·bli·est
pe·can'
pec'ca·ry
  ·ries
peck
pec'tin
pec'to·ral
pec'u·late'
  ·lat'ed ·lat'ing
pec'u·la'tion
pe·cu'liar
pe·cu'li·ar'i·ty
  ·ties
pe·cu'liar·ly
pe·cu'ni·ar'y
ped'a·gog'ic *or*
  ·gog'i·cal
ped'a·gogue' *or*
  ·gog
ped'a·gog'y
ped'al
  ·aled *or* ·alled
  ·al·ing *or* ·al·ling
  (*foot lever;* see
  PEDDLE)
ped'ant
pe·dan'tic
pe·dan'ti·cal·ly
ped'ant·ry
ped'dle
  ·dled ·dling
  (*sell;* see PEDAL)
ped'dler
ped'es·tal
pe·des'tri·an
pe'di·a·tri'cian
pe'di·at'rics
ped'i·cure'
ped'i·gree'
ped'i·greed'
ped'i·ment
pe·dom'e·ter
pe·dun'cle
peek
  (*look;* see PEAK,
  PIQUE)
peel
  (*skin;* see PEAL)
peel'ing
peen
peep
peep'er
peep'hole'
peer
  (*equal; look;* see
  PIER)
peer'age

peer'ess
peer'less
peeve
  peeved peev'ing
pee'vish
pee'vish·ly
pee'vish·ness
pee'wee'
peg
  pegged peg'ging
pej'o·ra'tion
pe·jo'ra·tive
pe'koe
pe·lag'ic
pelf
pel'i·can
pel·la'gra
pel'let
pell'-mell'
pel·lu'cid
pelt
pel'vic
pel'vis
  ·vis·es *or* ·ves'
pen
  penned *or* pent
  pen'ning
  (*enclose*)
pen
  penned pen'ning
  (*write with a pen*)
pe'nal
pe'nal·i·za'tion
pe'nal·ize'
  ·ized' ·iz'ing
pen'al·ty
  ·ties
pen'ance
pence
pen'chant
pen'cil
  ·ciled *or* ·cilled
  ·cil·ing *or* ·cil·ling
pend
pend'ant *n.*
pend'ent *adj.*
pend'ing
pen'du·lous
pen'du·lum
pen'e·tra·ble
pen'e·trate'
  ·trat'ed ·trat'ing
pen'e·trat'ing
pen'e·tra'tion
pen'guin
pen'i·cil'lin
pen·in'su·la
pen·in'su·lar
pe'nis
  ·nis·es *or* ·nes'
pen'i·tence
pen'i·tent
pen'i·ten'tial
pen'i·ten'tia·ry
  ·ries
pen'i·tent·ly
pen'knife'
  ·knives'
pen'light' *or* ·lite'

pen′man·ship′
pen′nant
pen′ni·less
pen′non
Penn′syl·va′ni·a
pen′ny
  ·nies *or* pence
pen′ny-pinch′ing
pen′ny·weight′
pe·nol′o·gist
pe·nol′o·gy
pen′sion
pen′sion·er
pen′sive
pen′sive·ly
pen′sive·ness
pent
pen′ta·cle
pen′ta·gon′
pen·tag′o·nal
pen·tam′e·ter
Pen′ta·teuch′
pen·tath′lete′
pen·tath′lon′
pent′house′
pent′-up′
pe·nul′ti·mate
pe·nu′ri·ous
pe·nu′ri·ous·ly
pen′u·ry
pe′on
  (*laborer;* see
  PAEAN)
pe′on·age
pe′o·ny
  ·nies
peo′ple
  ·ples
  ·pled ·pling
pep
  pepped pep′ping
pep′per
pep′per·corn′
pep′per·mint′
pep′per·o′ni
  ·nis *or* ·ni
pep′per·y
pep′pi·ness
pep′py
  ·pi·er ·pi·est
pep′sin
pep′tic
per
per′ad·ven′ture
per·am′bu·late′
  ·lat′ed ·lat′ing
per·am′bu·la′tor
per an′num
per·cale′
per cap′i·ta
per·ceiv′a·ble
per·ceive′
  ·ceived′ ·ceiv′ing
per·cent′
per·cent′age
per·cen′tile′
per′cept′
per·cep′ti·ble

per·cep′ti·bly
per·cep′tion
per·cep′tive
per·cep′tive·ly
per·cep′tive·ness
per·cep′tu·al
perch
per·chance′
per′co·late′
  ·lat′ed ·lat′ing
per′co·la′tor
per·cus′sion
per·cus′sion·ist
per·cus′sive
per di′em
per·di′tion
per·dure′
  ·dured′ ·dur′ing
per′e·gri·nate′
  ·nat′ed ·nat′ing
per′e·grine
per·emp′to·ry
per·en′ni·al
per·en′ni·al·ly
per′fect
per·fec′ta
  (*bet;* see
  PERFECTO)
per·fect′i·bil′i·ty
per·fect′i·ble
per·fec′tion
per·fec′tion·ism′
per·fec′tion·ist
per′fect·ly
per′fect·ness
per·fec′to
  ·tos
  (*cigar;* see PER-
  FECTA)
per·fid′i·ous
per′fi·dy
  ·dies
per′fo·rate′
  ·rat′ed ·rat′ing
per′fo·ra′tion
per′fo·ra′tor
per·force′
per·form′
per·form′ance
per·form′er
per·fume′
  ·fumed′ ·fum′ing
per·fum′er·y
  ·ies
per·func′to·ri·ly
per·func′to·ry
per′go·la
per·haps′
per′i·car′di·al
per′i·car′di·um
  ·di·a
per′i·gee′
per′i·he′li·on
  ·li·ons *or* ·li·a
per′il
  ·iled *or* ·illed
  ·il·ing *or* ·il·ling
per′il·ous
per′il·ous·ly

pe·rim′e·ter
  (*boundary of an
  area;* see PARAME-
  TER)
per′i·ne′um
  ·ne′a
pe′ri·od
pe′ri·od′ic
pe′ri·od′i·cal
pe′ri·od′i·cal·ly
pe′ri·o·dic′i·ty
pe′ri·od·i·za′tion
per′i·o·don′tal
per′i·pa·tet′ic
pe·riph′er·al
pe·riph′er·y
  ·ies
per′i·scope′
per′i·scop′ic
per′ish
  (*to die;* see PARISH)
per′ish·a·ble
per′i·stal′sis
per′i·stal′tic
per′i·to·ne′um
  ·ne′a *or* ·ne′ums
per′i·to·ni′tis
per′i·wig′
per′i·win′kle
per′jure
  ·jured ·jur·ing
per′jur·er
per′ju·ry
  ·ries
perk
perk′i·ness
perk′y
  ·i·er ·i·est
perm
per′ma·frost′
per′ma·nence
per′ma·nent
per′me·a·bil′i·ty
per′me·a·ble
per′me·ate′
  ·at′ed ·at′ing
per·mis′si·ble
per·mis′sion
per·mis′sive
per·mis′sive·ly
per·mis′sive·ness
per·mit′
  ·mit′ted ·mit′ting
per′mu·ta′tion
per·ni′cious
per·ni′cious·ly
per′o·ra′tion
per·ox′ide′
per′pen·dic′u·lar
per′pe·trate′
  ·trat′ed ·trat′ing
per′pe·tra′tion
per′pe·tra′tor
per·pet′u·al
per·pet′u·al·ly
per·pet′u·ate′
  ·at′ed ·at′ing
per·pet′u·a′tion

per′pe·tu′i·ty
  ·ties
per·plex′
per·plexed′
per·plex′ing
per·plex′i·ty
  ·ties
per′qui·site
  (*privilege;* see PRE-
  REQUISITE)
per′ se′
per′se·cute′
  ·cut′ed ·cut′ing
  (*harass;* see PROS-
  ECUTE)
per′se·cu′tion
per′se·cu′tor
per′se·ver′ance
per′se·vere′
  ·vered ·ver′ing
Per′sian
per·sim′mon
per·sist′
per·sist′ence
per·sist′ent
per·snick′e·ty
per′son
per′son·a·ble
per′son·age′
per′son·al
  (*private;* see PER-
  SONNEL)
per′son·al′i·ty
  ·ties
per′son·al·ize′
  ·ized′ ·iz′ing
per′son·al·ly
*per·so′na non
gra′ta*
per·son′i·fi·ca′tion
per·son′i·fy′
  ·fied′ ·fy′ing
per′son·nel′
  (*employees;* see
  PERSONAL)
per·spec′tive
  (*view;* see
  PROSPECTIVE)
per′spi·ca′cious
per′spi·ca′cious·ly
per′spi·cac′i·ty
per′spi·cu′i·ty
per·spic′u·ous
per′spi·ra′tion
per·spire′
  ·spired′ ·spir′ing
per·suad′a·ble
per·suade′
  ·suad′ed ·suad′ing
per·suad′er
per·sua′sion
per·sua′sive
per·sua′sive·ly
pert
per·tain′
per′ti·na′cious
per′ti·nac′i·ty
per′ti·nence
per′ti·nent
pert′ly

per·turb′
per′tur·ba′tion
pe·rus′al
pe·ruse′
  ·rused′ ·rus′ing
per·vade′
  ·vad′ed ·vad′ing
per·va′sive
per·verse′
per·verse′ly
per·verse′ness
per·ver′sion
per·ver′si·ty
per·vert′ *v.*
per′vert′ *n.*
pe·se′ta
pes′ki·ness
pes′ky
  ·ki·er ·ki·est
pe′so
  ·sos′
pes′si·mism′
pes′si·mist
pes′si·mis′tic
pes′si·mis′ti·cal·ly
pest
pes′ter
pest′hole′
pes′ti·cide′
pes′ti·lence
pes′ti·lent
pes′tle
pes′to
pet
  pet′ted pet′ting
pet′al
pet′cock′
pet′i·ole′
pe·tite′
pe·ti′tion
pe·ti′tion·er
pet′rel
  (*bird;* see PETROL)
pe′tri dish
pet′ri·fy′
  ·fied′ ·fy′ing
pet′ro·chem′i·cal
pet′ro·dol′lars
pet′rol
  (*gasoline;* see PE-
  TREL)
pet′ro·la′tum
pe·tro′le·um
pet′ti·coat′
pet′ti·ness
pet′tish
pet′tish·ly
pet′ty
  ·ti·er ·ti·est
pet′u·lance
pet′u·lant
pet′u·lant·ly
pe·tu′ni·a
pew
pe·wee′
pew′ter
pe·yo′te
pha′e·ton *or* ·ë·

phag′o·cyte′
pha·lan′ger
pha′lanx′
  ·lanx′es *or*
  pha·lan′ges′
phal′lic
phal′lus
  ·li′ *or* ·lus·es
phan′tasm′
phan·tas′ma·go′ri·a
phan′ta·sy
  ·sies
phan′tom
Phar′aoh
phar′i·sa′ic
phar′i·see′
phar′ma·ceu′ti·cal
phar′ma·ceu′tics
phar′ma·cist
phar′ma·col′o·gy
phar′ma·co·pe′ia
  or ·poe′·
phar′ma·cy
  ·cies
pha·ryn′ge·al
phar′yn·gi′tis
phar′ynx
  ·ynx·es *or*
  pha·ryn′ges′
phase
  phased phas′ing
  (*stage;* see FAZE)
phase′out′
pheas′ant
phe·nac′e·tin′
phe′no·bar′bi·tal′
phe′nol′
phe′nol·phthal′ein′
phe′nom
phe·nom′e·nal
phe·nom′e·non′
  ·na *or* ·nons′
pher′o·mone′
phi′al
phi·lan′der
phi·lan′der·er
phil′an·throp′ic
phi·lan′thro·pist
phi·lan′thro·py
  ·pies
phil′a·tel′ic
phi·lat′e·list
phi·lat′e·ly
phil′har·mon′ic
Phil·is′tine
phil′o·den′dron
phil′o·log′i·cal
phi·lol′o·gist
phi·lol′o·gy
phi·los′o·pher
phil′o·soph′ic *or*
  ·soph′i·cal
phi·los′o·phize′
  ·phized′ ·phiz′ing
phi·los′o·phy
  ·phies
phil′ter
  (*potion;* see
  FILTER)

phle·bi'tis
phlegm
phleg·mat'ic
phleg·mat'i·cal·ly
phlo'em'
phlox
pho'bi·a
pho'bic
phoe'be
phoe'nix
phone
  phoned phon'ing
pho'neme'
pho·ne'mic
pho·net'ic
pho·net'i·cal·ly
pho'ne·ti'cian
pho·net'ics
phon'ic
phon'ics
pho'ni·ness
pho'no·graph'
pho'no·graph'ic
pho'no·log'i·cal
pho·nol'o·gist
pho·nol'o·gy
pho'ny
  ·nies
  ·ni·er ·ni·est
phoo'ey
phos'phate'
phos'phor
phos'pho·res'-
  cence
phos'pho·res'cent
phos'pho·rus
pho'to
  ·tos
pho'to·cop'i·er
pho'to·cop'y
  ·ies
pho'to·e·lec'tric
pho'to·en·grave'
pho'to·en·grav'er
pho'to·en·grav'ing
pho'to·fin'ish·ing
pho'to·flash'
pho'to·gen'ic
pho'to·graph'
pho·tog'ra·pher
pho'to·graph'ic
pho·tog'ra·phy
pho'ton'
pho'to·off'set'
pho'to·sen'si·tive
pho'to·sen'si·tiv'i·ty
pho'to·stat'
  ·stat'ed or
  ·stat'ted
  ·stat'ing or
  ·stat'ting
pho'to·stat'ic
pho'to·syn'the·sis
pho'to·syn'the·size'
  ·sized' ·siz·ing
phras'al
phrase
  phrased phras'ing

phra'se·ol'o·gy
  ·gies
phre·net'ic
phre·nol'o·gy
phy·lac'ter·y
  ·ies
phyl'lo
phy·log'e·ny
  ·nies
phy'lum
  ·la
phys'ic
  ·icked ·ick·ing
phys'i·cal
phys'i·cal·ly
phy·si'cian
phys'i·cist
phys'ics
phys'i·og'no·my
phys'i·og'ra·phy
phys'i·o·log'i·cal
phys'i·ol'o·gist
phys'i·ol'o·gy
phys'i·o·ther'a·pist
phys'i·o·ther'a·py
phy·sique'
pi
pi'a·nis'si·mo'
pi·an'ist
pi·a'no
  ·nos
pi·an'o·for·te'
pi·as'ter
pi·az'za
  ·zas or ·ze
pi'ca
pic'a·dor'
pic'a·resque'
pic'a·yune'
pic'co·lo'
  ·los'
pick
pick'ax' or ·axe
pick'er
pick'er·el
pick'et
pick'ings
pick'le
  ·led ·ling
pick'pock'et
pick'up'
pick'y
  ·i·er ·i·est
pic'nic
  ·nicked ·nick·ing
pic'nick·er
pic'to·graph'
pic·to'ri·al
pic·to'ri·al·ly
pic'ture
  ·tured ·tur·ing
pic'tur·esque'
pid'dle
  ·dled ·dling
pid'dling
pid'dly
pidg'in English
pie
pie'bald'

piece
  pieced piec'ing
  (part; see PEACE)
piece'meal'
piece'work'
pied
pier
  (a structure; see
  PEER)
pierce
  pierced pierc'ing
pi'e·ty
pig
pi'geon
pi'geon·hole'
  ·holed' ·hol'ing
pi'geon-toed'
pig'gish
pig'gish·ness
pig'gy
  ·gies
pig'gy·back'
pig'head'ed
pig'ment
pig'men·ta'tion
pig'pen'
pig'skin'
pig'sty'
  ·sties'
pig'tail'
pike
pik'er
pi·laf' or ·laff'
pi·las'ter
pil'chard
pile
  piled pil'ing
piles
pile'up'
pil'fer
pil'fer·age
pil'fer·er
pil'grim
pil'grim·age
pill
pil'lage
  ·laged ·lag·ing
pil'lar
pill'box'
pil'lo·ry
  ·ries
  ·ried ·ry·ing
pil'low
pil'low·case'
pi'lot
pi'lot·house'
pi·men'to or
  ·mien'·
  ·tos
pimp
pim'ple
pim'ply
  ·pli·er ·pli·est
pin
  pinned pin'ning
pin'a·fore'
pi·ña'ta
pin'ball'
pin'cers

pinch
pinch'-hit'
pinch hitter
pin'cush'ion
pine
pin'e·al body
pine'ap'ple
pin'feath'er
ping
ping'-pong'
pin'head'
pin'hole'
pin'ion
pink
pink'eye'
pink'ie or ·y
  ·ies
pink'ing shears
pin'na·cle (acme)
pin'nate'
pi'noch'le or ·noc'·
  (card game)
pin'point'
pin'prick'
pint
pin'to
  ·tos
pin'up'
pin'wheel'
pi'o·neer'
pi'ous
pi'ous·ly
pip
pipe
  piped pip'ing
pipe'line'
pip'er
pi·pette' or ·pet'
pip'ing
pip'it
pip'pin
pip'squeak'
pi'quan·cy
pi'quant
pique
  piqued piqu'ing
  (provoke; see
  PEAK, PEEK)
pi'ra·cy
  ·cies
pi·ra'nha
pi'rate
  ·rat·ed ·rat·ing
pi·rat'i·cal
pi·ro'gi
pir'ou·ette'
  ·et'ted ·et'ting
pis·ca·to'ri·al
Pis'ces'
pis·tach'i·o
  ·os
pis'til (part of
  flower)
pis'tol (firearm)
pis'tol-whip'
pis'ton
pit
  pit'ted pit'ting

pi'ta
pitch
pitch'-black'
pitch'blende'
pitch'-dark'
pitch'er
pitch'fork'
pitch'man
pit'e·ous
pit'e·ous·ly
pit'fall'
pith
pith'i·ly
pith'y
  ·i·er ·i·est
pit'i·a·ble
pit'i·ful
pit'i·ful·ly
pit'i·less
pit'tance
pit'ter-pat'ter
Pitts'burgh'
pi·tu'i·tar'y
pit'y
  ·ies
  ·ied ·y·ing
piv'ot
piv'ot·al
pix'el
pix'ie or ·y
  ·ies
pi·zazz' or piz·
piz'za
piz'ze·ri'a
piz'zi·ca'to
plac'ard
pla'cate
  ·cat'ed ·cat'ing
pla·ca'tion
place
  placed plac'ing
pla·ce'bo
  ·bos or ·boes
place'ment
pla·cen'ta
  ·tas or ·tae
pla·cen'tal
plac'er
plac'id
pla·cid'i·ty
plac'id·ly
plack'et
pla'gia·rism'
pla'gia·rist
pla'gia·rize'
  ·rized' ·riz'ing
pla'gia·ry
plague
  plagued plagu'ing
plaid
plain
  (simple; see
  PLANE)
plain'clothes' man
plain'ly
plain'ness
plains'man
plain'song'

plain'tiff (legal
  term)
plain'tive (sad)
plain'tive·ly
plait
  (braid; see PLATE)
plan
  planned plan'ning
plane
  (airplane; surface;
  see PLAIN)
plan'et
plan'e·tar'i·um
  ·i·ums or ·i·a
plan'e·tar'y
plan'gent
plank
plank'ing
plank'ton
plan'ner
plant
plan'tain
plan'tar (of the sole)
plan·ta'tion
plant'er (one that
  plants)
plaque
plash
plas'ma
plas'ter
plas'ter·board'
plas'ter·er
plas'tic
plas·tic'i·ty
plat
  plat'ted plat'ting
plate
  plat'ed plat'ing
  (dish; see PLAIT)
pla·teau'
  ·teaus or ·teaux
plat'en
plate tec·ton'ics
plat'form'
plat'i·num
plat'i·tude'
pla·ton'ic
pla·ton'i·cal·ly
pla·toon'
plat'ter
plat'y
  ·ies
plat'y·pus
  ·pus·es or ·pi'
plau'dits
plau'si·bil'i·ty
plau'si·ble
plau'si·bly
play
play'act'
play'act'ing
play'back'
play'bill'
play'boy'
play'-by-play'
play'er
play'ful
play'ful·ly

play'ful·ness
play'go'er
play'ground'
play'house'
play'mate'
play'off'
play'pen'
play'thing'
play'wright'
pla'za
plea
plea'-bar'gain
plead
  plead'ed *or* pled *or*
  plead, plead'ing
pleas'ant
pleas'ant·ly
pleas'ant·ness
pleas'ant·ry
  ·ries
please
  pleased pleas'ing
pleas'ing
pleas'ing·ly
pleas'ur·a·ble
pleas'ure
pleat
ple·be'ian
pleb'i·scite'
plec'trum
  ·trums *or* ·tra
pled
pledge
  pledged pledg'ing
Pleis'to·cene'
ple'na·ry
plen'i·po·ten'ti·ar'y
  ·ies
plen'i·tude'
plen'te·ous
plen'ti·ful
plen'ti·ful·ly
plen'ty
pleth'o·ra
pleu'ra
  ·rae
pleu'ral
  (*of the pleura;* see
  PLURAL)
pleu'ri·sy
Plex'i·glas'
plex'us
  ·us·es *or* ·us
pli'a·bil'i·ty
pli'a·ble
pli'an·cy
pli'ant
pli'ers
plight
plod
  plod'ded plod'ding
plod'der
plop
  plopped plop'ping
plot
  plot'ted plot'ting
plot'ter
plov'er
plow

plow'man
plow'share'
ploy
pluck
pluck'i·ness
pluck'y
  ·i·er ·i·est
plug
  plugged plug'ging
plum (*fruit*)
plum'age
plumb (*lead weight*)
plumb'er
plumb'ing
plume
  plumed plum'ing
plum'met
plump
plump'ness
plun'der
plunge
  plunged plung'ing
plung'er
plunk
plu'per'fect
plu'ral
  (*more than one;*
  see PLEURAL)
plu'ral·ism'
plu'ral·is'tic
plu·ral'i·ty
  ·ties
plu'ral·ize'
  ·ized' ·iz'ing
plus
  plus'es *or* ·ses
plush
Plu'to
plu·toc'ra·cy
  ·cies
plu'to·crat'
plu'to·crat'ic
plu·to'ni·um
plu'vi·al
ply
  plies
  plied ply'ing
ply'wood'
pneu·mat'ic
pneu·mo'ni·a
poach
poached
poach'er
pock
pocked
pock'et
pock'et·book'
pock'et·ful'
  ·fuls'
pock'et·knife'
pock'mark'
pod
po·di'a·trist
po·di'a·try
po'di·um
  ·di·a *or* ·di·ums
po'em
po'et
po'et·as'ter

po'et·ess
po·et'ic
po·et'i·cal·ly
po'et·ry
po·grom'
poi
poign'an·cy
poign'ant
poin·set'ti·a
point
point'-blank'
point'ed
point'ed·ly
point'er
poin'til·lism'
poin'til·list
point'less
point'y
  ·i·er ·i·est
poise
  poised pois'ing
poi'son
poi'son·ous
poi'son·ous·ly
poke
  poked pok'ing
pok'er
pok'y
  ·i·er ·i·est
po'lar
po·lar'i·ty
  ·ties
po'lar·i·za'tion
po'lar·ize'
  ·ized' ·iz'ing
pole
  poled pol'ing
  (*rod;* see POLL)
pole'cat'
po·lem'ic
po·lem'i·cist
po·lem'ics
pole'star'
pole'-vault' *v.*
pole'-vault'er
po·lice'
  ·liced' ·lic'ing
po·lice'man
po·lice'wom'an
pol'i·clin'ic
  (*outpatient clinic;*
  see POLYCLINIC)
pol'i·cy
  ·cies
pol'i·cy·hold'er
po'li·o'
po'li·o·my'e·li'tis
pol'ish
Pol'ish
po·lite'
po·lite'ly
po·lite'ness
pol'i·tesse'
pol'i·tic'
  ·ticked' ·tick'ing
po·lit'i·cal
po·lit'i·cal·ly (*in a*
  political way)
political scientist

pol'i·ti'cian
po·lit'i·cize'
  ·cized' ·ciz'ing
pol'i·tic'ly
  (*shrewdly*)
po·lit'i·co'
  ·cos'
pol'i·tics
pol'i·ty
  ·ties
pol'ka
pol'ka dot
poll
  (*vote;* see POLE)
pol'len
pol'li·nate'
  ·nat'ed ·nat'ing
pol'li·na'tion
pol'li·wog'
poll'ster
pol·lu'tant
pol·lute'
  ·lut'ed ·lut'ing
pol·lu'tion
po'lo
pol'o·naise'
pol'ter·geist'
pol·troon'
pol'y·clin'ic
  (*hospital;* see POLI-
  CLINIC)
pol'y·es'ter
pol'y·eth'yl·ene'
po·lyg'a·mist
po·lyg'a·mous
po·lyg'a·my
pol'y·glot'
pol'y·gon'
po·lyg'o·nal
pol'y·graph'
pol'y·mer
po·lym'er·i·za'tion
po·lym'er·ize'
  ·ized' ·iz'ing
pol'y·no'mi·al
pol'yp
pol'y·phon'ic
po·lyph'o·ny
pol'y·rhythm'
pol'y·rhyth'mic
pol'y·syl·lab'ic
pol'y·syl'la·ble
pol'y·tech'nic
pol'y·the·ism'
pol'y·the·ist
pol'y·the·is'tic
pol'y·un·sat'u·rat'ed
pol'y·vi'nyl
pome'gran'ate
pom'mel
  ·meled *or* ·melled
  ·mel·ing *or*
  ·mel·ling
pomp
pom'pa·dour'
pom'pa·no'
pom'pom'
pom·pos'i·ty
pom'pous

pon'cho
  ·chos
pond
pon'der
pon'der·o'sa
pon'der·ous
pone
pon'tiff
pon·tif'i·cal
pon·tif'i·cate'
  ·cat'ed ·cat'ing
pon·toon'
po'ny
  ·nies
po'ny·tail'
pooch
poo'dle
pooh'-pooh'
pool
poop
poor
poor'house'
poor'ly
pop
  popped pop'ping
pop'corn'
pope
pop'gun'
pop'in·jay'
pop'lar
  (*tree;* see POPULAR)
pop'lin
pop'o'ver
pop'per
pop'py
  ·pies
pop'py·cock'
pops
pop'-top'
pop'u·lace
  (*the masses;* see
  POPULOUS)
pop'u·lar
  (*well-liked;* see
  POPLAR)
pop'u·lar'i·ty
pop'u·lar·i·za'tion
pop'u·lar·ize'
  ·ized' ·iz'ing
pop'u·lar·ly
pop'u·late'
  ·lat'ed ·lat'ing
pop'u·la'tion
pop'u·lism'
pop'u·list
pop'u·lous
  (*full of people;* see
  POPULACE)
por'ce·lain
porch
por'cine'
por'cu·pine'
pore
  pored por'ing
  (*ponder; tiny*
  opening; see POUR)
pork
pork'y
  ·i·er ·i·est
por'no

por'no·graph'ic
por·nog'ra·phy
po·ros'i·ty
po'rous
por'phy·ry
  ·ries
por'poise
por'ridge
port
port'a·bil'i·ty
port'a·ble
por'tage
  ·taged ·tag·ing
por'tal
port·cul'lis
por·tend'
por'tent'
por·ten'tous
por'ter
por'ter·house'
port·fo'li·o'
  ·os'
port'hole'
por'ti·co'
  ·coes' *or* ·cos'
por'tion
port'li·ness
port'ly
  ·li·er ·li·est
port·man'teau'
  ·teaus' *or* ·teaux'
por'trait
por'trai·ture
por·tray'
por·tray'al
pose
  posed pos'ing
pos'er
posh
pos'it
po·si'tion
pos'i·tive
pos'i·tive·ly
pos'i·tron'
pos'se
pos·sess'
pos·sessed'
pos·ses'sion
pos·ses'sive
pos·ses'sive·ness
pos·ses'sor
pos'si·bil'i·ty
  ·ties
pos'si·ble
pos'si·bly
pos'sum
post
post'age
post'al
post'card
post'date'
post'er
pos·te'ri·or
pos·ter'i·ty
post'grad'u·ate
post'haste'
post'hu·mous
post'hu·mous·ly

post'hyp·not'ic
post'in·dus'tri·al
post'man
post'mark'
post'mas'ter
post me·ri'di·em
post'mod'ern
post'-mor'tem
post'na'sal drip
post'na'tal
post'op'er·a·tive
post'paid'
post'par'tum
post·pone'
  ·poned' ·pon'ing
post·pone'ment
post'script'
pos'tu·late'
  ·lat'ed ·lat'ing
pos'ture
post'war'
po'sy
  ·sies
pot
  pot'ted pot'ting
po'ta·ble
pot'ash'
po·tas'si·um
po·ta'to
  ·toes
pot'bel'lied
pot'bel'ly
  ·lies
po'ten·cy
po'tent
po'ten·tate'
po·ten'tial
po·ten'ti·al'i·ty
  ·ties
po·ten'tial·ly
pot'ful'
  ·fuls'
pot'hold'er
pot'hole'
pot'hook'
po'tion
pot'luck'
pot'pie'
pot'pour·ri'
pot'sherd'
pot'shot'
pot'tage
pot'ter
pot'ter·y
  ·ies
pot'ty
  ·ties
pouch
poul'tice
  ·ticed ·tic·ing
poul'try
pounce
  pounced pounc'ing
pound
pound'cake'
pour
  (flow; see PORE)
pout
pout'er

pov'er·ty
pov'er·ty-strick'en
pow'der
pow'der·y
pow'er
pow'er·ful
pow'er·ful·ly
pow'er·house'
pow'er·less
pow'er·less·ly
pow'er·train'
pow'wow'
pox
prac'ti·ca·bil'i·ty
prac'ti·ca·ble
prac'ti·ca·bly
prac'ti·cal
prac'ti·cal'i·ty
  ·ties
prac'ti·cal·ly
prac'tice
  ·ticed ·tic·ing
prac'ticed
prac'ti·cum
prac·ti'tion·er
prag·mat'ic
prag·mat'i·cal·ly
prag'ma·tism'
prag'ma·tist
prai'rie
praise
  praised prais'ing
praise'wor'thi·ness
praise'wor'thy
prance
  pranced pranc'ing
pranc'er
prank
prank'ster
prate
  prat'ed prat'ing
prat'tle
  ·tled ·tling
prawn
pray
  (implore; see PREY)
prayer (an entreaty)
pray'er (one who
  prays)
prayer'ful
prayer'ful·ly
preach
preach'er
preach'ment
preach'y
  ·i·er ·i·est
pre·am'ble
pre·ar·range'
pre'can'cer·ous
pre·car'i·ous
pre·car'i·ous·ly
pre·cau'tion
pre·cau'tion·ar'y
pre·cede'
  ·ced'ed ·ced'ing
  (come before; see
  PROCEED)

prec'e·dence (pri-
  ority)
pre·ced'ent (exam-
  ple)
pre·ced'ing
pre'cept'
pre·cep'tor
pre·ces'sion
  (in astronomy; see
  PROCESSION)
pre'cinct'
pre'ci·os'i·ty
pre'cious
pre'cious·ly
pre'cious·ness
prec'i·pice
pre·cip'i·tant
pre·cip'i·tate'
  ·tat'ed ·tat'ing
pre·cip'i·ta'tion
pre·cip'i·tous
pré·cis' (summary)
pre·cise' (definite)
pre·cise'ly
pre·cise'ness
pre·ci'sion
pre·clude'
  ·clud'ed ·clud'ing
pre·clu'sion
pre·co'cious
pre·coc'i·ty
pre'cog·ni'tion
pre'cog'ni·tive
pre'-Co·lum'bi·an
pre'con·ceive'
  ·ceived' ·ceiv'ing
pre'con·cep'tion
pre'con·di'tion
pre·cur'sor
pre·cur'so·ry
pre·da'cious
pre'date'
pred'a·tor
pred'a·to'ry
pred'e·ces'sor
pre·des'ti·na'tion
pre·des'tine
  ·tined ·tin·ing
pre·de·ter'mine
pre·dic'a·ment
pred'i·cate'
  ·cat'ed ·cat'ing
pred'i·ca'tion
pre·dict'
pre·dict'a·ble
pre·dic'tion
pre·dic'tive
pre·dic'tor
pre'di·gest'
pred'i·lec'tion
pre'dis·pose'
  ·posed' ·pos'ing
pre'dis·po·si'tion
pre·dom'i·nance
pre·dom'i·nant
pre·dom'i·nant·ly
pre·dom'i·nate'
pre·em'i·nence

pre·em'i·nent
pre·em'i·nent·ly
pre·empt' or pre-
  empt'
pre·emp'tion
pre·emp'tive
preen
pre'ex·ist'
pre'ex·ist'ence
pre'fab'
pre·fab'ri·cate'
pref'ace
  ·aced ·ac·ing
pref'a·to'ry
pre'fect'
pre·fec'ture
pre·fer'
  ·ferred' ·fer'ring
pref'er·a·ble
pref'er·a·bly
pref'er·ence
pref'er·en'tial
pre·fer'ment
pre·fig'ure
  ·ured ·ur·ing
pre'fix'
preg'nan·cy
  ·cies
preg'nant
preg'nant·ly
pre·hen'sile
pre'his·tor'ic
pre'judge'
pre'judg'ment or
  ·judge'·
prej'u·dice
  ·diced ·dic·ing
prej'u·di'cial
prel'a·cy
  ·cies
prel'ate
pre·lim'i·nar'y
  ·ies
pre·lit'er·ate
prel'ude'
pre·mar'i·tal
pre'ma·ture'
pre'ma·ture'ly
pre'med'
pre·med'i·cal
pre·med'i·tate'
  ·tat'ed ·tat'ing
pre·med'i·ta'tion
pre·men'stru·al
pre'mier (first;
  prime minister)
pre·mière' or
  ·miere' (first per-
  formance)
prem'ise
  ·ised ·is·ing
pre'mi·um
pre·mo'lar
prem'o·ni'tion
pre·mon'i·to'ry
pre·na'tal
pre·nup'tial
pre·oc'cu·pa'tion

pre·oc'cu·pied'
pre·oc'cu·py'
pre'or·dain'
prep
  prepped prep'ping
pre'pack'age
pre'paid'
prep'a·ra'tion
pre·par'a·to'ry
pre·pare'
  ·pared' ·par'ing
pre·par'ed·ness
pre'pay'
  ·paid' ·pay'ing
pre·pon'der·ance
pre·pon'der·ant
pre·pon'der·ate'
  ·at'ed ·at'ing
prep'o·si'tion
prep'o·si'tion·al
pre'pos·sess'
pre'pos·sess'ing
pre·pos'ter·ous
prep'py or ·pie
  ·pies
  ·pi·er ·pi·est
pre'puce
pre·re'cord'
pre·re·cord'ed
pre·req'ui·site
  (requirement; see
  PERQUISITE)
pre·rog'a·tive
pres'age
  ·aged' ·ag'ing
pres'by·ter
Pres'by·te'ri·an
pre'school'
pre'school'er
pres'ci·ence
pres'ci·ent
pre·scribe'
  ·scribed' ·scrib'ing
  (to order; see PRO-
  SCRIBE)
pre'script'
pre·scrip'tion
pre·scrip'tive
pres'ence
pres'ent
pre·sent'a·ble
pres'en·ta'tion
pres'ent-day'
pre·sen'ti·ment
  (premonition)
pres'ent·ly
pre·sent'ment (pre-
  sentation)
pres'er·va'tion
pres'er·va'tion·ist
pre·serv'a·tive
pre·serve'
  ·served' ·serv'ing
pre·serv'er
pre'set'
pre'shrink'
pre'shrunk'
pre·side'
  ·sid'ed ·sid'ing

pres'i·den·cy
  ·cies
pres'i·dent
pres'i·den'tial
pre·sid'i·o'
  ·os'
pre·sid'i·um
  ·i·a or ·i·ums
press
press'er
press'ing
press'man
pres'sure
  ·sured ·sur·ing
pres'sur·i·za'tion
pres'sur·ize'
  ·ized' ·iz'ing
pres'sur·iz'er
pres'ti·dig'i·ta'tion
pres'ti·dig'i·ta'tor
pres·tige'
pres·ti'gious
pres'to
pre'stressed'
pre·sum'a·ble
pre·sum'a·bly
pre·sume'
  ·sumed' ·sum'ing
pre·sump'tion
pre·sump'tive
pre·sump'tu·ous
pre'sup·pose'
pre'sup·po·si'tion
pre'tax'
pre'teen'
pre·tend'
pre·tend'er
pre·tense'
pre·ten'sion
pre·ten'tious
pre·ten'tious·ly
pre·ten'tious·ness
pret'er·it or ·ite
pre'ter·nat'u·ral
pre'test'
pre'text'
pre'tri'al
pret'ti·fy'
  ·fied' ·fy'ing
pret'ti·ly
pret'ti·ness
pret'ty
  ·ti·er ·ti·est
  ·tied ·ty·ing
pret'zel
pre·vail'
pre·vail'ing
prev'a·lence
prev'a·lent
pre·var'i·cate'
  ·cat'ed ·cat'ing
pre·var'i·ca'tion
pre·var'i·ca'tor
pre·vent'
pre·vent'a·ble or
  ·i·ble
pre·ven'tion

pre·ven'tive *or* ·vent'a·tive
pre'view'
pre'vi·ous
pre'vi·ous·ly
pre'war'
prex'y
·ies
prey
(*victim;* see PRAY)
pri·ap'ic
price
priced pric'ing
price'less
prick
prick'er
prick'le
·led ·ling
prick'ly
·li·er ·li·est
pride
prid'ed prid'ing
pride'ful
pride'ful·ly
pri'er
(*one that pries;* see PRIOR)
priest
priest'ess
priest'hood'
priest'ly
·li·er ·li·est
prig
prig'gish
prim
prim'mer
prim'mest
pri'ma·cy
·cies
pri'ma don'na
pri'ma don'nas
pri'ma fa'ci·e'
pri'mal
pri·mar'i·ly
pri'mar'y
·ries
pri'mate'
prime
primed prim'ing
prim'er
pri·me'val
prim'i·tive
prim'ly
prim'ness
pri'mo·gen'i·ture
pri·mor'di·al
primp
prim'rose'
prince
prince'li·ness
prince'ly
·li·er ·li·est
prin'cess
prin'ci·pal (*chief*)
prin'ci·pal'i·ty
·ties
prin'ci·pal·ly
prin'ci·ple (*basic rule*)

prin'ci·pled
print
print'er
print'ing
print'out'
pri'or
(*previous;* see PRIER)
pri'or·ess
pri·or'i·tize'
·tized' ·tiz'ing
pri·or'i·ty
·ties
pri'o·ry
·ries
prism
pris·mat'ic
pris'on
pris'on·er
pris'si·ness
pris'sy
·si·er ·si·est
pris'tine'
pri'va·cy
·cies
pri'vate
pri'va·teer'
pri'vate·ly
pri·va'tion
pri'va·ti·za'tion
pri'va·tize'
·tized' ·tiz'ing
priv'et
priv'i·lege
·leged ·leg·ing
priv'y
·ies
prize
prized priz'ing
prize'fight'er
pro
pros
pro-am
prob'a·bil'i·ty
·ties
prob'a·ble
prob'a·bly
pro'bate'
·bat'ed ·bat'ing
pro·ba'tion
pro·ba'tion·ar'y
pro·ba'tion·er
pro'ba·tive
probe
probed prob'ing
pro'bi·ty
prob'lem
prob'lem·at'ic *or* ·at'i·cal
pro·bos'cis
·cis·es *or* ci·des'
pro'caine'
pro·ce'dur·al
pro·ce'dure
pro·ceed'
(*go on;* see PRECEDE)
pro·ceed'ing
pro'ceeds'
proc'ess'

pro·ces'sion
(*parade;* see PRECESSION)
pro·ces'sion·al
pro'cess·or *or* ·er
pro'-choice'
pro·claim'
proc'la·ma'tion
pro·cliv'i·ty
·ties
pro·cras'ti·nate'
·nat'ed ·nat'ing
pro·cras'ti·na'tion
pro·cras'ti·na'tor
pro'cre·ate'
pro'cre·a'tion
proc·tol'o·gist
proc·tol'o·gy
proc'tor
pro·cur'a·ble
proc'u·ra'tor
pro·cure'
·cured' ·cur'ing
pro·cure'ment
pro·cur'er
prod
prod'ded prod'ding
prod'i·gal
prod'i·gal'i·ty
·ties
pro·di'gious
pro·di'gious·ly
prod'i·gy
·gies
pro·duce'
·duced' ·duc'ing
pro·duc'er
prod'uct'
pro·duc'tion
pro·duc'tive
pro·duc'tive·ly
pro·duc'tive·ness
pro'duc·tiv'i·ty
prof
prof'a·na'tion
pro·fane'
·faned' ·fan'ing
pro·fane'ly
pro·fane'ness
pro·fan'i·ty
·ties
pro·fess'
pro·fessed'
pro·fes'sion
pro·fes'sion·al
pro·fes'sion·al·ly
pro·fes'sor
pro·fes·so'ri·al
pro·fes'sor·ship'
prof'fer
pro·fi'cien·cy
pro·fi'cient
pro·fi'cient·ly
pro'file'
·filed' ·fil'ing
prof'it
(*gain;* see PROPHET)
prof'it·a·ble

prof'it·a·bly
prof'it·eer'
prof'li·ga·cy
prof'li·gate
pro for'ma
pro·found'
pro·found'ly
pro·fun'di·ty
·ties
pro·fuse'
pro·fuse'ly
pro·fu'sion
pro·gen'i·tor
prog'e·ny
·nies
pro·ges'ter·one'
prog'na·thous
prog·no'sis
·ses'
prog·nos'tic
prog·nos'ti·cate'
·cat'ed ·cat'ing
prog·nos'ti·ca'tion
prog·nos'ti·ca'tor
pro'gram
·grammed' *or* ·gramed'
·gram'ming *or* ·gram'ing
pro'gram·ma·ble
pro'gram·mat'ic
pro'gram·mer *or* ·er
prog'ress *n.*
pro·gress' *v.*
pro·gres'sion
pro·gres'sive
pro·gres'sive·ly
pro·hib'it
pro'hi·bi'tion
pro'hi·bi'tion·ist
pro·hib'i·tive *or* ·i·to'ry
proj'ect' *n.*
pro·ject' *v.*
pro·jec'tile
pro·jec'tion
pro·jec'tion·ist
pro·jec'tor
pro'le·tar'i·an
pro'le·tar'i·at
pro'-life'
pro·lif'er·ate'
·at'ed ·at'ing
pro·lif'er·a'tion
pro·lif'ic
pro·lif'i·cal·ly
pro·lix'
pro·lix'i·ty
pro'logue'
pro·long'
pro·lon'gate'
·gat'ed ·gat'ing
pro'lon·ga'tion
prom
prom'e·nade'
·nad'ed ·nad'ing
prom'i·nence

prom'i·nent
prom'i·nent·ly
prom'is·cu'i·ty
pro·mis'cu·ous
pro·mis'cu·ous·ly
prom'ise
·ised ·is·ing
prom'is·so'ry
pro'mo
·mos
prom'on·to'ry
·ries
pro·mote'
·mot'ed ·mot'ing
pro·mot'er
pro·mo'tion
pro·mo'tion·al
prompt
prompt'er
prompt'ly
prompt'ness *or* promp'ti·tude'
prom'ul·gate'
·gat'ed ·gat'ing
prom'ul·ga'tion
prone
prong
pronged
prong'horn'
pro·nom'i·nal
pro'noun'
pro·nounce'
·nounced' ·nounc'ing
pro·nounce'a·ble
pro·nounced'
pro·nounce'ment
pron'to
pro·nun'ci·a'tion
proof
proof'read'
proof'read'er
prop
propped prop'ping
prop'a·gan'da
prop'a·gan'dist
prop'a·gan'dize
prop'a·gate'
·gat'ed ·gat'ing
prop'a·ga'tion
prop'a·ga'tor
pro'pane'
pro·pel'
·pelled' ·pel'ling
pro·pel'lant *or* ·lent
pro·pel'ler
pro·pen'si·ty
·ties
prop'er
prop'er·ly
prop'er·tied
prop'er·ty
·ties
proph'e·cy *n.*
·cies
proph'e·sy' *v.*
·sied' ·sy'ing

proph'et
(*one who predicts;* see PROFIT)
proph'et·ess
pro·phet'ic
pro·phet'i·cal·ly
pro'phy·lac'tic
pro'phy·lax'is
pro·pin'qui·ty
pro·pi'ti·ate'
·at'ed ·at'ing
pro·pi'ti·a'tion
pro·pi'ti·a'tor
pro·pi'ti·a·to'ry
pro·pi'tious
pro·po'nent
pro·por'tion
pro·por'tion·al
pro·por'tion·ate
pro·pos'al
pro·pose'
·posed' ·pos'ing
prop'o·si'tion
pro·pound'
pro·pri'e·tar'y
pro·pri'e·tor
pro·pri'e·tor·ship'
pro·pri'e·tress
pro·pri'e·ty
·ties
pro·pul'sion
pro·pul'sive
pro·rate'
pro·sa'ic
pro·sce'ni·um
·ni·ums *or* ·ni·a
pro·scribe'
·scribed' ·scrib'ing
(*forbid;* see PRESCRIBE)
pro·scrip'tion
prose
pros'e·cute'
·cut'ed ·cut'ing
(*legal term;* see PERSECUTE)
pros'e·cu'tion
pros'e·cu'tor
pros'e·lyte'
pros'e·lyt·ism'
pros'e·lyt·ize'
·ized' ·iz'ing
pros'e·lyt·iz'er
pro·sim'i·an
pros'o·dy
·dies
pros'pect'
pro·spec'tive
(*expected;* see PERSPECTIVE)
pros'pec'tor
pro·spec'tus
pros'per
pros·per'i·ty
pros'per·ous
pros'per·ous·ly
pros'tate'
(*gland;* see PROSTRATE)

pros'the·sis
·ses'
pros'thet'ic
pros'ti·tute'
·tut'ed ·tut'ing
pros'ti·tu'tion
pros'trate'
·trat'ed ·trat'ing
(prone; see
PROSTATE)
pros·tra'tion
pros'y
·i·er ·i·est
pro·tag'o·nist
pro'te·an
(changeable; see
PROTEIN)
pro·tect'
pro·tec'tion
pro·tec'tive
pro·tec'tive·ness
pro·tec'tor
pro·tec'tor·ate
pro'té·gé'
pro'te·in'
(life substance;
see PROTEAN)
pro tem
pro tem'po·re'
pro·test' v.
pro'test' n.
Prot'es·tant
Prot'es·tant·ism'
prot'es·ta'tion
pro·test'er or ·tes'-
tor
pro'to·col'
pro'ton'
pro'to·plasm'
pro'to·plas'mic
pro'to·typ'al or
pro'to·typ'ic or
·typ'i·cal
pro'to·type'
pro'to·zo'an
·zo'a
pro·tract'
pro·trac'tion
pro·trac'tor
pro·trude'
·trud'ed ·trud'ing
pro·tru'sion
pro·tu'ber·ance
pro·tu'ber·ant
proud
proud'ly
prov'a·ble
prove
proved, proved or
prov'en, prov'ing
prov'e·nance
prov'en·der
prov'erb'
pro·ver'bi·al
pro·vide'
·vid'ed ·vid'ing
prov'i·dence
prov'i·dent
prov'i·den'tial

prov'i·den'tial·ly
pro·vid'er
prov'ince
pro·vin'cial
pro·vin'cial·ism'
pro·vi'sion
pro·vi'sion·al
pro·vi'sion·al·ly
pro·vi'so'
·sos' or ·soes'
prov'o·ca'tion
pro·voc'a·tive
pro·voc'a·tive·ly
pro·voke'
·voked' ·vok'ing
pro'vo·lo'ne
pro'vost
prow
prow'ess
prowl
prowl'er
prox'i·mate
prox·im'i·ty
prox'y
·ies
prude
pru'dence
pru'dent
pru·den'tial
prud'er·y
prud'ish
prune
pruned prun'ing
pru'ri·ence
pru'ri·ent
pry
pries
pried pry'ing
psalm
psalm'ist
pseu'do
pseu'do·nym'
pshaw
psi
pso·ri'a·sis
psych
psyched psych'ing
psy'che
psy'che·del'ic
psy'chi·at'ric
psy·chi'a·trist
psy·chi'a·try
psy'chic
psy'chi·cal·ly
psy'cho
psy'cho·a·nal'y·sis
psy'cho·an'a·lyst
psy'cho·an'a·lyt'ic
or ·lyt'i·cal
psy'cho·an'a·lyze'
·lyzed' ·lyz'ing
psy'cho·bab'ble
psy'cho·log'i·cal
psy·chol'o·gist
psy·chol'o·gy
·gies
psy'cho·path'
psy'cho·path'ic

psy·cho'sis
·ses'
psy'cho·so·mat'ic
psy'cho·ther'a·pist
psy'cho·ther'a·py
psy·chot'ic
ptar'mi·gan
pter'o·dac'tyl
pto'maine'
pub
pu'ber·ty
pu'bes'
pu·bes'cence
pu·bes'cent
pu'bic
pub'lic
pub'li·can
pub'li·ca'tion
pub'li·cist
pub·lic'i·ty
pub'li·cize'
·cized' ·ciz'ing
pub'lic·ly
pub'lic-spir'it·ed
pub'lish
pub'lish·er
puck
puck'er
puck'ish
pud'ding
pud'dle
pu·den'dum
·da
pudg'i·ness
pudg'y
·i·er ·i·est
pueb'lo
·los'
pu'er·ile
pu'er·il'i·ty
Puer'to Ri'can
puff
puff'ball'
puff'er
puf'fin
puff'i·ness
puff'y
·i·er ·i·est
pug
pu'gil·ism'
pu'gil·ist
pu'gil·is'tic
pug·na'cious
pug·nac'i·ty
pug'-nosed'
puke
puked puk'ing
pul'chri·tude'
pule
puled pul'ing
Pul'it·zer Prize
pull
pul'let
pul'ley
·leys
pull'out'
pull'o'ver
pull'-up' or pull'up'

pul'mo·nar'y
pul'mo·tor
pulp
pul'pit
pulp'y
·i·er ·i·est
pul'sar'
pul'sate'
·sat'ed ·sat'ing
pul·sa'tion
pulse
pulsed puls'ing
pul'ver·ize'
·ized' ·iz'ing
pu'ma
pum'ice
pum'mel
·meled or ·melled
·mel·ing or
·mel·ling
pump
pump'er
pum'per·nick'el
pump'kin
pun
punned pun'ning
punch
pun'cheon
punch'y
·i·er ·i·est
punc·til'i·ous
punc'tu·al
punc'tu·al'i·ty
punc'tu·al·ly
punc'tu·ate'
·at'ed ·at'ing
punc'tu·a'tion
punc'ture
·tured ·tur·ing
pun'dit
pun'gen·cy
pun'gent
pu'ni·ness
pun'ish
pun'ish·a·ble
pun'ish·ment
pu'ni·tive
punk
pun'ster or ·ner
punt
pu'ny
·ni·er ·ni·est
pup
pu'pa
·pae or ·pas
pu'pil
pup'pet
pup'pet·eer'
pup'pet·ry
pup'py
·pies
pur'chas·a·ble
pur'chase
·chased ·chas·ing
pur'chas·er
pure
pure'bred'

pu·rée' or ·ree'
·réed' or ·reed'
·rée'ing or ·ree'ing
pure'ly
pure'ness
pur'ga·tive
pur'ga·to'ri·al
pur'ga·to'ry
purge
purged purg'ing
purg'er
pu'ri·fi·ca'tion
pu'ri·fi'er
pu'ri·fy'
·fied' ·fy'ing
pur'ism'
pur'ist
Pu'ri·tan
pu'ri·tan'i·cal
pu'ri·tan·ism'
pu'ri·ty
purl
(stitch; see PEARL)
pur'lieu'
pur·loin'
pur'ple
pur·port'
pur·port'ed
pur·port'ed·ly
pur'pose
·posed ·pos·ing
pur'pose·ful
pur'pose·less
pur'pose·ly
purr
purse
pursed purs'ing
purs'er
pur·su'ance
pur·su'ant
pur·sue'
·sued' ·su'ing
pur·su'er
pur·suit'
pu'ru·lence
pu'ru·lent
pur·vey'
pur·vey'or
pur'view'
pus
(matter; see PUSS)
push
push'er
push'i·ness
push'o'ver
push'-up' or
push'up'
push'y
·i·er ·i·est
pu'sil·lan'i·mous
puss
(cat; see PUS)
pus'sy (having pus)
puss'y
·ies
(cat)
puss'y·cat'
puss'y·foot'
pus'tule

put
put put'ting
pu'ta·tive
put'-down'
put'-on'
pu'tre·fac'tion
pu'tre·fy'
·fied' ·fy'ing
pu·tres'cence
pu·tres'cent
pu'trid
putt
putt'er (golf club)
put'ter (dawdle)
put'ty
·tied ·ty·ing
puz'zle
·zled ·zling
puz'zle·ment
puz'zler
pyg'my
·mies
py·ja'mas
py'lon'
py'or·rhe'a
pyr'a·mid
py·ram'i·dal
pyre
py·ret'ic
py'rite'
py'ro·ma'ni·a
py'ro·ma'ni·ac'
py'ro·tech'nics
Py·thag'o·re'an
py'thon'
pyx

Q

qua
quack
quack'er·y
quad
quad'ran'gle
quad·ran'gu·lar
quad'rant
quad·rat'ic
quad·ren'ni·al
quad'ri·ceps'
quad'ri·lat'er·al
qua·drille'
quad'ri·ple'gi·a
quad'ri·ple'gic
quad'ru·ped'
quad·ru'ple
·pled ·pling
quad·ru'plet
quaff
quag'mire'
qua'hog' or ·haug'
quail
quaint
quaint'ly
quaint'ness
quake
quaked quak'ing
Quak'er

quak'y
·i·er ·i·est
qual'i·fi·ca'tion
qual'i·fied'
qual'i·fi·er
qual'i·fy'
·fied' ·fy'ing
qual'i·ta'tive
qual'i·ta'tive·ly
qual'i·ty
·ties
qualm
quan'da·ry
·ries
quan'ti·fy'
·fied' ·fy'ing
quan'ti·ta'tive
quan'ti·ty
·ties
quan'tum
·ta
quar'an·tine'
·tined' ·tin'ing
quark
quar'rel
·reled or ·relled
·rel·ing or ·rel·ling
quar'rel·er or **·ler**
quar'rel·some
quar'ry
·ries
quart
quar'ter
quar'ter·back'
quar'ter·deck'
quar'ter·fi'nal
quar'ter·ly
·lies
quar'ter·mas'ter
quar·tet' or **·tette'**
quar'to
·tos
quartz
qua'sar'
quash
qua'si'
quat'rain'
qua'ver
quay
(wharf; see KEY)
quea'sy
·si·er ·si·est
queen
queen'ly
·li·er ·li·est
queen'-size'
queer
quell
quench
quer'u·lous
quer'u·lous·ly
que'ry
·ries
·ried ·ry·ing
quest
ques'tion
ques'tion·a·ble
ques'tion·naire'

queue
queued queu'ing
(a line; see CUE)
quib'ble
·bled ·bling
quiche
quick
quick'en
quick'ie
quick'lime'
quick'ly
quick'ness
quick'sand'
quick'sil'ver
quick'-tem'pered
quick'-wit'ted
quid
qui·es'cence
qui·es'cent
qui'et
qui'et·ly
qui'e·tude'
qui·e'tus
quill
quilt
quilt'er
quince
qui·nel'la
qui'nine'
quin·tes'sence
quin·tet' or **·tette'**
quin'tu·ple
·pled ·pling
quin·tu'plet
quip
quipped quip'ping
quip'ster
quire
quirk
quirk'i·ness
quirk'y
·i·er ·i·est
quirt
quis'ling
quit
quit quit'ted
quit'ting
quit'claim'
quite
quit'tance
quit'ter
quiv'er
quix·ot'ic
quiz
quiz'zes
quizzed quiz'zing
quiz'zer
quiz'zi·cal
quiz'zi·cal·ly
quoin
(corner; see COIN)
quoit
quon'dam
Quon'set hut
quo'rum
quo'ta
quot'a·ble
quo·ta'tion

quote
quot'ed quot'ing
quo'tient

R

rab'bet
(cut or groove; see RABBIT)
rab'bi
·bis
rab'bin·ate
rab·bin'i·cal
rab'bit
(hare; see RABBET)
rab'ble
rab'ble-rous'er
rab'id
ra'bies
rac·coon'
race
raced rac'ing
race'horse'
ra·ceme'
rac'er
race'track'
race'way'
ra'cial
ra'cial·ly
rac'i·ness
rac'ism
rac'ist
rack
rack'et
rack'et·eer'
rack'et·eer'ing
rac'on·teur'
rac'quet
rac'quet·ball'
rac'y
·i·er ·i·est
rad
ra'dar'
ra'di·al
ra'di·ance
ra'di·ant
ra'di·ant·ly
ra'di·ate'
·at'ed ·at'ing
ra'di·a'tion
ra'di·a'tor
rad'i·cal
rad'i·cal·ism'
rad'i·cal·ly
ra·dic'chio
·chios
ra'di·o'
·os', ·oed' ·o'ing
ra'di·o·ac'tive
ra'di·o·ac·tiv'i·ty
ra'di·o·i'so·tope'
ra'di·ol'o·gist
ra'di·ol'o·gy
ra'di·o·ther'a·py
rad'ish
ra'di·um

ra'di·us
·di·i' or ·di·us·es
ra'don
raf'fi·a
raf'part
raff'ish
raf'fle
·fled ·fling
raft
raf'ter
rag
rag'a·muf'fin
rag'bag'
rage
raged rag'ing
rag'ged
rag'ged·ness
rag'ged·y
rag'lan
ra·gout'
rag'time'
rag'weed'
rah
raid
raid'er
rail
rail'ler·y
·ies
rail'road'
rail'road'er
rail'way'
rai'ment
rain
(falling water; see REIGN, REIN)
rain'bow'
rain'coat'
rain'drop'
rain'fall'
rain'storm'
rain'wa'ter
rain'y
·i·er ·i·est
raise
raised rais'ing
(lift; see RAZE)
rai'sin
rai'son d'être'
ra'jah or **·ja**
rake
raked rak'ing
rak'ish
rak'ish·ly
ral'ly
·lies
·lied ·ly·ing
ram
rammed ram'ming
ram'ble
·bled ·bling
ram'bler
ram·bunc'tious
ram·bunc'tious·ness
ram'e·kin or **·quin**
ram'i·fi·ca'tion
ram'i·fy'
·fied' ·fy'ing
ramp

ram·page'
·paged' ·pag'ing
ramp'ant
ram'part'
ram'rod'
ram'shack'le
ran
ranch
ranch'er
ran'cid
ran'cor
ran'cor·ous
ran'dom
ran'dom·ly
ran'dy
·di·er ·di·est
rang
range
ranged rang'ing
rang'er
rang'y
·i·er ·i·est
rank
ran'kle
·kled ·kling
rank'ness
ran'sack'
ran'som
rant
rap
rapped rap'ping
(strike; see WRAP)
ra·pa'cious
ra·pac'i·ty
rape
raped rap'ing
rape'seed'
rap'id
ra·pid'i·ty
rap'id·ly
ra'pi·er
rap'ine
rap'ist
rap·pel'
·pelled' ·pel'ling
(descend with ropes; see REPEL)
rap·port'
rap'proche·ment'
rap·scal'lion
rapt
rap'ture
rap'tur·ous
rare
rar'er rar'est
rare'bit
rar'e·fac'tion
rar'e·fy'
·fied' ·fy'ing
rare'ly
rare'ness
rar'i·ty
·ties
ras'cal
ras·cal'i·ty
ras'cal·ly
rash
rash'er
rash'ly

rash'ness
rasp
rasp'ber'ry
rasp'y
·i·er ·i·est
rat
rat'ted rat'ting
ratch'et
rate
rat'ed rat'ing
rath'er
raths'kel'ler
rat'i·fi·ca'tion
rat'i·fy'
·fied' ·fy'ing
ra'tio
·tios
ra'ti·oc'i·nate'
·nat'ed ·nat'ing
ra'ti·oc'i·na'tion
ra'tion
ra'tion·al
ra'tion·ale'
ra'tion·al·ism'
ra'tion·al·ist
ra'tion·al·is'tic
ra'tion·al'i·ty
ra'tion·al·i·za'tion
ra'tion·al·ize'
·ized' ·iz'ing
ra'tion·al·ly
rat'line'
rat·tan'
rat'tle
·tled ·tling
rat'tler
rat'tle·snake'
rat'trap'
rat'ty
·ti·er ·ti·est
rau'cous
rau'cous·ly
rau'cous·ness
raun'chy
·chi·er ·chi·est
rav'age
·aged ·ag·ing
rave
raved rav'ing
rav'el
·eled or ·elled
·el·ing or ·el·ling
ra'ven
rav'e·nous
rav'e·nous·ly
ra·vine'
ra·vi·o'li
rav'ish
rav'ish·ing
raw
raw'boned'
raw'hide'
raw'ness
ray
ray'on
raze
razed raz'ing
(demolish; see RAISE)

ra′zor
ra′zor·back′
razz
raz′zle-daz′zle
razz′ma·tazz′
reach
re·act′
re·act′ant
re·ac′tion
re·ac′tion·ar′y
·ies
re·ac′ti·vate′
·vat′ed ·vat′ing
re·ac′ti·va′tion
re·ac′tive
re·ac·tiv′i·ty
re·ac′tor
read
read read′ing
(interpret writing;
see REED)
read′a·bil′i·ty
read′a·ble
read′er
read′er·ship′
read′i·ly
read′i·ness
read′out′
read′y
·i·er ·i·est
·ied ·y·ing
read′y-made′
read′y-to-wear′
re·a′gent
re′al
(actual; see REEL)
re′al·ism′
re′al·ist
re′al·is′tic
re′al·is′ti·cal·ly
re·al′i·ty
·ties
(real thing; see RE-
ALTY)
re′al·i·za′tion
re′al·ize′
·ized ·iz′ing
re′al-life′
re′al·ly
realm
re′al·tor
re′al·ty
(real estate; see
REALITY)
ream
ream′er
re·an′i·mate′
·mat′ed ·mat′ing
re·an′i·ma′tion
reap
reap′er
re′ap·por′tion
re′ap·por′tion·ment
rear
rear-end′
re′ar·range′
·ranged′ ·rang′ing
rear′ward
rea′son

rea′son·a·ble
rea′son·a·bly
rea′son·ing
re′as·sur′ance
re′as·sure′
·sured′ ·sur′ing
re′bate′
·bat′ed ·bat′ing
reb′el n.
re·bel′ v.
·belled′ ·bel′ling
re·bel′lion
re·bel′lious
re′birth′
re·bound′
re·buff′
re·buke′
·buked′ ·buk′ing
re′bus
re·but′
·but′ted ·but′ting
re·but′tal
rec
re·cal′ci·trance
re·cal′ci·trant
re·call′
re·cant′
re′can·ta′tion
re·cap′
·capped′ ·cap′ping
re′ca·pit′u·late′
·lat′ed ·lat′ing
re′ca·pit′u·la′tion
re·cap′ture
·tured ·tur·ing
re·cede′
·ced′ed ·ced′ing
re·ceipt′
re·ceiv′a·ble
re·ceive′
·ceived′ ·ceiv′ing
re·ceiv′er
re·ceiv′er·ship′
re·cen′sion
re′cent
(just before; see
RESENT)
re′cent·ly
re·cep′ta·cle
re·cep′tion
re·cep′tion·ist
re·cep′tive
re·cep′tor
re′cess
re·ces′sion
re·ces′sion·al
re·ces′sion·ar′y
re·ces′sive
re·cher′ché
rec′i·pe′
re·cip′i·ent
re·cip′ro·cal
re·cip′ro·cate′
·cat′ed ·cat′ing
re·cip′ro·ca′tion
rec′i·proc′i·ty
re·cit′al
rec′i·ta′tion
rec′i·ta·tive′

re·cite′
·cit′ed ·cit′ing
reck′less
reck′less·ly
reck′less·ness
reck′on
re·claim′
rec′la·ma′tion
re·cline′
·clined′ ·clin′ing
re·clin′er
rec′luse
rec′og·ni′tion
rec′og·niz′a·ble
re·cog′ni·zance
rec′og·nize′
·nized′ ·niz′ing
re·coil′
rec′ol·lect′ (remem-
ber)
re′-col·lect′ (collect
again)
rec′ol·lec′tion
re·com′bi·nant
rec′om·mend′
rec′om·men·da′-
tion
re·com·mit′
·mit′ted ·mit′ting
rec′om·pense′
·pensed′ ·pens′ing
rec′on·cil′a·ble
rec′on·cile′
·ciled′ ·cil′ing
rec′on·cil′i·a′tion
rec′on·dite′
re′con·di′tion
rec′on·nais′sance
rec′on·noi′ter
re′con·sid′er
re·con′sti·tute′
·tut′ed ·tut′ing
re′con·struct′
re′con·struc′tion
re·cord′ v.
rec′ord n.
re·cord′er
re·cord′ing
re·count′ (narrate)
re′-count′ (count
again)
re·coup′
re′course′
re·cov′er (get back)
re′-cov′er (cover
again)
re·cov′er·y
·ies
rec′re·ant
rec′re·ate′
·at′ed ·at′ing
(relax)
re′-cre·ate′
·at′ed ·at′ing
(create anew)
rec′re·a′tion
re′-cre·a′tion
rec′re·a′tion·al

re·crim′i·nate′
·nat′ed ·nat′ing
re·crim′i·na′tion
re·cru·desce′
·desced′ ·desc′ing
re′cru·des′cence
re′cru·des′cent
re·cruit′
re·cruit′er
rec′tal
rec′tan′gle
rec·tan′gu·lar
rec′ti·fi·ca′tion
rec′ti·fi′er
rec′ti·fy′
·fied′ ·fy′ing
rec′ti·lin′e·ar
rec′ti·tude′
rec′tor
rec′to·ry
·ries
rec′tum
·tums or ·ta
re·cum′bent
re·cu′per·ate′
·at′ed ·at′ing
re·cu′per·a′tion
re·cu′per·a′tive
re·cur′
·curred′ ·cur′ring
re·cur′rence
re·cur′rent
re·cy′cle
·cled ·cling
red
red′der red′dest
re·dact′
re·dac′tion
re·dac′tor
red′-blood′ed
red′-car′pet
red′coat′
red′den
red′dish
re·deem′
re·deem′a·ble
re·deem′er
re·demp′tion
re′de·ploy′
re′de·ploy′ment
re′de·vel′op
re′de·vel′op·ment
red′-hand′ed
red′head′
red′-hot′
re·dis′trict
red′-let′ter
red′lin′ing
red′ness
re·do′
·did′ ·done′ ·do′ing
red′o·lence
red′o·lent
re·dou′ble
·bled ·bling
re·doubt′
re·doubt′a·ble
re·doubt′a·bly

re·dound′
re·dress′
re·duce′
·duced′ ·duc′ing
re·duc′er
re·duc′i·ble
re·duc′tion
re·dun′dan·cy
re·dun′dant
red′wood′
re·ech′o or re-
ech′o
·oes, ·oed ·o·ing
reed
(tall, thin grass;
see READ)
reed′y
·i·er ·i·est
reef
reek
(emit a smell; see
WREAK)
reel
(whirl; dance;
spool; see REAL)
re′e·lect′
re′e·lec′tion
re′em′pha·size′
re′en·act′
re′en·list′
re′en·ter
re′en·try or re-
re′es·tab′lish
re′e·val′u·ate′
re′ex·am′ine
ref
re·fec′tion
re·fec′to·ry
·ries
re·fer′
·ferred′ ·fer′ring
ref′er·ee′
·eed′ ·ee′ing
ref′er·ence
ref′er·en′dum
·dums or ·da
ref′er·ent
re·fer′ral
re·fer′rer
re·fill′
re·fill′a·ble
re·fine′
·fined′ ·fin′ing
re·fine′ment
re·fin′er·y
·ies
re·fin′ish
re·fin′ish·er
re·fit′
re·flect′
re·flec′tion
re·flec′tive
re·flec′tor
re·flex′
re·flex′ive
re·flex′ive·ly
re·for′est
re·for′est·a′tion

re·form′ (make bet-
ter)
re′-form′ (form
again)
ref′or·ma′tion
re·form′a·to·ry
·ries
re·form′er
re·fract′
re·frac′tion
re·frac′to·ry
·ries
re·frain′
re·fresh′
re·fresh′ment
re·frig′er·ant
re·frig′er·ate′
·at′ed ·at′ing
re·frig′er·a′tion
re·frig′er·a′tor
ref′uge
ref′u·gee′
re·ful′gent
re·fund′
re·fur′bish
re·fus′al
re·fuse′
·fused′ ·fus′ing
(decline)
ref′use (rubbish)
re·fut′a·ble
ref′u·ta′tion
re·fute′
·fut′ed ·fut′ing
re·gain′
re′gal
re·gale′
·galed′ ·gal′ing
re·ga′li·a
re·gard′
re·gard′less
re·gat′ta
re′gen·cy
·cies
re·gen′er·ate′
·at′ed ·at′ing
re·gen′er·a′tion
re·gen′er·a′tive
re′gent
reg′gae
reg′i·cide′
re·gime′ or
ré·gime′
reg′i·men
reg′i·ment
reg′i·men′tal
reg′i·men·ta′tion
re′gion
re′gion·al
re′gion·al·ism′
reg′is·ter
reg′is·trant
reg′is·trar′
reg′is·tra′tion
reg′is·try
·tries
reg′nant
re·gress′

re·gres'sion
re·gres'sive
re·gret'
  ·gret'ted ·gret'ting
re·gret'ful
re·gret'ta·ble
re·group'
reg'u·lar
reg'u·lar'i·ty
  ·ties
reg'u·lar·ize'
  ·ized' ·iz'ing
reg'u·lar·ly
reg'u·late'
  ·lat'ed ·lat'ing
reg'u·la'tion
reg'u·la'tor
reg'u·la·to'ry
re·gur'gi·tate'
  ·tat'ed ·tat'ing
re·gur'gi·ta'tion
re'hab'
  ·habbed' ·hab'bing
re'ha·bil'i·tate'
  ·tat'ed ·tat'ing
re'ha·bil'i·ta'tion
re'ha·bil'i·ta'tive
re'hash'
re·hears'al
re·hearse'
  ·hearsed'
  ·hears'ing
reign
  (*rule;* see RAIN,
  REIN)
re'im·burse'
  ·bursed' ·burs'ing
re'im·burse'ment
rein
  (*control;* see RAIN,
  REIGN)
re'in·car'nat·ed
re'in·car·na'tion
rein'deer'
  ·deer'
re'in·force'
  ·forced' ·forc'ing
re'in·force'ment
re'in·state'
  ·stat'ed ·stat'ing
re'in·state'ment
re·it'er·ate'
  ·at'ed ·at'ing
re·it'er·a'tion
re·it'er·a'tive
re·ject'
re·jec'tion
re·joice'
  ·joiced' ·joic'ing
re·join'
re·join'der
re·ju've·nate'
  ·nat'ed ·nat'ing
re·ju've·na'tion
re·lapse'
  ·lapsed' ·laps'ing
re·late'
  ·lat'ed ·lat'ing
re·la'tion
re·la'tion·ship'

rel'a·tive
rel'a·tive·ly
rel'a·tiv'i·ty
re·lax'
re·lax'ant
re·lax·a'tion
re·lax'er
re'lay'
  ·layed' ·lay'ing
re·lease'
  ·leased' ·leas'ing
rel'e·gate'
  ·gat'ed ·gat'ing
rel'e·ga'tion
re·lent'
re·lent'less
re·lent'less·ly
re·lent'less·ness
rel'e·vance
rel'e·van·cy
rel'e·vant
re·li'a·bil'i·ty
re·li'a·ble
re·li'a·bly
re·li'ance
re·li'ant
rel'ic
re·lief'
re·lieve'
  ·lieved' ·liev'ing
re·li'gion
re·li'gi·os'i·ty
re·li'gious
  ·gious
re·li'gious·ly
re·lin'quish
re·lin'quish·ment
rel'ish
re·live'
re·lo'cate'
re·lo·ca'tion
re·luc'tance
re·luc'tant
re·luc'tant·ly
re·ly'
  ·lied' ·ly'ing
re·main'
re·main'der
re·mand'
re·mark'
re·mark'a·ble
re·mark'a·bly
re·me'di·al
rem'e·dy
  ·dies
  ·died ·dy·ing
re·mem'ber
re·mem'brance
re·mind'
re·mind'er
rem'i·nisce'
  ·nisced' ·nisc'ing
rem'i·nis'cence
rem'i·nis'cent
re·miss'
re·mis'sion
re·mit'
  ·mit'ted ·mit'ting

re·mit'tance
rem'nant
re·mod'el
re·mon'strance
re·mon'strate'
  ·strat'ed ·strat'ing
re·mon'stra'tion
re·morse'
re·morse'ful
re·morse'less
re·mote'
  ·mot'er ·mot'est
re·mote'ly
re·mov'a·ble
re·mov'al
re·move'
  ·moved' ·mov'ing
re·mu'ner·ate'
  ·at'ed ·at'ing
re·mu'ner·a'tion
re·mu'ner·a'tive
ren'ais·sance'
re'nal
re·nas'cence
rend
  rent rend'ing
ren'der
ren'dez·vous'
  ·vous'
  ·voused' ·vous'ing
ren·di'tion
ren'e·gade'
re·nege'
  ·neged' ·neg'ing
re·new'
re·new'al
ren'net
re·nounce'
  ·nounced'
  ·nounc'ing
ren'o·vate'
  ·vat'ed ·vat'ing
ren'o·va'tion
ren'o·va'tor
re·nown'
re·nowned'
rent
rent'al
rent'er
re·nun'ci·a'tion
re·or'der
re·or'gan·i·za'tion
re·or'gan·ize'
  ·ized' ·iz'ing
rep
re·paid'
re·pair'
re·pair'a·ble
re·pair'man
rep'a·ra'tion
rep'ar·tee'
re·past'
re·pa'tri·ate'
  ·at'ed ·at'ing
re·pa'tri·a'tion
re·pay'
re·pay'ment
re·peal'
re·peat'

re·peat'ed·ly
re·peat'er
re·pel'
  ·pelled' ·pel'ling
  (*force back;* see
  RAPPEL)
re·pel'lent
re·pent'
re·pent'ance
re·pent'ant
re·per·cus'sion
rep'er·toire'
rep'er·to'ry
  ·ries
rep'e·ti'tion
rep'e·ti'tious
re·pet'i·tive
re·pine'
  ·pined' ·pin'ing
re·place'
re·place'a·ble
re·place'ment
re·plen'ish
re·plen'ish·ment
re·plete'
re·ple'tion
rep'li·ca
rep'li·cate'
  ·cat'ed ·cat'ing
rep'li·ca'tion
re·ply'
  ·plies'
  ·plied' ·ply'ing
re·port'
re·port'age
re·port'ed·ly
re·port'er
rep'or·to'ri·al
re·pose'
  ·posed' ·pos'ing
re·pos'i·to'ry
  ·ries
re·pos·sess'
re·pos·ses'sion
rep're·hend'
rep're·hen'si·ble
rep're·hen'si·bly
rep're·sent'
rep're·sen·ta'tion
rep're·sen·ta'tion·al
rep're·sent'a·tive
re·press'
re·pres'sion
re·pres'sive
re·prieve'
  ·prieved'
  ·priev'ing
rep'ri·mand'
re·pris'al
re·proach'
re·proach'ful
rep'ro·bate'
re'pro·duce'
re'pro·duc'tion
re'pro·duc'tive
re·proof'
re·prove'
  ·proved' ·prov'ing
rep'tile

rep·til'i·an
re·pub'lic
re·pub'li·can
re·pu'di·ate'
  ·at'ed ·at'ing
re·pu'di·a'tion
re·pug'nance
re·pug'nant
re·pulse'
  ·pulsed' ·puls'ing
re·pul'sion
re·pul'sive
re·pul'sive·ly
re·pul'sive·ness
rep'u·ta·bil'i·ty
rep'u·ta·ble
rep'u·ta·bly
rep'u·ta'tion
re·pute'
  ·put'ed ·put'ing
re·put'ed
re·put'ed·ly
re·quest'
Re'qui·em'
re·quire'
  ·quired' ·quir'ing
re·quire'ment
req'ui·site
req'ui·si'tion
re·quit'al
re·quite'
  ·quit'ed ·quit'ing
re'run'
re'sale'
re·scind'
re·scis'sion
res'cue
  ·cued ·cu·ing
res'cu·er
re'search'
re'search'er
re·sem'blance
re·sem'ble
  ·bled ·bling
re·sent'
  (*take offense at;*
  see RECENT)
re·sent'ful
re·sent'ful·ly
re·sent'ment
res'er·va'tion
re·serve'
  ·served' ·serv'ing
re·serv'ist
res'er·voir'
re·side'
  ·sid'ed ·sid'ing
res'i·dence
res'i·den·cy
  ·cies
res'i·dent
res'i·den'tial
re·sid'u·al
res'i·due
re·sign'
res'ig·na'tion
re·sign'ed·ly
re·sil'ience

re·sil'ient
res'in
res'in·ous
re·sist'
re·sist'ance
re·sist'ant
re·sist'er (*one who
  resists*)
re·sist'i·ble
re·sist'less
re·sis'tor (*electrical
  device*)
re·sole'
res'o·lute'
res'o·lute'ly
res'o·lu'tion
re·solve'
  ·solved' ·solv'ing
res'o·nance
res'o·nant
res'o·nate'
  ·nat'ed ·nat'ing
res'o·na'tor
re·sort'
re·sound'
re·sound'ing
re'source'
re·source'ful
re·source'ful·ness
re·spect'
re·spect'a·bil'i·ty
re·spect'a·ble
re·spect'ful
re·spect'ful·ly
re·spec'tive
re·spec'tive·ly
res'pi·ra'tion
res'pi·ra'tor
res'pi·ra·to'ry
re·spire'
  ·spired' ·spir'ing
res'pite
re·splend'ence
re·splend'ent
re·splend'ent·ly
re·spond'
re·spond'ent
re·sponse'
re·spon'si·bil'i·ty
  ·ties
re·spon'si·ble
re·spon'si·bly
re·spon'sive
re·spon'sive·ness
rest
res'tau·rant'
res'tau·ra·teur' *or*
  ·ran'teur'
rest'ful
res'ti·tu'tion
res'tive
res'tive·ly
res'tive·ness
rest'less
rest'less·ly
rest'less·ness
res'to·ra'tion

re·stor'a·tive
re·store'
  ·stored' ·stor'ing
re·strain'
re·straint'
re·strict'
re·stric'tion
re·stric'tive
rest'room'
re·struc'ture
re·sult'
re·sult'ant
re·sume'
  ·sumed' ·sum'ing
ré'su·mé'
re·sump'tion
re·sur'face
re·sur'gence
re·sur'gent
res'ur·rect'
res'ur·rec'tion
re·sus'ci·tate'
  ·tat'ed ·tat'ing
re·sus'ci·ta'tion
re·sus'ci·ta'tor
re'tail'
re'tail'er
re·tain'
re·tain'er
re·take'
re·tal'i·ate'
  ·at'ed ·at'ing
re·tal'i·a'tion
re·tal'i·a·to'ry
re·tard'
re·tard'ant
re'tar·da'tion
retch
  (*strain to vomit;*
  see WRETCH)
re·ten'tion
re·ten'tive
ret'i·cence
ret'i·cent
ret'i·na
  ·nas *or* ·nae'
ret'i·nue'
re·tire'
  ·tired' ·tir'ing
re·tir'ee'
re·tire'ment
re'tool'
re·tort'
re'touch'
re·trace'
re·tract'
re·tract'a·ble
re·trac'tion
re'tread'
re·treat'
re·trench'
re·trench'ment
ret'ri·bu'tion
re·trib'u·tive
re·triev'al
re·trieve'
  ·trieved' ·triev'ing
re·triev'er

ret'ro·ac'tive
ret'ro·ac'tive·ly
ret'ro·fire'
ret'ro·fit'
ret'ro·grade'
  ·grad'ed ·grad'ing
ret'ro·gress'
ret'ro·gres'sion
ret'ro·spect'
ret'ro·spec'tion
ret'ro·spec'tive
ret·si'na
re·turn'
re·turn'a·ble
re·u'ni·fi·ca'tion
re·u'ni·fy'
re·un'ion
rev
  revved rev'ving
re·vamp'
re·veal'
rev·eil'le
rev'el
  ·eled *or* ·elled
  ·el·ing *or* ·el·ling
rev'e·la'tion
rev'el·er *or* ·ler
rev'el·ry
  ·ries
re·venge'
  ·venged' ·veng'ing
re·venge'ful
rev'e·nue'
re·ver'ber·ate'
  ·at'ed ·at'ing
re·ver'ber·a'tion
re·vere'
  ·vered' ·ver'ing
rev'er·ence
  ·enced ·enc·ing
rev'er·end
rev'er·ent
rev'er·en'tial
rev'er·ent·ly
rev'er·ie
re·ver'sal
re·verse'
  ·versed' ·vers'ing
re·vers'i·ble
re·ver'sion
re·vert'
re·vet'ment
re·view'
  (*look back on;* see
  REVUE)
re·view'er
re·vile'
  ·viled' ·vil'ing
re·vile'ment
re·vil'er
re·vise'
  ·vised' ·vis'ing
re·vi'sion
re·vi'sion·ist
re·vi'sion·ism
re·viv'al
re·viv'al·ist
re·vive'
  ·vived' ·viv'ing

re·viv'i·fi·ca'tion
re·viv'i·fy'
  ·fied' ·fy'ing
rev'o·ca·ble
rev'o·ca'tion
re·voke'
  ·voked' ·vok'ing
re·volt'
rev'o·lu'tion
rev'o·lu'tion·ar'y
  ·ies
rev'o·lu'tion·ist
rev'o·lu'tion·ize'
  ·ized' ·iz'ing
re·volv'a·ble
re·volve'
  ·volved' ·volv'ing
re·volv'er
re·vue'
  (*musical show;* see
  REVIEW)
re·vul'sion
re·ward'
re·wind'
re·word'
re·write'
rhap·sod'ic
rhap'so·dize'
  ·dized' ·diz'ing
rhap'so·dy
  ·dies
rhe'a
rhe'o·stat'
rhet'o·ric
rhe·tor'i·cal
rhet'o·ri'cian
rheum
rheu·mat'ic
rheu'ma·tism'
rheu'ma·toid'
rhine'stone'
rhi·ni'tis
rhi'no
  ·nos *or* ·no
rhi·noc'er·os
  ·os·es *or* ·os
rhi'zome'
Rhode Is'land
rho'do·den'dron
rhom'boid'
rhom'bus
  ·bus·es *or* ·bi
rhu'barb'
rhyme
  rhymed rhym'ing
  (*verse;* see RIME)
rhym'er
rhyme'ster
rhythm
rhyth'mic *or*
  ·mi·cal
rhyth'mi·cal·ly
rib
  ribbed rib'bing
rib'ald
rib'ald·ry
rib'bon
ri'bo·fla'vin

rice
  riced ric'ing
ric'er
rich
rich'es
rich'ly
rich'ness
Rich'ter scale
rick
rick'ets
rick'et·y
rick'shaw' *or* ·sha'
ric'o·chet'
  ·cheted' ·chet'ing
ri·cot'ta
rid
  rid *or* rid'ded
  rid'ding
rid'dance
rid'dle
  ·dled ·dling
ride
  rode rid'den
  rid'ing
rid'er
rid'er·ship'
ridge
  ridged ridg'ing
ridge'pole'
rid'i·cule'
  ·culed' ·cul'ing
ri·dic'u·lous
ri·dic'u·lous·ly
ri·dic'u·lous·ness
rife
riff
rif'fle
  ·fled ·fling
riff'raff'
ri'fle
  ·fled ·fling
ri'fle·man
rift
rig
  rigged rig'ging
rig'a·ma·role'
right
  (*correct;* see RITE,
  WRITE)
right'eous
right'eous·ly
right'eous·ness
right'ful
right'ful·ly
right'ful·ness
right'-hand'ed
right'ist
right'ly
right'-mind'ed
right'ness
right'-to-lif'er
right'-wing'er
rig'id
ri·gid'i·ty
rig'id·ly
rig'id·ness
rig'ma·role'
rig'or
rig'or mor'tis

rig'or·ous
rig'or·ous·ly
rile
  riled ril'ing
rill
rim
  rimmed rim'ming
rime
  rimed rim'ing
  (*rhyme; frost;* see
  RHYME)
rim'less
rind
ring
  rang rung ring'ing
  (*sound*)
ring
  ringed ring'ing
  (*circle;* see WRING)
ring'er
ring'lead'er
ring'let
ring'mas'ter
ring'side'
ring'worm'
rink
rinse
  rinsed rins'ing
ri'ot
ri'ot·er
ri'ot·ous
rip
  ripped rip'ping
ri·par'i·an
ripe
rip'en
ripe'ness
rip'-off'
ri·poste' *or* ·post'
rip'per
rip'ple
  ·pled ·pling
rip'-roar'ing
rip'saw'
rip'tide'
rise
  rose ris'en ris'ing
ris'er
ris'i·ble
risk
risk'y
  ·i·er ·i·est
ris·qué'
rite
  (*solemn act;* see
  RIGHT, WRITE)
rit'u·al
rit'u·al·ism'
rit'u·al·ly
ri'val
  ·valed *or* ·valled
  ·val·ing *or*
  ·val·ling
ri'val·ry
  ·ries
riv'en
riv'er
riv'er·side'
riv'et
riv'et·er

riv'u·let
roach
road
road'bed'
road'block'
road'show'
road'side'
road'ster
road'way'
road'work'
roam
roam'er
roan
roar
roast
roast'er
rob
  robbed rob'bing
rob'ber
rob'ber·y
  ·ies
robe
  robed rob'ing
rob'in
ro'bot'
ro·bot'ics
ro·bust'
ro·bust'ly
ro·bust'ness
rock
rock'a·bil'ly
rock'-and-roll'
rock'er
rock'et
rock'et·ry
rock'i·ness
rock'y
  ·i·er ·i·est
ro·co'co
rod
rode
ro'dent
ro'de·o'
  ·os'
roe (*fish eggs*)
roe
  roe *or* roes
  (*deer;* see ROW)
roe'buck'
roent'gen
rogue
ro'guer·y
ro'guish
roil
  (*stir up;* see
  ROYAL)
roist'er
roist'er·er
role *or* rôle (*actor's
  part*)
roll (*revolve*)
roll'back'
roll'er
roll'er-skate'
rol'lick
roll'-top'
ro'ly-po'ly
ro·maine'

Ro'man
ro·mance'
 ·manced'
 ·manc'ing
ro·man'tic
ro·man'ti·cal·ly
ro·man'ti·cism
ro·man'ti·cize'
 ·cized' ·ciz'ing
Ro'me·o'
 ·os'
romp
romp'er
rood
 (cross; see RUDE)
roof
 roofs
roof'er
roof'top'
rook
rook'er·y
 ·ies
rook'ie
room
room'er
room·ette'
room'ful'
room'i·ness
room'mate'
room'y
 ·i·er ·i·est
roost
roost'er
root
root'let
rope
 roped rop'ing
Ror'schach' test
ro'sa·ry
 ·ries
rose (flower)
ro·sé' (wine)
ro'se·ate
rose'bud'
rose'bush'
rose'mar'y
ro·sette'
rose'wood'
Rosh' Ha·sha'na
ros'i·ly
ros'in
ros'i·ness
ros'ter
ros'trum
 ·trums or ·tra
ros'y
 ·i·er ·i·est
rot
 rot'ted rot'ting
ro'ta·ry
 ·ries
ro'tate
 ·tat·ed ·tat·ing
ro·ta'tion
rote
 (routine; see
 WROTE)
ro·tis'ser·ie
ro'to·gra·vure'

ro'tor
ro'to·till'er
rot'ten
rot'ten·ness
ro·tund'
ro·tun'da
ro·tun'di·ty
ro·tund'ness
rou·é'
rouge
 rouged roug'ing
rough
 (not smooth; see
 RUFF)
rough'age
rough'en
rough'-hewn'
rough'house'
 ·housed' ·hous'ing
rough'ly
rough'neck'
rough'ness
rough'shod'
rou·lette'
round
round'a·bout'
roun'de·lay'
round'house'
round'ly
round'ness
round'-
  shoul'·dered
round'-the-clock'
round'-trip'
round'up'
round'worm'
rouse
 roused rous'ing
roust'a·bout'
rout (defeat)
route
 rout'ed rout'ing
 (course)
rou·tine'
rou·tine'ly
rou·tin'ize'
 ·ized ·iz·ing
rove
 roved rov'ing
rov'er
row
 (line; propel a
 boat; see ROE)
row'boat'
row'di·ness
row'dy
 ·dies
 ·di·er ·di·est
row'el
roy'al
 (regal; see ROIL)
roy'al·ist
roy'al·ly
roy'al·ty
 ·ties
rub
 rubbed rub'bing
rub'ber

rub'ber·ize'
 ·ized' ·iz'ing
rub'ber·neck'
rub'ber-stamp'
rub'ber·y
rub'bish
rub'ble
 (stone; see RUBLE)
rub'down'
rube
ru·bel'la
ru'bi·cund'
ru'ble
 (money; see RUB-
 BLE)
ru'bric
ru'by
 ·bies
ruck'sack'
ruck'us
rud'der
rud'der·less
rud'di·ness
rud'dy
 ·di·er ·di·est
rude
 rud'er rud'est
rude'ly
rude'ness
ru'di·ment
ru'di·men'ta·ry
rue
 rued ru'ing
rue'ful
rue'ful·ly
ruff
 (collar; see ROUGH)
ruf'fi·an
ruf'fle
 ·fled ·fling
rug
rug'by
rug'ged
rug'ged·ly
rug'ged·ness
ru'in
ru'in·a'tion
ru'in·ous
rule
 ruled rul'ing
rul'er
rum
rum'ba
rum'ble
 ·bled ·bling
ru'mi·nant
ru'mi·nate'
 ·nat'ed ·nat'ing
ru'mi·na'tion
rum'mage
 ·maged ·mag'ing
rum'my
ru'mor
rump
rum'ple
 ·pled ·pling
rum'pus
run
 ran run run'ning

run'a·round'
run'a·way'
run'down' (sum-
 mary)
run'-down' (in poor
 condition)
rune
rung
 (crosspiece; form
 of ring; see
 WRONG)
run'-in'
run'nel
run'ner
run'ner-up'
 ·ners-up'
run'ny
 ·ni·er ·ni·est
run'off'
run'-of-the-mill'
runt
run'-through'
run'way'
rup'ture
 ·tured ·tur·ing
ru'ral
ruse
rush
rusk
rus'set
Rus'sian
rust
rus'tic
rus'ti·cal·ly
rus'ti·cate'
 ·cat'ed ·cat'ing
rus·tic'i·ty
rust'i·ness
rus'tle
 ·tled ·tling
rus'tler
rust'proof'
rust'y
 ·i·er ·i·est
rut
 rut'ted rut'ting
ru'ta·ba'ga
ruth'less
ruth'less·ly
ruth'less·ness
rut'tish
rut'ty
 ·ti·er ·ti·est
rye
 (grain; see WRY)

S

Sab'bath
sab·bat'i·cal
sa'ber
sa'ble
sa·bot'
sab'o·tage'
 ·taged' ·tag'ing
sab'o·teur'

sac
 (pouchlike part;
 see SACK)
sac'cha·rin' n.
sac'cha·rine' adj.
sac'er·do'tal
sa'chem
sa·chet'
 (scented packet;
 see SASHAY)
sack
 (bag; see SAC)
sack'cloth'
sack'ful'
 ·fuls'
sack'ing
sac'ra·ment
sac'ra·men'tal
sa'cred
sa'cred·ness
sac'ri·fice'
 ·ficed' ·fic'ing
sac'ri·fi'cial
sac'ri·lege'
sac'ri·le'gious
sac'ris·tan
sac'ris·ty
 ·ties
sac'ro·il'i·ac'
sac'ro·sanct'
sa'crum
 ·cra or ·crums
sad
 sad'der sad'dest
sad'den
sad'dle
 ·dled ·dling
sad'dle·bag'
sad'ism'
sad'ist
sa·dis'tic
sa·dis'ti·cal·ly
sad'ly
sad'ness
sad'o·mas'o·chism
sad'o·mas'o·chist
sa·fa'ri
 ·ris
safe
 saf'er saf'est
safe'-con'duct
safe'-de·pos'it
safe'guard'
safe'keep'ing
safe'ly
safe'ness
safe'ty
 ·ties
saf'flow'er
saf'fron
sag
 sagged sag'ging
sa'ga
sa·ga'cious
sa·gac'i·ty
sage
 sag'er sag'est
sage'brush'

sag'gy
 ·gi·er ·gi·est
Sag'it·tar'i·us
sa·gua'ro
 ·ros
sa'hib'
said
sail
 (go by boat; see
 SALE)
sail'boat'
sail'cloth'
sail'er (boat)
sail'fish'
sail'or (person)
sail'plane'
saint
saint'li·ness
saint'ly
 ·li·er ·li·est
sake (purpose)
sa'ke (rice wine)
sa·laam'
sal'a·ble
sa·la'cious
sa·la'cious·ly
sa·la'cious·ness
sal'ad
sal'a·man'der
sa·la'mi
sal'a·ried
sal'a·ry
 ·ries
sale
 (business ex-
 change; see SAIL)
sales'clerk'
sales'girl'
sales'man
sales'man·ship'
sales'peo'ple
sales'per'son
sales'wom'an
sal'i·cyl'ic acid
sa'lient
sa'line
sa·lin'i·ty
sa·li'va
sal'i·var'y
sal'i·vate'
 ·vat'ed ·vat'ing
sal'low
sal'ly
 ·lies
 ·lied ·ly·ing
salm'on
sal'mo·nel'la
 ·lae or ·la or ·las
sa·lon'
sa·loon'
sal'sa
salt
salt'cel'lar
salt'ed
salt'i·ly
salt·ine'
salt'i·ness
salt'pe'ter
salt'shak'er

salt'wa'ter
salt'y
·i·er ·i·est
sa·lu'bri·ous
sal'u·tar'y
sal'u·ta'tion
sa·lu'ta·to'ri·an
sa·lute'
·lut'ed ·lut'ing
sal'vage
·vaged ·vag·ing
sal'vage·a·ble
sal·va'tion
salve
salved salv'ing
sal'ver
sal'vo'
·vos or ·voes
Sa·mar'i·tan
sam'ba
same
same'ness
sam'o·var'
sam'pan'
sam'ple
·pled ·pling
sam'pler
sam'u·rai'
·rai
sanc'ti·fi·ca'tion
sanc'ti·fy'
·fied' ·fy'ing
sanc'ti·mo'ni·ous
sanc'ti·mo'ni·ous·ly
sanc'ti·mo'ny
sanc'tion
sanc'ti·ty
sanc'tu·ar'y
·ies
sanc'tum
sand
san'dal
san'dal·wood'
sand'bag'
sand'bar'
sand'blast'
sand'box'
sand'er
sand'lot'
sand'man'
sand'pa'per
sand'pip'er
sand'stone'
sand'storm'
sand'wich'
sand'y
·i·er ·i·est
sane
sane'ly
sang
sang'-froid'
san'gui·nar'y
san'guine
san'i·tar'i·um
·i·ums or ·i·a
san'i·tar'y
san'i·ta'tion

san'i·tize'
·tized' ·tiz'ing
san'i·ty
sank
sans
sap
sapped sap'ping
sa'pi·ent
sap'ling
sap'phire
sap'pi·ness
sap'py
·pi·er ·pi·est
sap'ro·phyte'
sap'suck'er
sa·ran'
sar'casm
sar·cas'tic
sar·cas'ti·cal·ly
sar·co'ma
·mas or ·ma·ta
sar·coph'a·gus
·gi' or ·gus·es
sar·dine'
sar·don'ic
sar·don'i·cal·ly
sa'ri
sa·rong'
sar'sa·pa·ril'la
sar·to'ri·al
sash
sa·shay'
(to walk; see SA-CHET)
sass
sas'sa·fras'
sass'y
·i·er ·i·est
sat
sa·tan'ic
satch'el
sate
sat'ed sat'ing
sa·teen'
sat'el·lite'
sa'ti·ate'
·at'ed ·at'ing
sa'ti·a'tion
sa·ti'e·ty
sat'in
sat'in·wood'
sat'in·y
sat'ire'
sa·tir'i·cal
sat'i·rist
sat'i·rize'
·rized' ·riz'ing
sat'is·fac'tion
sat'is·fac'to·ri·ly
sat'is·fac'to·ry
sat'is·fy'
·fied' ·fy'ing
sa·to'ri
sa'trap
sat'u·rate'
·rat'ed ·rat'ing
sat'u·ra'tion
Sat'ur·day
Sat'urn

sat'ur·nine'
sat'yr
sat'y·ri'a·sis
sauce
sauce'pan'
sau'cer
sau'ci·ly
sau'ci·ness
sau'cy
·ci·er ·ci·est
sau'er·bra'ten
sau'er·kraut'
sau'na
saun'ter
sau'ri·an
sau'ro·pod'
sau'sage
sau·té'
·téed' ·té'ing
sau·ternes'
sav'age
sav'age·ly
sav'age·ry
sa·van'na or ·nah
sa·vant'
save
saved sav'ing
sav'er
sav'ing
sav'ior or ·iour (rescuer)
sa'voir-faire'
sa'vor (taste or smell)
sa'vor·y
·i·er ·i·est
sav'vy
saw
saw'dust'
sawed'-off'
saw'horse'
saw'mill'
saw'-toothed'
saw'yer
sax
sax'o·phone'
sax'o·phon'ist
say
said say'ing
say'ing
say'-so'
scab
scabbed scab'bing
scab'bard
scab'by
·bi·er ·bi·est
sca'bies
scab'rous
scads
scaf'fold
scaf'fold·ing
scal'a·wag'
scald
scale
scaled scal'ing
sca'lene'
scal'i·ness
scal'lion

scal'lop
scal'op·pi'ne
scalp
scal'pel
scalp'er
scal'y
·i·er ·i·est
scam
scamp
scam'per
scam'pi
·pi or ·pies
scan
scanned scan'ning
scan'dal
scan'dal·ize'
·ized' ·iz'ing
scan'dal·mon'ger
scan'dal·ous
scan'dal·ous·ly
Scan·di·na'vi·an
scan'ner
scan'sion
scant
scant'i·ly
scant'y
·i·er ·i·est
scape'goat'
scape'grace'
scap'u·la
·lae' or ·las
scap'u·lar
scar
scarred scar'ring
scar'ab
scarce
scarce'ly
scar'ci·ty
·ties
scare
scared scar'ing
scare'crow'
scarf
scarves or scarfs
(neck cloth)
scarf
scarfs
(joint)
scar'i·fi·ca'tion
scar'i·fy'
·fied' ·fy'ing
scar'i·ness
scar'let
scar'y
·i·er ·i·est
scat
scat'ted scat'ting
scath'ing
scath'ing·ly
scat'o·log'i·cal
sca·tol'o·gy
scat'ter
scat'ter·brain'
scav'enge
·enged ·eng·ing
scav'eng·er
sce·nar'i·o'
·i·os'
sce·nar'ist

scene
sce'ner·y
sce'nic
sce'ni·cal·ly
scent
(smell; see CENT, SENT)
scent'ed
scep'ter
sched'ule
·uled ·ul·ing
sche·mat'ic
sche·mat'i·cal·ly
scheme
schemed schem'ing
schem'er
scher'zo
·zos or ·zi
schism
schis·mat'ic
schist
schiz'oid
schiz'o·phre'ni·a
schiz'o·phren'ic
schle·miel'
schlep or schlepp
schlepped schlep'ping
schlock
schmaltz
schnapps
schnapps
schnau'zer
schol'ar
schol'ar·ly
schol'ar·ship'
scho·las'tic
scho·las'ti·cal·ly
scho·las'ti·cism
school
school'book'
school'boy'
school'girl'
school'house'
school'ing
school'marm'
school'mate'
school'room'
school'teach'er
school'work'
school'yard'
schoon'er
schuss
schwa
sci·at'ic
sci·at'i·ca
sci'ence
sci'en·tif'ic
sci'en·tif'i·cal·ly
sci'en·tist
sci'-fi'
scim'i·tar
scin·til'la
scin'til·late'
·lat'ed ·lat'ing
scin'til·la'tion
sci'on

scis'sors
scle·ro'sis
scle·rot'ic
scoff
scoff'er
scoff'law'
scold
scold'ing
sco'li·o'sis
sconce
scone
scoop
scoot
scoot'er
scope
scorch
scorch'ing
score
scored scor'ing
score'board'
score'less
scor'er
scorn
scorn'ful
scorn'ful·ly
Scor'pi·o'
scor'pi·on
scotch
Scotch
scot'-free'
Scot'tish
scoun'drel
scour
scourge
scourged
scourg'ing
scout
scout'ing
scout'mas'ter
scow
scowl
scrab'ble
·bled ·bling
scrag'gly
·gli·er ·gli·est
scram'ble
·bled ·bling
scrap
scrapped
scrap'ping
scrap'book'
scrape
scraped scrap'ing
scrap'er
scrap'heap'
scrap'per
scrap'py
·pi·er ·pi·est
scratch
scratch'i·ness
scratch'y
·i·er ·i·est
scrawl
scraw'ny
·ni·er ·ni·est
scream
screech
screech'y
·i·er ·i·est

screen
screen'play'
screen'writ'er
screw
screw'ball'
screw'driv'er
screw'worm'
screw'y
 ·i·er ·i·est
scrib'ble
 ·bled ·bling
scribe
scrim
scrim'mage
 ·maged ·mag·ing
scrimp
scrimp'y
 ·i·er ·i·est
scrim'shaw'
scrip (certificate)
script (manuscript)
scrip'tur·al
scrip'ture
script'writ'er
scrod
scrof'u·la
scrof'u·lous
scroll
scro'tum
 ·ta or ·tums
scrounge
 scrounged
 scroung'ing
scroung'er
scroung'i·ness
scroung'y
 ·i·er ·i·est
scrub
 scrubbed
 scrub'bing
scrub'by
 ·bi·er ·bi·est
scruff
scruff'y
 ·i·er ·i·est
scrump'tious
scrunch
scru'ple
 ·pled ·pling
scru'pu·los'i·ty
scru'pu·lous
scru'pu·lous·ly
scru'ti·nize'
 ·nized' ·niz'ing
scru'ti·ny
scu'ba
scud
 scud'ded scud'ding
scuff
scuf'fle
 ·fled ·fling
scull
 (boat; see SKULL)
scul'ler·y
 ·ies
scul'lion
sculpt
sculp'tor
sculp'tur·al

sculp'ture
 ·tured ·tur·ing
scum
scum'my
 ·mi·er ·mi·est
scup'per
scurf
scurf'y
 ·i·er ·i·est
scur·ril'i·ty
 ·ties
scur'ri·lous
scur'ri·lous·ly
scur'ry
 ·ried ·ry·ing
scur'vy
 ·vi·er ·vi·est
scutch'eon
scut'tle
 ·tled ·tling
scut'tle·butt'
scythe
sea
sea'board'
sea'coast'
sea'far'er
sea'far'ing
sea'food'
sea'go'ing
seal
seal'ant
seal'er
seal'skin'
seam
 (line; see SEEM)
sea'man
sea'man·ship'
seam'less
seam'stress
seam'y
 ·i·er ·i·est
sé'ance
sea'plane'
sea'port'
sear
 (burn; see SEER)
search
search'er
search'ing
search'light'
sea'scape'
sea'shell'
sea'shore'
sea'sick'
sea'sick'ness
sea'side'
sea'son
sea'son·a·ble
sea'son·al
sea'son·al·ly
sea'son·ing
seat
sea'ward
sea'way'
sea'weed'
sea'wor'thy
se·ba'ceous

seb'or·rhe'a or
 ·rhoe'·
se'cant
se·cede'
 ·ced'ed ·ced'ing
se·ces'sion
se·ces'sion·ist
se·clude'
 ·clud'ed ·clud'ing
se·clu'sion
se·clu'sive
sec'ond
sec'ond·ar'i·ly
sec'ond·ar'y
sec'ond-class'
sec'ond-guess'
sec'ond·hand'
sec'ond·ly
sec'ond-rate'
sec'ond-string'er
se'cre·cy
se'cret
sec're·tar'i·al
sec're·tar'i·at
sec're·tar'y
 ·ies
se·crete'
 ·cret'ed ·cret'ing
se·cre'tion
se'cre·tive
se'cre·tive·ly
se'cre·tive·ness
se'cret·ly
sect
sec·tar'i·an
sec·tar'i·an·ism'
sec'tion
sec'tion·al
sec'tion·al·ism'
sec'tor
sec'u·lar
sec'u·lar·ism'
sec'u·lar·i·za'tion
sec'u·lar·ize'
 ·ized' ·iz'ing
se·cure'
 ·cured' ·cur'ing
se·cure'ly
se·cu'ri·ty
 ·ties
se·dan'
se·date'
 ·dat'ed ·dat'ing
se·date'ly
se·da'tion
sed'a·tive
sed'en·tar'y
Se'der
sedge
sed'i·ment
sed'i·men'ta·ry
sed'i·men·ta'tion
se·di'tion
se·di'tion·ist
se·di'tious
se·duce'
 ·duced' ·duc'ing
se·duc'er

se·duc'tion
se·duc'tive
se·duc'tress
sed'u·lous
se'dum
see
 saw seen see'ing
seed
seed'case'
seed'i·ness
seed'ling
seed'y
 ·i·er ·i·est
seek
 sought seek'ing
seem
 (appear; see SEAM)
seem'ing
seem'ing·ly
seem'li·ness
seem'ly
 ·li·er ·li·est
seen
seep
seep'age
seer
 (prophet; see
 SEAR)
seer'suck'er
see'saw'
seethe
 seethed seeth'ing
seg'ment
seg'men·ta'tion
seg're·gate'
 ·gat'ed ·gat'ing
seg're·ga'tion
seg're·ga'tion·ist
se'gue
 ·gued ·gue·ing
seine
 seined sein'ing
seis'mic
seis'mi·cal·ly
seis'mo·graph'
seis·mol'o·gist
seis·mol'o·gy
seize
 seized seiz'ing
sei'zure
sel'dom
se·lect'
se·lec'tion
se·lec'tive
se·lec'tiv'i·ty
se·lect'man
se·lec'tor
se·le'ni·um
self
 selves
self'-ad·dressed'
self'-ap·point'ed
self'-as·sur'ance
self'-as·sured'
self'-cen'tered
self'-con'fi·dence
self'-con'fi·dent
self'-con'scious
self'-con'scious·ly

self'-
 con'scious·ness
self'-con·tained'
self'-con·trol'
self'-de·fense'
self'-de·ni'al
self'-de·struc'tive
self'-de·struc'tion
self'-dis'ci·pline
self'-de·ter'mined
self'-dis·cov'er·y
self'-ed'u·cat'ed
self'-em·ployed'
self'-es·teem'
self'-ev'i·dent
self'-ex·plan'a
 ·to'ry
self'-ex·pres'sion
self'-ful·fill'ing
self'-gov'ern·ing
self'-gov'ern·ment
self'-help'
self'-im'age
self'-im·por'tance
self'-im·por'tant
self'-im·posed'
self'-in·dul'gence
self'-in·dul'gent
self'-in·flict'ed
self'-in'ter·est
self'ish
self'ish·ly
self'ish·ness
self'less
self'less·ly
self'less·ness
self'-made'
self'-pit'y
self'-pos·sessed'
self'-pres'er·va'-
 tion
self'-pro·pelled'
self'-reg'u·lat'ing
self'-re·li'ance
self'-re·li'ant
self'-re·spect'
self'-re·spect'ing
self'-re·straint'
self'-right'eous
self'-right'eous·ly
self'-right'eous·
 ness
self'-sac'ri·fice'
self'-sac'ri·fic'ing
self'same'
self'-sat'is·fac'tion
self'-sat'is·fied'
self'-seal'ing
self'-seek'ing
self'-serve'
self'-serv'ice
self'-serv'ing
self'-styled'
self'-suf·fi'cien·cy
self'-suf·fi'cient
self'-taught'
self'-willed'

self'-wind'ing
sell
 sold sell'ing
 (trade for money;
 see CELL)
sell'er
 (vendor; see CEL-
 LAR)
sell'out'
selt'zer
sel'vage or ·vedge
selves
se·man'tics
sem'a·phore'
sem'blance
se'men
se·mes'ter
sem'i'
sem'i·an'nu·al
sem'i·au'to·mat'ic
sem'i·cir'cle
sem'i·cir'cu·lar
sem'i·co'lon
sem'i·con·duc'tor
sem'i·con'scious
sem'i-de·tached'
sem'i·fi'nal
sem'i·month'ly
sem'i·nal
sem'i·nar'
sem'i·nar'i·an
sem'i·nar'y
 ·nar'ies
se'mi·ot'ics
sem'i·pre'cious
sem'i·pri'vate
sem'i·pro'
sem'i·skilled'
Se·mit'ic
sem'i·tone'
sem'i·trail'er
sem'i·trop'i·cal
sem'i·week'ly
sem'o·li'na
sen'ate
sen'a·tor
sen'a·to'ri·al
send
 sent send'ing
send'er
send'-off'
se'nile
se·nil'i·ty
sen'ior
sen·ior'i·ty
sen'na
se·ñor'
 se·ño'res
se·ño'ra
se·ño·ri'ta
sen·sa'tion
sen·sa'tion·al
sen·sa'tion·al·ism'
sense
 sensed sens'ing
sense'less
sen'si·bil'i·ty
 ·ties

sen'si·ble
sen'si·bly
sen'si·tive'
sen'si·tiv'i·ty
sen'si·tize'
·tized' ·tiz'ing
sen'sor
(sensing device; see CENSER, CEN-SOR, CENSURE)
sen'so·ry
sen'su·al
sen'su·al'i·ty
sen'su·al·ly
sen'su·ous
sent
(transmitted; see CENT, SCENT)
sen'tence
·tenced ·tenc·ing
sen·ten'tious
sen'tient
sen'ti·ment
sen'ti·men'tal
sen'ti·men'tal·ism'
sen'ti·men'tal·ist
sen'ti·men·tal'i·ty
sen'ti·men'tal·ly
sen'ti·nel
sen'try
·tries
se'pal
sep'a·ra·ble
sep'a·rate'
·rat'ed ·rat'ing
sep'a·rate·ly
sep'a·ra'tion
sep'a·ra·tism'
sep'a·ra·tist
sep'a·ra'tor
se'pi·a
sep'sis
Sep·tem'ber
sep·tet' or ·tette'
sep'tic
sep'ti·ce'mi·a
sep'tum
sep'ul·cher
se·pul'chral
se'quel
se'quence
se·quen'tial
se·ques'ter
se·ques·tra'tion
se'quin
se'quined or
·quinned
se·quoi'a
se·ra'pe
ser'aph
·aphs or ·a·phim'
se·raph'ic
ser'e·nade'
·nad'ed ·nad'ing
ser'en·dip'i·tous
ser'en·dip'i·ty
se·rene'
se·rene'ly

se·ren'i·ty
serf
(slave; see SURF)
serf'dom
serge
(fabric; see SURGE)
ser'geant
ser'geant-at-arms'
ser'geants-
se'ri·al
(in a series; see CEREAL)
se'ri·al·i·za'tion
se'ri·al·ize'
·ized' ·iz'ing
se'ries
·ries
se'ri·ous
se'ri·ous·ly
se'ri·ous·ness
ser'mon
ser'mon·ize'
·ized' ·iz'ing
se'rous
ser'pent
ser'pen·tine'
ser'rate'
ser'rat'ed
ser'ried
se'rum
serv'ant
serve
served serv'ing
serv'er
serv'ice
·iced ·ic·ing
serv'ice·a·ble
serv'ice·man'
ser'vi·ette'
ser'vile
ser·vil'i·ty
ser'vi·tor
ser'vi·tude'
ser'vo·mech'a·nism
ser'vo·mo'tor
ses'a·me'
ses'qui·cen·ten'ni·al
ses'sion
(meeting; see CES-SION)
set
set set'ting
set'back'
set'screw'
set·tee'
set'ter
set'ting
set'tle
·tled ·tling
set'tle·ment
set'tler
set'-to'
-tos'
set'up'
sev'en
sev'en·teen'
sev'en·teenth'
sev'enth

sev'en·ti·eth
sev'en·ty
·ties
sev'er
sev'er·al
sev'er·al·ly
sev'er·ance
se·vere'
·ver'er ·ver'est
se·vere'ly
se·ver'i·ty
sew
sewed, sewn or
sewed, sew'ing
(stitch; see SOW)
sew'age
sew'er
sew'er·age
sew'ing
sex
sex'a·ge·nar'i·an
sex'i·ly
sex'i·ness
sex'ism'
sex'ist
sex'tant
sex·tet' or ·tette'
sex'ton
sex'u·al
sex'u·al'i·ty
sex'u·al·ly
sex'y
·i·er ·i·est
shab'bi·ly
shab'bi·ness
shab'by
·bi·er ·bi·est
shack
shack'le
·led ·ling
shad
shad or shads
shade
shad'ed shad'ing
shad'i·ness
shad'ing
shad'ow
shad'ow·box'
shad'ow·y
shad'y
·i·er ·i·est
shaft
shag
shagged shag'ging
shag'gi·ness
shag'gy
·gi·er ·gi·est
shah
shake
shook shak'en
shak'ing
shake'down'
shake'out'
shak'er
Shake·spear'e·an or
·i·an
shake'-up'
shak'i·ly
shak'i·ness

shak'y
·i·er ·i·est
shale
shall
should
shal·lot'
shal'low
shalt
sham
shammed
sham'ming
sham'ble
·bled ·bling
sham'bles
shame
shamed sham'ing
shame'faced'
shame'ful
shame'ful·ly
shame'ful·ness
shame'less
sham·poo'
·pooed' ·poo'ing
sham'rock'
shang'hai'
·haied' ·hai'ing
shank
shan'tung'
shan'ty
·ties
shape
shaped shap'ing
shape'less
shape'less·ness
shape'li·ness
shape'ly
·li·er ·li·est
shard
share
shared shar'ing
share'crop'per
share'hold'er
shark
shark'skin'
sharp
sharp'en
sharp'en·er
sharp'er
sharp'-eyed'
sharp'ie
sharp'ly
sharp'ness
sharp'shoot'er
sharp'-wit'ted
shat'ter
shat'ter·proof'
shave
shaved, shaved or
shav'en, shav'ing
shav'er
shav'ing
shawl
shay
she
sheaf
sheaves
shear
sheared, sheared

or shorn,
shear'ing
(cut; see SHEER)
shears
sheath
sheaths
(a case)
sheathe
sheathed
sheath'ing
(put into a sheath)
sheath'ing
sheave
sheaved sheav'ing
she·bang'
shed
shed shed'ding
sheen
sheep
sheep
sheep'fold'
sheep'ish
sheep'ish·ly
sheep'ish·ness
sheep'skin'
sheer
(thin; steep; see SHEAR)
sheet
sheet'ing
sheik or sheikh
(Arab chief; see CHIC)
shek'el
shelf
shelves
shell
shel·lac' or ·lack'
·lacked' ·lack'ing
shell'fire'
shell'fish'
shel'ter
shelve
shelved shelv'ing
shelv'ing
she·nan'i·gans
shep'herd
shep'herd·ess
sher'bet
sher'iff
sher'ry
·ries
shib'bo·leth'
shied
shield
shift
shift'i·ly
shift'i·ness
shift'less
shift'less·ness
shift'y
·i·er ·i·est
shill
shil·le'lagh or
·la'lah
shil'ling
shil'ly-shal'ly
·lied ·ly·ing
shim
shim'mer

shim'mer·y
shim'my
·mied ·my·ing
shin
shinned shin'ning
shin'bone'
shin'dig'
shine
shone or shined
shin'ing
shin'er
shin'gle
·gled ·gling
shin'gles
shin'guard'
shin'i·ness
shin'ny
·nied ·ny·ing
shin'splints'
shin'y
·i·er ·i·est
ship
shipped ship'ping
ship'board'
ship'build'er
ship'mate'
ship'ment
ship'own'er
ship'per
ship'ping
ship'shape'
ship'wreck'
ship'yard'
shire
shirk
shirk'er
shirr
shirr'ing
shirt
shirt'tail'
shirt'waist'
shish' ke·bab'
shiv
shiv'a·ree'
shiv'er
shiv'er·y
shmaltz
shoal
shoat
shock
shock'er
shock'ing
shock'proof'
shod
shod'di·ly
shod'di·ness
shod'dy
·di·er ·di·est
shoe
shod or shoed
shoe'ing
shoe'horn'
shoe'lace'
shoe'mak'er
shoe'shine'
shoe'string'
sho'far
(Jewish horn; see CHAUFFER)

sho'gun'
sho'gun·ate
shone
shoo
  shooed shoo'ing
shoo'-in'
shook
shoot
  shot shoot'ing
shoot'er
shoot'out' *or*
  shoot'-out'
shop
  shopped shop'ping
shop'keep'er
shop'lift'
shop'lift'er
shoppe
shop'per
shop'talk'
shop'worn'
shore
shore'line'
shor'ing
shorn
short
short'age
short'bread'
short'cake'
short'change'
short'-cir'cuit
short'com'ing
short'cut'
short'en
short'en·ing
short'fall'
short'hand'
short'-hand'ed
short'horn'
short'-lived'
short'ly
short'ness
short'-range'
short'sight'ed
short'sight'ed·ness
short'stop'
short'-tem'pered
short'-term'
short'-waist'ed
short'wave'
short'-wind'ed
shot
shot'gun'
shot'-put'ter
should
shoul'der
shout
shout'er
shove
  shoved shov'ing
shov'el
  ·eled *or* ·elled
  ·el·ing *or* ·el·ling
shov'el·ful'
  ·fuls'
show
  showed, shown *or*
  showed, show'ing

show'boat'
show'case'
show'down'
show'er
show'er·y
show'i·ly
show'i·ness
show'ing
show'man
show'man·ship'
shown
show'off'
show'piece'
show'place'
show'room'
show'y
  ·i·er ·i·est
shrank
shrap'nel
shred
  shred'ded *or*
  shred, shred'ding
shred'der
shrew
shrewd
shrewd'ly
shrewd'ness
shriek
shrift
shrike
shrill
shrill'ness
shril'ly
shrimp
shrine
shrink
  shrank *or* shrunk,
  shrunk *or*
  shrunk'en,
  shrink'ing
shrink'age
shrink'-wrap'
shriv'el
  ·eled *or* ·elled
  ·el·ing *or* ·el·ling
shroud
shrub
shrub'ber·y
shrub'by
shrug
  shrugged
  shrug'ging
shrunk
shrunk'en
shtick
shuck
shud'der
shuf'fle
  ·fled ·fling
shuf'fle·board'
shuf'fler
shun
  shunned shun'n-
  ing
shunt
shush
shut
  shut shut'ting
shut'down'

shut'-eye'
shut'-in'
shut'out'
shut'ter
shut'tle
  ·tled ·tling
shut'tle·cock'
shy
  shy'er *or* shi'er
  shy'est *or* shi'est
  shied shy'ing
shy'ly
shy'ness
shy'ster
Si'a·mese'
sib'i·lance
sib'i·lant
sib'ling
sib'yl
sib'yl·line'
sic
  sicked sick'ing
  (*urge to attack*)
sick (*ill*)
sick'bed'
sick'en
sick'en·ing
sick'ish
sick'le
sick'li·ness
sick'ly
  ·li·er ·li·est
sick'ness
sick'room'
side
  sid'ed sid'ing
side'arm'
side'bar'
side'board'
side'burns'
side'car'
side'kick'
side'light'
side'line'
side'long'
side'piece'
si·de're·al
side'sad'dle
side'show'
side'split'ting
side'step'
side'stroke'
side'swipe'
side'track'
side'walk'
side'wall'
side'ways'
side'wise'
sid'ing
si'dle
  ·dled ·dling
siege
si·er'ra
si·es'ta
sieve
sift
sift'er
sigh

sight
  (*vision*; see CITE,
  SITE)
sight'ed
sight'less
sight'ly
  ·li·er ·li·est
sight'-read'
sight'see'ing
sight'se'er
sign
sign'age
sig'nal
  ·naled *or* ·nalled
  ·nal·ing *or*
  ·nal·ling
sig'nal·ize'
  ·ized' ·iz'ing
sig'nal·ly
sig'na·to'ry
  ·ries
sig'na·ture
sign'board'
sig'net
sig·nif'i·cance
sig·nif'i·cant
sig·nif'i·cant·ly
sig·ni·fi·ca'tion
sig'ni·fy'
  ·fied' ·fy'ing
sign'post'
si'lage
sild
  sild *or* silds
si'lence
  ·lenced ·lenc·ing
si'lenc·er
si'lent
si'lent·ly
sil'hou·ette'
  ·et'ted ·et'ting
sil'i·ca
sil'i·cate
si·li'ceous
sil'i·con (*chemical
  element*)
sil'i·cone' (*silicon
  compound*)
sil'i·co'sis
silk
silk'en
silk'i·ness
silk'-screen'
silk'worm'
silk'y
  ·i·er ·i·est
sill
sil'li·ness
sil'ly
  ·li·er ·li·est
si'lo
  ·los
silt
sil'ver
sil'ver·fish'
sil'ver·smith'
sil'ver·ware'
sil'ver·y
sim'i·an

sim'i·lar
sim'i·lar'i·ty
  ·ties
sim'i·lar·ly
sim'i·le'
si·mil'i·tude'
sim'mer
sim·pa'ti·co
sim'per
sim'ple
  ·pler ·plest
sim'ple-mind'ed
sim'ple·ton
sim·plic'i·ty
sim·pli·fi·ca'tion
sim·pli·fi'er
sim'pli·fy'
  ·fied' ·fy'ing
sim·plis'tic
sim·plis'ti·cal·ly
sim'ply
sim'u·late'
  ·lat'ed ·lat'ing
sim'u·la'tion
si'mul·cast'
  ·cast' *or* ·cast'ed
  ·cast'ing
si'mul·ta·ne'i·ty
si'mul·ta'ne·ous
si'mul·ta'ne·ous·ly
sin
  sinned sin'ning
since
sin·cere'
sin·cere'ly
sin·cer'i·ty
si'ne·cure'
sin'ew
sin'ew·y
sin'ful
sing
  sang sung sing'ing
sing'-a·long'
singe
  singed singe'ing
sing'er
sin'gle
  ·gled ·gling
sin'gle-breast'ed
sin'gle-hand'ed
sin'gle-hand'·ed·ly
sin'gle-mind'ed
sin'gle-mind'·ed·ly
sin'gle·ness
sin'gle·ton
sin'gle·tree'
sin'gly
sing'song'
sin'gu·lar
sin'gu·lar'i·ty
sin'gu·lar·ly
sin'is·ter
sink
  sank *or* sunk sunk
  sink'ing
sink'er
sink'hole'
sin'ner

sin·u·os'i·ty
sin'u·ous
si'nus
si'nus·i'tis
sip
  sipped sip'ping
si'phon
sir
sire
  sired sir'ing
si'ren
sir'loin'
si·roc'co
  ·cos
sir·ree' *or* ·ee'
sis
si'sal
sis'sy
  ·sies
sis'ter
sis'ter·hood'
sis'ter-in-law'
  sis'ters-in-law'
sis'ter·ly
sit
  sat sit'ting
si·tar'
sit'com'
sit'-down'
site
  (*location*; see CITE,
  SIGHT)
sit'-in'
sit'ter
sit'ting
sit'u·ate'
  ·at'ed ·at'ing
sit'u·a'tion
sit'-up' *or* sit'up'
sitz bath
six
six'-pack'
six'-shoot'er
six'teen'
six'teenth'
sixth
six'ti·eth
six'ty
  ·ties
siz'a·ble *or* size'·
size
  sized siz'ing
siz'ing
siz'zle
  ·zled ·zling
skate
  skat'ed skat'ing
skate'board'
skat'er
ske·dad'dle
  ·dled ·dling
skeet
skein
skel'e·tal
skel'e·ton
skep'tic
skep'ti·cal
skep'ti·cal·ly
skep'ti·cism'

sketch
sketch'book'
sketch'i·ly
sketch'i·ness
sketch'y
  ·i·er ·i·est
skew
skew'er
ski
  skis
  skied ski'ing
skid
  skid'ded skid'ding
ski'er
skiff
skill
skilled
skil'let
skill'ful
skim
  skimmed
  skim'ming
skimp
skimp'i·ly
skimp'i·ness
skimp'y
  ·i·er ·i·est
skin
  skinned skin'ning
skin'-deep'
skin'flint'
skin'less
skin'ni·ness
skin'ny
  ·ni·er ·ni·est
skin'ny-dip'
  -dipped' -dip'ping
skin'tight'
skip
  skipped skip'ping
ski'plane'
skip'per
skir'mish
skirt
skit
skit'ter
skit'tish
skiv'vy
  ·vies
skoal
skul·dug'ger·y or
  skull·
skulk
skull
  (head; see SCULL)
skull'cap'
skunk
sky
  skies
sky'cap'
sky'-high'
sky'jack'
sky'jack'er
sky'lark'
sky'light'
sky'line'
sky'rock'et
sky'scrap'er
sky'ward

sky'ways'
sky'writ'ing
slab
slack
slack'en
slack'er
slack'ness
slacks
slag
slain
slake
  slaked slak'ing
sla'lom
slam
  slammed
  slam'ming
slam'-bang'
slam'-dunk'
slam'mer
slan'der
slan'der·er
slan'der·ous
slang
slang'y
  ·i·er ·i·est
slant
slap
  slapped slap'ping
slap'dash'
slap'-hap'py
slap'stick'
slash
slash'er
slat
slate
  slat'ed slat'ing
slath'er
slat'tern
slat'tern·ly
slaugh'ter
slaugh'ter·er
slaugh'ter·house'
slave
  slaved slav'ing
slav'er
slav'er·y
slav'ish
slav'ish·ly
slaw
slay
  slew slain slay'ing
  (kill; see SLEIGH)
slay'er
sleaze
slea'zi·ly
slea'zi·ness
slea'zy
  ·zi·er ·zi·est
sled
  sled'ded sled'ding
sledge
sledge'ham'mer
sleek
sleek'ly
sleek'ness
sleep
  slept sleep'ing
sleep'er

sleep'i·ly
sleep'i·ness
sleep'less
sleep'less·ness
sleep'walk'er
sleep'walk'ing
sleep'wear'
sleep'y
  ·i·er ·i·est
sleet
sleeve
sleeve'less
sleigh
  (snow vehicle; see
  SLAY)
sleight
  (skill; see SLIGHT)
slen'der
slen'der·ize'
  ·ized' ·iz'ing
slept
sleuth
slew
  (a lot; see SLUE)
slice
  sliced slic'ing
slic'er
slick
slick'er
slick'ly
slick'ness
slide
  slid slid'ing
slid'er
slight
  (frail; see SLEIGHT)
slight'ly
slight'ness
slim
  slim'mer
  slim'mest
  slimmed
  slim'ming
slime
slim'i·ness
slim'ness
slim'y
  ·i·er ·i·est
sling
  slung sling'ing
sling'shot'
slink
  slunk slink'ing
slink'y
  ·i·er ·i·est
slip
  slipped slip'ping
slip'case'
slip'cov'er
slip'knot'
slip'page
slip'per
slip'per·i·ness
slip'per·y
  ·i·er ·i·est
slip'shod'
slip'-up'
slit
  slit slit'ting
slith'er

sliv'er
slob
slob'ber
sloe
  (fruit; see SLOW)
sloe'-eyed'
slog
  slogged slog'ging
slo'gan
sloop
slop
  slopped slop'ping
slope
  sloped slop'ing
slop'pi·ly
slop'pi·ness
slop'py
  ·pi·er ·pi·est
slosh
slot
  slot'ted slot'ting
sloth
sloth'ful
sloth'ful·ness
slouch
slouch'y
  ·i·er ·i·est
slough
slov'en·li·ness
slov'en·ly
  ·li·er ·li·est
slow
  (not fast; see SLOE)
slow'down'
slow'ly
slow'-mo'tion
slow'ness
slow'poke'
slow'-wit'ted
sludge
slue
  slued slu'ing
  (turn; see SLEW)
slug
  slugged slug'ging
slug'gard
slug'ger
slug'gish
slug'gish·ness
sluice
  sluiced sluic'ing
slum
  slummed
  slum'ming
slum'ber
slum'lord'
slump
slung
slunk
slur
  slurred slur'ring
slurp
slur'ry
slush
slush'y
  ·i·er ·i·est
slut
slut'tish

sly
  sli'er or sly'er
  sli'est or sly'est
sly'ly or sli'ly
sly'ness
smack
smack'er
small
small'-mind'ed
small'ness
small'pox'
small'-scale'
small'-time'
smart
smart al'eck or
  smart al'ec
smart'en
smart'ly
smart'ness
smash
smash'ing
smash'up'
smat'ter·ing
smear
smear'y
  ·i·er ·i·est
smell
  smelled or smelt
  smell'ing
smell'i·ness
smell'y
  ·i·er ·i·est
smelt
smelt'er
smidg'en
smile
  smiled smil'ing
smil'ing·ly
smirch
smirk
smite
  smote, smit'ten or
  smote, smit'ing
smith
smith'er·eens'
smith'y
  ·ies
smock
smock'ing
smog
smog'gy
  ·gi·er ·gi·est
smok'a·ble or
  smoke'·
smoke
  smoked smok'ing
smoke'house'
smoke'less
smok'er
smoke'stack'
smok'i·ness
smok'y
  ·i·er ·i·est
smol'der
smooch
smooth
smooth'bore'
smooth'ly
smooth'ness

smooth'-shav'en
smor'gas·bord' or
  smör'gås·
smote
smoth'er
smudge
  smudged
  smudg'ing
smudg'i·ness
smudg'y
  ·i·er ·i·est
smug
  smug'ger
  smug'gest
smug'gle
  ·gled ·gling
smug'gler
smug'ly
smug'ness
smut
smut'ty
  ·ti·er ·ti·est
snack
snaf'fle
sna·fu'
snag
  snagged snag'ging
snail
snake
  snaked snak'ing
snak'y
  ·i·er ·i·est
snap
  snapped
  snap'ping
snap'drag'on
snap'per
snap'pish
snap'py
  ·pi·er ·pi·est
snap'shot'
snare
  snared snar'ing
snarl
snarl'y
  ·i·er ·i·est
snatch
sneak
  sneaked or snuck
  sneak'ing
sneak'er
sneak'i·ly
sneak'i·ness
sneak'y
  ·i·er ·i·est
sneer
sneer'ing·ly
sneeze
  sneezed sneez'ing
snick'er
snide
sniff
snif'fle
  ·fled ·fling
snif'ter
snig'ger
snip
  snipped snip'ping
snipe
  sniped snip'ing

snip'er
snip'pet
snip'py
  ·pi·er ·pi·est
snit
snitch
sniv'el
  ·eled or ·elled
  ·el·ing or ·el·ling
snob
snob'ber·y
snob'bish
snob'bish·ness
snood
snoop
snoop'y
  ·i·er ·i·est
snoot
snoot'i·ness
snoot'y
  ·i·er ·i·est
snooze
  snoozed snooz'ing
snooz'er
snore
  snored snor'ing
snor'er
snor'kel
  ·keled ·kel·ing
snor'kel·er
snort
snot
snot'ty
  ·ti·er ·ti·est
snout
snow
snow'ball'
snow'bank'
snow'blind'
snow'bound'
snow'drift'
snow'drop'
snow'fall'
snow'flake'
snow'man'
snow'mo·bile'
  ·biled' ·bil'ing
snow'plow'
snow'shoe'
  ·shoed' ·shoe'ing
snow'storm'
snow'suit'
snow'-white'
snow'y
  ·i·er ·i·est
snub
  snubbed
  snub'bing
snub'-nosed'
snuck
snuff
snuff'box'
snuff'er
snuf'fle
  ·fled ·fling
snug
  snug'ger snug'gest
snug'gle
  ·gled ·gling

snug'ly
soak
so'-and-so'
  so'-and-sos'
soap
soap'box'
soap'stone'
soap'suds'
soap'y
  ·i·er ·i·est
soar
  (fly; see SORE)
sob
  sobbed sob'bing
so'ber
so'ber·ly
so'ber·ness
so·bri'e·ty
so'bri·quet'
so'-called'
soc'cer
so·cia·bil'i·ty
so'cia·ble
so'cia·bly
so'cial
so'cial·ism'
so'cial·ist
so'cial·is'tic
so'cial·ite'
so'cial·i·za'tion
so'cial·ize'
  ·ized' ·iz'ing
so'cial·ly
so·ci'e·tal
so·ci'e·ty
  ·ties
so'ci·o·e·co·nom'ic
so'ci·o·log'i·cal
so'ci·ol'o·gist
so'ci·ol'o·gy
so'ci·o·path'
sock
  socks or sox
sock'et
sock'eye salmon
So·crat'ic
sod
  sod'ded sod'ding
so'da
sod'den
so'di·um
sod'om·y
so'fa
soft
soft'ball'
soft'-boiled'
soft'en
soft'en·er
soft'heart'ed
soft'ly
soft'ness
soft'-ped'al
soft'-spo'ken
soft'ware'
soft'wood'
sog'gi·ness
sog'gy
  ·gi·er ·gi·est

soil
soi·ree' or ·rée'
so'journ
so'journ·er
sol'ace
  ·aced ·ac·ing
so'lar
so·lar'i·um
  ·i·a
sold
sol'der (to bond
  metal)
sol'dier (member of
  an army)
sol'dier·ly
sole
  soled sol'ing
  (single; foot part;
  see SOUL)
sole
  sole or soles
  (fish)
sol'e·cism'
sole'ly
sol'emn
so·lem'ni·fy'
  ·fied' ·fy'ing
so·lem'ni·ty
  ·ties
sol'em·nize'
  ·nized' ·niz'ing
sol'emn·ly
sol'e·noid'
so·lic'it
so·lic'i·ta'tion
so·lic'i·tor
so·lic'i·tous
so·lic'i·tude'
sol'id
sol'i·dar'i·ty
so·lid'i·fi·ca'tion
so·lid'i·fy'
  ·fied' ·fy'ing
so·lid'i·ty
sol'id·ly
sol'id·ness
sol'id-state'
so·lil'o·quize'
  ·quized' ·quiz'ing
so·lil'o·quy
  ·quies
sol'i·taire'
sol'i·tar'y
sol'i·tude'
so'lo
  ·los
  ·loed ·lo·ing
so'lo·ist
sol'stice
sol·u·bil'i·ty
sol'u·ble
sol'ute'
so·lu'tion
solv'a·ble
solve
  solved solv'ing
sol'ven·cy
sol'vent
solv'er

so·mat'ic
som'ber
som'ber·ly
som·bre'ro
  ·ros
some
some'bod'y
  ·bod'ies
some'day'
some'how'
some'one'
som'er·sault'
some'thing
some'time'
some'times'
some'way'
some'what'
some'where'
som·nam'bu·lism'
som·nam'bu·list
som'no·lence
som'no·lent
son
so'nar'
so·na'ta
song
song'bird'
song'fest'
song'ster
song'stress
son'ic
son'-in-law'
  sons'-in-law'
son'net
son'net·eer'
so·nor'i·ty
so·no'rous
soon
soot
sooth (truth)
soothe
  soothed sooth'ing
  (make calm)
sooth'ing
sooth'say'er
sooth'say'ing
soot'y
  ·i·er ·i·est
sop
  sopped sop'ping
soph'ism'
soph'ist
so·phis'ti·cate'
  ·cat'ed ·cat'ing
so·phis'ti·cat'ed
so·phis'ti·ca'tion
soph'ist·ry
  ·tries
soph'o·more'
soph'o·mor'ic
sop·o·rif'ic
sop'ping
sop'py
  ·pi·er ·pi·est
so·pra'no
  ·nos
sor'bet
sor'cer·er

sor'cer·ess
sor'cer·y
  ·ies
sor'did
sor'did·ly
sor'did·ness
sore
  sor'er sor'est
  (painful; see SOAR)
sore'ly
sore'ness
sor'ghum
so·ror'i·ty
  ·ties
sor'rel
sor'ri·ly
sor'ri·ness
sor'row
sor'row·ful
sor'row·ful·ly
sor'ry
  ·ri·er ·ri·est
sort
sor'tie
so'-so'
sot
sot'tish
souf·flé'
sought
soul
  (spirit; see SOLE)
soul'ful
soul'ful·ly
soul'ful·ness
sound
sound'ing
sound'less
sound'ly
sound'ness
sound'proof'
sound'track'
soup
soup·çon'
soup'y
  ·i·er ·i·est
sour
source
sour'dough'
sour'ly
sour'ness
sour'puss'
souse
  soused sous'ing
south
South Car'o·li'na
South Da·ko'ta
south'east'
south'east'er·ly
south'east'ern
south'east'ward
south'east'wards
south'er·ly
south'ern
south'ern·er
south'paw'
south'ward
south'west'
south'west'er·ly

south'west'ern
south'west'ward
south'west'wards
sou've·nir'
sov'er·eign
sov'er·eign·ty
so'vi·et
sow
  sowed, sown or
  sowed, sow'ing
  (plant; see SEW)
sow'er
sox
soy
soy'bean'
spa
space
  spaced spac'ing
space'craft'
  ·craft'
space'flight'
space'man'
space'ship'
space'suit'
space'y or spac'y
  ·i·er ·i·est
spac'i·ness
spa'cious
spa'cious·ly
spa'cious·ness
spack'le
  ·led ·ling
spack'ling
spade
  spad'ed spad'ing
spa'dix
  ·dix·es or ·di·ces'
spaet'zle
spa·ghet'ti
spake
span
  spanned span'ning
span'dex'
span'gle
  ·gled ·gling
span'iel
Span'ish
spank
spar
  sparred spar'ring
spare
  spared spar'ing
spare'ly
spare'ribs'
spar'ing·ly
spark
spar'kle
  ·kled ·kling
spar'kler
spar'row
sparse
sparse'ly
sparse'ness
spar'si·ty
Spar'tan
spasm
spas·mod'ic
spas·mod'i·cal·ly
spas'tic

spat
  spat'ted spat'ting
spate
spathe
spa'tial
spat'ter
spat'u·la
spav'ined
spawn
spay
speak
  spoke spo'ken
  speak'ing
speak'-eas'y
  ·ies
speak'er
spear
spear'fish'
spear'head'
spear'mint'
spec
spe'cial
spe'cial·ist
spe'cial·i·za'tion
spe'cial·ize'
  ·ized' ·iz'ing
spe'cial·ly
spe'cial·ty
  ·ties
spe'cie (coin)
spe'cies
  ·cies
  (kind)
spe·cif'ic
spe·cif'i·cal·ly
spec'i·fi·ca'tion
spec'i·fy
  ·fied' ·fy'ing
spec'i·men
spe'cious
spe'cious·ly
speck
speck'le
  ·led ·ling
spec'ta·cle
spec·tac'u·lar
spec·tac'u·lar·ly
spec'ta'tor
spec'ter
spec'tral
spec'tro·scope'
spec'tro·scop'ic
spec·tros'co·py
spec'trum
  ·tra or ·trums
spec'u·late'
  ·lat'ed ·lat'ing
spec'u·la'tion
spec'u·la'tive
spec'u·la'tor
speech
speech'less
speed
  sped or speed'ed
  speed'ing
speed'boat'
speed'er
speed'i·ly
speed·om'e·ter

speed'ster
speed'way'
speed'y
  ·i·er ·i·est
spe'le·ol'o·gist
spe'le·ol'o·gy
spell
  spelled or spelt
  spell'ing
  (name the letters
  of)
spell
  spelled, spell'ing
  (work in place of)
spell'bind'er
spell'bound'
spell'er
spe·lunk'er
spend
  spent spend'ing
spend'a·ble
spend'er
spend'thrift'
spent
sperm
sper'ma·to·zo'on
  ·zo'a
sperm'i·cid'al
sperm'i·cide'
spew
sphag'num
sphere
spher'i·cal
sphe'roid
sphinc'ter
sphinx
  sphinx'es or
  sphin'ges'
spice
  spiced spic'ing
spic'i·ness
spick'-and-span'
spic'ule'
spic'y
  ·i·er ·i·est
spi'der
spi'der·y
spiel
spig'ot
spike
  spiked spik'ing
spill
  spilled or spilt
  spill'ing
spill'age
spin
  spun spin'ning
spi'na bi'fi·da
spin'ach
spi'nal
spin'dle
spin'dly
  ·dli·er ·dli·est
spine
spine'less
spin'et
spin'ner
spin'ner·et'
spin'off'
spin'ster

spin'ster·hood'
spin'y
  ·i·er ·i·est
spi'ra·cle
spi'ral
  ·raled or ·ralled
  ·ral·ing or ·ral·ling
spi'ral·ly
spire
spi·re'a
spir'it
spir'it·ed
spir'it·less
spir'it·u·al
spir'it·u·al·ism'
spir'it·u·al·ist
spir'it·u·al·is'tic
spir'it·u·al'i·ty
spir'it·u·al·ly
spi'ro·chete'
spit
  spit or spat spit'ting
spit'ball'
spite
  spit'ed spit'ing
spite'ful
spit'fire'
spit'tle
spit·toon'
spitz
splash
splash'i·ly
splash'i·ness
splash'y
  ·i·er ·i·est
splat
splat'ter
splay
splay'foot'
splay'foot'ed
spleen
splen'did
splen'did·ly
splen'dor
sple·net'ic
splice
  spliced splic'ing
splint
splin'ter
split
  split split'ting
split'-lev'el
splotch
splotch'y
  ·i·er ·i·est
splurge
  splurged
  splurg'ing
splut'ter
spoil
  spoiled or spoilt
  spoil'ing
spoil'age
spoil'er
spoil'sport'
spoke
spo'ken
spokes'man
spokes'per'son

spokes'wom'an
spo'li·a'tion
sponge
  sponged spong'ing
sponge'cake'
spong'er
spon'gy
  ·gi·er ·gi·est
spon'sor
spon'sor·ship'
spon·ta·ne'i·ty
  ·ties
spon·ta'ne·ous
spon·ta'ne·ous·ly
spoof
spook
spook'y
  ·i·er ·i·est
spool
spoon
spoon'bill'
spoon'er·ism'
spoon'-feed'
  ·fed' ·feed'ing
spoon'ful'
  ·fuls'
spoor
spo·rad'ic
spo·rad'i·cal·ly
spore
  spored spor'ing
sport
spor'tive
spor'tive·ly
sports'cast'
sports'cast'er
sports'man
sports'man·like'
sports'man·ship'
sport'y
  ·i·er ·i·est
spot
  spot'ted spot'ting
spot'-check'
spot'less
spot'light'
spot'ter
spot'ty
  ·ti·er ·ti·est
spous'al
spouse
spout
sprain
sprang
sprat
sprawl
spray
spray'er
spread
  spread spread'ing
spread'-ea'gled
spread'er
spread'sheet'
spree
sprig
spright'li·ness
spright'ly
  ·li·er ·li·est

spring
  sprang or sprung,
  sprung, spring'ing
spring'board'
spring'bok'
spring'i·ness
spring'time'
spring'y
  ·i·er ·i·est
sprin'kle
  ·kled ·kling
sprin'kler
sprint
sprint'er
sprite
spritz
spritz'er
sprock'et
sprout
spruce
  spruced spruc'ing
spry
  spri'er or spry'er
  spri'est or spry'est
spry'ly
spry'ness
spud
spume
  spumed spum'ing
spu·mo'ni
spun
spunk
spunk'y
  ·i·er ·i·est
spur
  spurred spur'ring
spurge
spu'ri·ous
spu'ri·ous·ly
spu'ri·ous·ness
spurn
spurt
sput'ter
spu'tum
spy
  spies
  spied spy'ing
spy'glass'
squab
squab'ble
  ·bled ·bling
squab'bler
squad
squad'ron
squal'id
squall
squal'or
squa'mous
squan'der
square
  squar'er squar'est
  squared squar'ing
square'-dance'
square'ly
square'ness
squash
squash'y
  ·i·er ·i·est

squat
  squat'ted squat'ting
squat'ter
squaw
squawk
squawk'er
squeak
squeak'er
squeak'y
  ·i·er ·i·est
squeal
squeal'er
squeam'ish
squeam'ish·ness
squee'gee
squeez'a·ble
squeeze
  squeezed
  squeez'ing
squelch
squib
squid
squig'gle
  ·gled ·gling
squint
squire
  squired squir'ing
squirm
squirm'y
squir'rel
  ·reled or ·relled
  ·rel·ing or ·rel·ling
squirt
squish
squish'y
  ·i·er ·i·est
stab
  stabbed stab'bing
sta·bil'i·ty
sta'bi·li·za'tion
sta'bi·lize'
  ·lized' ·liz'ing
sta'bi·liz'er
sta'ble
  ·bler ·blest
stac·ca'to
stack
sta'di·um
  ·di·ums or ·di·a
staff
  staffs or staves
  (stick; music)
staff
  staffs
  (people)
staff'er
stag
stage
  staged stag'ing
stage'coach'
stage'hand'
stage'-struck'
stag'ger
stag'nant
stag'nate'
  ·nat'ed ·nat'ing
stag·na'tion
staid
stain
stain'less

stair
   (*steps; see* STARE)
stair'case'
stair'way'
stair'well'
stake
   staked stak'ing
   (*post; share; see*
   STEAK)
stake'out'
sta·lac'tite
sta·lag'mite'
stale
   stal'er stal'est
stale'mate'
   ·mat'ed ·mat'ing
stale'ness
stalk
stall
stal'lion
stal'wart
sta'men
   sta'mens *or*
   stam'i·na
stam'i·na
stam'mer
stam'mer·er
stamp
stam·pede'
   ·ped'ed ·ped'ing
stamp'er
stance
stanch
   (*stop the flow of;*
   see STAUNCH)
stan'chion
stand
   stood stand'ing
stand'ard
stand'ard-bear'er
stand·ard·i·za'tion
stand'ard·ize'
   ·ized' ·iz'ing
stand'by'
   ·bys'
stand·ee'
stand'er
stand'-in'
stand'ing
stand'off'
stand'off'ish
stand'out'
stand'pipe'
stand'point'
stand'still'
stand'-up'
stank
stan'za
staph
staph'y·lo·coc'cus
   ·coc'ci'
sta'ple
   ·pled ·pling
sta'pler
star
   starred star'ring
star'board
starch
starch'y
   ·i·er ·i·est

star'-crossed'
star'dom
star'dust'
stare
   stared star'ing
   (*intent look; see*
   STAIR)
star'er
star'fish'
star'gaze'
star'gaz'er
stark
stark'-nak'ed
stark'ness
star'less
star'let
star'light'
star'ling
star'lit'
star'ry
   ·ri·er ·ri·est
star'ry-eyed'
star'-span'gled
start
start'er
star'tle
   ·tled ·tling
star·va'tion
starve
   starved starv'ing
stash
sta'sis
stat
state
   stat'ed stat'ing
state'craft'
state'hood'
state'house'
state'li·ness
state'ly
   ·li·er ·li·est
state'ment
state'-of-the-art'
state'room'
state'side'
states'man
states'man·ship'
state'wide'
stat'ic
stat'ick·y
sta'tion
sta'tion·ar'y (*not
   moving*)
sta'tion·er
sta'tion·er'y (*writ-
   ing paper*)
sta·tis'tic
sta·tis'ti·cal
sta·tis'ti·cal·ly
stat'is·ti'cian
stat'u·ar'y
stat'ue
stat'u·esque'
stat'u·ette'
stat'ure
sta'tus
   ·tus·es
sta'tus quo'

stat'ute
stat'u·to'ry
staunch
   (*loyal; stop the
   flow of;* see
   STANCH)
staunch'ly
stave
   staved *or* stove
   stav'ing
stay
stead
stead'fast'
stead'fast'ly
stead'i·ly
stead'y
   ·i·er ·i·est
   ·ied ·y·ing
steak
   (*meat; see* STAKE)
steal
   stole stol'en
   steal'ing
   (*take; see* STEEL)
stealth
stealth'i·ly
stealth'y
   ·i·er ·i·est
steam
steam'boat'
steam'er
steam'fit'ter
steam'roll'er
steam'ship'
steam'y
   ·i·er ·i·est
steed
steel
   (*metal; see* STEAL)
steel'work'er
steel'y
   ·i·er ·i·est
steel'yard'
steep
stee'ple
stee'ple·chase'
stee'ple·jack'
steep'ly
steep'ness
steer
steer'age
steg'o·sau'rus
   ·ri
stein
stel'lar
stem
   stemmed
   stem'ming
stem'ware'
stench
sten'cil
   ·ciled *or* ·cilled
   ·cil·ing *or* ·cil·ling
ste·nog'ra·pher
sten'o·graph'ic
ste·nog'ra·phy
sten·to'ri·an
step
   stepped step'ping
step'broth'er

step'child'
   ·chil'dren
step'daugh'ter
step'-down'
step'fa'ther
step'lad'der
step'moth'er
step'par'ent
steppe
step'per
step'ping·stone'
step'sis'ter
step'son'
step'-up'
ster'e·o'
   ·os'
ster'e·o·phon'ic
ster'e·o·scope'
ster'e·o·type'
   ·typed' ·typ'ing
ster'e·o·typ'i·cal
ster'ile
ste·ril'i·ty
ster'i·li·za'tion
ster'i·lize'
   ·lized' ·liz'ing
ster'i·liz'er
ster'ling
stern
stern'ly
stern'ness
ster'num
   ·nums *or* ·na
ster'oid'
stet
   stet'ted stet'ting
steth'o·scope'
ste've·dore'
stew
stew'ard
stew'ard·ess
stew'ard·ship'
stick
   stuck stick'ing
stick'er
stick'-in-the-mud'
stick'le·back'
stick'ler
stick'pin'
stick'um
stick'up'
stick'y
   ·i·er ·i·est
stiff
stiff'en
stiff'en·er
stiff'ly
stiff'ness
sti'fle
   ·fled ·fling
sti'fling
stig'ma
   ·mas *or* stig·ma·ta
stig'ma·tize'
   ·tized' ·tiz'ing
stile
   (*steps; see* STYLE)
sti·let'to
   ·tos *or* ·toes

still
still'birth'
still'born'
still'ness
stilt
stilt'ed
stim'u·lant
stim'u·late'
   ·lat'ed ·lat'ing
stim'u·la'tion
stim'u·lus
   ·li'
sting
   stung sting'ing
sting'er
stin'gi·ly
stin'gi·ness
sting'ray'
stin'gy
   ·gi·er ·gi·est
stink
   stank *or* stunk,
   stunk, stink'ing
stink'er
stint
sti'pend
stip'ple
   ·pled ·pling
stip'u·late'
   ·lat'ed ·lat'ing
stip'u·la'tion
stir
   stirred stir'ring
stir'-cra'zy
stir'-fry'
   -fried' -fry'ing
stir'rer
stir'ring
stir'rup
stitch
stoat
stock
stock·ade'
stock'bro'ker
stock'hold'er
stock'i·ness
stock'ing
stock'pile'
   ·piled' ·pil'ing
stock'room'
stock'-still'
stock'y
   ·i·er ·i·est
stock'yard'
stodg'i·ness
stodg'y
   ·i·er ·i·est
sto'gie *or* ·gy
   ·gies
sto'ic
sto'i·cal
sto'i·cal·ly
sto'i·cism'
stoke
   stoked stok'ing
stok'er
stole
stol'en
   (*form of* steal)

stol'id
stol'id·ly
stol'len (*bread*)
sto'lon' (*plant stem*)
stom'ach
stom'ach·ache'
stomp
stone
   stoned ston'ing
stoned
stone'wall'
stone'ware'
ston'i·ly
ston'y
   ·i·er ·i·est
stood
stooge
stool
stoop
   (*porch; bend; see*
   STOUP)
stop
   stopped stop'ping
stop'cock'
stop'gap'
stop'light'
stop'o'ver
stop'page
stop'per
stop'ple
   ·pled ·pling
stop'watch'
stor'age
store
   stored stor'ing
store'front'
store'house'
store'keep'er
store'room'
sto'ried
stork
storm
storm'i·ly
storm'i·ness
storm'y
   ·i·er ·i·est
sto'ry
   ·ries
sto'ry·board'
sto'ry·book'
sto'ry·tell'er
sto'ry·tell'ing
stoup
   (*basin; see* STOOP)
stout
stout'heart'ed
stout'ly
stout'ness
stove
stove'pipe'
stow
stow'age
stow'a·way'
strad'dle
   ·dled ·dling
strad'dler
strafe
   strafed straf'ing

strag'gle
  ·gled ·gling
strag'gler
strag'gly
straight
  (*not bent;* see
  STRAIT)
straight'a·way'
straight'edge'
straight'en
straight'ened
  (*made straight;*
  see STRAITENED)
straight'en·er
straight'-faced'
straight'for'ward
straight'ness
strain
strained
strain'er
strait
  (*waterway;* see
  STRAIGHT)
strait'ened
  (*limited;* see
  STRAIGHTENED)
strait'jack'et
strait'-laced'
strand
strange
  strang'er
  strang'est
strange'ly
strange'ness
stran'ger
stran'gle
  ·gled ·gling
stran'gle·hold'
stran'gler
stran'gu·late'
  ·lat'ed ·lat'ing
stran'gu·la'tion
strap
  strapped
  strap'ping
strap'less
strapped
strap'ping
stra'ta
strat'a·gem
stra·te'gic
stra·te'gi·cal·ly
strat'e·gist
strat'e·gy
  ·gies
strat'i·fi·ca'tion
strat'i·fy'
  ·fied' ·fy'ing
strat'o·sphere'
stra'tum
  ·ta *or* ·tums
stra'tus
  ·ti
straw
straw'ber'ry
  ·ries
stray
streak
streak'i·ness

streak'y
  ·i·er ·i·est
stream
stream'er
stream'line'
  ·lined' ·lin'ing
stream'lined'
street
street'car'
street'-smart'
street'walk'er
street'wise'
strength
strength'en
strength'en·er
stren'u·ous
stren'u·ous·ly
stren'u·ous·ness
strep
strep'to·coc'cus
  ·coc'ci
strep'to·my'cin
stress
stretch
stretch'a·ble
stretch'er
stretch'y
  ·i·er ·i·est
streu'sel
strew
  strewed, strewed
  or strewn,
  strew'ing
stri'at·ed
strick'en
strict
strict'ly
strict'ness
stric'ture
stride
  strode strid'den
  strid'ing
stri'dent
stri'dent·ly
strife
strike
  struck, struck *or*
  strick'en, strik'ing
strik'er
strik'ing
string
  strung string'ing
strin'gen·cy
strin'gent
string'er
string'y
  ·i·er ·i·est
strip
  stripped strip'ping
stripe
  striped strip'ing
strip'ling
strip'-search'
strip'tease'
strive
  strove *or* strived
  striv'en *or* strived,
  striv'ing
strobe
strode

stroke
  stroked strok'ing
stroll
stroll'er
strong
strong'box'
strong'hold'
strong'ly
stron'ti·um
strop
  stropped
  strop'ping
stro'phe
strove
struck
struc'tur·al
struc'ture
  ·tured ·tur·ing
stru'del
strug'gle
  ·gled ·gling
strum
  strummed
  strum'ming
strung
strut
  strut'ted strut't-
  ing
strych'nine
stub
  stubbed stub'bing
stub'ble
stub'bly
stub'born
stub'born·ness
stub'by
  ·bi·er ·bi·est
stuc'co
  ·coes *or* ·cos
  ·coed ·co·ing
stuck
stuck'-up'
stud
  stud'ded stud'ding
stu'dent
stud'ied
stu'di·o
  ·os'
stu'di·ous
stud'y
  ·ies
  ·ied ·y·ing
stuff
stuff'i·ness
stuff'ing
stuff'y
  ·i·er ·i·est
stul'ti·fy'
  ·fied' ·fy'ing
stum'ble
  ·bled ·bling
stum'bler
stump
stump'y
  ·i·er ·i·est
stun
  stunned stun'ning
stung
stunk
stun'ning

stunt
stu'pe·fac'tion
stu'pe·fy'
  ·fied' ·fy'ing
stu·pen'dous
stu'pid
stu·pid'i·ty
  ·ties
stu'por
stur'di·ly
stur'di·ness
stur'dy
  ·di·er ·di·est
stur'geon
stut'ter
stut'ter·er
sty
  sties stied sty'ing
  (*pig pen*)
sty *or* stye
  sties
  (*eyelid swelling*)
style
  styled styl'ing
  (*mode;* see STILE)
styl'ish
styl'ist
sty·lis'tic
sty·lis'ti·cal·ly
styl'ize'
  ·ized' ·iz'ing
sty'lus
  ·lus·es *or* ·li
sty'mie
  ·mied ·mie·ing
styp'tic
sty'ro·foam'
sua'sion
suave
suave'ly
suav'i·ty
sub
  subbed sub'bing
sub'as·sem'bly
sub'a·tom'ic
sub'base'ment
sub'com·mit'tee
sub'com·pact'
sub·con'scious
sub·con'scious·ly
sub·con'ti·nent
sub'con'tract
sub'con'trac·tor
sub'cul'ture
sub'cu·ta'ne·ous
sub'dis'trict
sub'di·vide'
sub'di·vi'sion
sub·due'
  ·dued' ·du'ing
sub·fam'i·ly
sub'head'
sub'ject
sub·jec'tion
sub·jec'tive
sub'jec·tiv'i·ty
sub·join'
sub'ju·gate'
  ·gat'ed ·gat'ing

sub'ju·ga'tion
sub'ju·ga'tor
sub·junc'tive
sub·lease'
sub·let'
  ·let' ·let'ting
sub'li·mate'
  ·mat'ed ·mat'ing
sub'li·ma'tion
sub·lime'
  ·limed' ·lim'ing
sub·lim'i·nal
sub·lim'i·ty
sub·ma·chine' gun
sub·mar'gin·al
sub'ma·rine'
sub·merge'
  ·merged'
  ·merg'ing
sub·mer'gence
sub·mer'gi·ble
sub·merse'
  ·mersed' ·mers'ing
sub·mers'i·ble
sub·mer'sion
sub·mis'sion
sub·mis'sive
sub·mit'
  ·mit'ted ·mit'ting
sub·nor'mal
sub·or'bit·al
sub·or'di·nate'
  ·nat'ed ·nat'ing
sub·or'di·na'tion
sub·orn'
sub'plot'
sub·poe'na
  ·naed ·na·ing
sub·scribe'
  ·scribed' ·scrib'ing
sub·scrib'er
sub'script'
sub·scrip'tion
sub'se·quent'
sub'se·quent·ly
sub·ser'vi·ence
sub·ser'vi·ent
sub·set'
sub·side'
sub·sid'ence
sub·sid'i·ar'y
  ·ies
sub'si·di·za'tion
sub'si·dize'
  ·dized' ·diz'ing
sub'si·dy
  ·dies
sub·sist'
sub·sist'ence
sub'soil'
sub·son'ic
sub'stance
sub·stand'ard
sub·stan'tial
sub·stan'tial·ly
sub·stan'ti·ate'
  ·at'ed ·at'ing
sub·stan'ti·a'tion
sub·stan·tive

sub'sta'tion
sub'sti·tut'a·ble
sub'sti·tute'
  ·tut'ed ·tut'ing
sub'sti·tu'tion
sub'stra'tum
  ·ta *or* ·tums
sub'struc'ture
sub·sume'
  ·sumed' ·sum'ing
sub'teen'
sub·ten'an·cy
sub·ten'ant
sub'ter·fuge'
sub'ter·ra'ne·an
sub'text'
sub'ti'tle
sub'tle
  ·tler ·tlest
sub'tle·ty
  ·ties
sub'tly
sub·to'tal
sub·tract'
sub·trac'tion
sub·tra·hend'
sub·trop'i·cal
sub'urb
sub·ur'ban
sub·ur'ban·ite'
sub·ur'bi·a
sub·ver'sion
sub·ver'sive
sub·vert'
sub'way'
suc·ceed'
suc·cess'
suc·cess'ful
suc·cess'ful·ly
suc·ces'sion
suc·ces'sive
suc·ces'sive·ly
suc·ces'sor
suc·cinct'
suc·cinct'ly
suc·cinct'ness
suc'cor
  (*help;* see SUCKER)
suc'co·tash'
suc'cu·lence *or*
  ·len·cy
suc'cu·lent
suc·cumb'
such
such'like'
suck
suck'er
  (*one that sucks;*
  see SUCCOR)
suck'le
  ·led ·ling
suck'ling
su'crose'
suc'tion
sud'den
sud'den·ly
sud'den·ness
su·dor·if'ic

suds
suds'y
  ·i·er ·i·est
sue
  sued su'ing
suede *or* suède
su'et
suf'fer
suf'fer·ance
suf'fer·er
suf'fer·ing
suf·fice'
  ·ficed' ·fic'ing
suf·fi'cien·cy
suf·fi'cient
suf·fi'cient·ly
suf'fix
suf'fo·cate'
  ·cat'ed ·cat'ing
suf'fo·ca'tion
suf'frage
suf'fra·gette'
suf'fra·gist
suf·fuse'
  ·fused' ·fus'ing
suf·fu'sion
sug'ar
sug'ar·coat'
sug'ar·less
sug'ar·plum'
sug'ar·y
sug·gest'
sug·gest'i·bil'i·ty
sug·gest'i·ble
sug·ges'tion
sug·ges'tive
sug·ges'tive·ly
su'i·ci'dal
su'i·cide'
suit
  (*a set; to be right for;* see SUITE)
suit'a·bil'i·ty
suit'a·ble
suit'a·bly
suit'case'
suite
  (*rooms; furniture;* see SUIT, SWEET)
suit'ing
suit'or
su'ki·ya'ki
sul'fa
sul'fate'
sul'fide'
sul'fur
sul·fu'ric
sul'fu·rous
sulk
sulk'i·ly
sulk'i·ness
sulk'y
  ·ies
  ·i·er ·i·est
sul'len
sul'len·ly
sul'len·ness
sul'ly
  ·lied ·ly·ing

sul'phur
sul'tan
sul·tan'a
sul'tan·ate
sul'try
  ·tri·er ·tri·est
sum
  summed
  sum'ming
su'mac' *or* ·mach'
sum·mar'i·ly
sum'ma·rize'
  ·rized' ·riz'ing
sum'ma·ry
  ·ries
  (*brief account*)
sum·ma'tion
sum'mer
sum'mer·house'
sum'mer·time'
sum'mer·y (*like summer*)
sum'mit
sum'mon
sum'mon·er
sum'mons
  ·mons·es
su'mo wrestling
sump
sump'tu·ous
sun
  sunned sun'ning
sun'bathe'
sun'bath'er
sun'beam'
sun'bon'net
sun'burn'
sun'burst'
sun'dae
Sun'day
sun'der
sun'di'al
sun'down'
sun'-dried'
sun'dries
sun'dry
sun'fish'
sun'flow'er
sung
sun'glass'es
sunk
sunk'en
sun'lamp'
sun'light'
sun'lit'
sun'ni·ness
sun'ny
  ·ni·er ·ni·est
sun'rise'
sun'roof'
sun'screen'
sun'set'
sun'shade'
sun'shine'
sun'shin'y
sun'spot'
sun'stroke'
sun'suit'

sun'tan'
sun'-tanned'
sun'up'
sup
  supped sup'ping
su'per
su'per·a·bun'·dance
su'per·a·bun'dant
su'per·an'nu·at'ed
su·perb'
su·perb'ly
su'per·car'go
  ·goes *or* ·gos
su'per·charge'
su'per·charg'er
su'per·cil'i·ous
su'per·con·duc·tiv'i·ty
su'per·e'go
  ·gos
su'per·e·rog'a·to'ry
su'per·fi'cial
su'per·fi'ci·al'i·ty
  ·ties
su'per·fi'cial·ly
su'per·flu'i·ty
su·per'flu·ous
su'per·high'way'
su'per·hu'man
su'per·im·pose'
  ·posed' ·pos'ing
su'per·in·tend'
su'per·in·tend'ent
su·pe'ri·or
su·pe'ri·or'i·ty
su·per'la·tive
su·per'la·tive·ly
su'per·man'
su'per·mar'ket
su'per·nal
su'per·nat'u·ral
su'per·no'va
  ·vae *or* ·vas
su'per·nu'mer·ar'y
  ·ies
su'per·sat'u·rate'
su'per·sat'u·ra'tion
su'per·scribe'
su'per·script'
su'per·sede'
  ·sed'ed ·sed'ing
su'per·sen'si·tive
su'per·son'ic
su'per·star'
su'per·sti'tion
su'per·sti'tious
su'per·struc'ture
su'per·tank'er
su'per·vene'
  ·vened' ·ven'ing
su'per·vise'
  ·vised' ·vis'ing
su'per·vi'sion
su'per·vi'sor
su'per·vi'so·ry
su'pine'
sup'per
sup·plant'

sup'ple
  ·pler ·plest
sup'ple·ment
sup'ple·men'tal
sup'ple·men'ta·ry
sup'pli·ant
sup'pli·cant
sup'pli·cate'
  ·cat'ed ·cat'ing
sup'pli·ca'tion
sup·pli'er
sup·ply'
  ·plies'
  ·plied' ·ply'ing
sup·ply'-side'
sup·port'
sup·port'a·ble
sup·port'er
sup·port'ive
sup·pose'
  ·posed' ·pos'ing
sup·posed'
sup·pos'ed·ly
sup'po·si'tion
sup·pos'i·to'ry
  ·ries
sup·press'
sup·pres'sant
sup·press'i·ble
sup·pres'sion
sup·pres'sor
sup'pu·rate'
  ·rat'ed ·rat'ing
su'pra·na'tion·al
su·prem'a·cist
su·prem'a·cy
su·preme'
su·preme'ly
sur·cease'
sur'charge'
sure
  sur'er sur'est
sure'-fire'
sure'-foot'ed
sure'ly
  (*certainly;* see SURLY)
sure'ness
sur'e·ty
  ·ties
surf
  (*waves;* see SERF)
sur'face
  ·faced ·fac·ing
surf'board'
sur'feit
surf'er
surf'ing
surge
  surged surg'ing
  (*sudden increase;* see SERGE)
sur'geon
sur'ger·y
  ·ies
sur'gi·cal
sur'gi·cal·ly
sur'li·ness

sur'ly
  ·li·er ·li·est
  (*rude;* see SURELY)
sur·mise'
  ·mised' ·mis'ing
sur·mount'
sur·mount'a·ble
sur'name'
sur·pass'
sur'plice (*cloak*)
sur'plus' (*excess*)
sur·prise'
  ·prised' ·pris'ing
sur·pris'ing·ly
sur·re'al
sur·re'al·ism'
sur·re'al·ist
sur·re'al·is'tic
sur·ren'der
sur'rep·ti'tious
sur'rey
  ·reys
sur'ro·gate'
sur·round'
sur·round'ings
sur'tax'
sur·veil'lance
sur·vey'
  ·veys
sur·vey'ing
sur·vey'or
sur·viv'a·ble
sur·viv'al
sur·viv'al·ist
sur·vive'
  ·vived' ·viv'ing
sur·vi'vor
sus·cep'ti·bil'i·ty
sus·cep'ti·ble
su'shi
sus·pect'
sus·pend'
sus·pend'ed ani-mation
sus·pend'ers
sus·pense'
sus·pense'ful
sus·pen'sion
sus·pi'cion
sus·pi'cious
sus·tain'
sus·tain'a·ble
sus'te·nance
sut'ler
su'ture
  ·tured ·tur·ing
su'ze·rain'
svelte
swab
  swabbed
  swab'bing
swad'dle
  ·dled ·dling
swag'ger
swal'low
swal'low-tailed'
swam
swa'mi
  ·mis

swamp
swamp'y
  ·i·er ·i·est
swan
swank
swap
  swapped
  swap'ping
swarm
swarth'y
  ·i·er ·i·est
swash'buck'ler
swash'buck'ling
swas'ti·ka
swat
  swat'ted swat'ting
swatch
swath n. (*strip*)
swathe v., n.
  swathed
  swath'ing
  (*bandage*)
swat'ter
sway
sway'backed'
swear
  swore sworn
  swear'ing
swear'er
swear'word'
sweat
  sweat *or* sweat'ed,
  sweat'ing
sweat'band'
sweat'er
sweat'shop'
sweat'y
  ·i·er ·i·est
Swed'ish
sweep
  swept sweep'ing
sweep'er
sweep'ing
sweep'ings
sweep'stakes'
  ·stakes'
sweet
  (*like sugar;* see SUITE)
sweet'bread'
sweet'en
sweet'en·er
sweet'heart'
sweet'ish
sweet'ly
sweet'meat'
sweet'ness
sweet'-talk'
swell
  swelled, swelled
  or swol'len,
  swell'ing
swell'head'ed
swell'ing
swel'ter
swel'ter·ing
swept
swerve
  swerved swerv'ing
swift

swift'ly
swift'ness
swig
  swigged swig'ging
swill
swim
  swam swum
  swim'ming
swim'mer
swim'suit'
swin'dle
  ·dled ·dling
swin'dler
swine
  swine
swing
  swung swing'ing
swing'er
swipe
  swiped swip'ing
swirl
swirl'y
swish
Swiss
switch
switch'back'
switch'blade'
switch'board'
switch'er
switch'-hit'ter
swiv'el
  ·eled or ·elled
  ·el·ing or ·el·ling
swiz'zle stick
swob
  swobbed
  swob'bing
swol'len
swoon
swoop
sword
sword'fish'
sword'play'
swords'man
swore
sworn
swum
swung
syb'a·rit'ic
syc'a·more'
syc'o·phan·cy
syc'o·phant
syl·lab'ic
syl·lab'i·fi·ca'tion
syl·lab'i·fy'
  ·fied' ·fy'ing
syl'la·ble
syl'la·bus
  ·bus·es or ·bi'
syl'lo·gism'
sylph
syl'van
sym·bi·o'sis
sym·bi·ot'ic
sym'bol
  (a sign; see CYM-
  BAL)
sym·bol'ic
sym·bol'i·cal·ly

sym'bol·ism'
sym'bol·ize'
  ·ized' ·iz'ing
sym·met'ri·cal
sym·met'ri·cal·ly
sym'me·try
  ·tries
sym·pa·thet'ic
sym·pa·thet'i·cal·ly
sym'pa·thize'
  ·thized' ·thiz'ing
sym'pa·thiz'er
sym'pa·thy
  ·thies
sym·phon'ic
sym'pho·ny
  ·nies
sym·po'si·um
  ·si·ums or ·si·a
symp'tom
symp'to·mat'ic
syn'a·gogue'
syn'apse'
sync or synch
  synced or synched,
  sync'ing or
  synch'ing
syn'chro·ni·za'tion
syn'chro·nize'
  ·nized' ·niz'ing
syn'chro·nous
syn'co·pate'
  ·pat'ed ·pat'ing
syn'co·pa'tion
syn'di·cate'
  ·cat'ed ·cat'ing
syn'di·ca'tion
syn'drome'
syn'er·gism'
syn'er·gis'tic
syn'od
syn'o·nym
syn·on'y·mous
syn·on'y·my
  ·mies
syn·op'sis
  ·ses
syn·tac'tic or ·ti·cal
syn·tac'ti·cal·ly
syn'tax'
syn'the·sis
  ·ses'
syn'the·size'
  ·sized' ·siz'ing
syn'the·siz'er
syn·thet'ic
syn·thet'i·cal·ly
syph'i·lis
syph'i·lit'ic
sy·ringe'
  ·ringed' ·ring'ing
syr'up
syr'up·y
sys'tem
sys'tem·at'ic
sys'tem·at'i·cal·ly
sys'tem·a·tize'
  ·tized' ·tiz'ing
sys·tem'ic

sys'to·le'
sys·tol'ic

T

tab
tab'by
  ·bies
tab'er·nac'le
ta'ble
  ·bled ·bling
tab'leau'
  ·leaux' or ·leaus
ta'ble·cloth'
ta'ble d'hôte'
ta'ble-hop'
ta'ble·land'
ta'ble·spoon'
ta'ble·spoon'ful
  ·fuls
tab'let
ta'ble·ware'
tab'loid'
ta·boo'
  ·boos
  ·booed'
  ·boo'ing
tab'u·lar
tab'u·late'
  ·lat'ed ·lat'ing
tab'u·la'tion
tab'u·la'tor
ta·chom'e·ter
tac'it
tac'it·ly
tac'i·turn'
tack
tack'i·ness
tack'le
  ·led ·ling
tack'ler
tack'y
  ·i·er ·i·est
ta'co
  ·cos
tact
tact'ful
tact'ful·ly
tac'ti·cal
tac·ti'cian
tac'tics
tac'tile
tact'less
tad
tad'pole'
taf'fe·ta
taf'fy
tag
  tagged tag'ging
tag'board'
tai' chi'
tai'ga
tail
  (rear end; see
  TALE)
tail'back'
tail'gate'
  ·gat'ed ·gat'ing

tail'ings
tail'less
tail'light'
tai'lor
tai'lor-made'
tail'pipe'
tail'spin'
taint
taint'ed
take
  took tak'en
  tak'ing
take'off'
take'out'
take'o'ver
tak'er
tak'ing
talc
tal'cum
tale
  (story; see TAIL)
tale'bear'er
tal'ent
tal'ent·ed
tal'is·man
  ·mans
talk
talk'a·tive
talk'er
talk'ing-to'
talk'y
  ·i·er ·i·est
tall
tal'low
tal'ly
  ·lies ·lied ·ly·ing
tal'ly·ho'
Tal'mud
tal'on
tam
tam'a·ble or tame'·
ta·ma'le
tam'a·rack'
tam'bou·rine'
tame
  tam'er tam'est
  tamed tam'ing
tame'ly
tame'ness
tam'-o'-shan'ter
tamp
tam'per
tam'pon'
tan
  tan'ner tan'nest
  tanned tan'ning
tan'a·ger
tan'dem
tang
tan'gent
tan·gen'tial
tan·ge·rine'
tan'gi·ble
tan'gi·bly
tan'gle
  ·gled ·gling
tan'go
  ·gos

tang'y
  ·i·er ·i·est
tank
tank'ard
tank'er
tank'ful'
  ·fuls
tan'ner
tan'ner·y
  ·ies
tan'nic
tan'nin
tan'ta·lize'
  ·lized' ·liz'ing
tan'ta·mount'
tan'trum
Tao'ism'
tap
  tapped tap'ping
tap'-dance'
  -danced' -danc'ing
tap'-danc'er
tape
  taped tap'ing
ta'per
  (candle; decrease;
  see TAPIR)
tape'-re·cord'
tap'es·try
  ·tries
tape'worm'
tap'i·o'ca
ta'pir
  (animal; see
  TAPER)
tap'pet
tap'room'
tap'root'
taps
tar
  tarred tar'ring
tar'an·tel'la
ta·ran'tu·la
tar'di·ly
tar'di·ness
tar'dy
  ·di·er ·di·est
tare
  tared tar'ing
  (weight deduction;
  see TEAR)
tar'get
tar'iff
tar'nish
ta'ro
  ·ros
  (plant)
tar'ot (playing
  cards)
tarp
tar·pau'lin
tar'pon
tar'ra·gon'
tar'ry
  ·ri·er ·ri·est
  (covered with tar)
tar'ry
  ·ried ·ry·ing
  (delay)
tart

tar'tan
tar'tar
task
task'mas'ter
tas'sel
taste
  tast'ed tast'ing
taste'ful
taste'less
tast'er
tast'i·ness
tast'y
  ·i·er ·i·est
tat'ter
tat'tered
tat'tle
  ·tled ·tling
tat'tler
tat'tle·tale'
tat·too'
  ·toos'
  ·tooed' ·too'ing
tau
taught
  (form of teach; see
  TAUT)
taunt
Tau'rus
taut
  (tight; see TAUGHT)
tau·to·log'i·cal
tau·tol'o·gy
  ·gies
tav'ern
taw'dry
  ·dri·er ·dri·est
taw'ny
  ·ni·er ·ni·est
tax
tax'a·ble
tax·a'tion
tax'-de·duct'i·ble
tax'-ex·empt'
tax'i
  ·is
  ·ied
  ·i·ing or ·y·ing
tax'i·cab'
tax'i·der'mist
tax'i·der'my
tax'i·me'ter
tax·on'o·mist
tax·on'o·my
  ·mies
tax'pay'er
T'-bone' steak
tea
  (beverage; see
  TEE)
tea'ber'ry
  ·ries
teach
  taught teach'ing
teach'a·ble
teach'er
teach'ing
tea'cup'
tea'cup·ful'
  ·fuls'
teak

tea'ket'tle
teal
team
   (*group;* see TEEM)
team'mate'
team'ster
team'work'
tea'pot'
tear
   tore torn tear'ing
   (*rip;* see TARE)
tear
   teared tear'ing
   (*eye fluid;* see
   TIER)
tear'drop'
tear'ful
tear'ful·ly
tear'-gas'
tea'room'
tear'y
   ·i·er ·i·est
tease
   teased teas'ing
tea'sel
teas'er
tea'spoon'
tea'spoon·ful'
   ·fuls'
teat
tech'ni·cal
tech'ni·cal'i·ty
   ·ties
tech'ni·cal·ly
tech·ni'cian
tech'ni·col'or
tech·nique'
tech'noc·ra·cy
tech'no·crat'
tech'no·log'i·cal
tech·nol'o·gy
te'di·ous
te'di·um
tee
   teed tee'ing
   (*ball-holder; to*
   anger; see TEA)
teem
   (*abound;* see
   TEAM)
teen
teen'age'
teen'ag'er
tee'ny
   ·ni·er ·ni·est
teen'y-bop'per
tee'ny-wee'ny
tee'pee
tee'ter
tee'ter-tot'ter
teeth
   (*pl. of* tooth)
teethe
   teethed teeth'ing
   (*grow teeth*)
tee'to'tal·er *or*
   ·tal·ler
tef'lon'
tek'tite'

tel'e·cast'
   ·cast' *or* ·cast'ed
   ·cast'ing
tel'e·cast'er
tel'e·com·mu'ni·ca
   'tion
tel'e·con'fer·ence
tel'e·gram'
tel'e·graph'
te·leg'ra·pher
tel'e·graph'ic
te·leg'ra·phy
tel'e·ki·ne'sis
tel'e·mar'ket·ing
tel'e·me'ter
te·lem'e·try
te'le·o·log'i·cal
te·le·ol'o·gy
tel'e·path'ic
te·lep'a·thy
tel'e·phone'
   ·phoned' ·phon'ing
tel'e·phon'ic
te·leph'o·ny
tel'e·pho'to
tel'e·pho'to·graph'
tel'e·pho·tog'ra·phy
tel'e·proc'ess·ing
tel'e·promp'ter
tel'e·scope'
   ·scoped' ·scop'ing
tel'e·scop'ic
tel'e·thon'
tel'e·type'writ'er
tel'e·vise'
   ·vised' ·vis'ing
tel'e·vi'sion
tel'ex'
tell
   told tell'ing
tell'a·ble
tell'er
tell'ing
tell'ing·ly
tell'tale'
tem'blor'
te·mer'i·ty
tem'per
tem'per·a
tem'per·a·ment
tem'per·a·men'tal
tem'per·ance
tem'per·ate
tem'per·a·ture
tem'pered
tem'pest
tem·pes'tu·ous
tem'plate
tem'ple
tem'po
   ·pos *or* ·pi
tem'po·ral
tem'po·rar'i·ly
tem'po·rar'y
tem'po·rize'
   ·rized' ·riz'ing
tempt
temp·ta'tion

tempt'er
tempt'ing
tempt'ress
ten
ten'a·ble
te·na'cious
te·nac'i·ty
ten'an·cy
ten'ant
tend
tend'en·cy
   ·cies
ten·den'tious
ten'der (*soft; offer*)
tend'er (*one who*
   tends)
ten'der·foot'
   ·foots' *or* ·feet'
ten'der·heart'ed
ten'der·ize'
   ·ized' ·iz'ing
ten'der·iz'er
ten'der·loin'
ten'di·ni'tis
ten'don
ten'dril
ten'e·ment
ten'et
ten'fold'
Ten'nes·see'
ten'nis
ten'on
ten'or
   (*tendency; singer;*
   see TENURE)
ten'pins'
tense
   tens'er tens'est
   tensed tens'ing
tense'ly
tense'ness *or*
   ten'si·ty
ten'sile
ten'sion
tent
ten'ta·cle
ten'ta·tive
ten'ta·tive·ly
tenth
ten'u·ous
ten'ure
   (*time held;* see
   TENOR)
te'pee
tep'id
te·qui'la
ter'cen·te'nar·y
   ·ies
term
ter'ma·gant
ter'mi·na·ble
ter'mi·na·bly
ter'mi·nal
ter'mi·nate'
   ·nat'ed ·nat'ing
ter'mi·na'tion
ter'mi·nol'o·gy
   ·gies

ter'mi·nus
   ·ni' *or* ·nus·es
ter'mite'
   (*bird;* see TURN)
ter'na·ry
ter'race
   ·raced ·rac·ing
ter'ra cot'ta
ter'ra fir'ma
ter·rain'
ter'ra·pin
ter·rar'i·um
   ·i·ums *or* ·i·a
ter·raz'zo
ter·res'tri·al
ter'ri·ble
ter'ri·bly
ter'ri·er
ter·rif'ic
ter·rif'i·cal·ly
ter'ri·fy'
   ·fied' ·fy'ing
ter'ri·to'ri·al
ter'ri·to'ry
   ·ries
ter'ror
ter'ror·ism'
ter'ror·ist
ter'ror·is'tic
ter'ror·i·za'tion
ter'ror·ize'
   ·ized' ·iz'ing
ter'ry
terse
   ters'er ters'est
ter'ti·ar'y
test
test'a·ble
tes'ta·ment
tes'ta·men'ta·ry
tes'tate'
tes'ta'tor
test'er
tes'ti·cle
tes'ti·fi'er
tes'ti·fy'
   ·fied' ·fy'ing
tes'ti·ly
tes'ti·mo'ni·al
tes'ti·mo'ny
   ·nies
tes'ti·ness
tes'tis
   ·tes'
tes·tos'ter·one'
tes'ty
   ·ti·er ·ti·est
tet'a·nus
tête'-à-tête'
teth'er
tet'ra
tet'ra·cy'cline
tet'ra·he'dron
   ·drons *or* ·dra
Tex'as
text
text'book'
tex'tile'

tex'tu·al
tex'tur·al
tex'ture
thal'a·mus
   ·mi'
tha·lid'o·mide'
thal'lo·phyte'
than
   (*compared to;* see
   THEN)
thank
thank'ful
thank'ful·ly
thank'less
thanks
thanks'giv'ing
that
   those
thatch
thaw
the
the'a·ter *or* ·tre
the·at'ri·cal
thee
theft
their
   (*form of* they; see
   THERE, THEY'RE)
theirs
   (*belonging to*
   them; see THERE'S)
the'ism'
the'ist
the·is'tic
them
the·mat'ic
theme
them·selves'
then
   (*at that time;* see
   THAN)
thence'forth'
the·oc'ra·cy
   ·cies
the'o·lo'gi·an
the'o·log'i·cal
the·ol'o·gy
   ·gies
the'o·rem
the'o·ret'i·cal
the'o·ret'i·cal·ly
the'o·re·ti'cian *or*
   the'o·rist
the'o·rize'
   ·rized' ·riz'ing
the'o·ry
   ·ries
the·os'o·phist
the·os'o·phy
ther'a·peu'tic
ther'a·peu'tics
ther'a·pist
ther'a·py
   ·pies
there
   (*at that place;* see
   THEIR, THEY'RE)
there'a·bouts'
there·af'ter
there·at'

there·by'
there·for' (*for it*)
there'fore' (*for that*
   reason)
there·in'
there·of'
there·on'
there's
   (*there is;* see
   THEIRS)
there·to'
there'to·fore'
there'up·on'
there·with'
ther'mal
ther'mo·dy·nam'ic
ther'mo·dy·nam'ics
ther·mom'e·ter
ther'mo·nu'cle·ar
ther'mo·plas'tic
ther'mos
ther'mo·stat'
ther'mo·stat'ic
the·sau'rus
   ·ri' *or* ·rus·es
these
the'sis
   ·ses'
thes'pi·an
they
they're
   (*they are;* see
   THEIR, THERE)
thi'a·mine'
thick
thick'en
thick'en·ing
thick'et
thick'ness
thick'set'
thick'-skinned'
thief
   thieves
thieve
   thieved thiev'ing
thiev'er·y
   ·ies
thiev'ish
thigh
thigh'bone'
thim'ble
thim'ble·ful'
   ·fuls'
thin
   thin'ner thin'nest
   thinned thin'ning
thine
thing
think
   thought think'ing
think'er
thin'ner
thin'-skinned'
third
third'-class'
third'-rate'
thirst
thirst'i·ly
thirst'i·ness

thirst'y
  ·i·er ·i·est
thir'teen'
thir'teenth'
thir'ti·eth
thir'ty
  ·ties
this
  these
this'tle
this'tle·down'
thith'er
thong
tho·rac'ic
tho'rax'
  ·rax'es *or* ·ra·ces'
tho'ri·um
thorn
thorn'y
  ·i·er ·i·est
thor'ough
thor'ough·bred'
thor'ough·fare'
thor'ough·go'ing
thor'ough·ly
thor'ough·ness
those
thou
though
thought
thought'ful
thought'ful·ly
thought'ful·ness
thought'less
thought'less·ly
thought'less·ness
thou'sand
thou'sandth
thrall
thrall'dom *or*
  thral'dom
thrash
thrash'er
thread
thread'bare'
thread'y
  ·i·er ·i·est
threat
threat'en
three
three'-deck'er
three'-
  di·men'sion·al
three'fold'
three'-quar'ter
three'some
three'-way'
three'-wheel'er
thresh
thresh'er
thresh'old'
threw
  (*form of* throw; see
  THROUGH)
thrice
thrift
thrift'i·ness

thrift'y
  ·i·er ·i·est
thrill
thrill'er
thrive
  thrived *or* throve,
  thrived *or*
  thriv'en, thriv'ing
throat
throat'y
  ·i·er ·i·est
throb
  throbbed
  throb'bing
throe
  (*pang;* see THROW)
throm·bo'sis
throm'bus
  ·bi'
throne
throng
throt'tle
  ·tled ·tling
through
  (*from end to end
  of;* see THREW)
through·out'
through'way'
throve
throw
  threw thrown
  throw'ing
  (*hurl;* see THROE)
throw'a·way'
throw'back'
throw'er
thrum
  thrummed
  thrum'ming
thrush
thrust
  thrust thrust'ing
thru'way'
thud
  thud'ded thud'd·
  ing
thug
thumb
thumb'nail'
thumb'screw'
thumb'tack'
thump
thump'ing
thun'der
thun·der·bolt'
thun·der·clap'
thun·der·cloud'
thun·der·head'
thun·der·ous
thun·der·show'er
thun·der·storm'
thun·der·struck'
Thurs'day
thus
thwart
thy
thyme
  (*herb;* see TIME)
thy'mo·sin
thy'mus

thy'roid'
thy·self'
ti·ar'a
tib'i·a
  ·i·ae *or* ·i·as
tic (*muscle spasm*)
tick (*click; insect*)
tick'er
tick'et
tick'ing
tick'le
  ·led ·ling
tick'ler
tick'lish
tick'-tack-toe' *or*
  tic'-tac-toe'
tick'tock'
tid'al
tid'bit'
tid'dly·winks'
tide
  tid'ed tid'ing
tide'land'
tide'wa'ter
ti'di·ly
ti'di·ness
ti'dings
ti'dy
  ·di·er ·di·est
  ·died ·dy·ing
tie
  tied, ty'ing *or*
  tie'ing
tie'back'
tie'break'er
tie'-dye'
  -dyed' -dye'ing
tie'-in'
tier
  (*row;* see TEAR)
ti'er
  (*one that ties;* see
  TIRE)
tie'-up'
tiff
ti'ger
tight
tight'en
tight'fist'ed
tight'fit'ting
tight'knit'
tight'-lipped'
tight'rope'
tights
tight'wad'
ti'gress
til'de
tile
  tiled til'ing
til'ing
till
till'age
till'er
tilt
tilt'-top'
tim'ber (*wood*)
tim'bered
tim'ber·line'

tim'bre (*quality of
  sound*)
time
  timed tim'ing
  (*duration;* see
  THYME)
time'card'
time'-con·sum'ing
time'-hon'ored
time'keep'er
time'-lapse'
time'less
time'li·ness
time'ly
  ·li·er ·li·est
time'out'
time'piece'
tim'er
times
time'sav'ing
time'ta'ble
time'-test'ed
time'worn'
tim'id
ti·mid'i·ty
tim'ing
tim'or·ous
tim'o·thy
tim·pa'ni
tin
  tinned tin'ning
tinc'ture
  ·tured ·tur·ing
tin'der
tin'der·box'
tine
tin'foil'
tinge
  tinged tinge'ing *or*
  ting'ing
tin'gle
  ·gled ·gling
tin'gly
  ·glier ·gli·est
tin'ker
tin'ker·er
tin'kle
  ·kled ·kling
tin'ni·ness
tin'ny
  ·ni·er ·ni·est
tin'sel
tin'smith'
tint
tin'tin·nab'u·la'-
  tion
ti'ny
  ·ni·er ·ni·est
tip
  tipped tip'ping
tip'-off'
tip'per
tip'ple
  ·pled ·pling
tip'pler
tip'ster
tip'sy
  ·si·er ·si·est

tip'toe'
  ·toed' ·toe'ing
tip'top'
ti'rade'
tire
  tired tir'ing
  (*weary; rubber
  hoop;* see TIER)
tired
tired'ly
tired'ness
tire'less
tire'less·ly
tire'some
tis'sue
ti'tan
ti·tan'ic
ti·ta'ni·um
tithe
  tithed tith'ing
ti'tian
tit'il·late'
  ·lat'ed ·lat'ing
tit'il·la'tion
ti'tle
  ·tled ·tling
ti'tled
ti'tle·hold'er
ti'tlist
tit'mouse'
  ·mice'
tit'ter
tit'u·lar
tiz'zy
  ·zies
to
  (*toward;* see TOO,
  TWO)
toad
toad'stool'
toad'y
  ·ies
  ·ied ·y·ing
to'-and-fro'
toast
toast'er
toast'mas'ter
toast'y
  ·i·er ·i·est
to·bac'co
  ·cos
to·bac'co·nist
to·bog'gan
to·day'
tod'dle
  ·dled ·dling
tod'dler
tod'dy
  ·dies
to-do'
  ·dos
toe
  toed toe'ing
  (*part of foot;* see
  TOW)
toed
toe'-dance'
toe'-danc'er
toe'hold'
toe'less

toe'nail'
tof'fee *or* ·fy
to'fu
to'ga
  ·gas *or* ·gae
to·geth'er
to·geth'er·ness
tog'gle
  ·gled ·gling
togs
toil
toil'er
toi'let
toi'let·ry
  ·ries
toils
toil'some
to'ken
to'ken·ism'
told
tol'er·a·ble
tol'er·a·bly
tol'er·ance
tol'er·ant
tol'er·ate'
  ·at'ed ·at'ing
tol'er·a'tion
toll
toll'booth'
toll'gate'
tol'u·ene'
tom
tom'a·hawk'
to·ma'to
  ·toes
tomb
tom'boy'
tomb'stone'
tom'cat'
tome
tom'fool'er·y
to·mor'row
tom'-tom'
ton
ton'al
to·nal'i·ty
  ·ties
ton'al·ly
tone
  toned ton'ing
tone'arm'
tone'-deaf'
tone'less
ton'er
tong
tongs
tongue
tongue'-lash'ing
tongue'-tied'
ton'ic
to·night'
ton'nage
ton'sil
ton'sil·lec'to·my
  ·mies
ton'sil·li'tis
ton·so'ri·al

ton'sure
  ·sured ·sur·ing
to'nus
ton'y
  ·i·er ·i·est
too
  (also; see TO, TWO)
took
tool
tool'mak'er
toot
tooth
  teeth
tooth'ache'
tooth'brush'
toothed
tooth'less
tooth'paste'
tooth'pick'
tooth'some
tooth'y
  ·i·er ·i·est
top
  topped top'ping
to'paz'
top'coat'
top'-draw·er'
top'-flight'
top'-heav'y
top'ic
top'i·cal
top'less
top'-lev'el
top'most'
top'-notch'
top'o·graph'ic or
  ·i·cal
top'o·graph'i·cal·ly
to·pog'ra·phy
  ·phies
  (surface features;
  see TYPOGRAPHY)
top'per
top'ping
top'ple
  ·pled ·pling
top'sail'
top'-se'cret
top'side'
top'soil'
top'sy-tur'vy
to'rah or ·ra
torch
torch'bear'er
torch'light'
tore
tor'e·a·dor'
tor'ment'
tor·ment'ing·ly
tor·men'tor or
  ·ment'er
torn
tor·na'do
  ·does or ·dos
tor·pe'do
  ·does
  ·doed ·do·ing
tor'pid
tor'por

torque
tor'rent
tor·ren'tial
tor'rid
tor'sion
tor'so
  ·sos or ·si
tort (wrongful act)
torte (cake)
tor·til'la
tor'toise
tor'toise-shell'
tor'tu·ous (winding)
tor'ture
  ·tured ·tur·ing
tor'tur·er
tor'tur·ous (agoniz-
  ing)
toss
toss'up'
tot
to'tal
  ·taled or ·talled
  ·tal·ing or ·tal·ling
to·tal'i·tar'i·an
to·tal'i·tar'i·an·ism'
to·tal'i·ty
  ·ties
to'tal·ly
tote
  tot'ed tot'ing
to'tem
tot'ter
tou'can'
touch
touch-and-go
touch'down'
tou·ché'
touched
touch'ing
touch'stone'
touch'-type'
touch'y
  ·i·er ·i·est
tough
tough'en
tough'en·er
tough'-mind'ed
tou·pee'
tour
tour' de force'
  tours' de force'
tour'ism'
tour'ist
tour'ma·line
tour'na·ment
tour'ney
  ·neys
tour'ni·quet
tou'sle
  ·sled ·sling
tout
tow
  (pull; see TOE)
to'ward
tow'el
  ·eled or ·elled
  ·el·ing or ·el·ling

tow'el·ing or
  ·el·ling'
tow·er
tow'er·ing
tow'head'
tow'head'ed
tow'hee
tow'line'
town
town'ship
towns'man
towns'peo'ple
tow'rope'
tox·e'mi·a
tox'ic
tox'i·col'o·gist
tox'i·col'o·gy
tox'in
toy
trace
  traced trac'ing
trace'a·ble
trac'er
tra'che·a
  ·ae or ·as
tra'che·al
tra'che·ot'o·my
  ·mies
trac'ing
track (trace)
track'less
tract (land; leaflet)
trac'ta·ble
trac'tion
trac'tor
trac'tor-trail'er
trad'a·ble or
  trade'a·ble
trade
  trad'ed trad'ing
trade'-in'
trade'mark'
trade'-off'
trad'er
trades'man
trades'wom'an
tra·di'tion
tra·di'tion·al
tra·di'tion·al·ism'
tra·di'tion·al·ist
traf'fic
  ·ficked ·fick·ing
traf'fick·er
tra·ge'di·an
trag'e·dy
  ·dies
trag'ic
trag'i·cal·ly
trail
trail'blaz'er
trail'er
train
train·ee'
train'er
train'ing
traipse
  traipsed traips'ing
trait

trai'tor
trai'tor·ous
tra·jec'to·ry
  ·ries
tram
tram'mel
  ·meled or ·melled
  ·mel·ing or
  ·mel·ling
tramp
tram'ple
  ·pled ·pling
tram'po·line'
trance
tran'quil
  ·quil·er or
  ·quil·ler, ·quil·est
  or ·quil·lest
tran'quil·ize' or
  ·quil·lize'
  ·ized' or ·lized'
  ·iz'ing or ·liz'ing
tran'quil·iz'er or
  ·quil·liz'er
tran·quil'li·ty or
  ·quil'i·ty
tran'quil·ly
trans·act'
trans·ac'tion
trans'at·lan'tic
trans·ceiv'er
tran·scend'
tran·scend'ent
tran'scen·den'tal
tran'scen·den'tal·
  ism'
tran'scen·den'tal·ly
trans'con·ti·nen'tal
tran·scribe'
  ·scribed' ·scrib'ing
tran'script'
tran·scrip'tion
trans·duc'er
tran'sept'
trans·fer'
  ·ferred' ·fer'ring
trans·fer'a·ble
trans·fer'al
trans'fer·ence
trans·fig'u·ra'tion
trans·fig'ure
trans·fix'
trans·form'
trans'for·ma'tion
trans·form'er
trans·fuse'
trans·fu'sion
trans·gress'
trans·gres'sion
trans·gres'sor
tran'si·ence or
  ·en·cy
tran'si·ent
tran'si·ent·ly
tran·sis'tor
tran·sis'tor·ize'
  ·ized' ·iz'ing
trans'it
tran·si'tion

tran·si'tion·al
tran·si'tion·al·ly
tran'si·tive
tran'si·to'ry
trans·lat'a·ble
trans·late'
  ·lat'ed ·lat'ing
trans·la'tion
trans·la'tor
trans·lit'er·ate'
  ·at'ed ·at'ing
trans·lit'er·a'tion
trans·lu'cence or
  ·cen·cy
trans·lu'cent
trans·mi'grate'
trans'mi·gra'tion
trans·mis'si·ble
trans·mis'sion
trans·mit'
  ·mit'ted ·mit'ting
trans·mit'ta·ble
trans·mit'tal
trans·mit'tance
trans·mit'ter
trans'mu·ta'tion
trans·mute'
  ·mut'ed ·mut'ing
trans·na'tion·al
trans'o·ce·an'ic
tran'som
trans·par'en·cy
  ·cies
trans·par'ent
tran'spi·ra'tion
tran·spire'
  ·spired' ·spir'ing
trans·plant'
trans'plan·ta'tion
tran·spon'der
trans·port'
trans'por·ta'tion
trans·pos'a·ble
trans·pose'
  ·posed' ·pos'ing
trans'po·si'tion
trans·sex'u·al
trans·ship'
trans·ship'ment
tran'sub·stan'ti·a'·
  tion
trans·ver'sal
trans·verse'
trans·ves'tite'
trap
  trapped trap'ping
trap'door'
tra·peze'
tra·pe'zi·um
  ·zi·ums or ·zi·a
trap'e·zoid'
trap'e·zoi'dal
trap'per
trap'pings
trap'shoot'ing
trash
trash'y
  ·i·er ·i·est

trau'ma
  ·mas or ·ma·ta
trau·mat'ic
trau·mat'i·cal·ly
trau'ma·tize'
  ·tized' ·tiz'ing
trav·ail' (hard work)
trav'el
  ·eled or ·elled
  ·el·ing or ·el·ling
  (journey)
trav'el·er or
  trav'el·ler
trav'e·logue' or
  ·log'
tra·vers'a·ble
tra·verse'
  ·versed' ·vers'ing
trav'es·ty
  ·ties
  ·tied ·ty·ing
trawl
trawl'er
tray
  (holder; see TREY)
treach'er·ous
treach'er·y
  ·ies
tread
  trod, trod'den or
  trod, tread'ing
trea'dle
  ·dled ·dling
tread'mill'
trea'son
trea'son·a·ble
trea'son·ous
treas'ure
  ·ured ·ur·ing
treas'ur·er
treas'ure-trove'
treas'ur·y
  ·ies
treat
treat'a·ble
trea'tise
treat'ment
trea'ty
  ·ties
tre'ble
  ·bled ·bling
tree
  treed tree'ing
tree'less
tree'like'
tree'top'
tre'foil'
trek
  trekked trek'king
trel'lis
trem'a·tode'
trem'ble
  ·bled ·bling
tre·men'dous
trem'o·lo'
  ·los'
trem'or
trem'u·lous
trench
trench'ant

trend
trend'y
  ·i·er ·i·est
trep'i·da'tion
tres'pass
tres'pass·er
tress
tres'tle
trey
  (a three; see TRAY)
tri'a·ble
tri'ad'
tri·age'
tri'al
tri'an'gle
tri·an'gu·lar
tri·an'gu·late'
  ·lat'ed ·lat'ing
tri·an'gu·la'tion
tri·ath'lon'
trib'al
trib'al·ism'
trib'al·ly
tribe
tribes'man
trib'u·la'tion
tri·bu'nal
trib'une'
trib'u·tar'y
  ·ies
trib'ute
trice
tri·cen·ten'ni·al
tri'ceps'
  ·ceps' or ·ceps'es
tri·cer'a·tops'
trich'i·no'sis
trick
trick'er·y
  ·ies
trick'i·ly
trick'i·ness
trick'le
  ·led ·ling
trick'le·down'
trick'ster
trick'y
  ·i·er ·i·est
tri'col'or
tri'cy·cle
tri'dent
tried
tri·en'ni·al
tri·en'ni·al·ly
tri'er
tri'fle
  ·fled ·fling
tri'fler
tri'fling
tri'fo'cals
trig
trig'ger
tri·glyc'er·ide'
trig'o·no·met'ric
trig'o·nom'e·try
tri·lin'gual
trill
tril'lion

tril'lionth
tril'li·um
tril'o·gy
  ·gies
trim
  trim'mer
  trim'mest
  trimmed
  trim'ming
tri·mes'ter
trim'mer
trim'ming
trim'ness
trin'i·ty
  ·ties
trin'ket
tri·no'mi·al
tri'o
  ·os
trip
  tripped trip'ping
tri·par'tite'
tripe
trip'ham'mer
tri'ple
  tri'pled tri'pling
tri'plet
trip'li·cate
tri'ply
tri'pod'
trip'per
trip'tych
tri·sect'
trite
  trit'er trit'est
trite'ly
trite'ness
trit'i·um
tri'umph
tri·um'phal
tri·um'phant
tri·um'vi·rate
tri·va'lent
triv'et
triv'i·a
triv'i·al
triv'i·al'i·ty
  ·ties
triv'i·al·ize'
  ·ized' ·iz'ing
triv'i·al·ly
trod
trod'den
troi'ka
troll
trol'ley
  ·leys
trol'lop
trom'bone'
trom·bon'ist
troop
  (of soldiers; see
  TROUPE)
troop'er
trope
tro'phy
  ·phies
trop'ic

trop'i·cal
tro'pism
tro'po·sphere'
trot
  trot'ted trot'ting
trot'ter
trou'ba·dour'
trou'ble
  ·bled ·bling
trou'ble·mak'er
trou'ble-shoot'er
trou'ble·some
trough
trounce
  trounced
  trounc'ing
trounc'er
troupe
  trouped troup'ing
  (of actors; see
  TROOP)
troup'er
trou'sers
trous·seau'
  ·seaux' or ·seaus'
trout
trow'el
  ·eled or ·elled
  ·el·ing or ·el·ling
troy
tru'an·cy
  ·cies
tru'ant
truce
truck
truck'er
truc'u·lence
truc'u·lent
trudge
  trudged trudg'ing
true
  tru'er tru'est
  trued, tru'ing or
  true'ing
true'-blue'
true'-life'
true'love'
truf'fle
tru'ism'
tru'ly
trump
trumped'-up'
trump'er·y
  ·ies
trum'pet
trum'pet·er
trun'cate'
  ·cat'ed ·cat'ing
trun·ca'tion
trun'cheon
trun'dle
  ·dled ·dling
trunk
truss
trust
trust·ee'
  (manager; see
  TRUSTY)
trust·ee'ship
trust'ful

trust'ful·ly
trust'ing
trust'wor'thi·ness
trust'wor'thy
  ·thi·er ·thi·est
trust'y
  ·i·er ·i·est
  (relied upon; see
  TRUSTEE)
truth
truth'ful
truth'ful·ly
truth'ful·ness
try
  tries
  tried try'ing
try'ing
try'ing·ly
try'out'
tryst
tsar
tsa·ri'na
tset'se fly
T'-shirt'
tsu·na'mi
tub
tu'ba
tub'al
tub'by
  ·bi·er ·bi·est
tube
tube'less
tu'ber
tu'ber·cle
tu·ber'cu·lar
tu·ber'cu·lin
tu·ber'cu·lo'sis
tu·ber'cu·lous
tu'ber·ous
tub'ing
tu'bu·lar
tu'bule'
tuck
tuck'er
Tues'day
tuft
tuft'ed
tug
  tugged tug'ging
tug'boat'
tu·i'tion
tu'la·re'mi·a
tu'lip
tum'ble
  ·bled ·bling
tum'ble·down'
tum'bler
tum'ble·weed'
tu·mes'cence
tu·mes'cent
tu'mid
tum'my
  ·mies
tu'mor
tu'mor·ous
tu'mult'
tu·mul'tu·ous
tun

tu'na
tun'a·ble or tune'·
tun'dra
tune
  tuned tun'ing
tune'ful
tune'less
tun'er
tune'up' or tune'-
  up'
tung'sten
tu'nic
tun'nel
  ·neled or ·nelled
  ·nel·ing or
  ·nel·ling
tu'pe·lo'
  ·los'
tur'ban (headdress)
tur'bid
tur'bine (engine)
tur'bo·charge'
tur'bo·fan'
tur'bo·jet'
tur'bo·prop'
tur'bot
tur'bu·lence
tur'bu·lent
tu·reen'
turf
tur'gid
tur·gid'i·ty
tur'gid·ly
tur'key
tur'moil'
turn
  (change direction;
  see TERN)
turn'a·bout'
turn'a·round'
turn'buck'le
turn'coat'
turn'down'
turn'er
turn'ing
tur'nip
turn'key'
  ·keys'
turn'off'
turn'out'
turn'o'ver
turn'pike'
turn'stile'
turn'ta'ble
tur'pen·tine'
tur'pi·tude'
tur'quoise'
tur'ret
tur'tle
tur'tle·dove'
tur'tle·neck'
tusk
tus'sle
  ·sled ·sling
tu'te·lage
tu'tor
tu·to'ri·al
tut'ti-frut'ti

tux
  tux'es
tux·e'do
  ·dos
TV
  TVs or TV's
twang
twang'y
  ·i·er ·i·est
tweak
tweed
tweed'y
  ·i·er ·i·est
tweet
tweet'er
tweez'ers
twelfth
twelve
twen'ti·eth
twen'ty
  ·ties
twerp
twice
twid'dle
  ·dled ·dling
twig
twi'light'
twill
twilled
twin
twine
  twined twin'ing
twin'-en'gined or
  ·gine
twinge
  twinged twing'ing
twi'-night' or
  twi'night'
twin'kle
  ·kled ·kling
twin'kling
twirl
twist
twist'er
twitch
twitch'y
  ·i·er ·i·est
twit'ter
two
  (a number; see TO,
  TOO)
two'-bit'
two'-edged'
two'-faced'
two'-fist'ed
two'fold'
two'-hand'ed
two'-leg'ged'
two'-piece'
two'-ply'
two'-sid'ed
two'some
two'-time'
two'-tim'er
two'-way'
ty·coon'
ty'ing
tyke
tym'pa·ni

tym·pan'ic
tym'pa·nist
typ'a·ble *or* type'·
type
  typed typ'ing
type'cast'
  ·cast' ·cast'ing
  (*in acting*)
type'-cast'
  -cast' -cast'ing
  (*in printing*)
type'script'
type'set'
type'set'ter
type'write'
type'writ'er
ty'phoid'
ty·phoon'
ty'phus
typ'i·cal
typ'i·cal·ly
typ'i·fi·ca'tion
typ'i·fy'
  ·fied' ·fy'ing
typ'ist
ty'po
  ·pos
ty·pog'ra·pher
ty'po·graph'i·cal
ty'po·graph'i·cal·ly
ty·pog'ra·phy
  (*setting of type;*
  see TOPOGRAPHY)
ty·ran'ni·cal
ty·ran'ni·cal·ly
tyr'an·nize'
  ·nized' ·niz'ing
ty·ran'no·saur'
tyr'an·nous
tyr'an·ny
  ·nies
ty'rant
tzar
tza·ri'na

U

u·biq'ui·tous
u·biq'ui·tous·ly
u·biq'ui·ty
ud'der
UFO
  UFOs *or* UFO's
ug'li·ness
ug'ly
  ·li·er ·li·est
u'kase
u'ku·le'le
ul'cer
ul'cer·ate'
  ·at'ed ·at'ing
ul'cer·a'tion
ul'cer·ous
ul'na
  ·nae *or* ·nas
ul'nar
ul'ster
ul·te'ri·or

ul'ti·mate
ul'ti·mate·ly
ul'ti·ma'tum
  ·tums *or* ·ta
ul'tra
ul'tra·con·serv'a·tive
ul'tra·ma·rine'
ul'tra·son'ic
ul'tra·sound'
ul'tra·vi'o·let
ul'u·late'
  ·lat'ed ·lat'ing
um'bel
um'ber
um·bil'i·cal
um·bil'i·cus
  ·ci'
um'bra
  ·brae *or* ·bras
um'brage
um·brel'la
u'mi·ak'
um'laut
ump
um'pire'
  ·pired' ·pir'ing
ump'teen'
ump'teenth'
un·a'ble
un'a·bridged'
un'ac·cept'a·ble
un'ac·com'pa·nied
un'ac·count'a·ble
un'ac·count'·
  ed-for'
un'ac·cus'tomed
un'a·dul'ter·at·ed
un'ad·vised'
un'af·fect'ed
un'-A·mer'i·can
u'nan·im'i·ty
u·nan'i·mous
u·nan'i·mous·ly
un·armed'
un'as·sum'ing
un'at·tached'
un'at·tend'ed
un'au·thor·ized'
un'a·vail'ing
un'a·ware'
un'a·wares'
un·backed'
un·bal'anced
un·beat'a·ble
un·beat'en
un'be·com'ing
un'be·known'
un'be·liev'a·ble
un'be·liev'er
un·bend'
  ·bent' *or* ·bend'ed
  ·bend'ing
un·bend'ing
un·bi'ased *or*
  ·assed
un·bid'den
un·bleached'
un·blem'ished

un·blush'ing
un·bolt'
un·born'
un·bound'ed
un·bri'dled
un·bro'ken
un·bur'den
un·but'ton
un·but'toned
un·called'-for'
un·can'ny
un·ceas'ing
un'cer·e·mo'ni·ous
un·cer'tain
un·cer'tain·ty
  ·ties
un·changed'
un·chang'ing
un·char'i·ta·ble
un·char'i·ta·bly
un·chart'ed
un·checked'
un·chris'tian
un'ci·al
un·civ'i·lized'
un·clasp'
un·clas'si·fied'
un'cle
un·clothe'
  ·clothed' *or* ·clad',
  ·cloth'ing
un·coil'
un·com'fort·a·ble
un·com'fort·a·bly
un·com·mit'ted
un·com'mon
un'com·mu'ni·ca'tive
un'com·pro·mis'ing
un'con·cerned'
un'con·di'tion·al
un'con·firmed'
un·con'scion·a·ble
un·con'scion·a·bly
un·con'scious
un'con·sti·tu'tion·al
un'con·vinced'
un·cork'
un·count'ed
un·cou'ple
  ·pled ·pling
un·couth'
un·cov'er
unc'tion
unc'tu·ous
unc'tu·ous·ness
un·cut'
un·daunt'ed
un'de·cid'ed
un'de·feat'ed
un'de·ni'a·ble
un'de·ni'a·bly
un'der
un'der·a·chieve'
  ·chieved'
  ·chiev'ing
un'der·a·chiev'er
un'der·age'
un'der·arm'

un'der·bel'ly
un'der·bid'
  ·bid' ·bid'ding
un'der·brush'
un'der·car'riage
un'der·charge'
  ·charged'
  ·charg'ing
un'der·class'
un'der·class'man
un'der·clothes'
un'der·coat'
un'der·cov'er
un'der·cur'rent
un'der·cut'
  ·cut' ·cut'ting
un'der·de·vel'oped
un'der·dog'
un'der·done'
un'der·em·ployed'
un'der·em·ploy'-
  ment
un'der·es'ti·mate'
  ·mat'ed ·mat'ing
un'der·es'ti·ma'-
  tion
un'der·foot'
un'der·gar'ment
un'der·go'
  ·went' ·gone'
  ·go'ing
un'der·grad'u·ate
un'der·ground'
un'der·growth'
un'der·hand'
un'der·hand'ed
un'der·hand'ed·ly
un'der·lay'
  ·laid' ·lay'ing
un'der·lie'
  ·lay' ·lain' ·ly'ing
un'der·line'
  ·lined' ·lin'ing
un'der·ling
un'der·ly'ing
un'der·mine'
  ·mined' ·min'ing
un'der·most'
un'der·neath'
un'der·nour'ished
un'der·pants'
un'der·pass'
un'der·paid'
un'der·pin'ning
un'der·priv'i·leged
un'der·rate'
  ·rat'ed ·rat'ing
un'der·score'
  ·scored' ·scor'ing
un'der·sea'
un'der·sec're·tar'y
  ·ies
un'der·sell'
  ·sold' ·sell'ing
un'der·shirt'
un'der·shorts'
un'der·shot'
un'der·side'
un'der·signed'

un'der·sized'
un'der·skirt'
un'der·staffed'
un'der·stand'
  ·stood' ·stand'ing
un'der·stand'a·ble
un'der·stand'a·bly
un'der·stand'ing
un'der·state'
  ·stat'ed ·stat'ing
un'der·stat'ed
un'der·state'ment
un'der·stud'y
  ·ies
un'der·take'
un'der·tak'er
un'der·tak'ing
un'der·things'
un'der·tone'
un'der·tow'
un'der·val'ue
  ·ued ·u·ing
un'der·wa'ter
un'der·way'
un'der·wear'
un'der·weight'
un'der·world'
un'der·write'
un'der·writ'er
un'de·served'
un'de·sir'a·ble
un'dies'
un·dis'ci·plined'
un'dis·cov'ered
un'dis·put'ed
un'dis·turbed'
un'di·vid'ed
un·do'
un·doc'u·ment'ed
un·do'ing
un·done'
un·doubt'ed
un·doubt'ed·ly
un·dress'
un·due'
un'du·lant
un'du·late'
  ·lat'ed ·lat'ing
un'du·la'tion
un·du'ly
un·dy'ing
un·earned'
un·earth'
un·earth'ly
un·eas'i·ly
un·eas'i·ness
un·eas'y
  ·i·er ·i·est
un·ed'u·cat'ed
un'em·ployed'
un'em·ploy'ment
un·end'ing
un·e'qual
un·e'qualed *or*
  ·qualled
un'e·quiv'o·cal
un'e·quiv'o·cal·ly

un·err'ing
un'es·sen'tial
un·e'ven
un·e'ven·ly
un'ex·cep'tion·a·ble
un'ex·cep'tion·al
un'ex·cep'tion·al·ly
un'ex·pect'ed
un'ex·pect'ed·ly
un·ex'pur·gat'ed
un·fail'ing
un·faith'ful
un'fa·mil'iar
un·feel'ing
un·feel'ing·ly
un·feigned'
un·fin'ished
un·fit'
un·flap'pa·ble
un·flinch'ing
un·fold'
un'for·get'ta·ble
un'for·giv'ing
un·for'tu·nate
un·for'tu·nate·ly
un·found'ed
un·friend'ly
un·ful·filled'
un·furl'
un·gain'ly
un·god'ly
un·gov'ern·a·ble
un·gra'cious
un·guard'ed
un'guent
un'gu·late
un·hand'
un·hap'pi·ly
un·hap'pi·ness
un·hap'py
  ·pi·er ·pi·est
un·health'y
  ·i·er ·i·est
un·heard'
un·heard'-of'
un·heed'ed
un·hinge'
  ·hinged' ·hing'ing
un·ho'ly
  ·li·er ·li·est
un·horse'
  ·horsed' ·hors'ing
u'ni·cam'er·al
u'ni·corn'
u'ni·cy'cle
u'ni·den'ti·fied'
u'ni·fi·ca'tion
u'ni·form'
u'ni·form'i·ty
u'ni·form'ly
un·fur'nished
u'ni·fy'
  ·fied' ·fy'ing
u'ni·lat'er·al
un'im·paired'
un'im·peach'a·ble
un'in·formed'

un·in·hab′it·ed
un·in·hib′it·ed
un′in·spired′
un′in·sured′
un·in′ter·est·ed
un·in′ter·est·ing
un′in·vit′ed
un′in·vit′ing
un′ion
un′ion·ize′
  ·ized′ ·iz′ing
u·nique′
u′ni·sex′
u′ni·son
u′nit
U′ni·tar′i·an
u′ni·tar′y
u·nite′
  ·nit′ed ·nit′ing
u′nit·ize′
  ·ized′ ·iz′ing
u′ni·ty
  ·ties
u′ni·va′lent
u′ni·valve′
u′ni·ver′sal
u′ni·ver·sal′i·ty
u′ni·ver′sal·ly
u′ni·verse′
u′ni·ver′si·ty
  ·ties
un·just′
un·just′ly
un·kempt′
un·kind′
un·kind′ly
un·kind′ness
un·know′ing
un·known′
un·lace′
  ·laced′ ·lac′ing
un·law′ful
un·law′ful·ly
un·law′ful·ness
un·lead′ed
un·learn′
un·learn′ed
un·leash′
un·leav′ened
un·less′
un·let′tered
un·like′
un·like′li·hood′
un·like′ly
un·lim′ber
un·lim′it·ed
un·lined′
un·list′ed
un·load′
un·lock′
un·looked′-for′
un·loose′
  ·loosed′ ·loos′ing
un·luck′y
  ·i·er ·i·est
un·make′
un·man′ly
  ·li·er ·li·est

un·manned′
un·marked′
un·mask′
un·mean′ing
un·men′tion·a·ble
un·mer′ci·ful
un′mis·tak′a·ble
un′mis·tak′a·bly
un·mit′i·gat′ed
un·nat′u·ral
un·nat′u·ral·ly
un·nec′es·sar′i·ly
un·nec′es·sar′y
un·nerve′
  ·nerved′ ·nerv′ing
un·num′bered
un′ob·served′
un′ob·struct′ed
un·oc′cu·pied′
un′op·posed′
un·or′gan·ized′
un·pack′
un·par′al·leled′
un·pleas′ant
un·pleas′ant·ly
un·pleas′ant·ness
un·plumbed′
un·pop′u·lar
un′pop·u·lar′i·ty
un·prac′ticed
un·prec′e·dent′ed
un·prej′u·diced
un′pre·pared′
un·prin′ci·pled
un·print′a·ble
un′pro·fes′sion·al
un′pro·tect′ed
un′pro·voked′
un·pun′ished
un·qual′i·fied′
un·ques′tion·a·ble
un·ques′tion·a·bly
un·ques′tioned
un·ques′tion·ing
un·quote′
un·rav′el
  ·eled or ·elled
  ·el·ing or ·el·ling
un·read′
un·re′al
un·re′al·ized′
un·rea′son·a·ble
un·rea′son·a·bly
un·rea′son·ing
un′re·gen′er·ate
un·reg′u·lat′ed
un′re·lat′ed
un′re·lent′ing
un′re·lieved′
un′re·mit′ting
un′re·served′
un′re·serv′ed·ly
un·rest′
un·ripe′
un·ri′valed or
  ·valled
un·roll′

un·ruf′fled
un·rul′i·ness
un·rul′y
  ·i·er ·i·est
un·sad′dle
  ·dled ·dling
un·said′
un·sat′u·rat′ed
un·sa′vor·y
un·scathed′
un·schooled′
un·scram′ble
  ·bled ·bling
un·screw′
un·scru′pu·lous
un·seal′
un·sea′son·a·ble
un·seat′
un·see′ing
un·seem′ly
un·seen′
un·set′tle
  ·tled ·tling
un·set′tled
un·shav′en
un·sheathe′
  ·sheathed′
  ·sheath′ing
un·sight′ly
un·skilled′
un·skill′ful
un·snap′
  ·snapped′
  ·snap′ping
un·snarl′
un′so·lic′it·ed
un′so·phis′ti·cat′ed
un·sound′
un·spar′ing
un·speak′a·ble
un·speak′a·bly
un·sta′ble
un·stead′y
un·stop′
  ·stopped′
  ·stop′ping
un·struc′tured
un·strung′
un·stuck′
un·stud′ied
un′sub·stan′tial
un·sung′
un·sweet′ened
un·swerv′ing
un·tamed′
un·tan′gle
  ·gled ·gling
un·taught′
un·think′a·ble
un·think′ing
un·ti′dy
  ·di·er ·di·est
un·tie′
  ·tied′, ·ty′ing or
  ·tie′ing
un·til′
un·time′li·ness
un·time′ly
un·tir′ing

un′to
un·told′
un·touch′a·ble
un·to′ward
un·trav′eled or
  ·elled
un·tried′
un·trou′bled
un·truth′
un·truth′ful
un·tu′tored
un·twist′
un·used′
un·u′su·al
un·u′su·al·ly
un·ut′ter·a·ble
un·var′nished
un·var′y·ing
un·veil′
un·ver′i·fied′
un·voiced′
un·want′ed
  (*not wanted;* see
  UNWONTED)
un·war′rant·ed
un·war′y
un·wa′ver·ing
un·wed′
un·well′
un·whole′some
un·wield′y
un·will′ing
un·will′ing·ly
un·wind′
  ·wound′ ·wind′ing
un·wise′
un·wit′ting
un·wont′ed
  (*not usual;* see UN-
  WANTED)
un·wor′thi·ness
un·wor′thy
  ·thi·er ·thi·est
un·wrap′
  ·wrapped′
  ·wrap′ping
un·writ′ten
un·yield′ing
up
  upped up′ping
up′-and-com′ing
up′beat′
up·braid′
up·bring′ing
up·chuck′
up′com′ing
up′coun′try
up·date′
  ·dat′ed ·dat′ing
up·end′
up′front′
up·grade′
  ·grad′ed ·grad′ing
up·heav′al
up′hill′
up·hold′
  ·held′ ·hold′ing
up·hol′ster
up·hol′ster·er

up·hol′ster·y
  ·ies
up′keep′
up′land
up′lift′
up·on′
up′per
up′per·case
up′per·class′man
up′per·cut′
up′per·most′
up′pi·ty
up·raise′
  ·raised′ ·rais′ing
up·rear′
up′right′
up·ris′ing
up·roar′
up·roar′i·ous
up·root′
up′scale′
up·set′
  ·set′ ·set′ting
up′shot′
up′side′
up′side′-down′
up·stage′
  ·staged′ ·stag′ing
up′stairs′
up·stand′ing
up′start′
up·state′
up′stream′
up·surge′
up·swing′
up′take′
up·tight′
up′-to-date′
up′town′
up·turn′
up′turned′
up′ward
up′ward·ly
up′wind′
u·ra′ni·um
U′ra·nus
ur′ban (*of the city*)
ur·bane′ (*socially
  poised*)
ur·ban′i·ty
ur′ban·i·za′tion
ur′ban·ize′
  ·ized′ ·iz′ing
ur′chin
u·re′a
u·re′mi·a
u·re′mic
u·re′ter
u′re·thane′
u·re′thra
  ·thrae or ·thras
urge
  urged urg′ing
ur′gen·cy
ur′gent
ur′gent·ly
u′ric
u′ri·nal

u′ri·nal′y·sis
  ·ses′
u′ri·nar′y
u′ri·nate′
  ·nat′ed ·nat′ing
u′ri·na′tion
u′rine
urn
u′ro·gen′i·tal
u·rol′o·gist
u·rol′o·gy
ur′sine′
ur·ti·car′i·a
us′a·bil′i·ty or use′·
us′a·ble or use′·
us′age
use
  used us′ing
used
use′ful
use′ful·ly
use′ful·ness
use′less
use′less·ly
use′less·ness
us′er
us′er-friend′ly
ush′er
u′su·al
u′su·al·ly
u′su·rer
u·su′ri·ous
u·surp′
u′sur·pa′tion
u·surp′er
u′su·ry
  ·ries
U′tah′
u·ten′sil
u′ter·ine
u′ter·us
  ·ter·i′
u·til′i·tar′i·an
u·til′i·tar′i·an·ism′
u·til′i·ty
  ·ties
u′ti·li·za′tion
u′ti·lize′
  ·lized′ ·liz′ing
ut′most′
u·to′pi·a
u·to′pi·an
ut′ter
ut′ter·ance
ut′ter·ly
ut′ter·most′
U′-turn′
u′vu·la
  ·las or ·lae′
u′vu·lar
ux·o′ri·ous

V

va′can·cy
  ·cies
va′cant

va'cant·ly
va'cate'
  ·cat'ed ·cat'ing
va·ca'tion
va·ca'tion·er
vac'ci·nate'
  ·nat'ed ·nat'ing
vac'ci·na'tion
vac·cine'
vac'il·late'
  ·lat'ed ·lat'ing
vac'il·la'tion
va·cu'i·ty
  ·ties
vac'u·ous
vac'u·ous·ly
vac'u·um
  ·ums or ·a
vag'a·bond'
va·gar'y
  ·ies
va·gi'na
  ·nas or ·nae
vag'i·nal
va'gran·cy
  ·cies
va'grant
vague
  va'guer va'guest
vague'ly
vague'ness
vain
  (futile; conceited;
  see VANE, VEIN)
vain'glo'ri·ous
vain'glo'ry
vain'ly
val'ance
  (drapery; see VA-
  LENCE)
vale
  (valley; see VEIL)
val'e·dic·to'ri·an
val'e·dic'to·ry
  ·ries
va'lence
  (combining capac-
  ity; see VALANCE)
val'en·tine'
val'et
val'e·tu·di·nar'i·an
val'iance
val'iant
val'iant·ly
val'id
val'i·date'
  ·dat'ed ·dat'ing
va·lid'i·ty
  ·ties
val'id·ly
va·lise'
Val'i·um
val'ley
  ·leys
val'or
val'or·ous
val'u·a·ble
val'u·a'tion
val'ue
  ·ued ·u·ing

val'ue-add'ed tax
val'ue·less
valve
va·moose'
  ·moosed'
  ·moos'ing
vamp
vam'pire'
van
va·na'di·um
van'dal
van'dal·ism'
van'dal·ize'
  ·ized' ·iz'ing
vane
  (blade; see VAIN,
  VEIN)
van'guard'
va·nil'la
van'ish
van'i·ty
  ·ties
van'quish
van'tage
vap'id
va·pid'i·ty
vap'id·ness
va'por
va'por·i·za'tion
va'por·ize'
  ·ized' ·iz'ing
va'por·iz'er
va'por·ous
va·que'ro
  ·ros
var'i·a·bil'i·ty
var'i·a·ble
var'i·ance
var'i·ant
var'i·a'tion
var'i·col'ored
var'i·cose'
var'i·e·gat'ed
va·ri'e·tal
va·ri'e·ty
  ·ties
var'i·ous
var'i·ous·ly
var'mint or ·ment
var'nish
var'si·ty
  ·ties
var'y
  var'ied var'y·ing
  (change; see VERY)
vas'cu·lar
vase
vas·ec'to·my
  ·mies
vas'e·line'
vas'o·mo'tor
vas'sal
  (servant; see VES-
  SEL)
vas'sal·age
vast
vast'ly
vast'ness
vat

vaude'ville
vault
vaunt
veal
vec'tor
veer
veg'e·ta·ble
veg'e·tar'i·an
veg'e·tate'
  ·tat'ed ·tat'ing
veg'e·ta'tion
veg'e·ta'tive
ve'he·mence
ve'he·men·cy
ve'he·ment
ve'he·ment·ly
ve'hi·cle
ve·hic'u·lar
veil
  (screen; see VALE)
vein
  (blood vessel; min-
  eral deposit; see
  VAIN, VANE)
Vel'cro
veld or veldt
vel'lum
  (parchment; see
  VELUM)
ve·loc'i·ty
  ·ties
ve·lour' or ·lours'
  ·lours'
ve'lum
  ·la
  (soft palate; see
  VELLUM)
vel'vet
vel'vet·een'
vel'vet·y
ve'nal
  (corrupt; see VE-
  NIAL)
ve·nal'i·ty
ve'nal·ly
vend
vend'er
ven·det'ta
ven'dor
ve·neer'
ven'er·a·bil'i·ty
ven'er·a·ble
ven'er·ate'
  ·at'ed ·at'ing
ven'er·a'tion
ve·ne're·al
Ve·ne'tian blind
venge'ance
venge'ful
ve·ni'al
  (pardonable; see
  VENAL)
ve·ni're·man
ven'i·son
ven'om
ven'om·ous
ve'nous
vent
ven'ti·late'
  ·lat'ed ·lat'ing

ven'ti·la'tion
ven'ti·la'tor
ven'tral
ven'tri·cle
ven·tric'u·lar
ven·tril'o·quism
ven·tril'o·quist
ven'ture
  ·tured ·tur·ing
ven'ture·some
ven'tur·ous
ven'ue'
Ve'nus
ve·ra'cious
  (truthful; see VO-
  RACIOUS)
ve·rac'i·ty
ve·ran'da or ·dah
verb
ver'bal
ver'bal·ize'
  ·ized' ·iz'ing
ver'bal·ly
ver·ba'tim
ver·be'na
ver'bi·age'
ver·bose'
ver·bos'i·ty
ver'dant
ver'dict
ver'di·gris'
ver'dure
verge
  verged verg'ing
verg'er
ver'i·fi'a·ble
ver'i·fi·ca'tion
ver'i·fy'
  ·fied' ·fy'ing
ver'i·ly
ver'i·si·mil'i·tude'
ver'i·ta·ble
ver'i·ty
  ·ties
ver'mi·cel'li
ver·mic'u·lite'
ver'mi·form'
ver·mil'ion
ver'min
  ·min
Ver·mont'
ver'mouth'
ver·nac'u·lar
ver'nal
ver'ni·er
ver'sa·tile
ver'sa·til'i·ty
verse
ver'si·fi·ca'tion
ver'si·fy'
  ·fied' ·fy'ing
ver'sion
ver'sus
ver'te·bra
  ·brae' or ·bras
ver'te·bral
ver'te·brate

ver'tex'
  ·tex'es or ·ti·ces'
ver'ti·cal
ver·tig'i·nous
ver'ti·go'
verve
ver'y
  (complete; exceed-
  ingly; see VARY)
ves'i·cant
ves'i·cle
ve·sic'u·lar
ve·sic'u·late
ves'pers
ves'sel
  (container; ship;
  see VASSAL)
vest
ves'tal
ves'ti·bule'
ves'tige
ves·tig'i·al
vest'ment
vest'-pock'et
ves'try
  ·tries
vetch
vet'er·an
vet'er·i·nar'i·an
vet'er·i·nar'y
  ·ies
ve'to
  ·toes
  ·toed ·to·ing
vex
vex·a'tion
vex·a'tious
vi'a
vi'a·bil'i·ty
vi'a·ble
vi'a·duct'
vi'al
  (bottle; see VILE,
  VIOL)
vi'and
vibes
vi'bra·harp'
vi'bran·cy
vi'brant
vi'bra·phone'
vi'bra·phon'ist
vi'brate'
  ·brat'ed ·brat'ing
vi·bra'tion
vi·bra'to
  ·tos
vi'bra'tor
vi'bra·to'ry
vi·bur'num
vic'ar
vic'ar·age
vi·car'i·ous
vi·car'i·ous·ly
vice
  (evil conduct;
  flaw; see VISE)
vice'ge'rent
vice'-pres'i·den·cy
vice'-pres'i·dent

vice'roy'
vi'ce ver'sa
vi'chys·soise'
vi·cin'i·ty
  ·ties
vi'cious
vi'cious·ly
vi'cious·ness
vi·cis'si·tudes'
vic'tim
vic'tim·ize'
  ·ized' ·iz'ing
vic'tor
Vic·to'ri·an
vic·to'ri·ous
vic'to·ry
  ·ries
vict'uals
vi·cu'ña
  ·ñas or ·ña
vi'de
vid'e·o'
  ·os'
vid'e·o'cas·sette'
vid'e·o·disc'
vid'e·o·tape'
  ·taped' ·tap'ing
vie
  vied vy'ing
view
view'er
view'find'er
view'point'
vig'il
vig'i·lance
vig'i·lant
vig'i·lan'te
vig'i·lan'tism'
vi·gnette'
vig'or
vig'or·ous
vig'or·ous·ly
vik'ing
vile
  (evil; offensive;
  see VIAL, VIOL)
vile'ness
vil'i·fi·ca'tion
vil'i·fy'
  ·fied' ·fy'ing
vil'la
vil'lage
vil'lag·er
vil'lain
  (scoundrel; see
  VILLEIN)
vil'lain·ous
vil'lain·y
  ·ies'
vil'lein
  (serf; see VILLAIN)
vim
vin
vin'ai·grette'
vin'di·cate'
  ·cat'ed ·cat'ing
vin'di·ca'tion
vin'di·ca'tor
vin·dic'tive

vin·dic'tive·ly
vin·dic'tive·ness
vine
vin'e·gar
vin'e·gar·y
vine'yard
vi'no
vin'tage
vint'ner
vi'nyl
vi'ol
  (*stringed instru-
  ment;* see VIAL,
  VILE)
vi·o'la
vi'o·la·ble
vi'o·late'
  ·lat'ed ·lat'ing
vi·o·la'tion
vi'o·la'tor
vi'o·lence
vi'o·lent
vi'o·lent·ly
vi'o·let
vi·o·lin'
vi·o·lin'ist
vi·ol'ist
vi·o·lon'cel'lo
  ·los
vi'per
vi'per·ous
vi·ra'go
  ·goes *or* ·gos
vi'ral
  (*of a virus;* see
  VIRILE)
vir'e·o'
  ·os'
vir'gin
vir'gin·al
Vir·gin'ia
vir·gin'i·ty
Vir'go'
vir'gule'
vir'ile
  (*manly;* see VIRAL)
vi·ril'i·ty
vi·rol'o·gist
vi·rol'o·gy
vir'tu·al
vir'tu·al·ly
vir'tue
vir·tu·os'i·ty
vir'tu·o'so
  ·sos *or* ·si
vir'tu·ous
vir'tu·ous·ly
vir'u·lence
vir'u·lent
vi'rus
vi'sa
vis'age
vis'-à-vis'
vis'cer·a
vis'cer·al
vis'cid
vis'cose'
vis·cos'i·ty
  ·ties

vis'count'
vis'count'ess
vis'cous
vise
  vised vis'ing
  (*clamp;* see VICE)
vis·i·bil'i·ty
  ·ties
vis'i·ble
vis'i·bly
vi'sion
vi'sion·ar'y
  ·ies
vis'it
vis'it·ant
vis·it·a'tion
vis'i·tor
vi'sor
vis'ta
vis'u·al
vis·u·al·i·za'tion
vis'u·al·ize'
  ·ized' ·iz'ing
vi'ta
  ·tae
vi'tal
vi·tal'i·ty
  ·ties
vi'tal·ize'
  ·ized' ·iz'ing
vi'tal·ly
vi'ta·min
vi'ti·ate'
  ·at'ed ·at'ing
vi'ti·a'tion
vit'i·cul'ture
vit're·ous
vit'ri·fy'
  ·fied' ·fy'ing
vit·rine'
vit'ri·ol
vit'ri·ol'ic
vi·tu'per·ate'
  ·at'ed ·at'ing
vi·tu'per·a'tion
vi·tu'per·a'tive
vi'va
vi·va'ce
vi·va'cious
vi·vac'i·ty
vi·va'cious·ness
vive
viv'id
viv'id·ly
viv'id·ness
viv'i·fy'
  ·fied' ·fy'ing
vi·vip'a·rous
viv'i·sect'
viv'i·sec'tion
viv'i·sec'tion·ist
vix'en
vix'en·ish
vi·zier'
viz'or
vo·cab'u·lar'y
  ·ies
vo'cal
vo·cal'ic

vo'cal·ist
vo'cal·ize'
  ·ized' ·iz'ing
vo'cal·ly
vo·ca'tion
vo·ca'tion·al
voc'a·tive
vo·cif'er·ate'
  ·at'ed ·at'ing
vo·cif'er·a'tion
vo·cif'er·ous
vod'ka
vogue
voice
  voiced voic'ing
voice'less
voice'-o'ver
void
void'a·ble
voi·là'
voile
vol'a·tile
vol'a·til'i·ty
vol·can'ic
vol·ca'no
  ·noes *or* ·nos
vole
vo·li'tion
vo·li'tion·al
vol'ley
  ·leys
  ·leyed ·ley·ing
vol'ley·ball'
volt
volt'age
vol·ta'ic
volt'me'ter
vol·u·bil'i·ty
vol'u·ble
vol'u·bly
vol'ume
vo·lu'mi·nous
vol'un·tar'i·ly
vol'un·ta·rism
vol'un·tar'y
vol'un·teer'
vo·lup'tu·ar'y
  ·ar'ies
vo·lup'tu·ous
vo·lute'
vom'it
vom'i·tous
voo'doo'
  ·doos'
voo'doo·ism'
vo·ra'cious
  (*greedy;* see VERA-
  CIOUS)
vo·rac'i·ty
vor'tex'
  ·tex'es *or* ·ti·ces'
vo'ta·ry
  ·ries'
vote
  vot'ed vot'ing
vot'er
vo'tive
vouch
vouch'er

vouch·safe'
  ·safed' ·saf'ing
vow
vow'el
voy'age
  ·aged ·ag·ing
voy'ag·er
voy·eur'
voy'eur·ism'
voy'eur·is'tic
vul'can·i·za'tion
vul'can·ize'
  ·ized' ·iz'ing
vul'gar
vul·gar'i·an
vul'gar·ism'
vul·gar'i·ty
  ·ties
vul'gar·ize'
  ·ized' ·iz'ing
vul'gar·ly
vul'ner·a·bil'i·ty
vul'ner·a·ble
vul'ner·a·bly
vul'pine
vul'ture
vul'tur·ous
vul'va
vy'ing

W

wab'ble
  ·bled ·bling
wack'i·ness
wack'o
  ·os
wack'y
  ·i·er ·i·est
wad
  wad'ded wad'ding
wad'ding
wad'dle
  ·dled ·dling
wade
  wad'ed wad'ing
wad'er
wa'di
  ·dis *or* ·dies
wa'fer
waf'fle
waft
wag
  wagged wag'ging
wage
  waged wag'ing
wa'ger
wag'gish
wag'gle
  ·gled ·gling
wag'on
waif
wail
  (*cry;* see WALE,
  WHALE)
wain'scot
  ·scot'ed *or*
  ·scot'ted

  ·scot'ing *or*
  ·scot‹ting
wain'scot'ing *or*
  ·ting
wain'wright'
waist
  (*middle section;*
  see WASTE)
waist'band'
waist'coat'
waist'line'
wait
wait'er
wait'ing
wait'ress
waive
  waived waiv'ing
  (*give up;* see WAVE)
waiv'er
  (*a relinquishing;*
  see WAVER)
wake
  woke *or* waked,
  waked *or* wok'en,
  wak'ing
wake'ful
wake'ful·ness
wak'en
wale
  waled wal'ing
  (*ridge;* see WAIL,
  WHALE)
walk
walk'er
walk'ie-talk'ie
walk'out'
walk'-up'
walk'way'
wall
wal'la·by
  ·bies
wall'board'
wal'let
wall'eye'
wall'eyed'
wall'flow'er
wal'lop
wal'low
wall'pa'per
wall'-to-wall'
wal'nut'
wal'rus
waltz
wam'pum
wan
  wan'ner wan'nest
  (*pale;* see WON)
wand
wan'der
wan'der·er
wan'der·lust'
wane
  waned wan'ing
wan'gle
  ·gled ·gling
want
  (*desire;* see WONT)
want'ing
wan'ton
wan'ton·ness

wap'i·ti
war
  warred war'ring
war'ble
  ·bled ·bling
war'bler
ward
war'den
war'er
ward'robe'
ward'room'
ware
ware'house'
war'fare'
war'head'
war'horse'
war'i·ly
war'i·ness
war'like'
war'lock'
war'lord'
warm
warm'blood'ed
warmed'-o'ver
warm'er
warm'heart'ed
warm'ish
warm'ly
war'mon'ger
war'mon'ger·ing
warmth
warm'-up'
warn
  (*caution;* see
  WORN)
warn'ing
warp
war'path'
war'rant
war'ran·ty
  ·ties
war'ren
war'ri·or
war'ship'
wart
war'time'
war'y
  ·i·er ·i·est
was
wash
wash'a·ble
wash'-and-wear'
wash'ba'sin
wash'board'
wash'bowl'
wash'cloth'
washed'-out'
washed'-up'
wash'er
wash'er·wom'an
wash'ing
Wash'ing·ton
wash'out'
wash'rag'
wash'room'
wash'stand'
wash'tub'

wasp
WASP *or* Wasp
wasp'ish
was'sail
wast'age
waste
 wast'ed wast'ing
 (*squander; see*
 WAIST)
waste'bas'ket
wast'ed
waste'ful
waste'ful·ly
waste'ful·ness
waste'land'
waste'pa'per
wast'er
wast'rel
watch
watch'band'
watch'dog'
watch'er
watch'ful
watch'ful·ly
watch'ful·ness
watch'man
watch'tow'er
watch'word'
wa'ter
wa'ter·col'or
wa'ter·course'
wa'ter·craft'
wa'ter·cress'
wa'ter·fall'
wa'ter·fowl'
wa'ter·front'
wa'ter·i·ness
wa'ter·lil'y
wa'ter·line'
wa'ter·logged'
wa'ter·mark'
wa'ter·mel'on
wa'ter·proof'
wa'ter·re·pel'lent
wa'ter·shed'
wa'ter·side'
wa'ter·ski'
wa'ter·spout'
wa'ter·tight'
wa'ter·way'
wa'ter·works'
wa'ter·y
WATS
watt
watt'age
wat'tle
 ·tled ·tling
wave
 waved wav'ing
 (*curving motion;*
 see WAIVE)
wave'length'
wave'let
wa'ver
 (*falter; see* WAIVER)
wav'i·ness
wav'y
 ·i·er ·i·est

wax
wax'en
wax'i·ness
wax'wing'
wax'works'
wax'y
 ·i·er ·i·est
way
 (*ship's movement;*
 see WEIGH)
way'far'er
way'far'ing
way'lay'
 ·laid' ·lay'ing
way'side'
way'ward
way'ward·ly
way'ward·ness
we
 sing. I
weak
weak'en
weak'-kneed'
weak'ling
weak'ly
 ·li·er ·li·est
 (*in a weak way;*
 see WEEKLY)
weak'ness
weal
 (*ridge; see* WHEAL)
wealth
wealth'i·ness
wealth'y
 ·i·er ·i·est
wean
weap'on
weap'on·less
weap'on·ry
wear
 wore worn
 wear'ing
wear'a·ble
wear'er
wea'ri·ly
wea'ri·ness
wea'ri·some
wea'ry
 ·ried ·ry·ing
 ·ri·er ·ri·est
wea'sel
wea'sel·ly
weath'er
 (*atmospheric con-*
 ditions; see
 WHETHER)
weath'er-beat'en
weath'er·cock'
weath'er·ing
weath'er·ize'
 ·ized' ·iz'ing
weath'er·man'
weath'er·proof'
weath'er·strip'
weave
 wove, wo'ven *or*
 wove, weav'ing
 (*interlace*)
weave
 weaved weav'ing

(*move from side to*
side)
weav'er
web
 webbed web'bing
web'bing
web'foot'
 ·feet'
web'-foot'ed
wed
 wed'ded, wed'ded
 or wed, wed'ding
wed'ded
wed'ding
wedge
 wedged wedg'ing
wedg'ie
wed'lock'
Wednes'day
wee
 we'er we'est
weed
weed'er
weed'less
weeds
weed'y
 ·i·er ·i·est
week
week'day'
week'end' *or*
 week'-end'
week'ly
 ·lies
 (*every week; see*
 WEAKLY)
ween
weep
 wept weep'ing
weep'er
weep'ing
weep'y
 ·i·er ·i·est
wee'vil
weft
weigh
 (*hoist anchor; see*
 WAY)
weight
weight'i·ness
weight'less
weight'less·ness
weight'y
 ·i·er ·i·est
weir
weird
weird'ly
weird'ness
weird'o
 ·os
wel'come
 ·comed ·com·ing
weld
weld'er
wel'fare'
well
well'-ad·vised'
well'-ap·point'ed
well'-bal'anced
well'-be·haved'
well'-be'ing

well'-born'
well'-bred'
well'-dis·posed'
well-done'
well'-fed'
well'-found'ed
well'-ground'ed
well'head'
well'-heeled'
well'-in·formed'
well'-in·ten'·tioned
well'-knit'
well'-known'
well'-made'
well'-man'nered
well'-mean'ing
well'meant'
well'-nigh'
well'-off'
well'-pre·served'
well'-read'
well'-round'ed
well'-spo'ken
well'spring'
well'-timed'
well'-to-do'
well'-wish'er
well'-worn'
Welsh
welt
wel'ter
wel'ter·weight'
wen
wench
wend
 wend'ed wend'ing
went
wept
were
we're
were'wolf'
 ·wolves'
west
west'er·ly
west'ern
west'ern·er
west'ern·ize'
 ·ized' ·iz'ing
West Virginia
west'ward
wet
 wet'ter wet'test
 wet *or* wet'ted
 wet'ting
 (*moisten; see*
 WHET)
wet'land'
wet'ness
wet'-nurse'
wet'ter
whack
whack'er
whack'y
 ·i·er ·i·est
whale
 whaled whal'ing
 (*sea mammal; see*
 WAIL, WALE)
whale'bone'

whal'er
wham
 whammed
 wham'ming
wharf
 wharves *or* wharfs
what
what·ev'er
what'not'
what's
what'so·ev'er
wheal
 (*pimple; see* WEAL,
 WHEEL)
wheat
whee'dle
 ·dled ·dling
wheel
 (*disk; see* WHEAL)
wheel'bar'row
wheel'base'
wheel'chair'
wheeled
wheel'er-deal'er
wheel'house'
wheel'wright'
wheeze
 wheezed
 wheez'ing
wheez'y
 ·i·er ·i·est
whelk
whelp
when
whence
when·ev'er
where
where'a·bouts'
where·as'
where·at'
where·by'
where'fore'
where·in'
where·of'
where'up·on'
wher·ev'er
where·with'
where·with·al'
wher'ry
 ·ries
whet
 whet'ted
 whet'ting
 (*sharpen; see* WET)
wheth'er
 (*if; see* WEATHER)
whet'stone'
whew
whey
which
 (*a pronoun; see*
 WITCH)
which·ev'er
whiff
while
 whiled whil'ing
 (*time; spend time;*
 see WILE)
whim
whim'per

whim'si·cal
whim'si·cal'i·ty
whim'si·cal·ly
whim'sy
 ·sies'
whine
 whined whin'ing
whin'ny
 ·nies
 ·nied ·ny·ing
whip
 whipped *or* whipt
 whip'ping
whip'cord'
whip'lash'
whip'per·snap'per
whip'pet
whip'poor·will'
whir *or* whirr
 whirred whir'ring
whirl
 (*spin; see* WHORL)
whirl'i·gig'
whirl'pool'
whirl'wind'
whisk
whisk'er
whis'key
 ·keys *or* ·kies
whis'per
whist
whis'tle
 ·tled ·tling
whis'tler
whis'tle-stop'
whit
 (*bit; see* WIT)
white
 whit'er whit'est
white'cap'
white'-col'lar
white'fish'
whit'en
whit'en·er
white'ness
whit'en·ing
white'wall'
white'wash'
whith'er
 (*where; see*
 WITHER)
whit'ing
whit'tle
 ·tled ·tling
whiz *or* whizz
 whizzed whiz'zing
who
whoa
who·dun'it
who·ev'er
whole
 (*entire; see* HOLE)
whole'heart'ed
whole'ness
whole'sale'
 ·saled' ·sal'ing
whole'sal'er
whole'some
whole'some·ness

whol'ly
   (*entirely;* see HO-
   LEY, HOLY)
whom
whom·ev'er
whoop
whoop'ing cough
whop'per
whop'ping
whore
whor'ish
whorl
   (*spiral design;* see
   WHIRL)
who's (*who is; who
   has*)
whose
   (*possessive form
   of* who)
who'so·ev'er
why
wick
wick'ed
wick'ed·ly
wick'ed·ness
wick'er
wick'er·work'
wick'et
wide
   wid'er wid'est
wide'-an'gle
wide'-a·wake'
wide'-eyed'
wide'ly
wid'en
wide'-o'pen
wide'spread'
widg'eon
widg'et
wid'ow
wid'ow·er
wid'ow·hood'
width
wield
wie'ner
wife
   wives
wife'ly
wig
wi'geon
wig'gle
   ·gled ·gling
wig'gly
   ·gli·er ·gli·est
wight
wig'let
wig'wag'
wig'wam'
wild
wild'cat'
   ·cat'ted ·cat'ting
wil'de·beest'
wil'der·ness
wild'-eyed'
wild'fire'
wild'flow'er
wild'life'
wild'ly

wild'ness
wile
   wiled wil'ing
   (*trick;* see WHILE)
wil'i·ness
will
will'ful *or* wil'·
will'ful·ly
will'ful·ness
will'ing
will'ing·ly
will'ing·ness
wil'li·waw' *or* ·ly·
will'-o'-the-wisp'
wil'low
wil'low·y
will'pow'er
wil'ly-nil'ly
wilt
wil'y
   ·i·er ·i·est
wimp
wim'ple
wimp'y *or* ·ish
win
   won win'ning
wince
   winced winc'ing
winch
wind
   wound wind'ing
wind'bag'
wind'blown'
wind'break'er
wind'burn'
wind'chill' factor
wind'ed
wind'er
wind'fall'
wind'i·ness
wind'ing sheet
wind'jam'mer
wind'lass
wind'mill'
win'dow
win'dow·pane'
win'dow-shop'
win'dow·sill'
wind'pipe'
wind'row'
wind'shield'
wind'sock'
wind'storm'
wind'surf'ing
wind'up'
wind'ward
wind'y
   ·i·er ·i·est
wine
   wined win'ing
win'er·y
   ·ies
wing
wing'ding'
winged
wing'less
wing'span'
wing'spread'

wink
win'ner
win'ning
win'now
win'some
win'ter
win'ter·green'
win'ter·ize'
   ·ized ·iz'ing
win'ter·time'
win'try
   ·tri·er ·tri·est
wipe
   wiped wip'ing
wip'er
wire
   wired wir'ing
wired
wire'hair'
wire'-haired'
wire'less
wire'tap'
wir'i·ness
wir'ing
wir'y
   ·i·er ·i·est
Wis·con'sin
wis'dom
wise
   wis'er wis'est
wise'a'cre
wise'crack'
wise'ly
wish
wish'bone'
wish'er
wish'ful
wish'ful·ly
wish'y-wash'y
wisp
wisp'y
   ·i·er ·i·est
wis·te'ri·a
wist'ful
wist'ful·ly
wist'ful·ness
wit
   (*humor;* see WHIT)
witch
   (*sorceress;* see
   WHICH)
witch'craft'
witch'er·y
   ·ies
with
with·al'
with·draw'
   ·drew' ·drawn'
   ·draw'ing
with·draw'al
with·drawn'
with'er
   (*wilt;* see WHITHER)
with'ers
with·hold'
   ·held' ·hold'ing
with·in'
with·out'

with·stand'
   ·stood' ·stand'ing
wit'less
wit'less·ly
wit'ness
wit'ti·cism'
wit'ti·ly
wit'ti·ness
wit'ting·ly
wit'ty
   ·ti·er ·ti·est
wives
wiz'ard
wiz'ard·ry
wiz'ened
wob'ble
   ·bled ·bling
wob'bli·ness
wob'bly
   ·bli·er ·bli·est
woe
woe'be·gone'
woe'ful
woe'ful·ly
wok
woke
wok'en
wolf
   wolves
   (*a canine;* see
   WOOF)
wolf'hound'
wolf'ish
wol'ver·ine'
wolves
wom'an
   wom'en
wom'an·hood'
wom'an·ish
wom'an·ize'
   ·ized' ·iz'ing
wom'an·iz'er
wom'an·kind'
wom'an·ly
womb
wom'bat'
wom'en
wom'en·folk'
won
   (*form of* win; see
   WAN)
won'der
won'der·ful
won'der·ful·ly
won'der·land'
won'der·ment
won'drous
won'drous·ly
wont
   (*accustomed;* see
   WANT, WON'T)
won't (*will not*)
won' ton'
woo
wood
wood'bine'
wood'carv'er
wood'carv'ing
wood'chuck'

wood'cock'
wood'craft'
wood'cut'
wood'cut'ter
wood'ed
wood'en
wood'en·ly
wood'i·ness
wood'land'
wood'man
wood'peck'er
wood'pile'
wood'shed'
wood'si·ness
woods'man
wood'sy
   ·si·er ·si·est
wood'wind'
wood'work'
wood'work'ing
wood'y
   ·i·er ·i·est
woo'er
woof
   (*to bark; weft;* see
   WOLF)
woof'er
wool
wool'en
wool'gath'er·ing
wool'ly *or* ·y
   ·li·er *or* ·i·er
   ·li·est *or* ·i·est
wooz'i·ness
wooz'y
   ·i·er ·i·est
Worces'ter·shire'
word
word'age
word'i·ness
word'ing
word'-of-mouth'
word'y
   ·i·er ·i·est
wore
work
   worked *or*
   wrought, work'ing
work'a·ble
work'a·day'
work'a·hol'ic
work'bench'
work'book'
work'day'
work'er
work'fare'
work'horse'
work'house'
work'ing
work'ing·man'
work'load'
work'man
work'man·like'
work'man·ship'
work'out'
work'place'
work'shop'
work'sta'tion

work'week'
world
world'-class'
world'li·ness
world'ly
   ·li·er ·li·est
world'ly-wise'
world'-shak'ing
world'view'
world'-wea'ry
world'wide'
worm
worm'wood'
worm'y
   ·i·er ·i·est
worn
   (*form of* wear; see
   WARN)
worn'-out'
wor'ri·er
wor'ri·ment
wor'ri·some
wor'ry
   ·ries
   ·ried ·ry·ing
wor'ry·wart'
worse
wor'sen
wor'ship
   ·shiped *or*
   ·shipped
   ·ship·ing *or*
   ·ship·ping
wor'ship·er *or* ·per
wor'ship·ful
worst
wor'sted
worth
wor'thi·ly
wor'thi·ness
worth'less
worth'less·ness
worth'while'
wor'thy
   ·thi·er ·thi·est
would
would'-be'
wound
wove
wo'ven
wow
wrack
wraith
wran'gle
   ·gled ·gling
wran'gler
wrap
   wrapped *or* wrapt
   wrap'ping
   (*cover;* see RAP)
wrap'per
wrap'ping
wrapt
wrath
wrath'ful
wreak
   (*inflict;* see REEK)

wreath *n.*
 wreaths
wreathe *v.*
 wreathed
 wreath'ing
wreck
wreck'age
wreck'er
wren
wrench
wrest
wres'tle
 ·tled ·tling
wres'tler
wres'tling
wretch
 (*miserable person;*
 see RETCH)
wretch'ed
wretch'ed·ly
wretch'ed·ness
wrig'gle
 ·gled ·gling
wrig'gler
wrig'gly
 ·gli·er ·gli·est
wright
wring
 wrung wring'ing
 (*twist;* see RING)
wring'er
wrin'kle
 ·kled ·kling
wrin'kly
 ·kli·er ·kli·est
wrist
wrist'band'
wrist'watch'
writ
write
 wrote writ'ten
 writ'ing
 (*inscribe;* see
 RIGHT, RITE)
write'-in'
write'-off'

writ'er
write'-up'
writhe
 writhed writh'ing
writ'ing
writ'ten
wrong
wrong'do'er
wrong'do'ing
wrong'ful
wrong'ful·ly
wrong'ful·ness
wrong'head'ed
wrong'head'ed·ly
wrong'head'ed·ness
wrong'ly
wrote
 (*form of* write; see
 ROTE)
wroth
wrought
wrought'-i'ron
wrung
 (*form of* wring; see
 RUNG)
wry
 wri'er *or* wry'er
 wri'est *or* wry'est
 (*ironic;* see RYE)
wry'ly
wry'ness
Wy·o'ming

X

xe'non'
xen'o·phobe'
xen'o·pho'bi·a
xen'o·pho'bic
xe·ro·graph'ic
xe·rog'ra·phy
xe'rox'
X'mas
X'-ray'

xy'lem
xy'lo·phone'
xy'lo·phon'ist

Y

yacht
yachts'man
yak
yam
yam'mer
yank
Yan'kee
yap
 yapped yap'ping
yard
yard'age
yard'arm'
yard'man'
yard'stick'
yar'mul·ke
yarn
yat'ter
yaw
yawl
yawn
yay
yea
yeah
year
year'book'
year'ling
year'ly
yearn
year'-round'
yeast
yeast'y
 ·i·er ·i·est
yell
yel'low
yel'low·ish
yelp

yen (*Japanese
 money*)
yen (*strong longing*)
yeo'man
yeo'man·ry
yes
 yessed yes'sing
ye·shi'va
 ·vas *or* ye·shi·vot'
yes'ter·day'
yes'ter·year'
yet
yew
 (*tree;* see EWE)
Yid'dish
yield
yip
 yipped yip'ping
yo'del
 ·deled *or* ·delled
 ·del·ing *or*
 ·del·ling
yo'del·er *or* ·del·ler
yo'ga
yo'gi
 ·gis
yo'gurt *or* ·ghurt
yoke
 yoked yok'ing
 (*harness*)
yo'kel
yolk (*yellow part of
 egg*)
Yom Kip'pur
yon
yon'der
yoo'-hoo'
yore
you
young
young'ish
young'ster
your
your·self'
youth

youth'ful
youth'ful·ly
youth'ful·ness
yowl
yo'-yo'
yt'tri·um
yuc'ca
yuck
yuck'y
 ·i·er ·i·est
yuk
 yukked yuk'king
yule
yule'tide'
yum'my
 ·mi·er ·mi·est
yup
yup'pie

Z

za'ni·ness
za'ny
 ·nies
 ·ni·er ·ni·est
zap
 zapped zap'ping
zeal
zeal'ot
zeal'ous
zeal'ous·ly
ze'bra
ze'bu'
zed
Zen
ze'nith
zeph'yr
zep'pe·lin
ze'ro
 ·ros *or* ·roes
 ·roed ·ro·ing

zest
zest'ful
zig'gu·rat'
zig'zag'
 ·zagged'
 ·zag'ging
zilch
zil'lion
zinc
zin'fan·del'
zing
zing'er
zin'ni·a
Zi'on·ism'
Zi'on·ist
zip
 zipped zip'ping
zip'per
zip'py
 ·pi·er ·pi·est
zir'con'
zir·co'ni·um
zit
zith'er
zo'di·ac'
zo·di'a·cal
zom'bie
zon'al
zone
 zoned zon'ing
zonked
zoo
zo'o·log'i·cal
zo·ol'o·gist
zo·ol'o·gy
zoom
zo'o·phyte'
zo'o·phyt'ic
zuc·chi'ni
 ·ni *or* ·nis
zwie'back
zy'de·co
zy'gote'
zy'mur·gy